MANAGING
COMMUNITY
COLLEGES

ARTHUR M. COHEN
FLORENCE B. BRAWER
AND ASSOCIATES

MANAGING COMMUNITY COLLEGES

A Handbook for Effective Practice

Jossey-Bass Publishers · San Francisco

Substantial discounts on bulk quantities of Jossey-Bass books are available to corporations, professional associations, and other organizations. For details and discount information, contact the special sales department at Jossey-Bass Inc., Publishers. (415) 433-1740; Fax (415) 433-0499.

For sales outside the United States, contact Maxwell Macmillan International Publishing Group, 866 Third Avenue, New York, New York 10022.

Manufactured in the United States of America. Nearly all Jossey-Bass books, jackets, and periodicals are printed on recycled paper that contains at least 50 percent recycled waste, including 10 percent postconsumer waste. Many of our materials are also printed with vegetable-based ink; during the printing process these inks emit fewer volatile organic compounds (VOCs) than petroleum-based inks. VOCs contribute to the formation of smog.

Library of Congress Cataloging-in-Publication Data

Cohen, Arthur M.
    Managing community colleges : a handbook for effective practice / Arthur M. Cohen, Florence B. Brawer, and associates.
       p. cm. — (The Jossey-Bass higher and adult education series)
    Includes bibliographical references and index.
    ISBN 1-55542-620-4
    1. Community colleges—United States—Administration—Handbooks, manuals, etc. I. Brawer, Florence B., date. II. Title. III. Series.
LB2341.C555   1994
378.1'00973—dc20
                                          93-43162
                                            CIP

FIRST EDITION
HB Printing   10 9 8 7 6 5 4 3 2 1   *Code 9417*

THE JOSSEY-BASS
HIGHER AND ADULT EDUCATION SERIES

Clearinghouse for Community Colleges

The material in this publication is based on work sponsored wholly or in part by the Office of Educational Research and Improvement, U.S. Department of Education, under contract number RI–93–00–2003. Its contents do not necessarily reflect the views of the Department or any other agency of the U.S. Government.

Conten

Contents

Preface

In all institutions, both large and small, proper leadership is necessary for proper functioning. While some organizations may operate in the absence of obvious management, those that would act most effectively must have administrators who translate institutional vision and purpose into a strong operation. Whether the leaders overtly exercise their role or more subtly direct behind the scenes, their experiences, attitudes, and behaviors are reflected in the ways their organizations perform.

Given the importance of administration, leadership, and management, we assumed that these topics would represent a sizable portion of the literature found in the files of the ERIC Clearinghouse for Community Colleges. The data base, however, yielded fewer documents than expected. From 1982 through a portion of 1993, 5.9 percent of all community college articles available in ERIC were devoted to issues of administration. Articles focusing on college presidents generated another 2.0 percent, and documents pertaining to department heads and institutional leadership constituted another 0.6 percent. In all, 8.5 percent of the documents pertained to issues discussed in this handbook.

Over those years, there was no trend to suggest that a pattern exists — no consistent increase or decrease in this literature over a few years' time, for example. Interest in the subjects covered appears fairly steady, with no acceleration or apparent reduction. We do find some variation when the contents of the ERIC data base are broken down into specific areas: college remediation and governance; presidents, deans, and department heads; curriculum; administration and development; students; and faculty. Table P.1, which presents the actual ERIC documents input by this clearinghouse for the years 1987 through the time noted in 1993, explicates these changes.

The figures validated the idea of Gale Erlandson, senior editor of the Jossey-Bass Higher and Adult Education Series, that a handbook on community college administration would be both timely and useful — and hence this volume.

Who Should Read This Book?

Managing Community Colleges is for everyone interested in understanding the administration of contemporary community colleges. The staffing and functioning of the major offices are described, along with some of the pertinent issues affecting each area of work. College planners, active and aspiring administrators, and students of higher education will find the book particularly useful.

Overview of the Contents

Part One considers theories of leadership, organizational culture, and relations between the administration and the governing board and between the college and the state.

Part Two details the operations of various administrative units: the president's office, articulation and transfer, business and finances, personnel, instruction, extramural affairs, student services, institutional research, and campus planning.

Part Three is devoted to college functions, with chapters covering staff recruitment and evaluation, goal design and assessment, and staff performance appraisal.

Table P.1. Topics of Documents Processed by the ERIC Clearinghouse for Community Colleges, 1987–1993 (Includes Documents from Both *RIE* and *CIJE*).

Year	Total no. of documents for year	College administration, governance		Presidents, deans, department heads		Curriculum		Remediation, development		Students		Faculty		Other	
		No.	%	No.	%	No.	%	No.	%	No.	%	No.	%	No.	%
1993	222	10	4.5	6	2.7	9	4.1	7	3.2	65	29.3	28	12.6	97	43.7
1992	925	61	6.6	23	2.5	48	5.2	62	6.7	123	13.9	128	13.8	480	51.8
1991	933	50	5.4	35	3.8	20	2.1	77	8.3	233	25	94	10.1	424	45.4
1990	947	43	9.5	28	2.9	49	5.1	70	7.4	275	29	104	10	378	39.9
1989	970	62	6.4	30	3.1	70	7.2	58	5.9	245	25	110	11	395	40.7
1988	977	73	7.5	26	2.7	34	7.5	63	6.4	258	26.4	134	13.7	389	39.8
1987	969	54	5.6	37	3.8	44	4.5	75	7.7	276	28.5	125	12.9	358	36.9

Note: Figures for 1993 represent coverage of *Resources in Education (RIE)* documents through the April issue and of *Current Index to Journals in Education (CIJE)* documents through the June issue.

While the book consistently focuses on administration, it presents several approaches to the topic. Some chapters reflect the personal experiences of their authors, serving to teach by example. Other chapters deal with the programs and services the colleges offer (for example, student services and institutional research) that fall into a particular administrative sector. And still other chapters emphasize the theories and concepts that underlie leadership, presenting college administrators as personalities who adopt particular and individual approaches to their work. In all, the handbook addresses administration from a broad perspective. We hope that *Managing Community Colleges* will provide both incumbent and incipient administrators with ideas as well as with proactive approaches to their task as leaders in community colleges.

Acknowledgments

In a handbook of this size and with so many different authors, it is impossible to recognize publicly all the people who have helped in so many different capacities. The lead authors wish to thank particularly the chapter authors themselves for their astute contributions, as well as the staff members of the ERIC Clearinghouse for Community Colleges for their assistance.

This book is dedicated to future college administrators, who with wisdom and foresight will help manage the many important functions of the American community college.

Los Angeles, California   Arthur M. Cohen
February 1994   Florence B. Brawer

The Authors

Arthur M. Cohen has been professor of higher education at the University of California, Los Angeles (UCLA), since 1964. He received his B.A. (1949) and M.A. (1955) degrees from the University of Miami in history. He received his Ph.D. degree (1964) from Florida State University in higher education. He has been director of the ERIC Clearinghouse for Community Colleges since 1966 and president of the Center for the Study of Community Colleges since 1974. Cohen has served on the editorial boards of numerous journals and has written extensively about community colleges. His first book was *Dateline '79: Heretical Concepts for the Community College* (1969); his latest is *Perspectives on the Community College* (1992).

Florence B. Brawer is research director of the Center for the Study of Community Colleges. A former research educationist at UCLA, psychometrist, and counselor, she received her B.A. degree (1944) from the University of Michigan in psychology and her M.A. (1962) and Ed.D. (1967) degrees from UCLA in educational psychology. She is the author of *New Perspectives*

xvii

on Personality Development in College Students (1973) and the coeditor of *Developments in the Rorschach Technique,* vol. 3 (1970).

Cohen and Brawer together wrote *Confronting Identity: The Community College Instructor* (1972), *The Two-Year College Instructor Today* (1977), *The Collegiate Function of Community Colleges* (1987), and *The American Community College* (2nd ed., 1989). Together with other ERIC staff members, they also wrote *A Constant Variable: New Perspectives on the Community College* (1971) and *College Responses to Community Demands* (1975). Cohen and Brawer have edited several series of monographs published by the Center for the Study of Community Colleges and the ERIC Clearinghouse for Community Colleges. Since 1973, they have been editor-in-chief and associate editor, respectively, of the Jossey-Bass quarterly series New Directions for Community Colleges.

Hans A. Andrews is dean of instruction at Illinois Valley Community College. He received his B.S. degree (1960) from Central Michigan University in business education, his M.S. degree (1963) from Michigan State University in guidance and counseling, and his Ed.D. degree (1971) from the University of Missouri in counseling psychology. Andrews has published two books, *Evaluating for Excellence* (1985) and *Merit in Education* (1987). In addition, he has published over fifty professional articles in such journals as *Community/Junior College Quarterly of Research and Practice; Community Services Catalyst; Community College Review; Community, Technical, and Junior College Journal; School Administrator; Journal of Staff, Program, & Organization Development;* and *Journal of Personnel Evaluation Systems.*

Dan Angel is president of Stephen F. Austin State University in Nacogdoches, Texas. He received his B.S. (1961) and M.A. (1963) degrees from Wayne State University in education and his Ph.D. degree (1965) from Purdue University in communications. Angel has authored two books, edited two books, and published more than three dozen articles. He is a former state legislator from Michigan and has also served as president of three community colleges in California and Texas.

Jacquelyn A. Barber is currently employed by the Department of Specialized Support Services at Episcopal High School, Louisiana. A former graduate student in the higher education doctoral program at Texas Tech University, she received her M.S.Ed. degree (1980) from the University of Houston, Clear Lake. She has taught curriculum and instruction planning, instructional methods and classroom management, and teacher evaluation and mathematics at the University of Houston, Clear Lake; the University of Texas, El Paso; and El Paso Community College. She has also served as supervisor and field evaluator of student teachers and has presented papers and developed workshops on evaluation instruments and procedures in public schools.

Estela Mara Bensimon is associate professor and senior research associate at the Center for the Study of Higher Education, Pennsylvania State University. She received her B.A. (1970) and M.A. (1971) degrees from Montclair State College in Spanish and student personnel services, respectively, and her Ph.D. degree (1984) from Teachers College, Columbia University, in higher education. Bensimon is also affiliated with the National Center on Postsecondary Teaching, Learning, and Assessment. She writes on leadership and organizational change from cultural and feminist perspectives. She wrote *Redesigning Collegiate Leadership: Teams and Teamwork in Higher Education* (1993, with A. Neumann) and has just completed a source book on *Multicultural Teaching and Learning: Strategies for Change* (1993). She is also coeditor (with J. Glazer and B. Townsend) of *Women in Higher Education: A Feminist Perspective* (1993).

Trudy H. Bers is senior director of institutional research, curriculum, and strategic planning at Oakton Community College, Illinois. She received her Ph.D. degree (1973) from the University of Illinois, Urbana, in political science. Her professional responsibilities include being consulting editor for *Research in Higher Education* as well as serving on the executive council for the Association for Institutional Research and on the advisory committee for the AACC's *Community College Journal*. She has published articles in many journals and has planned, designed, and conducted numerous research and marketing studies.

James Brader is retired vice president for planning and development at Austin Community College, Texas. He received his B.S. (1956) and M.S. (1966) degrees from Stephen F. Austin State University in science education. Brader was at Austin Community College for twenty years, during which time he served as dean of continuing education and dean of occupational programs. He has extensive experience in all phases of the planning and construction of college facilities, and in his position as vice president, he oversaw the Research and Physical Plant Departments.

Charles R. Dassance is the president of Ashland Community College, Kentucky. He received his Ph.D. degree (1979) from the University of Virginia in higher education administration. Dassance worked in community college systems in New York, Maryland, Virginia, and Florida before coming to Kentucky and has an extensive background in the field of student affairs.

Alfredo G. de los Santos, Jr., is vice chancellor for educational development at Maricopa Community Colleges, Arizona, and co-principal investigator of the Maricopa Comprehensive Regional Center for Minorities. A graduate of Laredo Junior College, Texas, he has three degrees from the University of Texas: a B.A. (1957) in English, an M.L.S. (1959), and a Ph.D. (1965) in educational administration. He has served on the board of directors of numerous major educational organizations, including the American Council on Education and American College Testing Program.

Billie Wright Dziech is professor of English at the University of Cincinnati's University College, where she served as assistant to the dean. She received her Ed.D. degree (1975) from the University of Cincinnati in higher education and contemporary literature. Her works include *The Lecherous Professor: Sexual Harass-*

ment on Campus (1984, with L. Weiner), *On Trial: American Courts'*
Treatment of Sexually Abused Children (1989, with C. Schudson),
and publications in academic journals, books, and the *Chronicle*
of Higher Education. She lectures and consults at educational institutions and businesses throughout the United States and
Canada and has appeared on numerous radio and television
programs.

Judith S. Eaton currently serves as president of the Council for
Aid to Education in New York City. Before her appointment
at the council, she was vice president of the American Council
on Education in Washington, D.C. She is the former president
of the Community College of Philadelphia (1983–1989) and the
Community College of Southern Nevada (1979–1983) and has
been a member of the Pennsylvania State Board of Education
since 1987. She received her B.A. (1964) and M.A. (1966) degrees from the University of Michigan and her Ph.D. degree
(1975) from Wayne State University in education. She is editor
of *Women in Community Colleges* (1981), author and editor of *Col-*
leges of Choice: The Enabling Impact of the Community College (1988),
and author of *The Unfinished Agenda: Higher Education and the 1980s*
(1991). Her latest book is *Strengthening Collegiate Education in Com-*
munity Colleges (forthcoming).

Scott Finger is district manager of Novacare, a health care–related
organization in Wisconsin. Formerly an administrative assistant
in the Maricopa Community College District, Arizona, he also
coordinated the Fitness Center at Scottsdale Community College,
where he was an instructor. He received his M.S. degree (1985)
from the University of Wisconsin and is a doctoral student in Arizona State University's higher education administration program.

Earl Hale is executive director of the State Board for Community and Technical Colleges in Washington State. He has served
in that capacity since 1987 and previously held other administrative positions in the State Board office. He received his M.A.
degree (1968) from the University of Washington in public ad-

ministration. Hale was chair of the National Council of State Directors of Community and Junior Colleges in 1990–91. He has been actively engaged in the development and reorganization of the adult workforce training and education system in Washington, which involved the merger of community and technical colleges into a single system in 1991.

Barbara E. Janzen is a staff writer for the ERIC Clearinghouse for Community Colleges and has researched the operations and functions of community college administrative offices. She received her B.A. degree from the University of California, Los Angeles, and is a graduate student at California State University, Northridge.

Martha J. Kanter is president of De Anza College in Cupertino, California. A community college educator for nearly twenty years, she received her Ed.D. degree (1989) from the University of San Francisco in administration of higher education, with a specialization in psychometric theory and educational research methodologies. The former assistant deputy chancellor of the California Community Colleges, she is a nationally recognized expert on the effects of college placement testing on access to higher education for underrepresented students and related educational equity issues affecting community colleges.

Albert L. Lorenzo has been president of Macomb Community College, Michigan, since 1979. He received his M.B.A. degree (1966) from the University of Detroit. Prior to 1979 he spent eleven years in community college business management and worked for a Detroit-based CPA firm. He has served on several corporate boards and is a member of the Michigan Governor's Workforce Commission. His publications have addressed leadership and organizational issues, and he has received three national leadership awards. He is past chair of the Consortium for Institutional Effectiveness and Student Success, and he currently chairs the Commission on New Directions for Michigan Community Colleges.

John Losak is dean of research and planning and professor of higher education at Nova University. He received his Ph.D. degree (1969) from Florida State University in higher education and spent twenty-eight years at Miami-Dade Community College, the last fifteen as dean of institutional research. He has written extensively about the community college and has maintained an active teaching and consulting schedule.

Daniel F. Moriarty has been president of Portland Community College in Oregon since 1986. He received his Ed.D. degree (1974) from George Washington University. He has served as chair of the American Association of Community Colleges' (AACC) Presidents Academy and as president of COMBASE and is currently a board member of AACC. As chair of the Presidents Academy, he led the effort to develop the AACC Code of Ethics for Community College Presidents. He also teaches part-time at Portland State University.

James C. Palmer is assistant professor of educational administration and foundations at Illinois State University. He received his B.A. degree (1975) from Pacific University in English and German and his M.L.S. (1981) and Ph.D. (1987) degrees from UCLA in library science and higher education, respectively. Before joining the Illinois State faculty in 1992, he held positions at the ERIC Clearinghouse for Community Colleges, the Center for the Study of Community Colleges, the American Association of Community Colleges, and the Center for Community College Education at George Mason University.

Michael H. Parsons is dean of instruction at Hagerstown Junior College. He received his B.A. (1964) and M.A. (1965) degrees from Western Michigan University in English and history, respectively, and his Ed.D. degree (1971) from Western Michigan University in interdisciplinary higher education. Parsons has published articles on strategic planning, adjunct faculty, staff development, and ethics in community colleges. He has been a community college faculty and staff member in Michigan, Illinois, and Maryland.

William E. Piland is professor of education and director of doctoral programs in education at San Diego State University. He received his Ed.D. degree (1975) from Northern Illinois University in community college studies. Formerly, he held administrative positions in five community colleges in Illinois and later served as professor of education at Illinois State University.

Richard C. Richardson, Jr., has been professor of higher education and educational leadership and policy studies at Arizona State University since 1977. He received his B.S. degree (1954) from Castleton State College in education, his M.A. degree (1958) from Michigan State University in guidance and counseling, and his Ph.D. degree (1963) from the University of Texas in educational administration. Before 1977, Richardson served as the founding president of Northampton County Area Community College, Pennsylvania. His current research focuses on faculty effectiveness, minority academic achievement and success, and quality education at community colleges and universities. His publications include *Fostering Minority Access and Achievement in Higher Education* (1987, with L. Bender), *Achieving Quality and Diversity* (1991, with E. Skinner), and *Literacy in the Open Access College* (1983, with E. Fisk and M. Okun).

Albert B. Smith is coordinator of the higher education doctoral and master's programs at Texas Tech University. He received his Ph.D. degree (1970) from the University of Michigan in higher education. He is the author of *Faculty Development and Evaluation in Higher Education* (1976), co-author of *Meeting the Changing Needs: Undergraduate Curriculum and Instruction* (1984, with C. Clements) and editor of *Evaluating Faculty and Staff* in the New Directions for Community Colleges series (1983). Smith has also published numerous articles and book chapters in the community college field on faculty development and evaluation, curriculum development, college teaching, and staff development.

James D. Tschechtelin is president of the Baltimore City Community College. He received his Ed.D. degree (1977) from George

Washington University in higher education. He is a member of the Governor's Work Force Investment Board and the Urban Colleges Commission of the American Association of Community Colleges. Tschechtelin was at the Maryland State Board for Community Colleges for fourteen years, which included seven years as executive director, and was chair of the National Council of State Directors of the American Association of Community Colleges.

George B. Vaughan is professor and associate director of the Academy for Community College Leadership Advancement, Innovation, and Modeling (ACCLAIM) at North Carolina State University. He received his Ph.D. degree (1970) from Florida State University in higher education. A past president of two community colleges, Vaughan serves on the board of directors of the American Association of Community Colleges. In 1988, he was named one of the fifty most effective community college presidents in the nation.

Edwin E. Vineyard retired recently after twenty-five years as president of Northern Oklahoma College. Previously, he had professional and administrative duties at various universities, including Oklahoma State University, where he had received his Ed.D. degree (1955) in educational and counseling psychology. He is author of *The Pragmatic Presidency* (1993) and co-author of *The Profession of Teaching* (1961, with H. Massey). He has contributed chapters to *College and University Teaching* and *Readings in Guidance* and has published a number of articles in scholarly journals. He wrote the *Task Force Report on Rural Community Colleges,* has been a member of North Central Association's Commission on Institutions of Higher Education, and served as an accrediting consultant-evaluator for more than twenty years.

Geneva Waddell is a principal with GW Associates, a small business providing educational and management consulting services to educational institutions and businesses. She earned her Ph.D. degree (1984) from George Washington University in adult learning and higher education administration. She has served in a variety of capacities in a comprehensive community college for the past twenty-three years and previously was a human resource manager at Tracor, Inc., and the National Institutes of Health, Clinical Center. She edited *Economic and Work Force Development* (1991), no. 75 in the New Directions for Community Colleges series, and published "Tips for Training a World-Class Work Force" in *Community, Technical, and Junior College Journal* (1990). She received a College and University Personnel Association award for publications for co-authoring a handbook, *Personnel Administration in Higher Education* (1981, with R. T. Fortunato).

Mimi Wolverton serves as a research assistant for the Education Policy Studies Laboratory at Arizona State University. She holds an M.B.A. degree (1990) from Arizona State University and brings twenty-five years of corporate experience to her work on quality, leadership, and organizational change in higher education.

MANAGING
COMMUNITY
COLLEGES

PART ONE

LEADERSHIP AND ORGANIZATION

Administration has many dimensions. It has been described in terms of leadership, with leaders being the people with the vision to interpret trends, set goals, and inspire the staff to work toward the common good. It has been characterized as management, the process of translating goals into specific work plans and deploying staff so that the organization functions efficiently. And it has been portrayed as maintenance, the necessary activity of ensuring that schedules are built, bills paid, budgets balanced.

In Chapter One, Arthur M. Cohen and Florence B. Brawer provide an introductory overview.

Estela Mara Bensimon — in Chapter Two — discusses the split between theory and practice in managing colleges. Dealing informally with the conventional research theories of organization and leadership, she explains how those theories have provided insight for academic leaders into processes of leadership and organizational functioning. Bensimon proposes that leadership be viewed as a collective and interactional practice acting as a counterpoint to traditional theories, and that the idea of organization be perceived as a human and subjective entity in contrast to the rational and objective models of organizational theory.

Richard C. Richardson, Jr., and Mimi Wolverton take both a practical and a research-based approach in Chapter Three. Using the perspective of organizational culture together with the results of a study of twelve community colleges, they suggest context-specific leadership strategies for moving institutions toward more effective learning environments. Their focus on identifying leadership strategies that motivate instructors to perform in leadership roles will have special appeal to administrators who deal directly with the faculty.

In Chapter Four, George B. Vaughan stresses the president's role in understanding the institutions, appreciating the culture, and moderating disputes. Aware of the necessity for good management, he discusses personnel selection, the utilization of relevant information, and educational leadership. Describing various uses of power, he also emphasizes the use of research as a vehicle for leadership.

In Chapter Five—on the governing board—William E. Piland cites the importance of solid board-administrator relations. Noted here are the types of boards, demographics of trustees, trustee views on community college missions and functions, powers of state and local boards, the board's role in establishing institutional climate, and responsibilities that trustees and administrators share.

James D. Tschechtelin describes the dynamic tensions that affect the college and the state. Reviewing the patterns of interaction between these two forces in Chapter Six, he describes concepts that help to explain and predict the behavior of the groups and recommends steps to increase the community college's success.

With an emphasis on the college leader's policy role, Judith S. Eaton also focuses on issues related to the state. In Chapter Seven, she presents a case study of Pennsylvania's attempt to make a major public policy change that affects community colleges. The chapter examines the role of the community college president in responding to the effort of the state's department of education to remove state support for some noncredit full-time equivalent enrollments—a timely issue today for institutions in all states.

In Chapter Eight, Earl Hale argues that the role of a state office of community, junior, or technical colleges differs from that of a college administrative office. These differences have significant implications for staffing and structure as well as for various college functions. Among the issues that must be considered are centralization/decentralization, community responsiveness, state office functions, and the relationship between colleges and state government.

Chapter 1

The Challenging Environment: Context, Concepts, and Crises

Arthur M. Cohen, Florence B. Brawer

As we approach the twenty-first century, the community college, a twentieth-century phenomenon, is firmly set in the landscape of American education. With five million students enrolled and institutions in every state, the two-year colleges constitute an important sector. They have links to universities and secondary schools and to numerous job-training and community service enterprises in their local districts. But even though they interact with all those areas, they stand alone as important units of analysis, worthy of study in their own right.

The community colleges provide prebaccalaureate and occupational entry education for many students who would not otherwise participate in postsecondary studies. Most of the students and faculty are part-timers. More than half the curriculum is comprised of the liberal arts, with the rest dominated by courses in business, health fields, technologies, and trade and industry. Remedial and English as a second language studies are prominent.

Although there is variation among the states, the comprehensive community college is the dominant form. In some states, as many as 80 percent of the people starting postsecondary studies

5

do so in a community college. Tuition and entry requirements tend to be lower than in the public universities; graduation and program completion rates are lower as well. The colleges allow students to drop in and out repeatedly, taking classes as their circumstances and preferences permit over their life span.

These unique characteristics have led to forms of administration in the community colleges that are different from those in other sectors. With variation among the states again providing exceptions, the major form of governance includes a locally elected board; a president or chancellor; vice presidents for instructional, business, and student services; and instructional division or department chairs. State-level boards and administrative offices have grown in recent years, along with statewide faculty associations. Some national influences come through loosely affiliated organizations, including the Association of Community College Trustees and the American Association of Community Colleges, to which most of the colleges belong.

The history of administration shows that in states where the colleges grew out of the secondary school systems, college management derived directly from secondary school administration. In fact, in the early years the school board supervised the community colleges and the school superintendent was also superintendent for the colleges. Administrative positions followed lower-school organizational lines, with deans of students and curriculum coordinators prominent. As the colleges proceeded in their drive toward acceptance as members of higher education, most of the colleges separated from the lower schools, and the school superintendent gave way to a district chancellor or college president. Academic departments and divisions were organized with chairs in charge of faculty functioning. The dean of instruction, the community college's unique contribution to higher education management, moved toward vice presidential status.

The evolution continues, with administrative positions devoted to subcategories that did not exist even a few years ago. Affirmative action officers are essential within the personnel office. Financial aid officers are basic to student admission offices. Contracts managers, often legally trained, sit at the right hand of the board and the president to ensure that all decisions are undertaken within the framework of the contracts governing personnel relations. Each newly installed program demands a program coordinator, department chair, or similarly designated manager. Demands for data have given rise to institutional research officers or to data management personnel acting under the aegis of the registrar. One of the newest of these administrators is the enrollment management director, the person who tries to predict enrollment by viewing community demographics and to monitor the flow of students.

In brief, larger institutions, more diverse curricula, more demands for data coming from extramural agencies, greater expectations for data useful for internal management, and the flat institutional profile that is related to participatory management and governance have changed the shape of administration.

The chapters in this volume consider several aspects of leadership, management, and administration in community colleges. Directions for leaders to pursue are explored, and administrative contexts and concepts are examined. This chapter brings some of these themes together and relates them to the environment in which the colleges function. The first section highlights the major differences between management in community colleges and in other enterprises. The second reports on a few popular attempts to reform administration in the colleges. And the third discusses trends that have affected institutional directions.

Context of Administration

Administration in community colleges is both similar to and different from administration in business corporations. The commonalities begin with the importance of encouraging people to support the venture. Managers spend much time convincing their associates that they should work for the common good. A corollary is that the people must understand what that good is; thus, the administrators set goals, translate the goals into work plans, and seek to ensure that they are carried forward.

But several characteristics differentiate community colleges from business corporations. One difference is that the community college is a public agency, and its support depends on perceptions of its value by the public and its representatives. In this context, administration in community colleges is more accurately compared with administration in public schools and other public agencies, including municipal government and branches of state government, than with private sector enterprises.

A second difference is that lines of authority in the colleges are not clearly demarcated. Businesses usually have a boss and several strata of workers, but few people within the colleges view themselves in superior-subordinate relationships. Faculty, administrators, and to some extent students are more likely to act as though they were colleagues in a common venture. In this context, one does not give orders and expect them to be carried out; one explains, cajoles, and seeks cooperation.

A third difference is that the community college is a school, which means that it strives to enhance human learning. Its processes are similar to those of other schools; it engages staff, attracts students, and sustains an image as a learning environment. Because its main product — human learning — is infinite, it can always do better. More learning, a more efficient set of processes to stimulate learning, and a more pleasant set of conditions surrounding the learning process itself can always be sought.

These differences influence all attempts to explain community college administration to people within and outside the institution, to advise administrators on the conduct of their work, and to categorize patterns of management. As a public agency, the college's survival depends on patterns of support that may relate only tangentially to its outcomes. As an environment continually striving for collegiality, the relationships among people cannot be understood as though they reflect superiors addressing subordinates. As a learning environment, the college does not have a profit motive and its products cannot be readily classified.

College managers function within a political arena where public relations, coalitions, interinstitutional cooperation, and image guide decisions regarding support. Data on products or outcomes are useful only to the extent that they relate to these phenomena. But outcomes data are among the most elusive products of the institution, primarily because if each student is an individual and has particular needs and aspirations, there must be as many outcomes measures as there are students. Every call for institutional accountability clashes with calls for multiple measures of attainment. Thus community college outcomes data are rarely put forth because, the argument runs, no one set of data adequately portrays the institution's effects.

Because of the difficulty of displaying product in an institution with human learning as its goal and with the concept of individuality as its guiding value, the *process* of bringing individuals to greater understandings has become the institution's main *product*. Furthermore, because one of the colleges' primary functions is to serve everyone, college success is directly related to the number or percentage of the local population that it serves. This belief has given rise to using enrollment as a measure of institutional success, a measure that is embedded in the lore of the institution.

The idea of serving everyone in the district with any type of instructional program they may desire has been dominant in community colleges for the past fifty years. It has been rationalized repeatedly by college leaders, who point out that the institutions contribute to the well-being of their community by providing access for people who would not otherwise be able to participate in postsecondary education. The people served go on to baccalaureate studies or enter the workforce with greater skills than they would have had if the institution had not been available to them. Since these functions contribute to human well-being, the colleges are an agency of the public good.

These concepts of open access and unlimited growth in enrollments as a public good served the colleges well from the 1950s to the 1980s. In state after state, legislation was passed enabling the states or local districts within them to organize colleges, and arrangements were made for funding to support the institutions. The tacit assumption was that if the college managers could bring students in and provide staff to counsel and teach them, the money to pay for that would be forthcoming. Accordingly, the college leaders directed their efforts toward finding proper staff, planning new programs, and recruiting students. Most contemporary community college administrators began their careers in an era of support for continual growth.

Now the context has changed. Since the early 1980s, in one state after another, the legislatures have indicated that they will not continue reimbursing the colleges for as many students as they are able to attract. Limitations on enrollments have been detailed and the colleges instructed to restrict entry into certain programs and to cut out programs entirely. The era of unrestricted enrollment growth has ended.

The main reason for growth restrictions is that as the states run short of money, competition between the community colleges and other public agencies becomes more intense. As one example, between 1980 and 1992, the state prison population in California increased by 300 percent and the prisons' operating budget increased from 2 to 6 percent of the state budget. There are more than half the number of people incarcerated in prison or in local jails or on probation as there are taking classes in the state's community colleges. And the cost of operating the criminal justice system is eight times as high on a per capita basis (Petersilia, 1993). To sum up, while the community college leaders have been lobbying for new programs and additional support for their institutions, the fiscal ground has been eroding under them.

Despite this obvious shift in context, the notion that the community colleges should market their services and continue attempting to bring in more students has still not been abandoned by administrators who learned their craft in an environment of continued growth. Many have reacted slowly to the knowledge that the states are not going to provide funds for every student they can entice into the institution, that they are competing with other agencies for state dollars. Every call for new programs to serve new populations, with the state paying the lion's share of the cost, reveals their shortsightedness.

Concepts of Administration

Traditional concepts of college organization as hierarchical have viewed it as having a pyramidal form with the board and president at the top and the vice presidents, deans, and the rest of the staff arrayed below. Organizational charts have consisted of boxes with arrows flowing in both directions as orders went down and responses went up.

Whether or not this conception of college organization ever fit the realities of the institutions is not now in contention. But colleges now tend to be seen as having flatter profiles, with all staff members participating in a co-equal fashion. In this view, the institution encourages ideas from all staff members. Everyone has the opportunity to share and participate in decision making. Orders do not flow from one level to another; instead, people transmit ideas to each other as co-equals. This pattern tends to describe a more caring, nurturing, empowering environment, with everyone working to help each other's creativity.

The conception of the college organized in such a participatory fashion has been in the literature for some time. In 1972, Richardson, Blocker, and Bender described the ideal community college as having that form. Other writers have since put it forward as a desirable organizational pattern for an institution that purports to enhance the well-being of all its members, staff as well as students. Most recently, this conception has been advanced by those who argue that it reveals the female values of caring, nurturing, and empowering as contrasted with the male tendency to emphasize dominance and formalistic relationships. Regardless of the ownership of the idea or the motives of those who would argue on its behalf, the notion of a hierarchical organization has never quite fit the college environment. The faculty have always been autonomous. Within the confines of their classroom, they guard their right to teach and interact with the students as they choose. The personal interactions that govern the daily activities of all college staff members influence their behavior far more than does any organizational chart with arrows showing who reports to whom.

A few concepts of administration are of particular interest to observers of the contemporary community college: Total Quality Management (TQM), shared governance, and responsibility.

Total Quality Management

Program Evaluation and Review Technique (PERT), Program
Planning and Budget System (PPBS), and Management by Objectives (MBO): each in its day was put forward as the answer
to decision making. But all have disappeared from the contemporary community college literature. Few college managers
remember the enthusiasm with which each was greeted in its
time, or the musty closet where its reports have been filed and
forgotten.

Recently, TQM has become the talisman that will reform
administration. It reflects the attempts community college managers have made to align their administrations with those of the
corporate world. Business corporations have budgets, staff,
offices, purposes; colleges have budgets, staff, offices, purposes.
Therefore, the thinking goes, let us be like business corporations.

TQM's premises, as popularized by Deming (1982), center on constancy of purpose, intrinsic quality control, on-the-
job training, cooperation between people and various departments, removal of adversarial relationships, and attention to
the customer. Quality, then, is defined as the degree to which
customer needs or expectations are met. TQM further holds
that the institution is never functioning optimally, that it needs
continuous improvement, that it should set higher performance
levels each year. Every employee must be given the preparation and initiative to contribute to corporate goals. Work must
be organized around the preferences of the customers, not those
of the corporation. TQM would shift organizations to a focus
on everyone's intrinsic motivation to do better on behalf of the
customers.

TQM has received much attention in the literature of
higher education. An entire issue of *Change* magazine (Marchese,
1993) was devoted to it, and Gonzales (1989) related it specifically to community college administration. Many of the
reports suggest that the extent to which TQM has made inroads
in higher education are difficult to pinpoint. The concept is
applied most often in business and finance administrative units
and in computer centers, but in the academic arena only the

business administration and engineering faculties seem to embrace it. Entin (1993) found that in most applications, the initial enthusiasm for TQM has waned quickly, and that institutional leaders have not used its principles in analyzing and solving major problems.

TQM codifies certain truisms. It holds that change is inevitable, desirable, and welcome and that change must be planned for proactively with participation by the greatest number of staff members and people from the surrounding community. Furthermore the college must be responsive to its customers, defined as its students, local schools, employers, and social welfare and charitable agencies. TQM's admonition that we must convert from a posture of penalizing failure to one of rewarding success centers on the belief that people should be accepted for what they are. Cooperation, not conflict, is key.

It is difficult to mount an argument against these principles. Contemporary belief values the individual and seeks systems that enhance everyone's sense of dignity. Concepts in behavior modification are based on reward, not punishment. Cooperation is perceived as essential if societies are to function. And the colleges have operated on these principles. It is the rare institution now that has a patriarch at its head and a set of cowering subordinates staffing its offices. The vertically integrated committees comprised of administrators, counselors, support staff, instructors, and students are familiar arrangements. The profile of management has flattened out. Barriers between divisions have been broken in numerous instances — for example, between instructional and student services, where combinations of staff from both areas now often conduct orientation, study skills courses, and remedial education. Similarly, changes in library management and function are so widespread that few libraries now operate solely as book repositories; as the result of joint efforts by librarians and instructors, they also tend to include instructional media and other resources.

TQM has much in common with good-sense management technique. Because it focuses on process instead of on product, it squares with the thinking of process-oriented administrators. Because it glorifies innovation, it fits the history of community colleges. And because it directs the staff's attention toward their customers, it suggests the student-centeredness that community colleges have always favored. Many of its premises are being incorporated in places where PERT, PPBS, and MBO disappeared. These latter patterns centered on outcomes or products. They were linear techniques in a process-oriented, lateral institution and could not survive.

Shared Governance

By way of accelerating cooperation among the staff, the term *shared governance* has come into prominence. An assembly bill passed in California in 1987 directed the colleges to open up the management process to various intracampus constituencies. The rationalization was that shared governance is a decision-making process that contributes to the best interests of the students and the institution because those affected by the decisions participate in an environment of cooperation and trust. Thus, the entire campus community should be empowered to participate in any decision process, because every decision potentially affects everyone.

The quest for the proper combination of cooperation and goal furtherance never ends. One reason is that administration is similar to teaching. Asking teachers whether they teach subject matter or students is a conundrum in the teaching field. The astute respondent knows the answer: both. Teachers teach subject matter to students. The image of a teacher attempting to impart subject matter to an empty room is as ludicrous as that of a teacher in a room full of students with no conception of what is to be learned. Both subject and students are essential components of the teaching process.

Do administrators manage institutions or people? Like teaching, the answer is both. An institution has programs, functions, goals, and activities carried out by people. The people must be directed, inspired, and otherwise impelled toward furthering the purposes of the institution. Without people, the administrator has no possibility of managing. Without the institution and its mission and responsibilities, the people would have no reason for interacting.

This conception of administration in the colleges, link-ing institutional purposes and people, is at the heart of man-agement. Many people within the colleges have a low regard for structure. They are professionals and they do not want to be managed, nor do they want to manage anyone else. There is an understandable lack of consistency, because administra-tors, staff members, and students often have differing goals. Peo-ple in different occupational classifications at different stages of their own lives do not see things the same way. Being employed in an institution with multiple goals or missions does not help. Managing such a collectivity makes for challenges.

Many administrators find it difficult to resist the tempta-tion to make decisions and then pass the word along. After all, it is easier for one person to decide than it is to engage the sup-port of a large number of people. Furthermore, the delays that can arise from a process that seeks consensus before a decision is rendered can be paralyzing. Fortunately for the principles of shared governance, most of the decisions made within educa-tion institutions are not severely restricted by time. Markets, clientele, and personnel persevere. A change in procedure not implemented this year can always be installed later. The most successful administrators typically plan for changes to be made many years in the future. There is always time to engage the staff in the deliberative process. Like TQM's principles, those of shared governance fit well with the primary goals in com-munity colleges and the outlook of the college staff. They fit also with Galbraith's (1992, p. 66) observation: "The modern cor-poration or public agency has an internal intelligence and au-thority of its own; these are to some extent independent of, or superior to, those of the persons who are seen, and who see them-selves, as in command."

Responsibility

A concept rarely articulated in the literature is that of owner-ship or responsibility for the entire enterprise. Who is respon-sible for the institution's progress toward meeting the goals that participatory management sets forth? The answer typically supplied — "everybody" — does not sufficiently explore the mean-

ing of responsibility. Who *owns* the institution? How many people who have participated in the process of goal setting would
feel a deep sense of loss if the goals were not met? How many
people who participate in a decision to reorganize the work flow
would be distressed if the reorganization does not lead to greater
efficiency? Saying that everyone shares responsibility is not much
different from saying that no one is responsible.

Addressing the issue of ownership or responsibility leads
to the issues of administrator selection and evaluation. College
administrators are usually selected from a pool of applicants who
have served in the same or closely related positions. The advertisements usually specify a number of years of experience
within the institutions. Presidents move among presidencies
three, four, or more times in their careers with an average tenure of six years. If decisions important to the future of the institution should have five- or ten-year time lines, the outcomes
will often be realized after the incumbent has gone. Thus, few
colleges reveal the lengthened shadow of their chief executive
officers. Few offices within the colleges reflect the distinctiveness of their managers. A corollary is that the criteria for assessing administrative success tend to be of a negative sort. The
administrator whose institution or office has yielded few problems, a paucity of complaints, a dearth of disruption is a success. The well-functioning administrator does not exceed the
budget, does not make the community unhappy, does not en-
gender lawsuits.

The demands of administration and the relatively short
tenure for college presidents combine to reinforce short-term
perspectives. There is always another problem that must be
solved today; planning for next year can be set aside in good
conscience. The head of a registrar's office that has just lost a
couple of clerical positions is in no mood to provide student transcript data to a federal agency in the hope that such data collected uniformly from all the colleges of the nation will eventually influence the type of legislation regarding institutional
accountability that Congress enacts. Short-term problems are
finite; long-term trends are infinite. Budgets are immediate and
specific; benefits are diffuse and uncertain. The corporate cul-

ture stimulates most managers to prefer short-run inaction to long-run action; short-run comfort is a powerful force. Those who seek to turn the administrators' attention toward planning for the future are continually frustrated by their tendency to focus on the immediate and obvious.

Crisis Cycle

A sense of past and future time can be helpful to the administrators. This sense enables them to understand that each crisis is similar to one that has had to be faced previously and, most important, that each crisis tends to devour the one that preceded it. Viewing some of the crises of the past four decades and putting them in the context of the contemporary community college and its immediate future offers evidence.

In the 1950s, the overriding national issue concerned community college identity and the need to expand the idea of the community college into more states. Much of the state legislation authorizing community colleges developed in the 1950s and early 1960s, and in each case, as the legislation was written, questions of institutional identity came to the fore. Prebaccalaureate or technical? Remedial or collegiate? How much emphasis in each area?

The identity question remained open as the colleges continually sought new markets. By the 1960s, the need for campuses, buildings, and staff members was critical. Rapidly growing student populations, expanding at the rate of 15 percent and more a year (nationwide, enrollments more than doubled between 1963 and 1968) put questions of college identity in the background. The colleges had been authorized; now the problem was to get them opened with people to manage and teach in them. Campus construction and staff recruitment dominated.

By the 1970s, a new set of crises had appeared. Collective bargaining had begun its rapid spread as the faculty and, in some cases, the administrators in many states gained authorization to form bargaining units and negotiate for wages and working conditions. Coupled with the continual references to affirmative action, the search for new staff then took a different form. The contracts spelled out in great detail how staff members were to be sought, employed, and evaluated. The affirmative action guidelines forced attention on the types of staff members entering the institutions. These issues have still not been resolved.

By the 1980s, a shift from local control and funding to state management and finance had shouldered unionization and affirmative action out of the spotlight. Whereas in 1965 the proportion of income coming from the state and from the local community was balanced at around one-third each, by 1980 the ratio had shifted to 60 percent state, 11 percent local income. Along with the trend toward state financing came more state regulation. And along with state-level management issues came the expansion of statewide associations comprised of faculty members, administrators, trustees, and groups coalescing around specific issues or programs, all seeking and receiving a say in college management.

Most recently, in the early 1990s, questions of funding limitations have become central. Statewide enrollment caps, budget cuts, and restrictions on expenditures have consumed questions of local or state control. The state legislatures are the center of concern as the community colleges compete for funds with all other state-supported agencies. And changing demography looms. The ratio of high school graduates to the number of students in the secondary school system is increasing for the first time since the mid 1960s, and the absolute number of eighteen-year-olds in the American population, declining steadily from 1979 to 1991, has turned up and will continue increasing until 2003. Because all colleges thrive on eighteen-year-olds and recent high school graduates, the pressure for increased enrollment at community colleges will be great. This pressure will be exacerbated by the universities' budgetary problems, which are imposing limits on the number of entering freshmen they can matriculate. These forces demanding access to postsecondary study will create pressure on legislatures to fund community colleges, which are seen as providing low-cost opportunity for prebaccalaureate and occupational studies. The rising tide of enrollment will devour the budgetary crisis.

Beyond Crisis Management

The news media rarely carry stories about the tens of thousands of people who go to work and return home without incident. Instead, they report only on the ones who suffered mishaps along the way. The presentations made by community college administrators in writing and from conference platforms, formerly centering on self-serving reports of college accomplishments, are now more likely to offer cries of alarm regarding imminent changes in state funding policies, community demographics, or some other immutable ill. It seems suitable to close this chapter with a few words of solace.

Stability. The college has the same mission now that it has always had. Look at the statements of purpose in any college's handbook since that college was founded. College goals have not changed, either. A national survey of presidents, faculty members, and students in the early 1970s found the following top goals: "Serve higher education needs of youth from the local community," "Provide some form of education for any student regardless of academic ability," and "Encourage mutual trust and respect among faculty, students, and administrators" (Bushnell and Zagaris, 1972). Those still rank among the highest on any contemporary list.

Constancy. The colleges do many things in the same way. Each year's entrants must be recruited, screened, matriculated, educated, and evaluated. The generations pass through an accessible, safe, pleasant environment. The college is always available to anyone who wants to interact with it. People talking together are its essence.

Corporate amnesia. There is little cumulative knowledge in the college staff. Experienced administrators or instructors have little to teach to neophytes beyond a few office procedures and general principles regarding pitfalls to avoid. The experience of individuals far transcends that of the collectivity; the whole is less than the sum of its parts. That is why staff recruitment and selection are the most important activities administrators can pursue.

Individual autonomy. Each practitioner on the campus acts as an individual. The long-sought team teaching remains elusive and the administrative committees may be comprised of individuals from different job settings, but they are usually dominated by a few charismatic individuals. Instructors do not hold each other accountable for results. Administrators are successful if the staff is comfortable, if their attention is kept focused on the work they are doing. That is why staff evaluation is a pro forma exercise.

Open-ended goals. The introduction of concepts drawn for managing business corporations seems untoward in an institution that has open-ended goals. Colleges are more like religious organizations than they are like businesses; they help people toward a better life. To introduce the rhetoric of achievement indicators, customer focus, and quality control is to introduce a type of thinking that ill fits the sensibilities of most of the people within the organizations. Attained learning, degrees earned, and new jobs entered may be measured, but beyond these gross indicators, the process is the product. The staff have never accepted outcome measures as indicators of college worth. There is no profit, no bottom line. Knowledge is not a consumption item.

College form. After decades of calls for innovation, the community colleges still look like the public schools from which they emerged. They are grounded in a structure of teachers, students, classrooms, semesters, grades, libraries, campuses. Innovations have occurred repeatedly, but nearly all within that basic form. Claims for the economy and effectiveness of distance learning or technology in the classrooms are made continually, but people stubbornly want to interact with each other. Futurists dating back to George Leonard (1968) and Aldous Huxley (1932) have envisioned the isolated learner, alone at a computer station or interacting eagerly with an artificial environment. Each new application of technology brings forth another set of claims, but the image is as elusive as it ever was.

Exclusivity. No other publicly supported agency in the nation provides a comparable range of helpful services. The colleges educate, thus transmitting the culture. They enhance individual mobility in society. They support cohesive communities that have shared values. They serve as agents of hope for all people regardless of their past experience with the educational system.

Summary

Thus, administrative patterns are consistent because schools are schools. The major reorganizations that may become necessary as the context in which the colleges function continues shifting — developments that we examine in the last chapter — will be effected at the state level. The far-sighted administrators will manage their offices but also work with their counterparts elsewhere to influence the direction of these reorganizations.

References

Bushnell, D. S., and Zagaris, I. *Report from Project Focus: Strategies for Change.* Washington, D.C.: American Association of Community and Junior Colleges, 1972. (ED 061 929)

Deming, E. W. *Out of the Crisis.* Cambridge, Mass.: MIT Press, 1982.

Entin, D. H. "Case Study Number One. Boston: Less Than Meets the Eye." *Change,* 1993, *25*(3), 28–31.

Galbraith, J. K. *The Culture of Contentment.* Boston: Houghton Mifflin, 1992.

Gonzales, F. S. *Implementing Total Quality Management at El Camino College.* Torrance, Calif.: El Camino College, 1989. (ED 356 827)

Huxley, A. *Brave New World.* London: Chatto & Windus, 1932.

Leonard, G. *Education and Ecstasy.* New York: Delacorte Press, 1968.

Marchese, T. "TQM: A Time for Ideas." *Change,* 1993, *25*(3), 10–13.

Petersilia, J. "Crime and Punishment in California: Full Cells, Empty Pockets, and Questionable Benefits." *CPS Brief,* 1993, *5*(11), 1–12.

Richardson, R. C., Jr., Blocker, C. G., and Bender, L. W. *Governance for the Two-Year College.* Englewood Cliffs, N.J.: Prentice-Hall, 1972.

Chapter 2

Understanding Administrative Work

Estela Mara Bensimon

College administrators tend to be skeptical about the practical uses of theories on organizations and leadership. There is a significant body of literature, covering the gamut of theoretical perspectives on academic organizations and leadership (for example, functionalist, critical, feminist, and postmodernist). But most administrators are not familiar with this scholarship, or if they are, they tend to see it as interesting but not necessarily relevant to their day-to-day administrative work. In fact, college administrators are likely to be more conversant with popular books on leadership that are based on the corporate sector such as *In Search of Excellence: Lessons from America's Best-Run Companies* (Peters and Waterman, 1982) or *The Seven Habits of Highly Effective People* (Covey, 1989), than with works that are grounded on the realities of leadership and administration in colleges and universities.

Several reasons might be advanced for this split between theory and practice—that is, the apparent lack of connection between academic leadership and the research conducted by scholars of academic organizations. Three are listed here.

1. *Scholars' predilection for inaccessible language.* The kinds of terms—such as *cybernetics* or *postmodernism*—that scholars of higher

education use to elaborate their views of organizations and leadership are highly specialized. This terminology makes their works less accessible to the audiences that scholars of higher education need to engage in dialogue.

2. *Administrators' predilection for solutions.* Academic administrators have often criticized conceptual studies of administration as being neither relevant nor particularly instructive. Conceptual works on leadership are often ignored because, unlike popular works, they are not prescriptive. They do not delineate how to determine one's leadership style or tell one what to do. Instead of making things simpler, conceptual works tend to highlight the complexity and indeterminacy of leadership.

3. *Inadequate modes of dissemination.* Much of the current scholarly work on organizations and leadership in colleges and universities is published in scholarly journals that administrators rarely see. Or it is communicated through the presentation of formal papers at academic conferences that few administrators attend. Generally, the scholars are not particularly effective at transforming their academic writing into conversational presentations or workshops for practitioners.

This chapter has three sections. The first two discuss conventional research theories of organization and leadership informally and explain how these theories have provided academic leaders with insights into processes of leadership and organizational functioning. They show how theories of organization and leadership can help administrators understand what they do and how they do it. Thus, these sections discuss organizational models and leadership theories that implicitly influence conceptions of good administrative leadership.

The third section plants the idea that the traditional models of organization and leadership discussed earlier, while analytically useful, may not be pragmatically useful on today's changing campuses. It concludes with two proposals: the idea of leadership as a collective and interactional practice as a counterpoint to the individualistic model in traditional theories; and the idea of organizations as human and subjective entities as the counterpoint to the rational and objective model that informs much of our thinking about organizations.

Viewing Colleges Through Organizational Frames

Where do our definitions of leadership come from? How do we determine the appropriate role of leadership? How do we define good leadership? How do we make judgments about effective leadership? The answers to these questions depend on how we view the nature of social organizations. In *How Colleges Work,* Birnbaum (1988) shows that the leader who views the college primarily as an organizational chart will have a very different conception of good leadership than the leader who views the college as a political entity. Therefore, since administrators' conceptualization of leadership derives from the assumptions they make about the nature of social organizations, it is important to examine the organizational frames through which administrators make sense of the organizations they attempt to lead.

First, a word about the meaning of organizational frames. An organizational frame represents a distinctive cognitive lens that influences what leaders see and do. Organizational frames determine what questions might get asked, what information is collected, how problems are defined, and what courses of action should be taken (Goleman, 1985). According to Bolman and Deal (1984, p. 4), "Frames are windows on the world. Frames filter out some things while allowing others to pass through easily. Frames help us to order the world and decide what action to take. Every manager uses a personal frame, or image, of organizations to gather information, make judgments, and get things done." Bolman and Deal propose four different organizational frames through which managers can understand their organizations: structural, human resources, political, and symbolic. They suggest that organizations have multiple realities and that a manager who can use multiple lenses will likely be more effective than one who deals with problems from a single perspective. Similarly, Birnbaum (1988) suggests that administrators must recognize the interactions between the bureaucratic, collegial, political, and symbolic processes in colleges and universities if they are to be effective.

Four Types of Frames

Following is a review of the four kinds of frames just mentioned.

Bureaucratic Frame. This frame views organizations as mechanistic hierarchies with clearly established lines of authority. According to this model, (1) the organization's goals are clear, (2) the organization is a closed system insulated from external influences, and (3) administrative leaders have the power to analyze a problem, determine possible solutions, choose the best, and execute it. Administrative leaders who are guided by the bureaucratic frame are likely to emphasize their role in making decisions, getting results, and establishing systems of management.

Because bureaucracies are ultimately centralized systems, the bureaucratic leader has final authority and therefore may be cast as a larger-than-life, or heroic, leader. From the bureaucratic perspective, the president of a college is seen as the center of power, responsible for the welfare and outcomes of the institution (Kerr and Gade, 1986). A frame analysis of presidents' definitions of good leadership revealed that a president guided by the bureaucratic frame defined a leader as "the person who sets the pace and commands the respect of those that follow him and who accomplishes what he sets out to do. . . . The president's principal responsibility is to make decisions" (Bensimon, 1989, p. 113). In true bureaucratic form, this president described the leader as being at the top of the hierarchy. Implicit within this definition is the image of the president as decisive and as oriented toward action and results. The heroic image of leaders in higher education can be found in references to great presidential figures of the past as well as in current works that idealize the position (see, for example, Fisher, 1984; Fisher, Tack, and Wheeler, 1988).

Collegial Frame. Within this frame, organizations are viewed as collectives with organizational members as their primary resource. The emphasis is on human needs and on how organizations can be tailored to meet them.

This frame pictures colleges and universities as communities of scholars (Millett, 1962) who, by virtue of their professional expertise and a shared value system, control organizational goals. The collegial frame is useful for understanding stable organizations, or organizational subunits, in which preferences are developed by consensus through interaction (Birnbaum, 1988). Presidents who use a collegial frame seek participative, democratic decision making and strive to meet people's needs and help them realize their aspirations. Emphasis here is on interpersonal skills, motivating others, and putting the interests of the institution first.

A president who spoke about leadership almost exclusively through the collegial frame said, "I define a leader as a person who provides a vision or direction for a group which takes the capability of the group and potential benefits into account. . . . A [president] has to understand what the faculty is feeling and needing and address oneself to meeting the needs and getting people to feel good about the institution" (Bensimon, 1989, p. 113). Unlike the president who spoke from a bureaucratic perspective, this one emphasizes being responsive to group needs rather than being a decision maker. For her, strong leaders attend to people's need to build commitment and loyalty to the institution.

While decision making within the collegial frame may be understood as a rational process similar to that discussed with respect to the bureaucratic frame, leaders emphasize the processes involved in defining priorities, problems, goals, and tasks to which institutional energies and resources will be devoted. From this perspective, leaders are viewed as less concerned with hierarchical relationships. They believe that the organization's core is not its leadership so much as its membership. The job of leaders is to promote consensus within the community — and especially between administrators and faculty (Bensimon, Neumann, and Birnbaum, 1989).

Political Frame. This frame sees organizations as formal and informal groups vying for power to control institutional processes and outcomes. Decisions result from bargaining, influencing, and coalition building. This frame assumes that colleges and universities are pluralistic entities made up of groups with different interests and values and that conflict will erupt when resources are scarce (Baldridge, 1971). Conflict, not salient in the two previous frames, is here a central feature of organizational life.

In the political frame, the president is a mediator or negotiator between shifting power blocs. The president must "assemble a winning or dominant coalition that will support proposed actions — as one would in a parliamentary form of government" (Whetten, 1984, p. 40). Presidents should administer through persuasion and diplomacy, be open and communicative, and stay flexible on means but rigid on ends (Walker, 1979). Presidents with a political frame are also sensitive to external interest groups and their strong influence over the policy-making process.

A president speaking about his way of doing things said, "[You should] do your homework, get to know your immediate staff — their backgrounds, make them relax with you. Drop in around campus. Accept all speaking engagements. Go to the faculty leaders' offices and talk to them so they will know that you are willing to listen to them. Have a beer with them. But don't make any promises" (Bensimon, 1989, p. 115). This president's view of leadership is reflective of the political frame, particularly in the emphasis on understanding key individuals who could be potential friends or opponents.

Symbolic Frame. Within this frame, organizations are cultural systems of shared meanings and beliefs in which organizational structures and processes are socially constructed. Leaders construct and maintain "systems of shared meanings, paradigms, and shared languages and cultures" (Pfeffer, 1981, p. 9) by sustaining rituals, symbols, and myths that create a unifying system of belief for the institution (Dill, 1982). Presidents who adhere to this symbolic frame are primarily catalysts and facilitators of an ongoing process. They do not so much lead the institution as channel its activities in subtle ways. This perspective emphasizes the effect that leaders have on the expressive side rather than on the instrumental side of organizations (Pfeffer, 1981). An administrative leader might be seen as one who brings about a sense of organizational purpose and orderliness through interpretation, elaboration, and reinforcement of institutional culture.

The symbolic view of organizations challenges two basic beliefs about leadership. One is the belief in the efficacy of leadership, which presumes that leaders have the power and resources to make choices that will affect organizational outcomes. The other is the belief in differential success among leaders, which presumes that individuals possess attributes that determine their success or failure as leaders (March, 1982). The symbolic view stresses that administrative discretion is constrained by many factors. It also emphasizes, however, that academic leaders usually have more influence than other organizational participants and that they can use that influence to make marginal changes supporting their own desired outcomes (Birnbaum, 1988).

A president who spoke about leadership from a symbolic frame said that good leadership requires a president to "do a lot of listening and solicit the dreams and hopes from the people; tell the people about the good things you are finding and in three to six months take these things and report them as the things you would like to see happen" (Bensimon, 1989, p. 114). A good leader, in this president's eyes, searches among the activities of the institution and selects those that should be retained as institutional goals. For this president, the presidential role is sense making, and leadership is the management of meaning (Smircich and Morgan, 1982). Reality is constructed not by imposing the president's image of what the institution should be doing, but by transforming people's desires and ambitions for the institution (for example, "the good things you are finding") into its plans and goals (Bensimon, 1989).

How Frames Shape the Exercise of Leadership

These frames focus on different aspects of organizational behavior; they also function as cognitive blinders in that whatever is "out of frame" is likely to be ignored or overlooked. For example, the president who analyzes problems through the cognitive lens of the bureaucratic frame will probably propose solutions that stress efficiency but overlook impacts on institutional members, political ramifications, or symbolic interpretations others in the organization may attach to the solution.

The difference between effective and ineffective leaders may be related to cognitive complexity. That is, academic organizations have multiple realities, and leaders with the capacity to use multiple frames tend to be more effective than those who analyze and act on every problem using a single perspective. Leaders who incorporate elements of several frames are likely to have more flexible responses to different administrative tasks because they have different images of the organization and can interpret events in a variety of ways. Hence, if they are to be effective, academic leaders must recognize the interactions between the bureaucratic, collegial, political, and symbolic processes present in all colleges and universities at all times.

Bensimon (1989) examined the preferred cognitive frames implicit in presidents' interpretations of good leadership and found that the theories of leadership presidents espouse were more likely to have a single or paired-frame orientation than a multiframe orientation. That is, the majority of presidents provided definitions of leadership that reflected one or two of the frames rather than three or four of the frames.

The most distinct pattern emerging from this analysis involved the distribution of definitions of good leadership provided by presidents of community colleges. These presidents clustered in the single-frame category, possibly because structurally and administratively, community colleges are more closely aligned with the bureaucratic model of governance (Baldridge, Curtis, Ecker, and Riley, 1978; Bensimon, 1984; Reyes and Twombly, 1987). But only two of the five community college presidents with a single frame had a bureaucratic orientation. Two others had a collegial and one a symbolic frame.

The finding that four out of the five single-frame theories espoused by community college presidents have either a bureaucratic or collegial orientation may reveal tendencies to view the organization as a closed system. Presidents of community colleges are perhaps prone to closed-system views because decision making is centralized, and they, rather than the faculty, control transactions with the external environment.

Furthermore, three of the five community college presidents with a single-frame orientation were recent appointees, and none of them had a bureaucratic orientation. The two who did had served in their positions for some time. Possibly, as Vaughan (1986) has suggested, the newer generation of community college presidents favors leadership approaches encouraging greater participation and shared decision making.

Understanding Traditional Theories of Leadership

Leadership is an elusive concept. There are probably as many definitions of leaders and of leadership as there are people who have written about these topics. In their most recent book, *Reframing Organizations* (1991, p. 404), Bolman and Deal state that "despite tens of thousands of pages written about it, leadership remains an elusive concept. Social science research on leadership has provided few generalizations that are reliable and even fewer that are interesting." Conventional theories of leadership focus on the traits as well as on the power and influence of individuals.

Trait Theories

From a *trait theory* perspective, the focus would be on specific personal characteristics that contribute to a person's ability to assume leadership. The traits approach proposes that leaders are persons endowed with specific traits related to their effectiveness that differentiate them from followers. Traits may include physical characteristics (height, appearance, age, energy level), personality, social background, and ability (Bensimon, Neumann, and Birnbaum, 1989).

Trait theories are the most primitive of the theories of leadership in that they reduce the explanation of leadership to individual characteristics. Although scholars of leadership do not discount that many leaders may have certain traits in common, they suggest that a model emphasizing traits is too simple to explain a phenomenon as complex as leadership.

For example, Watkins (1989, p. 13) suggests that "the trait approach still finds favor because it often presents those idealized characteristics with which people would like to typify their imagined symbolic heroes." In addition, the approach has been nurtured by business magnates to justify their own position through myths and legends that endorse their prowess — witness the seductiveness of corporate heroes like Lee Iacocca and Donald Trump.

Power-and-Influence Theories

Power-and-influence theories emphasize the relationship between the leader and follower as one of reciprocity and mutual influence or one the leader initiates and controls. Some views of the power relationship suggest that leaders should cultivate charisma by remaining distant and remote from constituents. The importance attached to charismatic leadership has been questioned (Bensimon, Neumann, and Birnbaum, 1989; Drucker, 1988), and the wisdom of advice that directs leaders to remain aloof from constituents has also been challenged. A leader concerned with creating an image of mystery and separateness cannot be successful in building relationships, which after all is a critical part of leadership.

Within the domain of social influence theories of leadership, the transactional and transformational models hold the greatest interest. Transactional leadership considers the relationship between leader and followers as a two-way process of exchange and mutual influence (Hollander, 1987). Leaders accumulate power through their positions and their personalities, but their authority is constrained by follower expectations. Transformational leadership presents a one-way view of the relationship between the leader and followers. Leaders initiate relationships that raise followers to new levels of morality and motivation (Burns, 1978). While mention of transactional leadership conjures a managerial image, transformational leadership evokes images of extraordinary individuals such as Martin Luther King, Jr., or Mohandas K. Ghandi. Susan B. Anthony and Ida B. Wells can also be added to the list as female exemplars of transformational leadership.

The difference between fulfilling or changing expectations is at the heart of the distinction between transactional and transformational leadership (Burns, 1978; Bennis and Nanus, 1985; Bass, 1985). For example, transactional leaders are depicted as accepting and maintaining the culture of an organization as it exists—its belief system, language, and group norms (Bass, 1985). In contrast, transformational leaders alter organizational culture by introducing new beliefs and goals and by changing how group members define their roles.

Clarifying transformational leadership is difficult because it has been defined from at least two perspectives. The classic concept of transformational leadership, as proposed by Burns (1978), had powerful moral connotations. However, recently advocates of the corporatist culture who have made heroes out of CEOs have appropriated the term. When someone like Lee Iacocca is labeled a "transformational leader," the moral connotation of transformational leadership has been lost.

Some scholars are skeptical about the possibility of transformational leadership in colleges and universities. (For a discussion of organizational factors impeding transformational leadership in an academic organization, see Bensimon, Neumann, and Birnbaum, 1989.) But an imperative exists in higher education for formal and informal leaders to exercise transformational leadership. This is particularly true with respect to emancipatory or liberatory leadership to change structural factors that perpetuate inequities in the academy on the basis of race, gender, class, or sexual orientation.

Power-and-influence theories of leadership can be criticized for their excessive concern with how formal leaders accumulate power for the purposes of exercising control over others. Accordingly, individuals in leadership positions or individuals who aspire to such positions are advised that they can gain power by controlling access to information, dominating the budgetary process, and allocating resources to preferred projects.

To put it simply, these leadership theories promulgate a conception of power based on the idea of control and domination. On this point, Hartsock (1981, pp. 3–4) points out, "Most social scientists have based their discussions of power on definitions of power as the ability to compel obedience, or as control and domination. They link this definition with Bertrand Russell's statement that power is the production of intended effects, and add that power must be power over someone—something possessed, a property of an actor such that he can alter the will or actions of others in a way that produces results in conformity with his own will."

A more human understanding of leadership might be gained if power were to be conceptualized differently. A glaring omission from conventional theories of leadership is the conception of power as the empowerment of others. Alternative views of power are proposed by two renowned philosophers. Arendt noted that power relates to group interactions, that it is never the property of an individual (quoted in Greene, 1988). Greene—a philosopher of education—writes that "power may be thought of, then, as 'empowerment,' a condition of possibility for human and political life and, yes, for education as well" (1988, p. 134).

Reconceptualizing Leadership

The organizational and leadership models discussed so far, even though they result from different conceptions of the nature of social organizations, are similar in that they promulgate a view of leadership as individual centered. Such leadership models will become increasingly irrelevant, particularly as campuses are thrown into disequilibrium by new voices in academe among the faculty, administration, and student body—people of color, women, lesbians, gay men, and people whose social and economic origins would have barred them from American higher education during previous eras. On today's campuses, administration is no longer a matter of negotiating (as in the political model) concessions over the idiosyncratic concerns of special interest groups clamoring for equal treatment, or, as some would have it, their piece of the pie. Rather, the task of the administrator and any leader today is to discern and to act responsively from an understanding of differences among "a plurality of voices vying for the right to reality—to be accepted as legitimate expressions of the true and good" (Gergen, 1991, p. 7).

Accordingly, in a situation of so much flux, conflict, and uncertainty, a need exists for leadership that embraces a multiplicity of viewpoints rather than one that is based on the assumption of a single and shared reality. Leadership needs to be reconceptualized as a collective practice. This means that administrators will need to put aside the long-standing belief that leadership is a force for marshaling commonality and consensus to the point of excluding unique points of view and unique definitions of reality. Moreover, to conceive of leadership as a collective and interactive act, it is necessary to reconstruct our definitions of leadership—to build a "view of leadership which counters the emphasis on individualism, hierarchical relationships, bureaucratic rationality, and abstract moral principles" (Blackmore, 1989, p. 94), because all of these tend to exclude.

Recent scholarship on the moral development of women merits consideration as a theoretical base for the reconceptualization of leadership as a collective and interactive act. This is because it is grounded in the experience of people (women) whose background differs dramatically from the norm of leadership (which is male dominated and heavily individualistic). Blackmore (1989) shows how this scholarship on women's moral development can be used to reconstruct the conventional model of leadership. Rather than conceiving of leadership as unidimensional and as posited within one individual, she advocates "a view of power which is multi-dimensional and multi-directional" (p. 94), drawing others into the center rather than subordinating, marginalizing, or excluding them. She asserts a new view of leadership that builds on the following beliefs:

- Leadership can be practiced in different contexts by different people and not merely equated with formal roles. [p. 94]
- Leadership looks to empower others rather than have power over others. [p. 94]
- Leadership is concerned with communitarian and collective activities and values. Thus, the process of leading is both educative and conducive to democratic process. [p. 94]
- Leadership, and the power that accompanies it, [may] be redefined as the ability to act with others to do things that could not be done by an individual alone. [p. 123]

The scholarship on women's moral development also elaborates the concept of "taking the role of the other" in a way that concretizes the meaning of leadership as an interactive and relational practice — a view of leadership that is absent in traditional theories.

When an individual in a leadership position "takes the role" of an "other," she or he musters feelings of empathy that give rise to gestures signifying, to the "other," that "I am one with you in spirit" (Bensimon, 1991). Taking the role of a particular other goes against the grain of conventional theories of administration, which are grounded in the notion of the individual making decisions independently based on her or his impersonal judgment of the facts in relation to abstract principles of morality. From the perspective of conventional understandings of leadership, the individual strives to "take the role of the generalized other" — in effect, a disembodied, unreal abstraction — rather than taking the role of the real, particular person to whom one is relating at a particular moment in time (Harding, 1983; Gilligan, 1982). Building on Gilligan's (1982) studies of differences between women's and men's moral development, Harding (1983) differentiates further between taking the role of the particular other as opposed to the generalized other by proposing two different ways to view rationality, one typically associated with women, the other with men: "A rational person, for women, values highly her abilities to empathize and 'connect' with particular others and wants to learn more complex and satisfying ways to take the role of the particular other in relationships. . . . For men, in contrast, a rational person values highly his ability to separate himself from others and to make decisions independent of what others think — to develop 'autonomy.' And he wants to learn more complex and satisfying ways to take the role of the generalized other" (p. 55).

In sum, taking the role of the particular other is an attempt at genuine understanding of the lived experience of another person, while taking the role of the generalized other represents the abstract conceptualization of a person's or group's situation.

Even though taking the role of the particular other is associated strongly with how women construct their social world, the ability to take the role of the other should not be viewed as foreign to the experience of men. Nor should men be viewed as unable to learn, from the experience of women, how to interpret and understand the situations and circumstances that affect the lives of others.

Summary

Despite the increasing popularity of cultural theories of organization and leadership, most works on leadership are based on the belief that organizations are objective and rational entities, separate from ourselves, waiting to be discovered (Greenfield, 1980). This view informs the bureaucratic, collegial, and political models insofar as they are concerned with the instrumental value of structures, consultation, and power. Regrettably, our thinking about leadership is still very much a product of the view of organizations as rational entities pursuing clearly delineated goals in a linear fashion. Consequently, leadership is viewed as an objective act in which leaders influence the activities of followers through the display of specific traits, or the display of power, or the display of specific behaviors.

Feminist research on the moral development of women can provide a foundation for the reconceptualization of leadership as a collaborative and interactive practice. The imperative for such leadership will increase as campuses become more culturally diverse. Just as institutions of higher education are grappling with the transformation of the curriculum to be more inclusive of the voices, lives, and histories of the excluded "others," administrative practice will also have to be transformed to be more responsive to the multiple realities on our campuses. Our conceptions of the nature of organizations inform our conceptions of leadership. Just as there is a need to abandon the idea of leadership as an individualistic practice, so must we abandon the idea that organizations consist of rational entities existing outside ourselves.

Organizations may be better understood as human collectives. The college inevitably has an organizational chart with boxes and arrows showing who is in charge of what and who re-

ports to whom. But within those boxes are people: untidily thinking, mind-changing, goal-shifting, varying-daily people. The perspective that feminist research has brought to the study of organizations suggests that a view of the college as an association of
people with whom each administrator must empathize, interact, and collaborate will lead to a more productive environment.

References

Baldridge, J. V. *Power and Conflict in the University.* New York:
Wiley, 1971.

Baldridge, J. V., Curtis, D. V., Ecker, G., and Riley, G. L.
"Alternative Models of Governance in Higher Education."
In J. V. Baldridge, D. V. Curtis, G. Ecker, and G. L. Riley
(eds.), *Governing Academic Organizations: New Problems, New Perspectives.* Berkeley, Calif.: McCutchan, 1978.

Bass, B. M. *Leadership and Performance Beyond Expectation.* New
York: Free Press, 1985.

Bennis, W. G., and Nanus, B. *Leaders.* New York: HarperCollins, 1985.

Bensimon, E. M. "Selected Aspects of Governance: An ERIC
Review." *Community College Review,* 1984, *12*(2), 54–61.

Bensimon, E. M. "The Meaning of 'Good Presidential Leadership': A Frame Analysis." *Review of Higher Education,* 1989,
12(2), 107–123.

Bensimon, E. M. "The Social Processes Through Which Faculty
Shape the Image of a New President." *Journal of Higher Education,* 1991, *62*(6), 637–660.

Bensimon, E. M., Neumann, A., and Birnbaum, R. *Making
Sense of Administrative Leadership: The "L" Word in Higher Education.* ASHE-ERIC Higher Education Report No. 1. Washington, D.C.: School of Education and Human Development,
George Washington University, 1989.

Birnbaum, R. *How Colleges Work: The Cybernetics of Academic Organization and Leadership.* San Francisco: Jossey-Bass, 1988.

Blackmore, J. "Educational Leadership: A Feminist Critique
and Reconstruction." In J. Smyth (ed.), *Critical Perspectives
on Educational Leadership.* London: Falmer Press, 1989.

Bolman, L. G., and Deal, T. E. *Modern Approaches to Understanding and Managing Organizations.* San Francisco: Jossey-Bass, 1984.

Bolman, L. G., and Deal, T. E. *Reframing Organizations: Artistry, Choice, and Leadership.* San Francisco: Jossey-Bass, 1991.

Burns, J. M. *Leadership.* New York: HarperCollins, 1978.

Covey, S. *The Seven Habits of Highly Effective People.* New York: Simon & Schuster, 1989.

Dill, D. D. "The Management of Academic Culture: Notes on the Management of Meaning and Social Integration." *Higher Education,* 1982, *11,* 303–320.

Drucker, P. E. "Leadership: More Doing Than Dash." *Wall Street Journal,* Jan. 6, 1988, p. 14.

Fisher, J. L. *The Power of the Presidency.* New York: Macmillan, 1984.

Fisher, J. L., Tack, M. W., and Wheeler, K. J. "Leadership Behaviors of Effective College Presidents." Paper presented at the annual meeting of the American Education Research Association, New Orleans, Louisiana, Apr. 1988.

Gergen, K. J. *The Saturated Self: Dilemmas of Identity in Contemporary Life.* New York: Basic Books, 1991.

Gilligan, C. *In a Different Voice: Psychological Theory and Women's Development.* Cambridge, Mass.: Harvard University Press, 1982.

Goleman, D. *Vital Lies, Simple Truths: The Psychology of Self-Deception.* New York: Simon and Schuster, 1985.

Greene, M. *The Dialectic of Freedom.* New York: Teachers College Press, 1988.

Greenfield, T. B. "The Man Who Comes Back Through the Door in the Wall: Discovering Truth, Discovering Self, Discovering Organization." *Educational Administration Quarterly,* 1980, *16,* 26–59.

Harding, S. "Why Has the Sex-Gender System Become Visible Only Now?" In S. Harding and M. Hintikka (eds.), *Discovering Reality: Feminist Perspectives on Epistemology, Methodology, and Philosophy of Science.* Dordrecht: Reidel, 1983.

Hartsock, N. "Political Change: Two Perspectives on Power." In C. Bunch and others (eds.), *Building Feminist Theory.* White Plains, N.Y.: Longman, 1981.

Hollander, E. P. "College and University Leadership from a Social Psychological Perspective: A Transactional View." Prepared for the Invitational Interdisciplinary Colloquium on Leadership in Higher Education, Institutional Leadership Project, National Center for Postsecondary Governance and Finance, Teachers College, Columbia University, New York, 1987.

Kerr, C., and Gade, M. *The Many Lives of Academic Presidents.* Washington, D.C.: Association of Governing Boards of Universities and Colleges, 1986.

March, J. G. "Emerging Developments in the Study of Organizations." *Review of Higher Education,* 1982, *6,* 1–18.

Millett, J. D. *An Essay on Organization: The Academic Community.* New York: McGraw-Hill, 1962.

Morgan, G. *Images of Organization.* Newbury Park, Calif.: Sage, 1986.

Peters, T. J., and Waterman, R. H. *In Search of Excellence: Lessons from America's Best-Run Companies.* New York: HarperCollins, 1982.

Pfeffer, J. "Management as Symbolic Action: The Creation and Maintenance of Organizational Paradigms." *Research in Organizational Behavior,* 1981, *3,* 1–52.

Reyes, P., and Twombly, S. B. "Perceptions of Contemporary Governance in Community Colleges: An Empirical Study." *Community College Review,* 1987, *14,* 4–12.

Smircich, L., and Morgan, G. "Leadership: The Management of Meaning." *Journal of Applied Behavioral Science,* 1982, *18*(3), 257–273.

Vaughan, G. B. *The Community College President.* New York: American Council on Education/Macmillan, 1986.

Walker, D. E. *The Effective Administrator: A Practical Approach to Problem Solving, Decision Making, and Campus Leadership.* San Francisco: Jossey-Bass, 1979.

Watkins, P. "Leadership, Power, and Symbols in Educational Administration." In J. Smyth (ed.), *Critical Perspectives on Educational Leadership.* London: Falmer Press, 1989.

Whetten, D. A. "Effective Administrators: Good Management on the College Campus." *Change,* 1984, *16*(8), 38–43.

Chapter 3

Leadership Strategies

Richard C. Richardson, Jr.,
Mimi Wolverton

Community colleges differ from other forms of higher education in ways that have vast implications for leadership. In four-
year institutions, most academic leaders have been trained as
scholars within their respective disciplines, whereas in community colleges, a large number of leaders have their degrees in
education, often from leadership training programs housed in
departments of educational administration. While this trend may
be changing (Vaughan, 1989, p. 119), the effect of a large leadership cadre trained in approaches similar to those in use in the
public schools has supported perceptions of community colleges
as organizations deeply rooted in bureaucratic traditions (Birnbaum, 1988, pp. 105–127).

Given these conditions, it is somewhat surprising that the
three most recent volumes on leadership in the community college deal only peripherally with the topics of rationality and structure. Roueche, Baker, and Rose (1989, p. 11) argue for leadership as transformation or change. From their perspective, leaders
are individuals with vision who develop teams to make the vision real. Through this process, values are changed so that the

entire college moves toward a commonly accepted vision of the future (p. 10).

Vaughan (1989, pp. 8–11) speaks of presidents as educational leaders who, in addition to managing their institutions efficiently and effectively, create campus climates that preserve institutional integrity while maintaining a reasonable balance among institutional, community, and individual concerns and needs. Presidents are also responsible for interpreting and communicating the institutional mission.

Fryer and Lovas (1991, pp. 4–5) propose a more severe test by defining leadership in community colleges as a complex process or art that involves getting others to want to do something in an institutional setting that the leader believes is important.

Each of these views carries with it explicit or implicit leadership strategies. Moving from the conviction that effective leaders are transformational in character, Roueche, Baker, and Rose (1989) use reputational methods to identify "excellent" presidents. But in describing the qualities and attributes of leaders, the authors confine discussion of implications almost exclusively to graduate programs that train community college leaders (pp. 287–289).

Vaughan (1989) agrees that presidents as educational leaders need a vision of their institution and have a responsibility for interpreting, shaping, and communicating that vision. Presidents need a commitment to scholarship so they can lead by example. Presidents should include scholarship as an important part of the reward system, provide leadership in professional renewal, and take the lead in dispelling the image that community colleges are second best.

To a degree, Roueche and his colleagues and Vaughan discuss leadership from the trait perspective, although they also incorporate cultural perspectives. While Vaughan provides "advice for those who would be president" (pp. 125–139), most of his discussion focuses on how to get the job rather than what to do afterward. Thus, neither book offers much help in defining leadership strategies as these might involve ongoing efforts to improve the quality of an institution's performance.

Fryer and Lovas (1991, p. 43), by contrast, write from a behavioral perspective, devoting much of their attention to process and emphasizing leadership roles in planning, deciding, acting, reacting, and communicating. Consistent with the views of Roueche, Baker, and Rose and Vaughan, they believe leaders must articulate an ideal and empower people to pursue that ideal. Other leadership strategies they emphasize include sustaining standards of excellence, retaining responsibility and accountability for decisions even when these are delegated, and envisioning a partnership in decision making that incorporates all legitimate views and interests (pp. 149–150). Their discussion encompasses all levels of an institution rather than focusing on the president.

Other writers, especially those with a feminist perspective, take the study of leadership in a different direction. Bensimon, in her chapter in this volume and in her previous work (Bensimon, Neumann, and Birnbaum, 1989), identifies a half dozen ways of characterizing leadership, all with a view toward supporting empowerment of others as the most effective form.

Astin and Leland (1991), who studied successful women in colleges and universities, also define educational leadership as a "process of empowerment" or mobilizing energy—a holding of power jointly as a group (p. 8). "Members of a group are empowered to work together synergistically toward a common goal or vision that will create change, transform institutions, and improve the quality of life" (p. 8). Leaders build synergistic teams through open communication founded on active listening, influence based on trust, integrity, a sense of caring, and clearly stated values. How something gets done is just as important as what gets done. The leadership strategies most often employed by the women they studied included the following: meeting people on their own turf and listening to them, hiring strong people who complemented their own strengths and talents, and providing feedback and giving credit where credit was due. Above all, these women valued collegiality (p. 120).

Each of these views adds to our understanding of leadership, but, even taken as a group, the strategies described raise as many questions as they answer. What happens if a transformational leader encounters an institution dedicated to stability? What is it that education leaders do that improves learning conditions for students? Can leadership processes be separated from policies and practices?

In this chapter, we use the perspective of organizational culture and the results of a study of twelve community colleges to suggest context-specific leadership strategies for moving institutions toward more effective learning environments. The institutions were participants in a Ford Foundation–funded study of the relationship between effective faculty behaviors and administrative policies and practices. Through the report of the study, we translate theoretical concepts into observed behaviors. We then draw on these behaviors to suggest strategies through which leaders can shape learning environments.

The study began with the assumption that an excellent community college was one where variance between accepted standards for high-quality learning environments and actual conditions was minimized. We focused on identifying leadership strategies that motivated faculty members to perform in ways that diverse learners had already identified as important to achievement (Chickering and Gamson, 1987; McCabe, 1991).

Organizational Culture as a Framework for Leadership

Culture can be thought of as the persistent assumptions, values, and beliefs that shape the behavior of individuals in organizations (Kuh and Whitt, 1988, p. 3). Culture develops over time among a group with an identifiable history as learned responses to the problems of maintaining internal cohesion and relating to the external community (Schein, 1985, p. 6). Conceptually, culture is based on social construction; participants constantly interpret and create organizational reality. The approach stands in opposition to organizational reality as objective fact, the view that largely governs the perspectives of Roueche and his colleagues, Vaughan, and Fryer and Lovas, but not of Astin and Leland, who explicitly base their analysis on culture defined as a commonly arrived at sense of reality.

Within the cultures of complex organizations, subcultures may exist. The views of more than a single group may define organizational reality, and these separate views may or may not be congruent. In this chapter, we focus specifically on faculty and administrative subcultures because, in an open-door institution, instructional quality cannot be altered by changing the student mix through admissions policy.

Many discussions of leadership distinguish between transformational leaders who "do the right things" and transactional leaders who "do things right." In reality, as Gardner (1990, p. 5) notes, visionary leaders must understand how to allocate scarce resources, and the best managers think beyond short-term results. Implicit in the notion of doing the right things is the concept of creating a shared culture. As Gardner suggests, transactional processes are as important as their transformational counterparts in changing deeply held values and beliefs.

Kuh and Whitt (1988, p. 101) argue that institutional culture is difficult to modify intentionally. Nonetheless, Chaffee and Tierney (1988, pp. 10–26) suggest strategies through which leaders can influence culture, based on case studies of seven institutions. In their model, three dimensions of culture — structure, environment, and values — are acted on respectively by linear, adaptive, and interpretive strategies. Linear strategies are transactional; they aim at doing the right things to achieve organizational ends. Adaptive strategies seek planned organizational change to maintain or improve an institution's alignment with its environment. Interpretive strategies are transformational; they are designed to create the shared vision that recent books on leadership describe as essential to organizational excellence. In the Chaffee and Tierney model (p. 24), all three dimensions and their related strategies share three properties: all must be performed for an institution to be effective, they are not interactive in nature, and they are hierarchical but not necessarily sequential.

This discussion of culture as a theoretical perspective sets the stage for the description of a study that used culture to explain differences in the levels of effective practice reported by faculty members in twelve community colleges.

The Study

The study began by asking what faculty members do to help students persist and succeed in their institutions. We started with the insights developed in Miami-Dade Community College's Teaching/Learning Project (McCabe, 1991) and followed with intensive field work in the Maricopa Community College District, where we asked students, faculty members, and administrators to describe behaviors important to student success (Elliott, 1992). We also did an extensive review of the literature, including Chickering and Gamson's "Seven Principles for Good Practice in Undergraduate Education" (1987). The substantial agreement among all of these sources suggested a good working knowledge about how to promote student success.

Information on effective educational practices was incorporated in a survey that went to the faculty in a random, stratified, national sample of fifty-two community colleges. Institutions with substantial minority enrollments were oversampled. More than 67 percent of the faculty returned usable surveys. Faculty members in some institutions reported significantly higher levels of effective behaviors than their counterparts in other institutions. To find out why, we invited twelve community colleges from across the country to participate in case studies. The survey responses from faculty members in these twelve community colleges represented the full range of behaviors reported in the fifty-two-institution sample.

Survey results indicated that faculty performance differed significantly among the twelve institutions, and half or more of the differences could be explained by participation in professional development and governance opportunities. The case studies offered a more contextual explanation of how and why these differences occurred.

1. Higher-performing institutions had cultures that emphasized student achievement and brought people together. While these cultures in some instances tolerated a lack of involvement beyond the classroom, they did not encourage it. Among the lower-performing institutions, the presence of competing cultures and formal safeguards (in the form of compre-

hensive collective bargaining agreements or board policies) allowed or even encouraged faculty disengagement.

2. Higher-performing institutions expected more from their faculty and defined their roles to encompass a broader range of responsibilities. By contrast, some lower-performing institutions defined faculty responsibilities almost exclusively in terms of meeting classes and keeping posted office hours.

3. Faculty were evaluated more frequently in higher-performing institutions. Rewards and recognition were tied to the evaluation process and reflected the values faculty and administrators shared. In lower-performing institutions, evaluation for continuing faculty occurred at lengthy intervals and was typically unrelated to rewards or recognition. In these institutions, faculty were described as "very oriented toward minimum standards."

4. While all case-study institutions used some form of combined department and division structure, higher-performing institutions supported departments as places where faculty could gain leadership experience and incubate innovative ideas. Among lower-performing colleges, departments were tolerated or served as bastions of faculty autonomy.

5. Creative leadership is required to offset the effects of bureaucracies in multicampus districts. The many demands of large and complex district administrative staffs have the same deadening effects on the creativity and vitality of community college faculty that they have in the public schools.

6. Lower-performing districts had more extensive and complex governance arrangements, but faculty in higher-performing institutions were more likely to participate in governance. The complex structures seem to be better predictors of a lack of trust than of effective faculty involvement.

7. Professional development opportunities for faculty members in higher-performing institutions were linked in systematic ways to institutional priorities. In several lower-performing districts, faculty had no clear sense of priorities. Many were described as angry or alienated.

8. In higher-performing institutions, arrangements for involving faculty in decision making provided credible opportunities for both faculty and administrators to influence out-

comes. In lower-performing institutions, administrators persuaded, influenced, supported, or, in some instances, confronted, but they did not seem to lead or develop any sort of shared vision of what the institution hoped to achieve.

Characterizing Organizational Environments

The twelve case-study community colleges could be classified in four major domains based on the relative strength of faculty and administrative influences and the degree to which the values of the two subcultures were congruent.

Adversarial Domain

In the adversarial domain, discontent simmers below the surface and conflict erupts on a regular basis. Neither faculty nor administrators can muster sufficient levels of influence to move the institution beyond the conflict. Values differ. Each group spends considerable amounts of energy keeping the other in line. Conflict resolution sustains the organization and allows it to continue functioning.

Faculty-Dominated Domain

In the faculty-dominated domain, some combination of strong collective bargaining agreements, board policies, and frequent administrative turnover gives rise to a decision environment in which administrative views are unlikely to prevail unless faculty leaders first endorse them. Faculty preference for stability and continuity produce cumbersome governance procedures and administrative structures often embedded in collective bargaining agreements. Faculty remain well insulated from efforts to change the status quo. The environment, while nonthreatening, stifles initiative and creativity.

Administratively Dominated Domain

In the administratively dominated domain, nonresponsiveness to faculty concerns typifies a top-down, structured hierarchy.

Administrators seldom seek faculty input and, when they do, systematically ignore it. What the administrator sees as important determines what gets done, when it is done, and how it is done. Faculty roles are narrowly defined. Faculty distrust institutional processes and resist administratively defined values and priorities. Collective bargaining agreements or board policies that require faculty consultation for modification prevent conflict at the cost of limiting possibilities for organizational change.

Shared-Culture Domain

The shared-culture domain is characterized by an environment where administrative and faculty influences are balanced. Both groups are encouraged to participate in efforts to define priorities and plan for their achievement. Thus, balanced power in a shared culture leads to joint responsibility and authority. Together, faculty and administrators build a common history based on long-enduring assumptions, values, and beliefs that are communicated through the organization's rituals, activities, and practice. Creativity, innovation, and risk taking play key roles. Efforts to relate faculty and administrative behavior to well articulated institutional priorities promote a supportive, familylike atmosphere.

Quality and Leadership

In the case-study community colleges, levels of perceived quality in learning environments varied as a function of domain. Figure 3.1 superimposes a conceptualized quality boundary system over the four domains. Among lower-performing institutions, competing values and procedural safeguards produced environments where faculty members were significantly less likely to report engaging in success-related behaviors. Faculty-dominated and administratively dominated environments tended to provide average-quality opportunities that were neither particularly innovative nor consistently bad. Faculty were most likely to display high levels of student success-related behaviors in

Figure 3.1. Domain-Determined Institutional Quality.

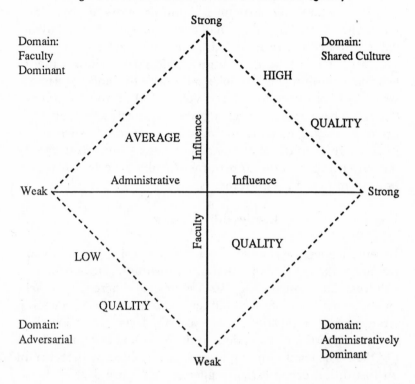

institutions with a shared culture. Clearly, conflict as well as an imbalance of faculty and administrative influence adversely affected institutional quality. While all community colleges identified student achievement as an important objective, conflict or the arrangements developed to prevent conflict affected the ability of leaders to pursue student achievement through changes that would alter the expectations held for faculty. By the same token, leadership strategies that moved institutions toward shared cultures also produced improved learning environments.

In community colleges with higher-quality learning environments, administrators create and defend cultures where faculty input is sought out, valued, and used. Priorities are clearly defined, and the focus is on teaching and learning. Administrators support rituals and tell stories that illustrate and reinforce the attitudes and beliefs that define culture. People are more important than structure. Administrators are open and fair in the internal distribution of available resources. Behaviors valued in faculty are modeled by administrators.

By contrast, in community colleges with lower-quality learning environments, complex administrative and governance structures substitute for shared values and mutual accommodation. There is no consensus about priorities. Faculty are oriented toward meeting the minimum standards spelled out in restrictive contracts or board policies. Administrators rely on extra compensation to encourage faculty to become involved beyond minimum requirements.

Leadership Strategies

Because leadership is a determining factor for quality, it is important to define strategies that move institutions toward shared cultures. Each domain suggests a somewhat different approach. In the remainder of this chapter, we outline five leadership strategies — revitalization, strategic realignment, strategic planning, synergistic collaboration, and Total Quality Management (TQM). The choice among them is determined by the domain an institution occupies, as suggested in Figure 3.2.

Revitalization

For colleges in the adversarial domain, conflict resolution consumes most of its members' energy. Revitalization provides a strategy for managing conflict that can move an institution toward a shared culture by defining conflict as an opportunity for change.

To revitalize an institution, leaders must develop a nonjudgmental, trusting atmosphere where faculty, staff, and administrators actively promote changes that challenge the existing conflict environment and create a culture that facilitates their acceptance (Mintzberg, 1989, p. 295). In other words, they manage conflict to the advantage of the organization. Revital-

Figure 3.2. Strategies for Changing Environments.

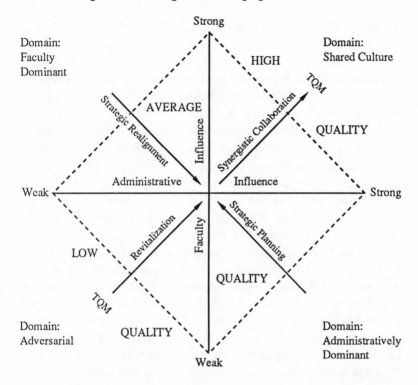

ization is a slow and careful process of incremental change. Initial success is crucial, so small changes that build toward larger environmental shifts must be identified. Revitalization begins with the identification of a possible problem area and the analysis of organizational assumptions. After defining the problem, a leader presents facts that document its existence and works with faculty and administrators to explore alternatives, searching out the strengths and weaknesses of each. They jointly arrive at an action agreement that defines goals, designs events to reach these goals, and determines the sequencing and timing of these events (Cornesky, 1990, pp. 70–71). Open lines of communication ensure that organizational members know why an action is being taken and what is expected of them.

Strategic Realignment

In the faculty-dominated domain, autonomy leads to isolation and pigeonholing designed to preserve the existing environment. A leader using strategic realignment seeks, through joint participation with the faculty, to facilitate renegotiation and repositioning to increase the defined leadership role. The differences between revitalization and strategic realignment are subtle but can significantly affect the probability of success. In revitalization, because influence among faculty and administrators remains balanced, administrators can assert themselves with relative ease. In strategic realignment, administrators hold an inferior influence position and must tread lightly. Consensus through negotiation is the key, and equal partnership in the educational process is the desired outcome.

The object of strategic realignment is to gain the emotional involvement of faculty by building coalitions where people can work within a group to derive a jointly supported set of objectives (Spanbauer, 1987; Whetten, 1984). Determining a common purpose leads to faculty and administrator acceptance of responsibility, both individually and communally. Leaders learn to distinguish between responsive action and acting responsively, between legitimate claims and political posturing (Seymour, 1992).

Leaders intent on organizational change assess the present organizational culture, determine where the organization should be, and articulate a mission. They identify the problem and strive for consensus among the faculty and administrators on its definition. Next, the problem must be incrementally redefined. Here, faculty acknowledgment of the need for action might hinge on the leader's ability to convince faculty that improved administrative effectiveness is really the desired result. The solutions proposed by faculty must be accepted. To reject them means destroying faculty trust and ensuring faculty rejection of leader-initiated alternatives. Revisions can always be made in the future. Leaders provide training, resources, and support but delegate the details of implementation. Once the solution is in place, they evaluate and redefine the process (Moomaw,

1984). Identifying the problem and evaluating its remedy are key leadership responsibilities in strategic realignment.

Strategic Planning

In the administratively dominated community college, change comes through administrative fiat. Strategic planning offers a systematic approach to integrating goals, policies, and actions into a sequenced, cohesive whole in a way that carries an institution closer to shared values. Strategic planning elaborates the basic organizational mission. It is deliberate and impersonal and may be more flexible than plans that emerge from collective choice. Basic elements of any strategic plan include the following: defining the goals and objectives to be achieved, identifying the significant policies guiding or limiting the proposed action, and developing the major action sequences needed to accomplish the defined goals within the set limits (Quinn, Mintzberg, and James, 1988).

In strategic planning, the mission sets the criteria for assessing the long-term effectiveness of the community college. The goals suggest future conditions that contribute to the fulfillment of the mission. And the objectives stipulate what the short-term accomplishments should be (Ivancevich and Matteson, 1987). The plan hinges on a few key concepts and tries to anticipate the unknowable. Failure often occurs because administrators hold no clear vision and substitute procedures for process. Marginal success results because they either extrapolate from existing strategies or copy the strategies of others (Mintzberg, 1989).

While the focus in each of the domains is on student achievement, the three leadership strategies discussed so far are designed for domains where rival environmental priorities exist. For institutions within the adversarial domain, resolving conflict provides a major challenge. In the faculty-dominated domain, there are pressures to protect the existing environment. Leaders in an administratively dominated institution try to impose change. The placement of blame for failure in reaching desired levels of student achievement also differs. Conflict-ridden institutions blame the students. Dominating faculty blame the students and the administrators. Dominating administrators target the faculty.

Synergistic Collaboration

The dominant priority in a shared culture is student achievement, and the system is blamed when desired results fail to materialize. Synergistic collaboration as a shared-culture strategy builds on the strengths of the first three strategies. It sees conflict as healthy. It thrives on the joint participation and collegiality of faculty and administrators, is founded on a well-defined mission and goals, and believes in systematic planning to achieve such goals. To these strengths, synergistic collaboration adds an overriding vision, or common caring, in order to develop the common values that sustain the shared culture. The leader serves as a guide to a jointly defined future and makes the vision both practicable and compelling (Cornesky, 1990). The gap between a shared vision and reality represents creative tension that leads to opportunity.

Synergistically collaborative leaders realize that the current reality is only one of several possible realities. They see patterns and parallels and intuitively follow hunches. They seek quality and break down barriers that impede progress toward reaching excellence. They energize their organizations. To them the vision is the "what" (the picture of the future we seek to create). The mission is the "why" (why do we exist?). And core values suggest "how we want to act" (Senge, 1990).

Six leadership substrategies support synergistic collaboration.

1. Empower others by clarifying values and providing the vision that guides organizational behavior. Power in the form of control is not the issue, influence is (Astin and Leland, 1991).
2. Clearly communicate the vision and its meaning for the organization to others.
3. Build seeds of understanding, identity, and commit-

ment into the very processes that create organizational strategies (Quinn, Mintzberg, and James, 1988, p. 678).

4. Model the behavior you want to see by building trust through honesty and integrity, and confidence through respect. Set high expectations for yourself and for those around you. Create an atmosphere that encourages risk taking. Recognize mistakes and failures as pathways to success (Cornesky, 1990, p. 5).

5. Provide faculty, staff, and administrators with the tools needed for self-leadership through professional development, training and education, and feedback. Lead others to lead themselves (Manz and Sims, 1989).

6. Encourage continuous, incremental improvement and innovation by promoting divergent thinking grounded in the interdependence of shared responsibility and authority.

Total Quality Management

"In industry, Total Quality Management (TQM) arose as a response to a real crisis of competitiveness and profitability. . . . Education feels no parallel crisis" (Ewell, 1991, p. 50). That TQM works only in times of crisis may or may not be true. That education feels no parallel crisis can be questioned.

Gitlow and Gitlow (1987) describe TQM as a long-term procedure that states an organization's goals and its philosophy (vision) and explains how they relate. It is a concept that revolves around a commitment to quality. Excellence, achieved through teamwork and a process of continuous improvement, hinges on long-term incremental change based on open communication among those involved with the service provided (Coate, 1990).

TQM attacks the system. The process, not the participants, harbors the problem. TQM strives to improve the system by systematically analyzing it for variance and by consciously defining the organization's internal and external customers and actively seeking input from both. It drives out fear by encouraging organization members to risk making mistakes in order to

learn more about the system. It removes organizational barriers by establishing clear and open lines of communication. It
educates and retrains employees. It thrives on teamwork and
interrelationships. Balance is important. Management guides
and facilitates. In other words, TQM creates a structure conducive to never-ending improvement by building cooperative
labor-management relations (Gitlow and Gitlow, 1987).

Clearly, much that occurs under TQM happens during
synergistic collaboration as well. TQM employed in a shared
culture fine-tunes synergistic collaboration and adds two dimensions, by (1) identifying primary internal and external customers,
and (2) providing analytical tools — flowcharting and counting
techniques — that aid the institution in searching its systems and
processes for variance that detracts from quality. TQM is administratively initiated because, in a shared culture, the initiation of a strategy to improve quality lies within the jointly accepted realm of administrative duties.

TQM may also have an application at the opposite end
of the balanced-influence continuum for the community college facing crisis. In the adversarial domain, TQM can provide a systematic process that fosters a vision and promotes incremental change to push the institution beyond crisis and
conflict toward a gradual increase in shared values. Even though
TQM begins with reform at the top of an institution, an antagonistic faculty may, over time, be persuaded to participate
in the search for shared values. Its members can be convinced,
however, that changes made will affect the way the institution
deals with them, as well as with students and customers in the
external environment.

Exhibit 3.1 summarizes the environmentally reactive and
proactive strategies, which can be employed in each of the four
domains.

Summary

Community colleges in the faculty-dominated and administratively dominated domains live lives of relative stability, yet
leadership strategies can be developed to encourage change that

Exhibit 3.1. Leadership Strategies by Domain.

Domain	Reactive strategy	Proactive strategy
Adversarial	Conflict resolution Conflict management	Revitalization In crisis: TQM
Faculty-dominated	Negotiation Consensus building	Strategic realignment
Administratively dominated	Administrative fiat	Strategic planning
Shared-culture	Collegiality	Synergistic collaboration: TQM

improves the learning conditions for students. Adversarial and shared cultures reflect much more dynamic situations where constant challenges are hurled at the status quo. Again, leadership plays an important role in defining solutions that improve the learning environment.

Each leadership strategy — revitalization, strategic realignment, strategic planning, synergistic collaboration, and Total Quality Management — strives for organizational transformation. Each defines leadership as a process intricately tied to the policies and practices of the organization.

References

Astin, H. S., and Leland, C. *Women of Influence, Women of Vision: A Cross-Generational Study of Leaders and Social Change.* San Francisco: Jossey-Bass, 1991.

Bensimon, E. M., Neumann, A., and Birnbaum, R. *Making Sense of Administrative Leadership: The "L" Word in Higher Education.* ASHE-ERIC Higher Education Report No. 1, Washington, D.C.: School of Education and Human Development, George Washington University, 1989.

Birnbaum, R. *How Colleges Work: The Cybernetics of Academic Organization and Leadership.* San Francisco: Jossey-Bass, 1988.

Chaffee, E. E., and Tierney, W. G. *Collegiate Culture and Leadership Strategies.* New York: American Council on Education/ Macmillan, 1988.

Chickering, A., and Gamson, Z. F. "Seven Principles for Good
    Practice in Undergraduate Education." *Wingspread Journal*
    (Johnson Foundation, Racine, Wis.), 1987, *9*(2).
Coate, L. E. *Implementing Total Quality Management in a Univer-
    sity Setting.* Oregon State University, 1990.
Cornesky, R. A. *Using Deming: Improving Quality in Colleges and
    Universities.* Madison, Wis.: Magna Publications, 1990.
Elliott, D. C. *Community College Faculty Behaviors Impacting Transfer
    Student Success: A Qualitative Study.* Unpublished doctoral dis-
    sertation, Division of Educational Leadership and Policy
    Studies, Arizona State University, 1992.
Ewell, P. T. "Assessment and TQM: In Search of Convergence."
    In L. A. Sherr and D. J. Teeter (eds.), *Total Quality Manage-
    ment in Higher Education.* New Directions for Institutional Re-
    search, no. 71. San Francisco: Jossey-Bass, 1991.
Fryer, T. W., Jr., and Lovas, J. C. *Leadership in Governance: Creat-
    ing Conditions for Successful Decision Making in the Community Col-
    lege.* San Francisco: Jossey-Bass, 1991.
Gardner, J. W. *On Leadership.* New York: Free Press, 1990.
Gitlow, H. S., and Gitlow, S. J. *The Deming Guide to Quality and
    Competitive Position.* Englewood Cliffs, N.J.: Prentice-Hall,
    1987.
Ivancevich, J. M., and Matteson, M. I. *Organizational Behavior
    and Management.* Plano, Tex.: Business Publications, 1987.
Kuh, G. D., and Whitt, E. J. *The Invisible Tapestry: Culture in
    American Colleges and Universities.* ASHE-ERIC Higher Edu-
    cation Report No. 1. Washington, D.C.: Association for the
    Study of Higher Education, 1988. (ED 299 934)
McCabe, R. *The Miami-Dade Community College's Teaching/Learning
    Project Summary Report.* Summary Report (Year 4), 1989–1990.
    Miami, Fla., 1991.
Manz, C. C., and Sims, H. P. *Superleadership.* New York: Berke-
    ley Books, 1898.
Mintzberg, H. *Mintzberg on Management: Inside Our Strange World
    of Organizations.* New York: Free Press, 1989.
Moomaw, W. E. "Participatory Leadership Strategy." In D. J.
    Brown (ed.), *Leadership Roles of Chief Academic Officers.* New
    Directions for Higher Education, no. 47. San Francisco:
    Jossey-Bass, 1984.

Quinn, J. B., Mintzberg, H., and James, R. M. *Strategic Process.* Englewood Cliffs, N.J.: Prentice-Hall, 1988.

Roueche, J. E., Baker, G. A. III, and Rose, R. R. *Shared Vision: Transformational Leadership in American Community Colleges.* Washington, D.C.: Community College Press, 1989.

Schein, E. H. *Organizational Culture and Leadership: A Dynamic View.* San Francisco: Jossey-Bass, 1985.

Senge, P. M. *The Fifth Discipline: The Art and Practice of the Learning Organization.* New York: Doubleday, 1990.

Seymour, D. *On Q: Causing Quality in Higher Education.* New York: American Council on Education/Macmillan, 1992.

Spanbauer, S. J. *Quality First in Education . . . Why Not? Using Quality and Productivity Methods to Improve Schools.* Appleton, Wis.: Fox Valley Technical College Foundation, 1987.

Vaughan, G. B. *Leadership in Transition: The Community College Presidency.* New York: American Council on Education/Macmillan, 1989.

Whetten, D. A. "Effective Administrators: Good Management on the College Campus." *Change,* 1984, *16*(8), 38–43.

Chapter 4

Effective Presidential Leadership: Twelve Areas of Focus

George B. Vaughan

The chief executive officer of a college or university—whether called president, chancellor, or chief administrator—must focus on twelve areas in order to be effective: understanding the institution, appreciating the culture, mediating disputes, understanding the necessity of good management, selecting personnel, utilizing information, acting as educational leader, functioning in the professional field, establishing political leadership, providing avenues for renewal, serving as an institutional symbol, and using power. This chapter discusses these areas in terms of the community college president.

In his influential work on leadership, Burns (1979) observes that we know too much about our *leaders,* including their hobbies, sleeping habits, eating preferences, sexual practices, and the names of their dogs. On the other hand, he continues, "We know far too little about *leadership*" (p. 1).

Both as a practitioner and as a scholar, I have attempted to learn more about leadership and to communicate that understanding to others. I have concluded that various skills, abilities, and personal attributes are considered important for effective presidential leadership. Ranking at the top of those personal attributes are integrity, judgment, courage, concern for others, and flexibility. Among the skills and abilities are the ability to produce results, select capable people, resolve conflicts, communicate effectively, and motivate others (Vaughan, 1986, p. 189). However, to enhance the leadership of community college presidents, one now needs to look at leadership from a perspective other than the skills, abilities, and personal attributes required of the effective leader.

Before beginning the discussion of areas of focus, it should be noted that the decision to choose twelve areas of focus was subjective; others choosing a similar approach to leadership might select ten areas, or thirteen, or nine. The point is not whether there is some magic number of areas, but rather that presidents devote their time, energy, and talents to those areas in which presidential leadership should be exercised. The twelve areas chosen here have no order of priority. Indeed, all are equally important and should be viewed as separate arenas in which to exercise presidential leadership.

Understanding and enhancing community college leadership in today's environment requires not so much identifying skills and abilities as determining *where* and *how* they should be utilized. Therefore, the following discussion identifies and discusses those arenas in which the president *exercises* leadership skills. It is an attempt to interpret what I have learned as a president and as a scholar in ways that will help others to look at leadership in terms of areas of focus rather than as tasks to be performed or skills to be applied. Defining presidential leadership in terms of broad areas in no way lessens the need for those skills and abilities normally associated with leadership, nor is the need to accomplish tasks diminished. Rather, the skills and abilities and the tasks to be accomplished are interwoven in the multidimensional fabric of presidential leadership included in the areas of focus. This approach assumes that by the time someone reaches the presidency, skills and abilities need only be acknowledged, honed, and applied. The result of broadening one's perspective on leadership, of concentrating on arenas in which to exercise leadership, will result in a more effective application of those skills, abilities,

and personal attributes that are so necessary for the effective
community college president.

Understanding the Institution

The effective community college president must fully comprehend the institution being led. One cannot effectively lead something that one does not understand: yet to understand a single
institution, the effective president cannot focus on the campus
alone, for a single institution's destiny is interwoven intricately
and permanently with similar institutions and with the broader
society. The effective president must be true to a single institution's mission, while at the same time discerning the broader
needs of society and the role the institution's mission plays in
meeting those needs.

Understanding the institution is more than knowing the
institution's organizational chart, budget, or funding source, or
knowing members of the college community by their first names.
Understanding the institution means knowing its history — knowing why it exists and why it would matter if it did not exist. It
means knowing something about its students and its programs,
seeing the institution through the perspective of the larger society and knowing its impact on that society. Through understanding an institution, one knows its potential and its limitations.

Understanding provides the basis for formulating a vision of what the institution can be in the future, a vision that
is educationally and morally sound, a vision that supports the
mission and is in turn supported by it. Through understanding
an institution, one knows what resources are required and are
available for making the vision a reality. Only through understanding can the president effectively communicate his or her
vision as well as the mission of the institution to both internal
and external constituents. The president's knowledge and support of the community college and of higher education must be
so compelling that others will understand, appreciate, and support equality and selectivity, access and high academic standards,
vocational-technical education, the arts and the sciences, developmental education, community services, and student ser-

vices. Communicating the understanding of the institution in ways that others buy into the mission is mandatory in "selling" the institution to funding sources, both private and public. Understanding is the basis of wisdom, a desirable characteristic in all leaders.

However, understanding the institution must be more than philosophical. The effective president must translate institutional understanding into practical acts. For example, the president who visits a potential donor must be able to illustrate the value of the institution to the area it serves. The value may be in economic terms: jobs created, industries attracted to the area served by the college, and skilled workers trained. Or the value may be in terms of human potential: How many students from disadvantaged socioeconomic groups attend the college? How many minorities attend? How many older women have been given a second chance for an education because the institution exists? Without translating the institutional vision into practical goals and objectives, little is accomplished. Yet without an understanding of the institution on the part of the president, it is unlikely that the vision and the goals required to accomplish the vision will be achieved.

The following example illustrates the importance of understanding the institution. An individual who had recently become the president of a relatively new community college located in an area whose economy depended on lumber was approached by an environmental group during his first week on the job. What, the group wanted to know, was he as president of the college going to do about the lumber industry's destruction of the environment? The president, who was himself sympathetic to the environmental movement, asked that he be allowed to think about the group's concerns, since he knew enough about the conflicts between the lumber interests and the environmentalists to approach the topic cautiously. He was correct in doing so, because two days later at a Chamber of Commerce reception in his honor, he was approached by a top executive of one of the leading logging companies in the region. What, the logging company executive demanded, is the college going to do about those people who would wreck the area's economy and in the process destroy the college's program in forestry? Again, the president of the college kept his cool and told the executive he would be in touch with him. The president kept his promise and met with both groups. He did not propose to mediate between the logging interests and the environmental groups at this stage of his presidency, but his understanding of the college's brief history and the tension existing between the two groups kept the college out of the middle of a dispute that could have literally destroyed part of its instructional program. Both the logging company executive and the environmental group members perceived the president as someone who was willing to listen to opposing views without passing judgment on who was right or wrong. Later, the president was able to bring the two groups together on the college campus for a major forum on the impact of the logging industry on the economy and the environment.

Appreciating the Culture

The effective president appreciates and contributes to an institution's culture. Appreciating the culture is a part of understanding the institution, yet institutional culture is so complex that the effective president should pay special attention to this facet of understanding the institution. Often, for example, institutional culture is confused with institutional climate. Effective presidents should realize that climate changes much more quickly than culture and that climate is more subject to individual attitudes and actions than institutional culture is.

Institutional culture grows out of and is a part of shared values, beliefs, and assumptions about an institution. Culture can be a strength or a liability (causing an institution to stagnate), but it is generally a strength in that it projects the image of the institution. Institutional image and culture have a symbiotic relationship, one constantly feeding and shaping the other. Institutional cultures change slowly. For example, racial attitudes have often dominated the culture of some institutions, religion others, and gender still others. While understanding is a rational process, appreciating an institution's culture can be an emotional process, one that demands sensitivity to what has gone before and to what may happen in the future — a sensitivity that often evokes chills and even tears when a certain song is sung or a certain place on campus is visited.

Culture consists of those things that make an institution distinct: its history, its traditions, its values, its interaction with the larger environment, its ceremonies, how it renews itself — including recruiting and selecting personnel — and how it evaluates itself. Is integrity maintained in all that the institution does? Or does the culture say that "anything goes" — for example, winning football games at any cost or padding enrollment figures to generate full-time equivalent students? Does the culture encourage, indeed reward, risk taking? Is the culture in tune with the times, especially in relation to diversity on campus and the roles of women and minorities in society? How do we know when to let parts of our culture die? Or when to kill them? Open access, an important aspect of a community college's culture, is in itself a form of risk taking, for many community college students have academic deficiencies. What does it mean when we say that the community college is a teaching institution?

Myths, legends, stories of the college's founding and of early institutional leaders, are part of an institution's culture, contribute to a sense of history and community, and inspire loyalty to that institution. The culture of an institution influences how members of both the college community and the community at large perceive it. The effective president understands and is sensitive to an institution's culture, respecting and preserving the good things of the past but always shaping the present and planning for the future. The effective leader, and especially the effective president, understands when and where to change an institution's culture, when to let go. The effective president discusses the institution's culture in ways that can be understood by much of the public, often using metaphors with which the audience identifies. Indeed, the highly successful president becomes one with the culture, both as its interpreter and as the symbol of the institution, absorbing and being absorbed by the institutional culture and ultimately becoming an integral part of that culture, often after passing from the scene.

Probably no single arena offers presidents more opportunities for error than does the failure to understand the institutional culture. For example, many presidents have made the mistake of failing to recognize an institution's governance structure as an aspect of its culture. For an autocratic president to move into an institution with a heritage of shared governance is often suicidal. The same thing is true when a president follows an autocratic president and attempts to govern by committee. In one situation in which the latter happened, the new president followed a strong and autocratic leader. The new president, with his student personnel background, decided that literally everyone should be involved in the decision-making process. The result was that few decisions were made and the president was "let go." Understanding the culture and moving within its framework could have saved him and members of the academic community much grief and perhaps ultimately accomplished the goal of shared governance.

Mediating Disputes

The effective president mediates disputes between and among various segments of the college community and, when necessary, the larger community. Mediation includes helping to resolve external disputes if they have the potential of influencing the direction of the institution. Serving as mediator requires a broad range of skills and abilities; thus, the effective president cannot become too specialized in terms of thought processes or actions. In mediating disputes, the president must not become involved with personalities and must not be drawn into the vortex of the arguments. Rather, the president must act quickly and courageously to exercise checks and balances in a timely fashion, thereby promoting institutional equilibrium, turning conflict into creativity. Issues are rarely so clear that one side is right and the other side wrong; therefore, many disputes should be placed in the perspective of the mission. The effective president helps all parties to understand and appreciate the perspective of others without destroying the confidence of either side. At the same time, it is essential to keep the overall welfare of the institution foremost in the minds of all parties. Serving as mediator enhances rather than diminishes the president's ability to lead. The effective president uses the appropriate skills and abilities to bring various constituents together for the common good, which is leadership at its best.

A personal example will illustrate the value of understanding the president's role in mediating disputes. The college where I was president inherited from the Commonwealth of Virginia a regional bicentennial center. A leading state senator led the city in which the college was located to believe that the city would inherit the building after the nation's bicentennial celebration ended. Indeed, the city had already joined hands with the county and the Chamber of Commerce in establishing the region's visitors' center in one part of the bicentennial center. Members of the college community saw little value in the building, since it was small and located some distance from the main campus. Members of the nursing faculty who were likely to be located in the building were especially disgruntled. Yet the governor ordered me, as president, to utilize the building. The years of coalition building among members of the college community, the community at large, and the political forces in the state capital were on the verge of crumbling. I moved to mediate the dispute, bringing to the table the chair of the college's local governing board, the city manager, the mayor, the county executive, the chair of the board of supervisors, the president of the Chamber, local members of the state legislative body, the president of a very influential nonprofit foundation, and a powerful state senator. Before negotiations could take place, it was necessary to mediate among the various special interest groups. To make a long and complicated story short, a new governor was elected, the building was sold to the county and leased to the nonprofit organization, and the college got a much-needed new building located on its main campus. Without mediation, the story would probably have a much different ending.

Necessity of Good Management

The effective president understands the necessity of good management and demands it on the part of all segments of the college community. One's ability to lead is related directly to one's credibility; the president who fails to ensure that the institution is managed well soon loses credibility, for the institution must be well managed.

Management functions are often the most visible aspects of the campus's operation and the ones audited, both formally and informally. The president must be a good manager in areas such as motivating people, establishing priorities, and creating a positive climate on campus. In this era of measuring educational outcomes and Total Quality Management, evaluation is a management function. Effective presidents should, as much as possible, concentrate on systems of management under the direction of others, thus freeing the president from day-to-day management activities.

A part of good management is the allocation of resources, because ultimately adequate resources are required if the president's vision is to become a reality. Resource allocation is of great concern to governing boards. How resources are allocated tests the president's ability to manage, for it often makes it necessary to say to the college community and to the board what is important and what is not. Resource allocation includes the allocation of time—both the president's time and that of the leadership team. The president's role must never be limited to that of a manager, however, for this would deny the institution the leadership in the critical area of linking resources, both human and financial, to the institutional mission.

The effective president brings leadership to bear on the management of the institution in ways that managers do not. That is, managerial skills represent just one group of leadership skills among the many the successful president possesses and utilizes. A president who uses good management to make the vision possible serves the institution and the larger society well.

While mismanagement of funds tends to get most of the headlines, the effective president realizes that management goes well beyond fiscal management. The president who fails to manage resources in ways that reflect community needs often encounters frustration, if not major problems. For example, one president failed to respond to the needs of the area's major industry and therefore the college was essentially isolated from the region's major employer. On the other hand, the president's successor went overboard in serving the leading industry, often neglecting other critical needs. In both cases, the presidents did not manage the curriculum well, and the college failed to achieve its full potential.

Selecting Personnel

The effective president selects members of the leadership team who are leaders themselves. Presidents use the selection process to shape institutional culture — for example, employing minorities and women can shape that culture. Among the attributes those selected should possess are competence, loyalty to the institution's mission, and a willingness to use assets in ways that complement and occasionally compete with other members of the leadership team. This team must be formulated, coached, and utilized by the president, because selecting excellent personnel is not good enough: they must be brought together as a unit with common goals.

In selecting members of the leadership team, presidents must not pick individuals who are mirror images of themselves. Yet in selecting individuals who march to different drummers, the president must understand that conflicts will develop, that the understanding of who has what power will emerge only after much debate, and that power will shift between and among leaders. The president must be willing and able to resolve conflicts among others and to use the conflicts to further the mission of the institution. The president must not be surrounded with myrmidons, for no one can be effective unless challenged. Hearing the truth, no matter how painful it may be at times, is essential.

In selecting personnel, the president must consider the total mission of the institution. To make an appointment that is politically expedient may not be the best decision in the long run. For example, to choose a member of the "old boys' network," when proclaiming to diversify the leadership team, is likely to be the wrong decision, no matter how well qualified the appointee may be.

Examples abound that illustrate the role personnel selection plays in shaping a college's mission and culture. A president with experience in and a commitment to occupational-technical education is likely to lead the college in a different direction than would a president committed to the arts. Selecting a woman as president may make the institution more sensitive to issues affecting women, just as a president who is a member of a minority group is likely to affect the institution in ways that a white male president would not.

Utilizing Information

The effective college leader selects, analyzes, and utilizes information of all types and from various sources. The president is responsible for selecting and sharing information that is candid, even if it is occasionally detrimental to the image of the college. The president must be well informed regarding what to read and what to do with what is learned. The president must know which experts can be trusted and who the charlatans are.

Realizing that the governing board cannot and should not read everything that is written about the college, the effective president must select information that is useful to the board. The once-popular approach whereby the president bombarded the board with information hoping that everything would be covered and nothing read is no longer acceptable. Board members want relevant information; the president is obligated to provide such information. How well presidents process and disseminate information may well determine how the board and members of the campus community view them.

One example of where processing and utilizing information effectively is critical to today's president is in the field of demographics. While most chief administrators read about national demographic trends, it is often those in regions of high demographic changes in minority population who use such information in their planning process. For example, how many presidents plan their curriculum around the out-migration of the young people in their service region? How many are planning to serve an aging population?

Educational Leadership

The effective president is the institution's educational leader. The educational leader is concerned with ideas, values, and goals that go well beyond the day-to-day affairs of the college. Educational leadership requires constant learning on the part of the president and all members of the college community. This is because educational leadership is broader than shaping the curriculum, broader than managing the institution, since the educational leader should be concerned with the distinctiveness of the institution's mission and with preserving that distinctiveness. Is the institution doing what it says it is doing? Teaching what it should?

A part of any institution of higher education's mission that sets it apart from other segments of society is scholarship; it follows that the educational leader is a scholar who demands a commitment to scholarship by all members of the academic community. Educational leadership is even broader than creating the vision, because educational leadership requires bringing together the assets of the institution in a way that makes achieving the vision possible, while at the same time creating new tensions that will result in new visions. Without tensions and without new visions, the edge is lost, not only for the president, but for the rest of the college community. An institution without tensions is an institution that faces no new challenges.

As an educational leader, the president never permits the college to become completely settled, is never satisfied that the college is as good as it can or should be. The effective educational leader is generous in giving credit to others in achieving goals and is subtle in taking credit. Educational leadership implies moral leadership in the sense that institutional integrity is maintained in all aspects of the college's operation.

In addition to serving as the educational leader on campus, it is the president's responsibility to function as the educational leader for the members of the institution's governing board. The board members should understand the mission of the institution in ways that permit them to interpret that mission to others, including legislators and private funding sources. It is also the president's responsibility to educate members of the board regarding their proper role in campus governance. In many cases, when board members get overly involved in the administrative process, it is because the president has not taken the time to educate them to their proper role. Educational leadership, then, is an important avenue for communicating with and leading all of the institution's constituents in ways that are in concert with the institutional mission.

Professional Leadership

Effective presidents are leaders in their professional fields. Every professional who proposes to lead must know the responsibilities associated with one's professional field. Moreover, professional leadership requires that the president be an active rather than a passive bystander in identifying, analyzing, and solving issues in higher education.

To be a leader in one's professional field, one must keep abreast of local, state, and national trends and issues affecting higher education. The issues must be viewed as more than problems and must be analyzed in light of the college's mission and acted on when warranted. The effective president joins and participates in state, regional, and national organizations, occasionally assuming a leadership role in these organizations. Scholarship, a key ingredient of educational leadership, is helpful in providing leadership in one's professional field, although in organizations such as the American Association of Community Colleges' Presidents Academy, scholarship is not a prerequisite to effective professional leadership.

To lead in one's profession requires the establishment, maintenance, and utilization of a network of peers. Peers are especially important in community colleges if one is to avoid becoming too provincial, a great danger in many institutions located in rural areas. In some respects, working with one's peers — leading one's peers — represents the ultimate in leadership, since to be a leader among leaders is the highest compliment to leaders.

Professional leadership requires the constant questioning of the status quo on campus and within society and relating the results of the questioning to the college's mission. From a practical point of view, professional leadership provides the avenue for keeping up with what is happening beyond one's own campus. Presidents who rarely leave the small, isolated campus are in a weak position when it comes to planning for the future, even if they process available information effectively. Much can be learned through professional activities that simply is not available elsewhere. For example, serving on a national board such as that of the American Association of Community Colleges broadens one's perspective in ways that are not available through reading or working only on one's own campus. Moreover, professional leadership enhances one's image on campus and nationally, assuming, of course, that things are not neglected on one's own campus.

Political Leadership

The effective president understands and works effectively with political leaders at the local, state, and in some cases, the national level. Working effectively in the political arena means more than being an effective lobbyist, although lobbying (maintaining one's political contacts may be a more appropriate term than lobbying) is an important part of working within the political hierarchy. Political leadership requires building bridges with unions, special interest groups, and other organizations.

The effective president defines and understands the political issues that have the potential of influencing the college's mission. Achieving the president's vision for the college requires building on past and present political support and cultivating new political support as it emerges. The president ensures that the college's mission moves in concert with the goals of the community, the state, and, when appropriate, the nation. If the state political leadership advocates industrial development, the effective president interprets the college's mission in light of the current political agenda, while at the same time making sure that the mission is not whiplashed by every political or social trend.

As is true with much of the rest of the presidency, working in the political arena involves living with ambiguity and moving with the political flow as long as that flow is in concert with the college's mission and involves going against the flow when necessary but in a way that does not alienate the college's political supporters. Although in the best of all worlds, the effective president is nonpartisan in working with all politicians in the world in which most presidents function, partisan politics is a reality and must be dealt with effectively but always in ways that enhance the institutional mission.

One example illustrates the need for effective political leadership. The founding chancellor of a statewide system of community colleges was on a first-name basis with every key member of the state legislative body during the formative years of the system. All the key leaders, including the governor, were members of the majority party. The chancellor was an astute politician when dealing with these key members; indeed, he got everything he requested for the system. But he failed to realize that new leadership was always emerging and older leaders were retiring or dying. In selecting the site for a new college, the chancellor went head to head with a first-term legislator from the minority party. The chancellor, with the backing of key political supporters, won the battle hands down. Fast forward to ten years later: the first-term legislator was now governor. The chancellor's tenure did not survive the governor's term in office. Needless to say, the system suffered a great deal during the period in which the chancellor clashed with the governor. This time, there were no members of the old guard to come to his aid. Had the chancellor worked effectively with the emerging political leadership, he could have perhaps saved both himself and the system much grief.

Avenues for Renewal

Perpetual self-renewal is mandatory for perpetual institutional renewal. The effective president provides avenues for renewal for all members of the college community, meshing individual needs with institutional needs, finding and making available resources for renewal such as travel, released time for faculty and administrators, and time for pursuing new fields of professional interest. The president should devote some time each day to being alone and thinking, an important source of renewal. Time should be devoted to introspection, because effective presidents must know themselves. Ironically, perhaps, introspection is in itself a leadership skill.

Renewal for the president can take the form of mentoring younger and less experienced administrators and faculty members. The president who uses the renewal process to advance the college and higher education in general is often a role model for other members of the college community. By ensuring one's own renewal, the effective president sets a pattern that others will emulate; by engaging in perpetual self-renewal, the president provides that spark of energy that lights the fires that must burn brightly in the vibrant institution. Renewal often requires that the president step back and view the institution from a distance, from a new perspective, a perspective that permits envisioning the possibilities and limitations of an institution, a perspective that lets the president see the humor or occasionally the tragedy in a given situation.

Presidents are infamous for seeking avenues of renewal for everyone except themselves. A president I know takes great pride in providing educational assistance for members of the faculty and administration, yet he has never taken a leave of absence, although he can do so with full pay. When asked why, his answer was that he did not have the time. It is possible that many presidents do not want to leave their campus for an extended period of time because they are insecure, feeling that they might not be missed. They get caught up in their roles and find it difficult to back away, fearing that things will slow down without their involvement. As the pressure mounts, effective presidents will find avenues for self-renewal as well as institutional renewal. To do any less may well jeopardize the future of the president's career.

Institutional Symbol

The effective president serves as a symbol of the institution. The symbolic role of the community college leader is often not used to its fullest. Presidents must let it be known that when they speak, they are speaking with the authority — the voice — of an important educational institution. They must realize that when they move among politicians, other college presidents, business leaders, and members of the public, the institution is present, at least symbolically. When the president publishes an article or a book, the institution's reputation is often enhanced.

The chief executive officer's and the institution's fortunes are always entwined, one with the other. At receptions, formal ceremonies, convocations, and other functions to which the head of the institution is invited, the president attends not as an individual, but as the institutional head, as the symbol of the institution. By being aware of the significance of the presidency as a symbol of the institution, presidents can enhance their role and therefore enhance the effectiveness of the institution.

In contrast to most four-year college leaders, community college presidents have not utilized the symbolic role to the fullest. For example, until recently, few presidents had formal inaugurations, thereby missing an opportunity to call attention to the institution. Few presidents write for the Sunday newspaper's op ed page, an excellent forum in which to exercise presidential leadership as both scholar and symbol.

Use of Power

The effective president understands power and uses it wisely and with discretion. The use of power is complex. The wise use of power means that the president never steps outside the rules and regulations, never uses power to punish or reward, and always uses power to promote the good of the institution and never to promote self.

The effective president understands that all power ultimately emanates from the office or the position and not from the individual who occupies the office. Even while recognizing its source, the president realizes that power is a formidable tool that must be used if the vision is to be accomplished, indeed if the president is to achieve the full potential of the presidency. The use of power, for example, is mandatory in establishing institutional priorities ranging from what programs are to be offered to what personnel are employed.

Power has moral and social connotations as well as political ones, in dealing with both the college community and the community at large. The president who fails to function effectively in the power arena is likely to falter in other areas as well.

To even attempt to discuss the uses and abuses of power by the community college president would fill volumes. Most of these people are public servants who play by the rules and use power wisely and with discretion. Yet some presidents misuse funds, others take liberties with employees, others take more time off than is authorized, and still others abuse travel privileges. Many of the abuses come about because presidents begin to think that they are above the law, that the president's office offers an immunity not afforded other members of the college community. The failure to understand power and use it effectively causes presidents even more problems than their failure to understand the institutional culture. Wise presidents use power to promote the institution's welfare and not themselves, while at the same time understanding that power must be used to achieve institutional goals.

Summary

The effective president of the future will need to choose carefully how and when to utilize these skills and attributes. College leadership requires planning and creative problem solving. It demands discernment and understanding in dealing with opposing points of view, and forethought enough to realize how different people will perceive different actions. The wise leader takes into account existing belief systems and works within an existing structure to bring about change, always being sensitive to the concerns of others.

The twelve areas described in this chapter provide the

focus for the use of the president's time, energy, creativity, and intellectual pursuits. Presidents who exercise their skills and abilities in the proper arenas will find that their leadership will improve, as will their effectiveness as presidents. Such leaders will direct colleges that are able to function smoothly, regardless of any sudden crises that may arise.

References

Burns, J. M. *Leadership*. New York: HarperCollins, 1979.

Vaughan, G. B. *The Community College Presidency*. New York: American Council on Education/Macmillan, 1986.

Chapter 5

The Governing Board

William E. Piland

The development of effective community colleges is related to the development and maintenance of effective board-administrator relations. While most boards rarely become involved with the day-to-day operations of a college, they have considerable long-term impact through their policy formation role. And, during times of financial exigency, board decisions may come to bear rather quickly and directly on all aspects of a community college's operations. The board ultimately makes decisions to eliminate programs, services, and personnel, usually with advice from many groups, most notably administrators. Whether it is the best of times or the worst of times, solid board-administrator relations are crucial for a community college to accomplish its mission.

The principal role of building effective board-administrator relations belongs to the college president. Often, the president, working in conjunction with the board chairperson, has the responsibility for guiding interactions and relationships between the board and the administration. While some presidents attempt to control communications with the board, others encourage the development of a board-administration team approach to college governance and management. Regardless of the situation, administrators at many organizational levels have contact with the board and with its individual members. In fact, the board-administrator team approach goes a long way toward diffusing the "divide-and-conquer" strategy sometimes used by external pressure groups, employee unions, rogue board members, and disgruntled teachers, support staff, and administrators. The college administration, and not the board, must recognize that it has the primary responsibility for developing and maintaining harmonious and effective board-administrator relations.

This chapter examines the role of the board. The first section discusses types of boards, including trustee demographics and opinions. The second section touches on ways the board influences institutional climate and points out how administrators can work with board members. The final section considers trends affecting types of boards and board-administrator relations.

Types of Boards

There are a number of different ways to describe the types of boards that govern the over 1,000 public community, technical, and junior colleges in the country. Two common descriptors are (1) level of control (state or local), and (2) board member selection (appointed or elected). Over 600 boards of trustees exist. Members of these boards are usually laypeople serving as volunteers without compensation, although in some states, board members are paid.

Exhibit 5.1 lists the types of boards in each state. More than half the states have local boards governing their community colleges. Generally these are the states with the largest populations and the most colleges. Eighteen states have state boards. Three states—New York, Colorado, and Georgia—have a combination of local and state governing boards. Two states—South Dakota and Alaska—do not have public community colleges.

In the states governed by state boards, most (sixteen) have appointed boards; only two have elected boards. There is more of a balance between elected (fifteen states) and appointed (twelve

Exhibit 5.1. Board Types by State.

State boards	Local elected boards	Local appointed boards
Alabama	Arizona	Florida
Colorado	Arkansas	Illinois[b]
Connecticut	California	Maryland
Delaware	Colorado[a]	Massachusetts
Georgia	Georgia[a]	Mississippi
Hawaii	Idaho	New Jersey
Indiana	Illinois	New Mexico[b]
Kentucky	Iowa	New York (CUNY)
Louisiana	Kansas	North Carolina
Maine	Michigan	Ohio
Minnesota	Missouri	Oklahoma[b]
Nevada	Montana	Pennsylvania
New Hampshire	New Mexico	South Carolina
New York (SUNY)	Oklahoma	Washington
North Dakota	Oregon	Wisconsin
Rhode Island	Texas	
Tennessee	Wyoming	
Utah		
Vermont		
Virginia		
West Virginia		

[a]Combination of state and local boards
[b]Combination of elected and appointed boards.

states) boards in those states with local governing boards. In the three combination states, the state boards are appointed; the local boards are also appointed in New York. Three of the four states with the most community college districts (California, Texas, and Illinois) have elected boards. Some states, like New Mexico and Oklahoma, have a combination of local elected and appointed boards. Only Oklahoma has more appointed than elected boards. Colleges existing in states with local, appointed boards usually have their board members appointed by the state governor.

Although criticizing local boards, especially ones elected by the citizenry, is akin to bashing democracy itself, sentimentality should not hinder the debate about the most desirable type of boards to govern our colleges. In far too many communities, voter turnout for community college board elections is dismally low. Candidates get elected by small special interest groups who get out the vote. Since the election process coincides with other local, state, and national elections, the process becomes politicized, requiring the blessing and backing of a political party to win an election. Running a campaign also takes money, which means fundraising and the political favors often attached to the money. In a recent board election in a metropolitan area, a candidate spent $40,000 to get elected! Running for board election also seems to appeal to certain types of individuals. More and more often, these types appear to be using the election to a local community college board as a stepping-stone to higher elective office. A 1987 study of elected trustees discovered that one-third of the sample would like to be elected to a different public office in the future (Whitmore, 1987). It is interesting to note that one of the contenders for the Democratic presidential nomination in 1992 began his political career as an elected community college trustee!

Some trustees attempt to govern the colleges to the level of administrative intrusion. Various factors lead to this posture. Trustees may be interested in making a name for themselves so they can achieve higher office; beholden to a special interest group such as the faculty union or a segment of the community that got them elected, loyal to a political party that might be interested in using the college as a patronage haven, or indebted to contributors who expect certain favors for their contributions. In these situations, the needs of the college may be secondary to the trustees' agenda. Nevertheless, altruistic community leaders often do decide to run for office, and they do win elections in many instances. These trustees generally are interested in the college and in helping it accomplish its mission.

The appointment process seems to have its drawbacks, too. Since trustees are usually appointed by a politician, this process can be highly political. Appointments can be payoffs for political favors rendered or benefits for party hacks. Appointed trustees are not without political ambitions, also, or they may represent a certain ideology held by the appointer. Of course, the more limited investment in time and money normally needed for appointment than for election could mean that the appointees are less interested in the college than their elected counterparts are. Appointed trustees do have the opportunity to be more independent than elected ones, and they seem to be less inclined to be associated with a special interest group attempting to use the college for some limited purpose. They also seem to be more reflective of a professional/managerial class than elected trustees.

States with state boards controlling their community colleges generally have less well-developed community college systems and institutions that function less independently. In fact, most states with state boards have either a board for all of higher education in the state, a board with responsibility for universities and community colleges, or a state board of education. Only eight states have state boards exclusively for two-year postsecondary institutions. From a college administrator's viewpoint, the state board may be considered a bureaucratic operation too far removed from local colleges or too involved with other segments of education to effectively govern locally oriented community colleges.

While the way a board operates typically is idiosyncratic, administrators must recognize the forces behind the type of board and the appointment or election of their board members. Especially in states with local boards, an understanding of the election or appointment process and its implications should shape administrator behaviors when developing and maintaining relations with the governing board.

Trustee Demographics

Studies of trustees in higher education go back to 1917 (Nearing, 1917). The early studies dealt only with university, and usually private university, board members. An important scholarly inquiry in 1947 entitled "Men Who Control Our Universities" indicated that 75 percent of trustees were businessmen, bankers, and lawyers. A 1967 Educational Testing Service study of 5,000 trustees, 261 from public community colleges, drew the following profile of trustees: male, fifty to sixty-five years

old, white, well-educated, financially well off, moderate Republican, business executive or professional (Rauh, 1969). In 1977,
a study of community college and university trustees found that
the subjects tended to be male, fifty to fifty-nine years old, with
a high income and employed in an executive or managerial position. The study also reported that 15 percent of trustees were
female and 6 percent black (Drake, 1977). A comprehensive
study of 175 community college trustees in Illinois in 1984 drew
the following trustee profile: male (78 percent); white (97 percent); thirty-seven to fifty-six years old (54 percent); professional
or business owner/manager (67 percent); above-average income,
in the range $30,000–$60,000 (51 percent); highly educated,
with a B.A. degree or above (56 percent); Republican (59 percent); and moderate or somewhat conservative politically (68
percent) (Petty and Piland, 1985).

    In 1987, a national survey of 522 elected and appointed
community college trustees from 24 states offered a more recent snapshot of trustee characteristics (Whitmore, 1987). This
study provided the following profile: male (71 percent), between
forty and sixty years of age (54 percent), white (90 percent),
B.A. degree or higher (73 percent), professional or business
managerial occupation (61 percent), and high income of $55,000
or more (52 percent). Some other interesting findings were that
7 percent of trustees were black, 20 percent listed education as
their profession, one-third had attended or had a family member attend a community college, 54 percent had experience in
public office, and 50 percent considered themselves politically
moderate. Overall, differences between trustees who were appointed and those who were elected were slight. Some noticeable
differences were that appointed trustees were somewhat older
than elected ones, not as highly educated, and slightly more
liberal than elected trustees (Whitmore, 1987). These studies
show that trustees tended to reflect the historical profile of trustees
in all of higher education throughout the twentieth century.

    Trustees in charge of governing community colleges have
not changed much over the years. While there have been increases in the number and percentages of women and minorities in education as an employment field, a shift of correspond-

ing magnitude in the characteristics of trustees has not occurred. Observers of the community college scene may conclude that trustees are not representative of the students served by community colleges, who tend to be female, younger, less wealthy and less educated, from a lower socioeconomic stratum, and more reflective of ethnic minorities. The trustees may be viewed, therefore, as out of step with and unresponsive to the needs of the students. They may also lack commitment to the community college mission, which reflects a democratization of higher education. How can white, upper-middle-class trustees govern an institution that might bring about a shift in power and undermine the existing social system? Insight into the trustees' views of the mission and function of community colleges might provide a partial response to this question.

Trustee Views on Community College Mission and Functions

There have been a number of state-level studies of trustee views on the mission and functions of the colleges they govern (Petty and Piland, 1985; Stevens and Piland, 1988; Wilbur and Sheldon, 1988, 1989; Watson and Winner, 1987). Recently there have been two national surveys concerning community college trustee views. One was a survey of 100 trustees attending the annual convention of the Association of Community College Trustees in September 1989. The trustees—representing twenty-three states and two Canadian provinces—provided views on financial, governance, and educational issues. Responses reflected similar views on educational issues and a number of split opinions on questions concerning governance (three out of seven items) and finance (four out of seven items).

On the whole, the educational views of trustees mirrored the current thinking by professionals in the higher education field. They reflected the importance of general education in a student's total educational program and the importance of learning critical thinking skills and the development of personal values. The trustees also agreed that some programs are outdated and should be eliminated; academic standards must be raised; the college should be the primary institution educating adult, non–high school graduates; and more focus should be placed on the transfer function. Trustee views on governance seemed to indicate an understanding of the boards' role in governance and support of a strong president. The advocacy of community college interests in the state executive branch and legislature were viewed as problematic. State and local practices and experiences probably explain discrepancies in views on governance. The trustees' opinions about funding issues were far from uniform. Different state funding schemes may account for some of those differences. The answers to "who pays" and "how much do they pay" are not easily agreed on. Trustees did agree that most community college funding should come from the state and that student tuition should be at least 25 percent of operating costs (Piland and Butte, 1991).

The other national survey of trustee views was conducted in 1986 and involved 522 elected and appointed trustees from 24 states (Whitmore, 1987–88). These respondents answered questions regarding college programs, finance, statewide concerns, and student issues. Responses to college programs (educational) and financial issues were similar to the other study's findings. With respect to student issues, trustees agreed that their colleges should have no academic entry requirements for most programs and courses, that academic assessment should be required of students, and that community colleges have done an excellent job of serving the underserved student. There were few differences of opinion between elected and appointed trustees.

The opinions of trustees, as reflected in these surveys, reveal that trustees tend to hold mainstream views concerning the mission and functions of their colleges. Many of their opinions reflect the literature describing the traditional role of community colleges. There is little doubt that community college administrators and faculty, as well as state and national trustee educational organizations (Association of Community College Trustees, Association of Governing Boards of Universities and Colleges, American Association of Community and Junior Colleges), have helped mold and shape trustees' attitudes. Further, if these opinions are translated into action at the board table, the continuity of the community college mission will be preserved. Trustee actions, building on the institution's traditions and strengths, can be viewed in a positive light. On the other hand, maintaining or, at best, extending the status quo through trustee decision making does little to address the concerns of the critics of community colleges.

Observers of the community college scene, including Zwerling (1976), Pincus (1980), Karabel (1972), and Clark (1960), have raised numerous criticisms concerning the role and performance of community colleges in our society. For these critics, the views and corresponding actions of trustees miss the mark and will not lead to much-needed reform. Taken in this light, the characteristics and views of trustees inhibit a reconstruction of an important segment of higher education that is necessary to change the existing social order. Societal inequities will continue to exist because the people who govern our institutions, overtly or otherwise, perpetuate the inequities through their actions or inaction, according to this alternative view. Here again, it is important to recognize the differences between boards and individual trustees. Those trustees who govern large, urban colleges may be different and hold different views from their counterparts at small, rural colleges. Ultimately, actions taken by community college boards must be in the best interests of local community members — interests determined by trustees and administrators with active input and assistance from faculty, staff, students, and community leaders and organizations.

State Board Powers

As shown earlier in this chapter, most community colleges are governed by locally elected or appointed boards. Yet a large number of colleges — approximately 213 — are governed by state boards. State boards typically have some powers different from local boards. Some common state board powers include approving new programs; conducting systemwide program review and evaluation; developing systemwide legislative budget requests; distributing state aid; approving capital construction; approving new colleges, branches, and centers; and performing financial accountability audits or establishing a uniform accounting system.

Some states have local advisory councils that supplement the state boards. Common local advisory board powers include approving budgets, recommending programs to the state board, working with local business/industry and legislatures, and providing liaison with the local community.

Local Board Powers

The following list summarizes typical powers of local community college boards of trustees.

- Establish policies, rules, and regulations for governance and operation of the college
- Maintain and operate the college
- Approve programs
- Award degrees, certificates, and diplomas
- Establish student fees/tuition
- Determine salaries and benefits and employ staff
- Develop and control the budget
- Hold, convey, manage, and control district property
- Enter into contracts for services
- Apply to federal and state agencies in order to obtain and accept funds
- Hire, evaluate, and terminate a president
- Conduct long- and short-range planning
- Set minimum standards for student academic requirements
- Set salary and benefits for employees or enter into collective bargaining over these matters

This list is not exhaustive. Some boards have all of these powers and more. Others possess only some of these powers. For example, local boards in California cannot influence fees or tuition. Yet in Illinois, local boards have total control of all student fees. It also should be recognized that some powers are more important than others to the institution and to its students

and employees. Some observers believe the hiring and evaluation of a president is the most important duty a board has to
perform. Since the president is the chief executive officer of the
college, it is the president who influences the direction of the
college through direct actions and close communications with
the board (Tatum, 1985). While some board members and community college practitioners see this as the single most important board power, others see a more intense board involvement
with hiring and evaluation of all college staff, particularly the
professional staff (Jasiek, Wisgoski, and Andrews, 1985; Andrews and Licata, 1991).

Establishing policies, rules, and regulations for college
operations also is viewed as a primary board function. In fact,
a traditional view of board-administrator-faculty relations illustrates this role as an overarching one that heavily influences college operations. Conversely, institutional policies have been in
existence for many years at most colleges. New policies are established from time to time, but they tend to be narrow in scope
and often are a reaction to some state or federal law or regulation. Existing policies are also changed periodically.

Numerous forces impinge on the board's power in establishing policy. The collective bargaining agreement supersedes
board policies and directs the types of changes made to existing
policies. While the board does have to approve a collective bargaining agreement, the end result is often a compromise reached
at a bargaining table without direct board involvement. Addi-
tionally, the board relies heavily on administrator involvement
in policy formation. In fact, some studies have shown that
trustees have little communications beyond the administrative
staff of the college when determining policy or policy changes
(Watson and Winner, 1987; Petty and Piland, 1985).

Some recent studies suggest that the boards' involvement
in planning is an area of board powers that is becoming more
important (Giles, 1991; Wilbur and Sheldon, 1988; Stevens and
Piland, 1988). Trustees recognize the importance of planning
as it affects the budget, programs and services, student fees, and
staff hiring and evaluation. Planning, particularly of a long-term
nature, is similar to setting or altering the mission and goals

of an institution. In a recent study of community college boards in California and British Columbia, Canada trustees emphasized long-term horizons and short-term planning. They saw the boards' role in planning as being one of setting the broad direction of the institution and then reviewing, revising, and approving short-term, strategic plans (Deas, 1992).

These examples of powers show that the community college boards have substantial authority. Many community college administrators, especially presidents, would agree with this point of view. In practice, however, boards do not seem to make substantial decisions as often as people believe. Studies of board practices and operations show that boards typically meet once or, at most, twice a month and that meetings last less than four hours per month (Griffin, 1989). About 80 percent of trustees spend less than ten hours per week on board business (Wilbur and Sheldon, 1988). Coupled with the fact that trustees get most of their information from college administrators, the perceived powers of boards may be overstated.

Attending a typical college board meeting can be a deadly experience. Few activities in life are as boring to visitors as board meetings. On the other hand, every board agenda contains some action items, and while most are routine matters, decisions are made that will affect the college, sometimes in a substantial way. Nevertheless, two forces are eroding local and, in some cases, state board powers. These factors, which will be discussed later in this chapter, are shared governance and state control.

Board's Role in Establishing Institutional Climate

Many forces merge to make a community college. Most forces are human ones, for colleges are largely about people: employees, students, and trustees. The degree to which a college can achieve excellence is largely due to the factors that contribute to the overall climate. According to studies by Roueche and Baker (1987), the climate for excellence in a community college centers on four basic factors: (1) leadership, (2) decisions, (3) motivation, and (4) communications. These factors seem to be the result of attitudes and actions of all constituents within a college. The board has a major role to play in establishing a climate of excellence. As O'Banion (1989, p. 8) notes, "Board members can challenge the president to expand the vision, take risks, and explore new approaches."

Board-Administrator Relations

The relationship between trustees and administrators consists of two factors: the established rules, policies, and practices; and the behavioral patterns exhibited by the participants. This second human factor, too often ignored in the literature, has a tremendous impact on institutional climate. The personalities, egos, ambitions, fears, goals, and styles of internal constituents can enhance or sabotage the quest for excellence.

What if the board really wants to run the college? What if a few trustees feel they can do a better job than the administrators? What if a trustee needs to make a big splash in order to gain reappointment or reelection? What if administrators consider themselves better qualified to shape the institutional direction than a group of laypeople? What if a president with one year left on the employment contract decides to acquiesce to the board's every wish to curry favors with the trustees? These scenarios could have a disruptive effect on institutional climate. According to the *Report of the Chancellor's Task Force on Community Colleges* in New York State, "The extent to which a college achieves a degree of excellence in accomplishing its mission and maintaining its academic integrity is due, in large measure, to the governance of the institution" (State University of New York, 1986, p. 1).

The board-administration relationship is at the leading edge of creating a climate of quality in a community college. The pursuit of excellence should bring the trustees and administrators together toward a common goal. Excellence can only be achieved in a climate of mutual trust and respect in which the board and administration want each other to be the best, mutually serving an institution that aims to be the best (O'Banion, 1989). Teamwork depends on a willingness to share power as well as on trust and open communications. This mutual support must be of a lasting nature in order for the board-administration team to gain momentum and reach peak performance. Board members and administrators in one study indicated that an informed and moderately active board supporting an active and innovative administration is the best balance for achieving a desirable institutional climate (Deas, 1992).

Shared Responsibilities of Trustees and Administrators

As previously observed, board powers are significant in establishing institutional climate. Yet boards do not operate in a vacuum. Rather, they tend to communicate and work closely with administrators in performing certain governance tasks. The tasks that require collaboration between board and administration have a large impact on the direction of the college. These tasks have been identified as important ones in a number of studies (Petty and Piland, 1985; Giles, 1991; Dowdy, 1987; Martens, 1985; Crews, 1985; Levin, 1991). Some tasks demand more action from one group than the other, but all seem to bring the trustees and administrators together in a joint initiative. The roles of each group are described for each task in Exhibit 5.2.

The board and administration roles identified in Exhibit 5.2 appear clearcut and easily understandable. In practice, this is not always the case. Overlap and gaps in the performance of these roles show up frequently. In the Giles study (1991) of fifteen governance activities, not a single activity was identified as being exclusively in the boards' or administrators' domain. The largest number of activities — seven — were identified as the administrations' responsibility with board involvement, and four activities were selected as having equal board and administrator responsibility.

According to John Gardner (1990), leadership is exercised by individuals working together as a team. The listing of administrator and trustee roles shows that teamwork is an absolute necessity in order to maintain a healthy organizational climate. Board-administration relationships must be bound together by trust, mutual respect, and clear understanding of each other's roles. These elements are at the forefront of an effective team. In undertaking governance tasks, the board and administration have the chance to contribute greatly to the climate from which excellence seems to emanate. The effectiveness of that contribution depends on the relationship molded between the trustees and the administrators.

Trends Affecting Governing Board Roles

Some noticeable trends affect the composition and role of community college governing boards, especially local boards. Listed below are a few of these trends and their impacts.

Board Member Diversity

While it is true that governing boards consist of people whose demographic characteristics are much like those of board members in years past, changes are taking place. More women, minorities, younger people, and representatives of a range of socioeconomic classes and occupational groups are being elected and appointed to boards. These newer members are bringing an underrepresented point of view to boards. They often champion the causes and represent the needs of groups that have not held power in the past but that make up sizable numbers of students. These board members frequently push agendas that might be different from or counter to the status quo for many institutions. They provide a counterpoint to the conservatism of most governing boards and provide a challenge to administrators to question current educational programs and services to make sure they meet the needs of the underrepresented in the community.

A smaller trend is the influence of the Christian right on governing boards. While "Christian candidates" have been more interested in obtaining seats on school, municipal, and county boards, some have begun appearing on community college boards. These members frequently espouse what they characterize as spiritual views or traditional values — for example, opposition to the separation of church and state or to abortion. They too feel that they express an underrepresented viewpoint. The potential for conflicts among these newer board members

Exhibit 5.2. Governance Tasks and Roles of Board and Administration.

Tasks	Board roles	Administration roles
1. Establish mission and goals	Provide input into formation of mission and goals Approve mission and goals	President identifies mission in consultation with others Develop mission and goals into a formal statement
2. Make short- and long-range plans	Set broad direction Review, revise, and approve plans Publicize plans	Involve constituents in process Develop plans Monitor plans
3. Make policy	Participate in policy-making, revision exercises Approve policies	Provide impetus and language for policies Involve constituents Review policies
4. Develop budgets	Articulate community needs/views in budget building Perform fiduciary role Set broad directions Review and approve budgets and financial statements	Involve constituents Prepare budget and financial resource details Provide information to the board Monitor budgets and recommend revisions
5. Evaluate programs, services, and staff	Provide support and resources Approve evaluation plan Review overall results Evaluate the president Evaluate board effectiveness	Involve constituents Develop evaluation system Conduct evaluations Present results to the board Recommend changes in system

6. Conduct community relations	Set broad directions
	Approve community relations plan
	Participate in community relations activities
	Participate in fundraising activities
	Participate in lobbying
	Involve constituents
	Prepare and implement plan
	Participate in community relations activities
	Work closely with foundation/fundraising enterprise
	Participate in lobbying
7. Make property transactions	Purchase, transfer, and sell land
	Select an architect
	Provide adequate resources for construction maintenance
	Communicate actions and rationale to public
	Involve constituents
	Provide detail background information
	Make recommendations to board
8. Formulate disciplinary procedures	Approve staff and student procedures
	Serve as court of appeal
	Make disciplinary decisions
	Involve constituents
	Interpret codes of behavior
	Develop staff and student disciplinary procedures
	Keep board informed of disciplinary actions
	Make disciplinary recommendations to board
9. Bargain collectively	Develop desired outcomes
	Review tentative settlement
	Sign the agreement
	Inform community of bargaining results
	Participate in developing desired outcomes
	Conduct bargaining sessions
	Share union proposals with board
	Make recommendation to board
	Implement the agreement

and existing trustees is readily apparent. Such diversity of opinion and backgrounds on governing boards usually is desirable.
However, internal strife and sometimes open warfare can dominate the workings of a board. These forces paralyze a college
and damage the institution's reputation in the community and
beyond. Administrators, and particularly the president, need
to work hard at developing trust, understanding, respect, and
collaboration among all trustees. The task is daunting.

State Control

The trend toward state control is well developed. Figure 5.1
shows that it is a reality, not a trend, in twenty-one states. In
many of the other states with local boards, increasing state control is eroding the power of these boards. State control usually
follows increased state funding. Shifting revenue sources from
the local property tax to state income and sales taxes portends
bigger state influences on local operations. Proposition 13, passed
in California in 1978, is the most dramatic illustration of a shift
from primarily local to exclusively state funding. Many observers
in California are convinced the legislature is running the community colleges by enacting a large number of laws that govern
the operations of the state's community colleges. In other states,
the power is shifting to a state coordinating board, such as a
board of higher education or a community college board. These
boards, through legislation and rules and regulations, are usurp-
ing traditional powers of local boards.

Increasing state control has some serious implications for
community college trustees. If the trend continues, local boards
may become merely advisory bodies to the college administration or could even cease to exist. During the recently enacted
reform of the California community college system (AB 1725),
some consideration was given to replacing local boards with
regional boards. Community college trustees should not ignore
the demand to eliminate local public school boards through
privatization of the schools (Chubb and Moe, 1990). Reform-
ing boards to strengthen policy-making authority and reduce
meddling in operations is more desirable than eliminating boards
or their powers.

Shared Governance

While community colleges now are recognized as partners in a state's higher education enterprise, they grew out of a public school tradition that separated the overseers (administrators) from the hired hands (teachers). The higher education tradition views teachers as partners in a shared decision-making environment.

Shared governance, at its most basic level, means power sharing. In many locales, the community college governing board retains the final decision by affirming or, in some cases, simply rejecting undesirable recommendations emanating from the shared governance system. The recent reforms in California have stipulated that local boards and local academic senates must jointly agree on policies governing the college. This change is true power sharing. Shared governance contains positives and negatives as a system of governance. If trustees focus on the negatives such as the tedious, lengthy, and difficult nature of the process, the lack of recognizable accountability for decisions, and role confusion, they may resist or subvert the concept. If they appreciate the positives such as the empowerment of participants, the development of collegial relationships, and the shared ownership of policies as a motivating force, they may actively embrace and guide the move to a shared governance system (Wirth, 1991). Administrators are responsible for helping trustees choose this second option.

Summary

Though governing boards are not usually directly involved in the day-to-day operations of the community college, they do have much influence on long-range planning through their policy formation role. The level of control of these boards can be state or local, and the members can be appointed or elected. Regardless of the type of governing board, administrators at many organizational levels have contact with the board and its individual members. The administration has the primary responsibility for developing and maintaining harmonious and effective board-administrator relations. Some trends that have an impact on governing board roles are board member diversity, increasing state control, and shared governance.

Board-administrator relations are at the leading edge of creating a climate of quality in a community college. The pursuit of excellence should bring the trustees and administrators to want each other to be the best, mutually serving an institution that aims to be the best. Teamwork depends on a willingness to share power, trust, and open communications. An informed, moderately active board supporting an active and innovative administration is the best balance for an effective institution.

References

Andrews, H., and Licata, C. "Administrative Perceptions of Existing Evaluation Systems." *Journal of Personnel Evaluation in the United States*, 1991, *5*, 69–76.

Chubb, J., and Moe, T. *Politics, Markets, and America's Schools.* Washington, D.C.: Brookings Institute, 1990.

Clark, B. R. "The 'Cooling-Out' Function in Higher Education." *American Journal of Sociology*, 1960, *65*(6), 569–576.

Crews, J. "Authority and Responsibility in Board/President Performance." *Trustee Quarterly*, 1985, *9*(1), 7–12.

Deas, E. "The Relationship Between the Board and Administration in Selected Activities Contributing to the Overall Climate of a Community College." Unpublished research report, Office for Research and Service in Postsecondary Education, San Diego State University, 1992.

Dowdy, H. B. *Manual for Trustees of the North Carolina Community College System.* Raleigh: North Carolina State Department of Community Colleges, 1987.

Drake, S. *A Study of Community and Junior College Boards of Trustees.* Washington, D.C.: American Association of Community and Junior Colleges, 1977.

Gardner, J. W. *On Leadership.* New York: Free Press, 1990.

Giles, R. "Governance and Leadership Expectations of Trustees and CEOs." *Trustee Quarterly*, 1991, *15*(2), 8–14.

Griffin, B. "Presidents' Survey of Board of Trustee Practices in Kansas Community Colleges." Unpublished research report,

Office of Institutional Research, Allen County Community College, Iola, Kans., 1989. (ED 324 060)

Jasiek, C. R., Wisgoski, A., and Andrews, H. A."The Trustee Role in College Personnel Management." In G. F. Petty (ed.), *Active Trusteeship for a Changing Era*. New Directions for Community Colleges, no. 51. San Francisco: Jossey-Bass, 1985.

Karabel, J. "Community Colleges and Social Stratification." *Harvard Educational Review*, 1972, *42*(4), 521–562.

Levin, J. "The Importance of the Board-President Relationship in Three Community Colleges." *Canadian Journal of Higher Education*, 1991, *6*(2), 63–69.

Martens, F. *Governance of the State University of New York Community Colleges*. New York: Office for Community Colleges, State University of New York, Albany, 1985. (ED 263 936)

Nearing, S. "Who's Who Among College Trustees." *School and Society*, 1917, *6*, 297–299.

O'Banion, T. "Retaining a Peak Performing President." *Trustee Quarterly*, 1989, *13*(4), 3–7.

Petty, G., and Piland, W. "The Illinois Public Community College Board Members." In G. F. Petty (ed.), *Active Trusteeship for a Changing Era*. New Directions for Community Colleges, no. 51. San Francisco: Jossey-Bass, 1985.

Piland, W., and Butte, H. "Trustee Views on Finance, Governance, and Educational Issues." *Community College Review*, 1991, *18*(4), 6–12.

Pincus, F. L. "The False Promise of Community Colleges: Class Conflict and Vocational Education." *Harvard Educational Review*, 1980, *50*(3), 332–361.

Rauh, M. *College and University Trusteeship*. New York: McGraw-Hill, 1969.

Roueche, J., and Baker, G. *Access and Excellence: The Open Door College*. Washington, D.C.: Community College Press, 1987.

State University of New York. *Report of the Chancellor's Task Force on Community Colleges*. New York: State University of New York, 1986.

Stevens, L., and Piland, W. "Reform in Community College Governance: The California Story." *Community/Junior College Quarterly of Research and Practice*, 1988, *12*(3), 251–261.

Tatum, J. "Active Trusteeship for a Changing Era." In G. F. Petty (ed.), *Active Trusteeship for a Changing Era.* New Directions for Community Colleges, no. 51. San Francisco: Jossey-Bass, 1985.

Watson, E., and Winner, L. "Participation and Content in Community and Technical College Board Meetings." *Community/Junior College Quarterly of Research and Practice,* 1987, *11*(4), 275–282.

Whitmore, L. "Results of a National Survey of Local Community College Trustees: Trustee Characteristics." *Trustee Quarterly,* 1987, *11*(4), 14–23.

Whitmore, L. "Results of a National Survey of Local Community College Trustees: Trustee Attitudes." *Trustee Quarterly,* 1987–88, *12*(1), 3–9.

Wilbur, L., and Sheldon, M. *What Price Local Control: California Community College Trustees.* Report no. 2. Los Angeles: School of Education, University of Southern California, 1988. (ED 305 094)

Wilbur, L., and Sheldon, M. *On California Community College Trustees: Expectations and Realities.* Report no. 3. Los Angeles: School of Education, University of Southern California, 1989. (ED 305 095)

Wirth, P. "Shared Governance: Promises and Perils." Unpublished manuscript, Yuba Community College District, Marysville, Calif., 1991. (ED 331 568)

Zwerling, L. S. *Second Best: The Crisis of the Community College.* New York: McGraw-Hill, 1976.

Chapter 6

The Community College and the State

James D. Tschechtelin

A state General Assembly holds a hearing about funding issues, including aid to community colleges. A community college president travels to the state capital to testify and, outlining the plight of the college, requests additional funds. The committee listens politely. The president continues, becoming more blunt, then concludes by expressing frustration with the lack of funding the college has received from the General Assembly. At that point, the mood in the room shifts. One legislator goes on the counteroffensive, questioning the president's data and the effectiveness of community colleges. As the hearing ends, both parties are angry. The president goes away upset that legislators do not understand the college's problems, and the legislators go away upset at the nerve of the president to take them to task for not being more sympathetic.

This incident illustrates the delicate and complicated boundary where the life of the community college meets the life of state government. It is the point at which people from different organizational cultures with separate personal agendas debate state policies and legislation about local community col-

101

leges. It is not unexpected, then, that a dynamic tension between community colleges and state government often exists.

There are several reasons for this tension. First, it is in the nature of community colleges to focus on the educational needs and concerns of a local, not a statewide, service area. In contrast to state universities, which exist to serve the citizens of the entire state, the mission statements of community colleges generally include a reference to the geographic area to be served. The area might be a county, a set of counties, a city, or a tax district. Responsiveness to local needs is one of the hallmarks of community colleges. The idea, then, of marching also to a statewide drummer can seem contrary or at least confusing to a community college. It has been said that the term *state community college system* is an oxymoron, that it is a contradiction in terms to speak of an institution simultaneously oriented to the needs of the local community and the state.

Second, tension often exists between community colleges and the state because, in many states, the role of the state in the affairs of all public institutions of higher education is increasingly active and directive. In search of increased efficiency and economy, many states have created new boards or granted additional authority to existing boards to plan and regulate the affairs of higher education institutions, including community colleges (Glenny, 1985). With enrollment growth in community colleges often outpacing the growth in four-year colleges, state agencies and legislatures have devoted additional attention to community colleges.

This chapter reviews the patterns of interaction between community colleges and the state, describes concepts that help to explain and predict the behavior of the two groups, and makes recommendations for steps that can be taken by both groups to increase the success of community colleges. The following definitions are used in this chapter:

> *Community college.* A two-year degree granting institution headed by a president or chancellor; a single community college campus or multicampus community college district; also refers to junior and technical colleges.

College official. A board member, president, administrator, faculty member, or anyone who represents the community college to a state policy maker.

State community college agency. A department of state government whose function it is to oversee, regulate, or represent the community colleges of the state, be it on a governance, coordinating, or planning basis.

State government. The legislative and regulatory bodies beyond the community college or community college district. It includes the legislative branch and the executive branch.

State policy maker. An official in state government whose decisions and influence affect state laws, financing, or regulations related to community colleges. Examples include the governor, chairs of legislative committees that deal with community college finance and policy, and the leaders of a state governing or coordinating board.

Variations in Governance

One of the defining characteristics of community colleges in the United States is variability. Because they are designed to meet local needs, community colleges take on many different shapes and functions, depending on local needs and traditions. College-state relations are greatly affected by these variations, and any discussion of college-state relations must take them into account. McGuinness (1986) reports that the systems governing colleges in the United States are of one of three types, based on the authority of the state board. Twenty-three states have a consolidated governing board (thirteen with one board for all public institutions and ten with a separate agency for community colleges), twenty-eight states have coordinating boards (nineteen with program approval authority and nine without such authority), and three states have planning agencies. The total is greater than fifty because a few states have a state agency in more than one category.

As an example of state variations, New Jersey community colleges have local governing boards that are coordinated by the New Jersey Department of Higher Education. College presidents are selected by each local board of trustees. Community college presidents and trustees in New Jersey have formed the New Jersey Council of County Colleges to represent the interests of the colleges and, in particular, to present the case for increased funding to the General Assembly. By contrast, in Virginia all community colleges are governed by a single state board whose chancellor selects the presidents for the individual colleges. Relationships between colleges and the state in these two states are quite different.

In addition to the variations in governance structure, there are also state-by-state differences in whether the community colleges have elected or appointed boards and whether the colleges have collective bargaining for the faculty. These differences can be significant in college-state relations, because boards of trustees and employee groups often form associations that organize to seek influence with state government. For example, Illinois has an active trustee organization, with paid executive staff and strategic plans for its legislative agenda. These separate groups may or may not argue for the same set of policies or legislative priorities sought by the state community college agency. Community colleges in ten states are part of a university system, which radically changes the governance relationship that the colleges have with state policy makers (Haeuser, 1988). The major sources of variability in college-state relations are illustrated in Exhibit 6.1. No two states are exactly alike in their community college systems. That fact makes simple generalizations about college-state relations difficult.

State and local funding patterns differ as well. In the late 1980s, the community colleges in eighteen states were receiving less than 5 percent of their financial support from local government. In a few other states, such as Arizona and Kansas, local government contributed nearly half of the operating funds (American Association of Community and Junior Colleges, 1991). The role of state government in setting policy is affected by the proportion of funding support it provides.

Exhibit 6.1. Major Sources of Variability in College-State Relations.

Dimension	Possible variations
Authority of state board	Governing board Coordinating board Planning agency
Organizational structure	Part of a university Not part of a university
Proportion of funding from state	17–81 percent
Local board status	Elected (taxing authority) Appointed No local boards
Faculty organization	Collective bargaining No agent
Trustee organization	Active and organized Minimally organized No local trustees

The community colleges in each state can be placed on the autonomy-responsiveness continuum in Exhibit 6.2 based on a composite of college-state relations. Three of the most critical dimensions of authority and autonomy are the responsibility for approval of the college budget, appointment of the college president, and approval of new instructional programs. The sources of authority for these three functions are barometers of the degree of state or local control. States also vary greatly in terms of the degree of state control over such things as budget flexibility, tuition level, total number of positions allowed, purchasing, salary schedules, and travel.

College-State Interactions

There are four types of issues about which colleges and the state interact: policy development, finance, instructional programs, and planning. In terms of policy development, states are concerned with systems and strategies that promote quality, access, efficiency, and economy in higher education. In an effort to create clear and distinctive roles for different institutions, the state

Exhibit 6.2. Autonomy-Responsiveness Continuum.

Local orientation	*State orientation*
Higher local autonomy	Lower local autonomy
Lower state responsiveness	Higher state responsiveness
Greater local identity	Greater state identity
Decentralized decision making	Centralized decision making

agency may have responsibility for approving or endorsing the mission of each public college and university. Many states have taken steps to encourage improved accountability and assessment. The number of states that are active in promoting assessment grew from four in 1985 to nearly forty in 1990 (Hutchings and Marchese, 1990).

Tuition policy is another example of state role in community college operations. In states with a state governing board, community college tuition can be set at one level for all community colleges, while in other states, legislation or state agency policy might establish an upper limit for tuition. In still other states, the setting of tuition is entirely a local community college board prerogative. Tuition policy represents a clear case where the dynamic tension between state and local concerns is manifested. Local boards may consider tuition their responsibility and may resent intrusion by the state in a decision that affects the total college budget. On the other hand, state agencies know that state aid is only one part of the college budget, and any deliberation about the need for increased state aid must be done in the context of tuition revenue. State policy makers might be concerned about a college with excessively high tuition (because of deleterious effects on student access) as well as a college with unusually low tuition (because the need for additional state aid would be less if more revenue were raised through tuition). The question of what groups (senior citizens, college employees, and so on) should receive tuition waivers is another policy issue often debated at the state level.

The second area of interaction between the college and the state is that of finance. In some states, community colleges receive state funding based on a statutory formula. The legislature enacts a statute that prescribes how funds will be allocated among the colleges, and the administration of the formula and the actual payment of the funds is the responsibility of the state community college agency. The development of these aid formulas is a complex process, involving a delicate balance of concerns that often include consideration of the enrollment of the college, the wealth of the local jurisdiction, types of instructional programs offered, enrollment projections, and flat grants for fixed costs. The development of community college formulas is generally a balancing act between simplicity and accommodation to special needs of certain colleges. The simplest formulas often do not take into account historical arrangements for assisting small and rural colleges, for example. On the other hand, the more the formula accommodates special needs, the more difficult it becomes to explain and administer. Many states also provide funds to construct or to share the construction costs for college facilities. Often states accompany these funds with guidelines about the types, size, and level of grandeur that will be supported with state funds. Some community colleges are audited on a regular basis by a state legislative auditor; alternatively, colleges might be audited by a commercial audit firm, with the results (including the management letter) submitted to the state community college agency.

The third subject for state-college relations is instructional programs. Often this concern arises in an effort to minimize duplication of high-cost, low-enrollment programs. A few states provide funding for noncredit courses and thus develop guidelines about what types of courses will be eligible for state aid. In addition to playing a role in the review and approval of new programs and courses, states often become involved in the review of existing programs. This is frequently contentious, especially if the state has and seeks to use the authority to order instructional programs to be eliminated. In many cases, states have developed data monitoring systems that track criteria such as enrollment and degrees awarded in each program over time. The state agency raises questions about programs that seem to be in a state of decline, and the colleges respond with an explanation of the situation or propose that the program be abolished. Community colleges in Maryland discontinued seventy-one associate degree programs using such a system during a seven-year period.

The fourth type of college involvement with the state is in the area of planning. Some states require community colleges to produce plans covering a wide range of subjects, including strategic plans, facilities plans, financial plans, cost containment plans, and minority student achievement plans. Often, these plans include a projection of new instructional programs. The majority of states (twenty-eight) have coordinating boards, and a majority of those (nineteen) have authority to approve new instructional programs (McGuinness, 1986). The foundation for sound planning is research and data collection. Some states have developed comprehensive data collection systems, in which individual student and employee information is transmitted from the college to the state agency by electronic means. Such data enable state agencies to perform policy analyses on issues such as student retention, enrollment trends, and affirmative action in employment.

The College Setting

Community colleges operate in an organizational culture that shapes their interaction with the state. One aspect of their culture is institutional autonomy. This independent spirit is a result of two deep roots. The first is that many community colleges were originally established by local school boards, which have a long tradition of independence in making decisions about the curriculum and other policy matters. The concept of a local school board is, by definition, to serve the needs of a limited area, and that sense of local responsiveness leads to perspectives that do not always react well to state requirements. A tension is created when a state agenda competes with a local agenda. As a branch of higher education, community colleges tap into a second root of independence and autonomy — academic freedom. Colleges and universities pay great tribute to academic freedom as one of the keystones of their success, unlike branches of state government such as the departments of transportation or agriculture, which operate without boards and without such a heritage.

Given their culture as locally responsive and autonomous, it is not surprising that the expectations that many community college officials have toward the state can be summarized as two great commandments: get us lots of money and stay out of our affairs. The financial expectation is based in the reality that states usually provide the largest portion of community college funds. According to the American Association of Community and Junior Colleges (1991), states provide an average of 55 percent of the operating budgets of community colleges, with 14 percent coming from local support, 18 percent from tuition and fees, and 13 percent from the federal government and other sources. The expectation to stay out of local policy matters stems from the tradition of local school boards as well as from the concept of academic freedom.

The word *intrusion* is often heard in discussions with college officials about the state role in community colleges. The implication is that the state does not belong there and has no right to tell local colleges what to do. Such an attitude is typified in a remark by a board member (from a state with local boards and a state coordinating board) who complained, "They are trying to push us to do those multicultural things, but they are five years behind the times." Local concern about state interference in college operations is not without foundation, however. One role that state policy makers often see for themselves is to promote efficiency and economy. In one state, a community college had obtained federal funds for upgrading its computer hardware. State procurement procedures called for each college to submit requests to the state capital before a purchase could be made. College officials requested two additional disk drives and had the funds in the federal grant to purchase them. The state agency rejected the request for two disk drives and authorized the purchase of one. College officials were astounded and frustrated at such an example of micromanagement from the capital. In another state, local community college officials are not permitted to change the college stationery without the permission of the state agency.

Another relevant part of the culture of the college that affects college-state relations is the expectation for the college president to be the flag bearer for the institution. Students, faculty, and the board of trustees (where there are local boards) generally want their president to be a leader who is visibly fighting for the college. They are well aware of the financial needs of the college, and they expect the president to be the person whose job it is to push the state to provide increased funding. College presidents are often evaluated, in part, on their ability to get increased funds from supporting government entities. Conversely, these local constituent groups do not want their flag-bearer president to call attention to things about the college that could be interpreted as negative, such as a high attrition rate.

Most community college employees and many presidents and board members spend little time in the state capital. Their concept of how political processes work and how decisions are made are often stereotypical or based on their experience with other decision-making systems. For example, many college officials think that funding is allocated on the basis of what is deserved in an absolute sense. Immersed in their own college's work, community college officials often consider that the justification for additional aid for the college is self-evident. This attitude leads to presentations that often carry the tone of "We need it, we deserve it, so give it to us." State policy makers are guided by what they think agencies deserve as well as myriad laws that mandate substantial portions of the state budget. The distinction between what agencies deserve in an absolute sense and what policy makers think agencies deserve is not subtle. It implies an obligation on the part of the college to make its case in an informative, positive, and convincing way to the policy makers.

In states with strong local boards, the assets of local control can become a liability in terms of decision making on state issues. In the absence of a strong formal and central authority, statewide decision making takes place in the context of a confederation, with each college having great negative power to stop a proposal. It is somewhat like the United Nations Security Council, where one country can veto a proposal. Because the only decision-making mechanism is the development of a consensus, one or two vocal and assertive colleges can effectively stop any action that is generally agreed on by the others. This problem becomes exaggerated in a state with a larger number of community colleges, each able to exercise its veto authority. Unless a group or an individual assumes a constructive and positive leadership role, community colleges in such states can exhibit a lack of organization and unity. State directors of community colleges in states with strong local boards sometimes speak of themselves as "trying to lead a choir of soloists."

The State Setting

State policy makers operate in the organizational culture of the state capital and state government, where the formal and informal rules of life are much different from those of the community college campus. Few state policy makers have worked on a community college campus, and state government bears little resemblance to what Cohen and March (1984) call the "organized anarchy" of the college campus, with its ambiguities of purpose, power, experience, and success. Legislative leaders wrestle with the question of what is in the common interest as well as the need to retain the power of their position through reelection. Their unit of organization is the legislative district, and they have periodic summative evaluation at the ballot box rather than a performance report from a supervisor. State policy makers certainly do not have tenure, as most faculty members do. Power and decision making are more clearly delineated, and success or failure is more concrete as bills pass or fail, budgets stand or are amended. In elective state government, axioms such as "there's always tomorrow" tend to govern relationships. There's always tomorrow counsels legislators not to burn bridges in pursuit of their bills, since win or lose, they will need each other to pass their own legislation at a later date.

Having a finger on the pulse of public opinion is the stock in trade for elected officials. They spend a great deal of time hearing from constituents through the mail, on the phone, and at public events. Other than perhaps the president and members of a board of trustees, few members of the college community spend as much time listening to what the public thinks and wants. Faculty and staff at most community colleges spend the greatest amount of time talking to each other. Elected officials tend to focus on perceptions, while college officials tend to look for truth in an absolute sense. This does not mean that elected officials are unconcerned about truth; they know that, to each person, the perception is the truth. If a large number of people think that tuition is too high, that perception becomes the reality with which the legislator deals.

Voters expect legislators not only to know about problems but to act on them. In the culture of state capitals, a perceived leadership vacuum eventually will be filled. If enough people perceive that a problem exists, the issue will be dealt with. It may be met sooner or later, and how it will be resolved is not preordained. One example of this phenomenon is the issue of the quality of education. There has been a growing disenchantment among the American public about the quality of our educational system, especially about its emphasis on process rather than results. Schools and colleges have generally reacted defensively to these charges, but the groundswell of public opinion was not to be denied, and most states have taken steps to deal with the issue. Hutchings and Marchese (1990) note that two-thirds of the states have established permissive policies whereby institutions conduct assessment in ways that they develop, rather than follow a strict state prescription. The policy goal would seem to be institutional improvement more than accountability. However, Hutchings and Marchese wonder how long this will last. In an interview, the head of a state board said, "It all depends on how the institutions respond . . . if they don't take the process seriously, there will be enormous pressure to centralize."

One special problem that community colleges face in state capitals is endemic to their mission. Many Americans seem to be preoccupied with status and prestige. Things that are expensive and hard to get are implicitly assigned a higher value. The community college mission is founded on low tuition and open-door admissions policies. These essential parts of the mission can give rise to what some people see as a "congenital status deficiency" for the community college. In this climate, the work of Ph.D.'s in selective research universities can take on a particular attraction while community colleges struggle for attention. In the words of a state senator who is quite supportive of community colleges, "They are not glamorous."

State agencies that are established to coordinate or govern community colleges are often confronted with a dualism of being both advocates and regulators. The governor and the legislature expect the agencies to push for quality, accountability, and attention to state needs, while the community colleges expect the agencies to be advocates for increased financial assistance and administrative independence. Who are the customers of a state community college agency? Who are they established to serve? The answer is that they walk a fine line in serving both groups, and this dual role often leads to misunderstanding and tension between the colleges and state community college agencies.

In contrast with a college expectation of "Get us lots of money and stay out of our affairs," the expectations of state community college agencies toward the colleges can often be summarized in their own two great commandments: set high standards and take a statewide view. The idea of setting high standards is an admonition for colleges to monitor their own quality and to take action to correct problems. This expectation of internal control can be related to any area, from ethical fundraising practices to graduation requirements to athletic recruiting. The idea of taking a statewide view establishes the expectation that the college will look and listen to a wider audience than itself, will pay attention to state issues, and will take an active role in seeking solutions to state problems even when it results in changing the college agenda to some degree.

Given their concern for quality and their approval authority, stage agencies can find themselves playing a gatekeeper function. From time to time, community colleges will submit proposals for instructional programs or capital projects that are either patently overly ambitious or of poor caliber. In such cases, the college administration neither wants to say no to a campus constituency nor to scrutinize the item before sending it to the state. This sets up the stage agency in a gatekeeping role, preserves the local status of the president with the faculty, allows the state agency to be the "bad guy," and plays on the tension between the college and the state.

Related Theory and Concepts

Given the different settings of the colleges and the state, what theoretical foundation can best explain the behavior of both groups in relation to each other and present a guide to the effective functioning of both? Jacobs (1971) has done an extensive review of the literature on the nature of leadership, and he draws distinctions between power, leadership, and authority. He concludes that leadership is a transaction between the leader and the group, which he calls *social exchange:* "The essence of social exchange is the development of relationships with other persons, such that benefits of mutual value can be 'traded' between participants of both equal and unequal status" (p. 339).

Based on this theory, tensions between the college and the state will rise when either party perceives the social exchange to be increasingly inequitable, and tensions will subside when both parties see the social exchange as fair. College officials need to perceive that there is a sufficient benefit or value obtained from the state. This benefit or value can take many forms, and financial resources are usually considered to be paramount. However, it could also include favorable policy actions, recognition for achievements, or protection from competitors. State policy makers need to perceive that the state receives satisfactory benefits from the colleges in return.

Where an imbalance exists in the expectations between parties about the extent to which the state provides funds or the college controls quality, the exchange of benefits will not be seen as of mutual value, and increased tension will result. The role of communication in the evaluation of the exchange is paramount. There may be a fair exchange, for example, between the state agency and the college president; however, the faculty and staff may not be aware of the other values exchanged and may therefore be dissatisfied with the exchange when they judge it only on a financial basis.

Exchange theory would suggest, for instance, that increasing state requirements in the same year that funds must be cut due to budgetary problems would increase tensions. It would suggest that a college seeking support to extricate it from a special problem would be well advised to include in the proposal a new initiative or change that would meet state needs in a specific way.

In a state where there is a single state governing board for community colleges or where community colleges are part of a university system, the colleges generally derive a sense of esteem from being a member of the larger system as part of the exchange. This value of state identity is not highly exchanged in a state with local governing boards. The exchange of value in these states is more ambiguous, and while the colleges still seek strong funding, the values returned to the state are not always as clear to state policy makers.

At an operational level, four factors determine the extent of state support for government agencies, be they a department such as the Department of Transportation, a state university, or community colleges. They are (1) perception of need and value among the policy makers, (2) sense of ownership by the funding authority, (3) strong and positive personal relationships with policy makers, and (4) perception of performance and public goodwill. The support derived from these four factors is both policy and financial support. For maximum state support, all four of the factors must be present in good measure.

The first factor for state support is a perception by state policy makers that the colleges have need and value. State policy makers need to perceive community colleges as being an important public interest to address, in the context of a wide variety of other worthy causes. A key word in this factor is *perception*. Most community college board members, faculty, and administrators deeply believe in their cause and consider it to be deserving of support. However, unless state policy makers share such a perception, there is no great chance of strong support. They want to know what the problem is that needs to be solved and how important that problem is in relation to other problems that need to be solved.

The perception of need is supported by Jacobs's social exchange theory in that the state policy makers need to believe that they are getting a favorable return on their commitment to the community colleges. The perception of need must be in two dimensions: there must be a sense that the colleges are highly needed as well as that they truly need additional funds and favorable policy action.

The second factor for state support of colleges is a sense of ownership and identity with the funding authority. In states where community colleges receive relatively balanced portions of their funds from both the state and the local government, the two sponsoring authorities can withhold additional support and advise the college to seek increased funds from the other sponsor. In some states, the university system enjoys greater support than community colleges in part because the university system has only one government sponsor, whereas the community colleges have both a state and a local government sponsor.

The third factor in determining state support for agencies is strong and positive personal relationships with policy makers. Does the college have close ties to the people who set budget priorities? Are the representatives of the college trusted and respected? Effective personal relationships will depend largely on the trust and integrity established between the college officials and the state policy makers. Direct and honest communications will build a foundation of trust that will promote mutual regard and support. Candid conversation and testimony is an unconventional approach in state capitals, and most college officials do not do it because their local constituencies do not want them to concede any negatives and because media stories generally feature any negative information more prominently over the positive. However, a lack of defensiveness and a willingness to discuss problems openly will build trust.

One incident that damaged relationships occurred in a state where legislation was proposed to have a member of the faculty be appointed to the board of regents of the state university. The university was opposed to the proposed legislation, and there were well-grounded arguments that the university could have used to make its case. Unfortunately, the text and the tone of the testimony the university gave were essentially that "it is none of your business to get involved with this." Although the bill received an unfavorable report from the committee, the university was perceived as arrogant and defensive; its credibility with the committee was damaged in the process.

Positive personal relationships can be established by first identifying key people in state government. While there are many delegates and senators, the committee structure of most assemblies dictates that key legislation is routed through certain committees. In addition, certain delegates and senators often become regarded as experts in given fields, and others defer to them for advice about particular topics. College officials need to meet with these specialists and with the chairs of the key committees. Meetings should be arranged while the legislature is *not* in session, when the pace is slower and there are fewer distractions. Another way to establish positive personal relationships is to invite to the campus state policy makers from the district in which the college is located. Many times, these persons have neither seen the inside of a community college nor met with its students, who are often the best spokespersons for the college.

College officials can take positive or negative approaches to informing state policy makers. Positive approaches include providing information about student transfer rates and the need for education and training to meet the requirements of the workforce. Negative approaches include implicit criticism of other agencies of government that are apparently getting more funding or favorable treatment from the state. In the long run, negative approaches are less effective, because they damage the integrity of the speaker and because they spawn retaliatory responses by the other agencies.

Common courtesies go a long way in establishing strong and positive personal relationships with state policy makers. State policy makers are seldom thanked for their role in establishing favorable policies or increasing funding levels. Letters of appreciation to key persons are highly valued.

The fourth factor in state support of community colleges is a perception of performance and goodwill on the part of the general public. The man and woman on the street must see the college as valuable and performing a useful service. Community colleges can help to ensure such a public perception by imposing strong quality controls from within the institution. They can also seek solid documentation of performance and then use effective means to inform the public about them. For example, a college can set high numerical goals for its job placement rate and student success in transfer institutions. As the college performs well on these dimensions, newspaper articles and speeches before local community groups can report the results. There needs to be an absence of "horror stories" about quality; such stories have a long life in the memory of the public. An article in the *Chronicle of Higher Education* about a community college course in one state titled "Fun with Jello" is an example of negative press that strikes at a reputation. In another state, a college copied names from a telephone book to increase registrations in noncredit courses. Even though the staff member was fired and the state aid returned, the damage to the image of the college, and to other colleges in the state as well, persisted for many years.

Recommendations

Recommendations for improving college-state relations are included in the four concepts for state support discussed above. In addition, college officials can enhance their relationships with state policy makers by adopting a role as effective salespersons. The analogy of selling is an apt description for this interaction, because the college is attempting to "sell" state policy makers on the value of the institution and because state policy makers have the power to decide whether to "buy" the values and services that the community college offers. The effective salesperson role is also consistent with social exchange theory, in which benefits of mutual value are traded. An effective salesperson listens well to understand the needs of the customer and then illustrates the benefits of the product or service. The basic message for college officials in the role of an effective salesperson is: I am here to learn about your needs and to demonstrate how our college can help you meet them.

Effective salespersons are positive and orient their presentations to the advantages of the product or service. In pursuit of this role, college officials give enthusiastic and spirited presentations, supported by clear, succinct graphics and brief handouts. Effective salespeople are candid about the strengths and weaknesses of their services, and they avoid defensiveness and misrepresentation. When they do not get a sale, effective salespersons do not blame the customer, but rather review how they need to improve their product or how they failed to show how their product could meet the customer's needs.

Unfortunately, some college officials adopt a role as ineffective salespersons. In this role, salespeople expect that customers will buy the product and then blame the customers if they do not. They consider themselves to be superior to their customers and respond defensively to any criticism of their product. Translated to the college setting, the basic message is: we do all of these good things for you, we deserve more money, and we expect you to give it to us. Ineffective salespeople are poor listeners and seem most intent on making long-winded and often boring presentations. They read testimony to committees in a sleepy monotone. They whine and complain when things do not go their way. It is not surprising that college officials who adopt such a role meet with little success in the state capital.

To be effective, community college officials must be credible. State policy makers know that colleges are imperfect institutions, and they do not expect them to be flawless. One way to be credible with state policy makers is to tell the unvarnished truth about the college. College officials must be willing to talk about real problems and not simply problems caused by lack of funding; it will make the requests for assistance more believable. To hear some college presidents describe it, there are no failures at community colleges. Most state policy makers would rather hear from and would be more supportive of a college official who openly discusses real problems than one who leaves the impression that there are no problems at the college.

For their part, state policy makers can take steps that will give community colleges their best chance for success. While they clearly have the legal authority to legislate or to regulate changes, they should appreciate that they also have great power of moral suasion. They can collect data about a key problem and assemble community college officials to discuss the options for addressing the problem. In many cases, astute community college officials will respond to such an overture with concrete action. If this approach fails, state policy makers may then need to use their regulatory and legislative authority to seek a remedy.

State policy makers need to be cautious of the "selectivity as quality" trap. Some state policy makers create a mental ladder of status and prestige based on admissions criteria that place the universities at the top, the state colleges in the middle, and the community colleges at the bottom. This implies a unitary definition of quality, and a definition that is based on reputation or resources, rather than results. It also implies a narrow view of the human resource challenges the United States faces. Studies of the projected needs in the work force indicate that by the year 2000, between 50 and 75 percent of entry-level jobs will require education and training beyond the secondary level, though not necessarily a baccalaureate degree (Coe, 1989). Community colleges are also playing a key role in training and retraining adults for changes in the workplace. Community colleges clearly have an important role to play in the economic health of the nation, but that role will not be realized if state policy makers associate funding and policy support with a traditional sense of organizational status.

State community college agencies need to be sure that they take a service orientation to their work. While community colleges do need to be urged to be responsive to state priorities and sometimes need to be pushed to seek new directions, state agencies should view themselves as helpers and facilitators of the mission of community colleges.

State policy makers need to confine their attention to policy development and not to the micromanagement of the colleges. There is a temptation for state legislatures and agencies to dig into the details of college operations rather than the broad questions of where they are going (mission), how they are getting there (programs), and how successful they are in reaching their goals (accountability). For example, if legislators are concerned that college students are not emerging with effective writing skills, a variety of appropriate steps can be taken to push colleges to improve that outcome. One state, though, enacted a law that students must write 6,000 words during their college courses. Such legislation is highly prescriptive and does not even guarantee that the writing skills of students will improve.

Summary

While the mission of community colleges is to serve local educational needs, they operate in a framework in which the state plays a major role. Because community colleges exist to meet local needs and the states have become more active in the affairs of community colleges, a dynamic tension often exists between the colleges and the state. While there is great variability among the states, most are involved with policy development, finance, instructional programs, and planning. The organizational culture of the community college is one that values autonomy and resists intrusion, while expecting strong financial support from the state. The organizational culture of state government expects community colleges to be accountable and to appreciate statewide priorities. State community college agencies are often confronted with a dualism of being both advocates on behalf of the colleges and regulators on behalf of the state.

Four factors determine the extent of public support for community colleges. They are (1) perception of need and value among the policy makers, (2) sense of ownership by the funding authority, (3) strong and positive personal relationships with policy makers, and (4) perception of performance and public goodwill. For maximum state support, all four of the factors must be present and dominant. College officials need to adopt the role of effective salespersons, listening to state policy makers and being responsive to their needs. Arrogance and defensiveness are the leading causes of problems in college-state relations. State policy makers need to focus on policy issues and resist the temptation to micromanage the colleges. The dynamic tension between community colleges and the state is functional and can lead to strengthened colleges and strengthened states. However, the attitudes of both parties will determine the tone of the dialogue and the soundness of the solutions. The question is not whether states will "intrude" in the lives of community colleges. They have a vested interest and they will continue to be involved. The question is whether states and colleges can agree on the legitimate areas of intervention, act in good faith, and leave the management to the colleges.

References

American Association of Community and Junior Colleges. *A Summary of Selected National Data Pertaining to Community, Technical, and Junior Colleges.* Washington, D.C.: American Association of Community and Junior Colleges, 1991.

Coe, M. A. *Education and U.S. Competitiveness: The Community College Role.* Austin, IC2 Institute, University of Texas, 1989.

Cohen, M. D., and March, J. G. "Leadership in an Organized Anarchy." *ASHE Reader in Organization and Governance in Higher Education.* Lexington, Mass.: Ginn, 1984.

Glenny, L. A. *State Coordination of Higher Education.* Denver, Colo.: State Higher Education Executive Officers, 1985.

Haeuser, P. "Explaining State Variations in Community College Policies." Unpublished doctoral dissertation, Department of Political Science, University of Wisconsin–Milwaukee, 1988.

Hutchings, P., and Marchese, T. "Watching Assessment— Questions, Stories, Prospects." *Change,* 1990, *5,* 12–38.

Jacobs, T. O. *Leadership and Exchange in Formal Organizations.* Alexandria, Va.: Human Resources Research Organization, 1971.

McGuinness, A. C., Jr. *The Search for More Effective State Policy Leadership in Higher Education.* Denver, Colo.: Education Commission of the States, 1986.

Chapter 7

How Presidents
Influence Public Policy

Judith S. Eaton

Community college presidents are frequently scrutinized for their leadership capacities in campus financial, governance, and instructional matters. Less attention is paid to the role of presidents away from the campus, especially in the development of public policy at the state level. Yet, with acute financial problems in virtually every state, the president's role in public policy is both expanding and becoming more critical.

This chapter presents a case study of an attempt to make a major public policy change affecting community colleges in the Commonwealth of Pennsylvania during 1992. It examines the role of the community college president in responding to the Pennsylvania Department of Education's (PDE) effort to remove state support for some noncredit full-time equivalent enrollments (FTEs) at the state's community colleges effective with

I am grateful for the generous cooperation of key individuals within the Pennsylvania Department of Education and the Pennsylvania Commission for Community Colleges. I thank Donald M. Carroll, Charles Fuget, Peter Garland, John Kraft, Edward Sweitzer, and Gust Zogas for their assistance in the preparation of this article.

123

the fiscal year 1993 budget. The Department's initiative was not adopted in the fiscal year 1993 budget.

This public policy issue of funding for the community college's mission displays many of the characteristics of public policy issues generally. As events unfolded, the issue itself was not always clear but became murky. What count as the "facts" of the issue differ, from time to time, among those involved. The two major disputants — the Department of Education and the Commission for Community Colleges — not only differed with each other but also sustained some differences of opinion within their own organizations. The perceptions of what was at stake, what could be won or lost, and who would benefit varied over time.

Four suggestions about the presidential role in public policy at the state level emerge from scrutiny of this important issue. First, presidents must be pivotal in the definition of the issue at hand. In this case, they had to answer whether the state was interested only in cost containment or in a more dramatic attempt at mission modification for the community colleges. Second, presidents must be strategically positioned to influence both locally based and state-based constituencies: they have a responsibility to the local community, local legislators, and the local press, as well as to their colleagues on the state level. Third, presidents must strengthen their state-level organizations to augment their individual efforts and build a sense of equity among institutions. Fourth, presidents need to be willing to take some risks to redesign and restructure the community college as part of the state's higher education enterprise — when and where appropriate.

Fiscal Scene

In the early 1990s, financial support for higher education was at its weakest point since the end of World War II. Federal support had been stable to declining for a decade. At the state level, higher education's percentage of general fund revenues was slipping (Ottinger, 1992). At the institutional level, the majority of colleges and universities experienced more than one budget reduction, and many were forced to cap enrollments. Two-thirds of the public institutions lost financial ground between 1990 and 1991 (El-Khawas, 1992). Federal student aid declined, and the ability to pay for college as measured by family income diminished as well.

In the early 1990s, community colleges, too, began to feel the impact of economic contraction. By any available standard of comparison, community colleges are less well funded than four-year institutions. The revenue per FTE student, support for educational and general expenses, and the total aid that students receive are all considerably less than the revenues consumed in the four-year sector. And even this least-well-financed sector of higher education had experienced multiple budget cuts by 1991.

With the declining financial viability of states have come discussions of change—not only of the enrollment levels and programming in community colleges, but also of changes in the colleges' place in the higher education structure of the respective states. Minnesota, for example, is considering a merger of its community colleges with four-year institutions and technical colleges (Rodriguez, 1992). Utah and Florida are considering allowing community colleges to offer baccalaureate degrees (Mercer, 1992). Connecticut is planning a merger of community colleges and technical colleges ("State Notes," 1992). In other states, the long-standing public policy commitment to access is challenged by funding reductions so extensive that community colleges are forced to deny admission to some students. North Carolina, for example, has discussed ending open enrollment (Rodriguez, 1991). Budget cuts have forced up community college tuition, further reducing access.

These circumstances are extraordinary. They will likely result in changes in community college education that go beyond operational or programmatic shifts to fundamental modifications of a structural or systemic nature. These considerations of structural or systemic changes in the community college will force community college presidents into the realm of public policy to a greater extent than ever before. This means going beyond annual efforts to increase operating budgets through enrollment growth to examining the basic principles of funding such as FTE student support and differential funding for higher-cost occupational programs. They also mean that governance will be scrutinized: Is there adequate state influence on community college boards and is state regulation appropriate for managing community colleges? It could be that the community college mission will shift as well.

Pennsylvania Community Colleges

In the fall of 1991, the thirteen comprehensive community colleges in Pennsylvania enrolled 112,518 students (Pennsylvania Department of Education, 1992) and had a combined operating and capital budget of $132,181,000 (Commonwealth of Pennsylvania, 1992). There is significant variation in size, student demographics, and programming among the thirteen institutions, with the Community College of Allegheny County in the Pittsburgh area enrolling almost 22,000 students and Reading Area Community College in central Pennsylvania enrolling 3,000 students. The Community College of Philadelphia is a predominantly minority institution, while all of the other colleges are predominantly white. The enrollment mix of the community colleges varies greatly: some schools have large numbers of credit occupational FTEs, while others have more enrollment in the arts and sciences. Significant for consideration here, noncredit FTE enrollments for 1992–93 varied dramatically, from 377 FTEs at Luzerne County Community College to 8,310 FTEs at the Community College of Allegheny County. Costs per FTE ranged from $2,830 to $4,262 in 1992–93 (Commission for Community Colleges . . . , 1992). The diversity among the community colleges makes it extremely difficult to develop public policy that is reasonably applicable to all institutions without harming at least one of them.

Pennsylvania community colleges are chartered and funded under 1963 state legislation that requires the state to pay one-third of the net operating costs of the community colleges, with a "local sponsor" paying one-third and students paying one-third in tuition. Capital expenditures (for example, books, debt service, leases, construction, equipment) are funded with 50 percent state and 50 percent local financing. A "local sponsor" might be a municipality, a county, or a school district. Community colleges do not have taxing authority, but must work through another governmental entity that does.

In return for agreeing to finance the community college, the local sponsor has the authority to appoint the governing board of each institution. This gives the local sponsor considerable latitude in determining the direction of the community colleges. Few restrictions have been placed on local control, either through the state department of education or the state board of education. In contrast to many states, Pennsylvania does not have a separate state board of community colleges or office for community colleges.

The Pennsylvania community colleges do not comprise a community college system. Instead, they form a voluntary federation outside state government. This federation has two arms: the Commission of Community Colleges, made up of the presidents of each of the community colleges, and the Pennsylvania Federation of Community College Trustees, comprised of the representatives of each of the governing boards of the community colleges. The commission and federation determine the legislative agenda for community colleges, sustain a public image campaign at the state level, and collect and analyze data related to community college operation. A single executive director for the federation and commission is the key individual at the state level with whom the department of education and the Pennsylvania legislature deal.

Pennsylvania provides state support to community colleges through FTE formula funding. Community colleges receive $1,000 per FTE or one-third the actual FTE cost, whichever is less. They receive stipends for higher-cost occupational programs that range from $500 to $1,100 per FTE. Most critical to considerations here, they are also in one of the few states in which community colleges receive support for noncredit FTE enrollments, based on a formula for converting contact hour enrollment to credit hour reimbursement. Noncredit programming is generally contact hour coursework in virtually any area — ranging from wine tasting to advanced technology. It includes short courses of six to eight weeks duration and programs that might take up to a year. It can involve subcontracting with other educational institutions, corporations, unions, or community groups.

In any budgetary year, to receive an increase in state support, the community colleges must lobby successfully not only for an increased appropriation for the community college line in the state budget, but also for "raising the cap" or increasing the limit on the FTE reimbursement through a separate change in the law. Even if the community colleges received additional funds for operating costs, they cannot claim reimbursement for these costs beyond the current $1,000 per FTE without this additional legislative action to raise this limit. This approach to state funding is generally contrasted with local support that is provided in a lump sum appropriation that carries fewer restrictions.

Pennsylvania Department of Education

This story has two main characters: the Pennsylvania Department of Education and the Commission for Community Colleges. In 1990, the Pennsylvania Department of Education decided to address the funding structure for the state's community colleges. At least three issues appeared to be at stake. First, the Department of Education was concerned about containing costs for community colleges. Since 1987–88, community colleges had experienced an 80 percent increase in credit enrollments and a 51 percent increase in noncredit continuing education programs (Commission for Community Colleges . . . , 1992). With significant enrollment increases and growing capital needs, some in the department were worried about how much the community college budget was growing. Commissioner of Higher Education Charles Fuget, for example, was greatly concerned about the consequences of ongoing enrollment increases in a climate of declining revenues to pay for them. Second, there was some question about the funding philosophy for the community colleges. In a number of the colleges (not all), state support accounted for most funding. In virtually all colleges, local support had been declining. Should the funding philosophy be adjusted to reflect this change in source of funds from the original community college legislation that recommended funding from state, local, and tuition sources in equal proportions? Third, there was a history of concern about the content of noncredit courses and programs offered by the community colleges. State auditors in particular had been raising a number of questions about the noncredit area for several years. One key public policy issue was not on the table: there was no significant interest in additional state investment in community college expansion.

Some in the department felt that noncredit FTE support was not adequately regulated. There were allegations of "double-dipping": were some community colleges managing externally funded, noncredit programs in such a way that they were receiving state aid as well as the external funds for the same programs? There was concern about the kinds of noncredit courses that were appropriate for state support. Should the stereotypical belly-dancing and basket-weaving short courses be supported as well as more occupationally focused short courses in word processing or real estate? The department said that it lacked adequate guidelines for the kind of noncredit FTEs the state should support and that it was uncomfortable funding what came to be called noncredit "avocational/recreational" courses: courses in fitness, crafts, art, and "leisure learning" (Commission for Community Colleges . . . , 1992). Some felt that it was inappropriate that noncredit FTE reimbursement be used to support credit FTEs. Discussions about these issues were pretty much confined within the department until late 1991.

In September 1991, however, Secretary of Education Donald Carroll met with the Commission for Community Colleges about their funding. He made it quite clear that, at least for him, a restructuring of funding for community colleges was essential. He wanted the colleges to move quickly to address the issue — hoping for a change in the fiscal year 1993 budget. The commission, following this meeting, set up a funding committee to further discuss this with the secretary or his designee. Both the department and the commission acknowledged that neither felt the issues were clearly stated and both were worried whether they could reach sound agreements. The commission's interim executive director, John Kraft, himself a former community college president, said that the commission never felt sure about what the department really wanted. Some commission members also felt that the department was only minimally responsive to requests for ongoing dialogue.

The governor's annual budget message to the Commonwealth in February 1992 set the stage for the next phase of the department-commission debate. With only one week's advance notice to the community colleges, the governor's message contained the good news that the community college line in the state budget would be increased from $132 million to $140 million for 1992–93 and that the reimbursement cap would be raised to $1,100 per FTE. The bad news was that all state funding for noncredit enrollments that did not have a public service component would be eliminated (Office of the Governor, Commonwealth of Pennsylvania, 1992). "Public service," according to the department, refers to police and fire training, emergency medical services, and hazardous materials training. The commission refers to these as "public safety" programs.

The commission reacted strongly to the governor's budget message. It had every reason to believe that he was serious — the budget also called for reduction in support to all other higher education institutions. Yet it had been told by at least some of the department staff that any change in funding structure would not be effective until fiscal year 1994. The staff were not lying; they were not aware of the change in timetable. But understandably, the commission was increasingly suspicious of the department's efforts.

The Commission Takes a Position

The Commission for Community Colleges and the Pennsylvania Federation of Community College Trustees held an emergency joint executive committee meeting just three days after the governor's message. Peter Garland, the acting commissioner of higher education, met with them and later with the commission presidents. The presidents argued that no college should get less state support, that comprehensiveness should be maintained, and that the colleges' mission should be preserved. Translated, this meant that the community colleges might be willing to give up state funding for some (not all) noncredit enrollments, provided that there would be no loss of operating revenues for any institution and that they could continue with much of their noncredit work. Under these circumstances they were willing to go along with the department's elimination of "avocational/recreational" noncredit offerings. They also pointed out that the enrollment growth they were experiencing meant that the $140 million for 1992–93 was not adequate; $143 million was needed. They maintained that they were willing to work on a longer-range funding proposal for the community colleges.

In May 1992, the commission formally adopted a four-point position:

- That the governor's recommended appropriation for 1992–93 of $140 million be sustained.
- That the current formula for reimbursement of noncredit or continuing education courses be maintained.
- That the colleges agree to delete avocational/recreational continuing education offerings as a category of reimbursement for noncredit offerings.
- That the current reimbursement of $1,000 per FTE be maintained (Commission for Community Colleges . . . , 1992).

The commission was pretty much opting for the status quo for 1992–93. This plan enabled it to take the $8 million increase and make little change in the current operation. Based on its own survey, only 3.8 percent of noncredit offerings were in the avocational/recreational category (Commission and Federation, 1992). Its primary response to this public policy issue was to prevent any major change in its current funding structure.

The commission's perception that it did not fully understand what was happening was based on actions taken by the department that appeared to be inconsistent with the department's previously stated commitment to retain full funding for community colleges. For example, the guarantee that the community colleges would be held harmless if they gave up some of the noncredit FTE support was, at one point, interpreted by the department to be only a one-year commitment. The commission had taken this to be a multiyear commitment. Further, the department said that the money to make up for the loss of noncredit FTE revenues would be channeled to the capital budget of each community college, not the operating budget. This meant that the state really retained control of the money: capital projects required state approval, while use of the money in operating would not require additional state authority. As the commission calculated it, this also meant huge losses in operating revenues for the community colleges.

By early spring of 1992, the differences between the department and the commission were such that the commission determined that getting the legislature on its side was essential to prevent the administration—through the department—from forcing its will on the community colleges. The legislature, after all, had to concur with the governor in order that these changes in community college funding would come about. The commission obtained the services of an influential Pennsylvanian who had access both to the governor's office and to key legislators. Through this intermediary, the commission came to believe that the governor's office had only a mild interest in changing the funding of community colleges, and even this interest diminished as the controversy surrounding the effort grew. The community colleges had, for example, mobilized key constituencies such as the state's emergency medical service personnel and led them to believe that loss of noncredit support meant that their training programs would no longer be offered at the community college. Also through this intermediary, the commission and the department exchanged proposals. The proposals addressed the issues described above: what "hold harmless" really meant, operating versus capital revenues, which noncredit offerings would no longer be supported, and the adequacy of the community college budget line.

The department, in spring 1992, perceived the situation somewhat differently. Secretary Carroll said that it had been receiving some legislative pressure for containing the cost of community college funding. And, from the secretary's perspective, the interest of the governor's office had not diminished.

The individual community college presidents did not stop with the commission activity in relation to the legislature. They were aggressive in individually dealing with their local representatives through visits, phone calls, and letters. Trustees undertook similar activities. Colleges from different areas of the state approached their respective legislative delegations.

What Happened?

State support for noncredit enrollments was not eliminated in the fiscal year 1993 budget. The budget passed by the legislature in June provided $140 million for the community colleges; it did not raise the FTE cap or change the funding structure for community colleges. There is no new capital funding in the budget for construction or leases. Although language to restrict noncredit funding was developed in the House Education Committee, it was not passed. Nothing was resolved. This does not end the issue, however. The Pennsylvania legislature passed the fiscal year 1993 budget fully aware that its work was not complete and that it would take up unresolved issues later, including the funding of community colleges.

Community colleges can claim to have made some gains. They maintained the status quo by preventing a change in the funding structure for community colleges to which they were opposed. Their total budget increased while all other sectors of higher education decreased. It is questionable whether this would have occurred if the discussion about changing funding structure was not taking place and Secretary Carroll had not vigorously argued on behalf of the community colleges. The community colleges, also, to paraphrase Director Kraft, found out how strong they were. They, after all, had prevented the department from achieving its goal. There was, also according to Kraft, an extraordinary level of cooperation among institutions. This is difficult to achieve at best: the variation among the community colleges in Pennsylvania means that any funding decision is bound to cause problems for at least one institution. There is a great temptation for that single institution to move out on its own to solve its problems.

The commission perceives that it lost as well: the $140 million cannot fund the enrollment increases that the colleges anticipate and precludes meeting any capital needs such as construction, renovation, leasing new facilities, or equipment purchase. There were longer-range concerns. President Sweitzer of Montgomery County Community College, for example, was worried that the community college resistance to change meant failure to take advantage of an opportunity to improve their financial circumstances by revising the funding structure for community colleges. The federation and commission had addressed the issue of long-range funding in both 1990 and 1991, seeking changes in the funding formula, a separate line for some capital, and separate funds for special projects (Pennsylvania Federation and Commission, 1991).

The department can also claim to have made some gains. Staff view the events of 1991 and 1992 as the opening round of a longer debate. During that opening round, they at least established the principle of not funding all noncredit enrollments and perhaps changing the funding structure of community colleges. They made the community colleges a more important issue within the department. There was a better understanding of community colleges, their enrollment categories, expenditures, and financing history. And, at least as perceived by Garland, the department was established as a force with which to be reckoned. The department also perceives the community colleges as being shortsighted. Their resistance to any change in funding could result in their forfeiting future budget increases. The commission, feeling that the pinch of inadequate resources would not be alleviated by pursuing the noncredit issue, might be happy not to take it up again soon.

Messages for the President

Several messages for community college presidents emerge from the Pennsylvania story.

First, it is important for a president to define the public policy issue for the campus, the governing board, and the community. Some of the presidents saw the noncredit issue as a financial move on the part of the department: reducing funding for community colleges. As these presidents defined the issue, this was not about the mission of the community college, but a fight for adequate resources. Others saw it as involving a fundamental public policy decision: would the state continue to support the comprehensive mission of the community college when that mission included noncredit instruction? President Zogas of Reading Area Community College, for example, described himself as placed between his community that badly wanted these noncredit offerings and the state that badly wanted not to pay for them. Yet others saw the noncredit issue as a strategy to increase state regulation in an undesirable way. This was a smokescreen to target a few "problem" institutions, those having large numbers of noncredit FTEs or those who structured external funding in such a way that the department believed they were "double-dipping."

Deciding what the issue is also means being clear about the facts. In the Pennsylvania case, there were several ways to calculate the state support for noncredit FTEs and the impact of external revenues derived from noncredit FTEs on an institution. These calculations were the difference between whether the "double-dipping" allegation had any merit or whether community colleges were making legitimate reimbursement claims for their noncredit offerings. The calculations that were used varied between the department and the commission — and among commission presidents themselves. This produced conflict in most instances and clouded the question of just what issue was being addressed.

The Pennsylvania community college presidents also had the power to determine the importance — or lack of importance — of this public policy issue within their communities. This involved some risks. If some presidents downplayed the issue by defining it only in terms of money, they ran the risk of appearing unconcerned about mission to their campuses, their boards, and their local communities. These local constituencies might wonder why the presidents lacked spirit for the fight at hand. If, on the other hand, presidents stressed the importance of the issue as a key mission challenge, they ran the risk of the campus, board, and community responding too strongly. In this partic-ular situation, presidents did well to articulate this issue on both levels of concern: funding and mission.

Second, the president is the essential link between the two arenas of state activity and the local community. The president is likely to be the only—or one of the few—individuals from the institution who is operating at both the local and state levels. At the local level, the president takes the lead in bringing local legislators into the issue. Personal contacts and influence pay off here. In the noncredit funding situation, individual presi-dents believed that both their access and their credibility with members of their particular legislative delegation were greater than the access and the credibility of the commission through which the colleges act in unison. People at the local level look to the president to interpret the activity at the state level as well as to represent local interests.

At the state level, people look to the president for an in-terpretation of local interests and to represent events at the state level to local constituencies. In the Pennsylvania situation, for example, individual presidents would bring back information about the work of the commission and the discussions with the department to the campus and the community. In turn, the po-sitions they took within the commission reflected their local com-munity concerns about elimination of noncredit course offer-ings that the community valued.

The president is also the focal point of accountability— often without commensurate authority. From the local perspec-tive, the president will be the target of praise or blame for deci-sions over which there is little control. The actions at the state level on noncredit enrollment funding are not usually within the scope of an individual president's powers. Individual presi-dents are not likely to decide the commission's position or drive the department's decisions or powerfully influence the legisla-ture. From the state perspective, the presidents will be praised or blamed based on the extent to which they have influenced individual legislators at the local level to contribute to the general cause. Presidents will be held responsible for either building community support or containing community animosity. Yet they cannot control either local legislative or community reaction.

Third, presidents need to be the architects of a stronger, more influential, and more effective state-level organization of community colleges that is not at odds with their own campus. This need was starkly clear in the Pennsylvania situation — and is not unique to this state. This calls for more careful and creative attention to strategies that balance statewide community college interests and individual campus interests. State organizations are only as strong as their capacity to resolve differences.

Because the funding needs of the thirteen community colleges vary so greatly, the commission did not develop a response to the department's challenge that strayed far from the status quo. The commission, appearing to affirm the status quo as much as possible, was perceived as offering a weak response in the face of serious financial difficulties for the state.

Each member of the commission was confronted with a dilemma. The presidents had to deal with at least the likelihood that the commission would take a position on the funding challenge that was not in the best interests of their individual campuses. Questions would be raised at the local level if a president subordinated individual institutional interests to a commission-wide position. At the state level, there was a political price if the president put the best interests of the campus ahead of the commission. On the one hand, the value of working through the commission diminished when it meant that an individual president's institution would suffer as a result of commission action. On the other hand, presidents could not function as trustworthy and viable members of the commission if they pursued legislative goals independently of the others.

The commission thus found it very difficult — if not impossible — to address the general funding issues for community colleges so that no one was dissatisfied. The combination of general FTE support, occupational stipends, noncredit reimbursement, and capital funding — all in the same state budget line — made redesigning state support for community colleges quite complex. Yet the presidents had not come up with suggestions that maximized revenues for each institution where possible and preserved a sense of equitable treatment for all when revenues were not adequate. This must be tackled for the long-term financial viability of the colleges.

Fourth, the public policy arena is a place in which a president must be willing to take some risks by thinking differently about the future. In the Pennsylvania situation, community college presidents were reluctant to redesign state funding because some institutions might lose some revenues. These revenues, in the eyes of the presidents, were essential to preserving access. Yet, in the long run, all institutions might be better served by funding changes. In a tight fiscal situation, it is reasonable to reexamine the principle of access and reconsider whether offerings that are an enhancement for some students but not essential to educational and economic gain for many (such as some noncredit work) is as important as degree programs leading to first-time employment and future education. With limited resources, "access" cannot be reasonably defined as meeting all and every community need, and the colleges need to set some priorities.

Presidents can also take the risk of rethinking community college governance. If, as Secretary Carroll points out, the state is the principal community college benefactor, are there ways to structure additional state involvement in the governing of community colleges that will build advocacy at the state level? The suggestion that has been offered in Pennsylvania for many years is the addition of a few governor-appointed trustees to community college boards. This has been strongly resisted — and for good reasons. These appointments can diminish the role of the local sponsor and dilute the community college's central commitment to meeting local needs. On the other hand, the Pennsylvania local sponsors have been willing to gain from the local mission commitment of the community college without honoring their financial obligation by providing the revenues required by law. If these appointments were made in collaboration with the local sponsor, they might prove beneficial in encouraging the sponsors to match their desire for community college services with the needed financial support and in building additional state-community programming of value to the Commonwealth.

Summary

Community college presidents have a great responsibility in influencing public policy. They not only define the public policy issue for the campus, the governing board, and the two arenas of state activity and the local community. Presidents can also have great impact on public policy when they are a force in state-level community college organizations that support aims of the college.

    Presidents need to take risks in planning for the future in the areas of public policy and college governance. Their role in public policy is complex, central, and filled with decisions. Public policy challenges for presidents are opportunities for excitement, for really making a difference, and for helping to bring about major change. The only certainty is that these challenges will increase in frequency and magnitude.

References

Commission for Community Colleges and Pennsylvania Federation of Community College Trustees. *1992–93 Budget Brief.* Harrisburg: Commission for Community Colleges and Pennsylvania Federation of Community College Trustees, 1992.

Commonwealth of Pennsylvania. *Department of Education Budget.* Harrisburg: Commonwealth of Pennsylvania, 1992.

El-Khawas, E. *Campus Trends 1992.* Washington, D.C.: American Council on Education, 1992.

"Gov. Casey Proposes 1992–93 Budget." Press release. Harrisburg: Office of the Governor, Commonwealth of Pennsylvania, Feb. 5, 1992.

Mercer, J. "States Turn to Community Colleges as Route to Bachelor's Degree as 4-Year Campuses Face Tight Budgets and Overcrowding." *Chronicle of Higher Education,* May 6, 1992, pp. A1, A28.

Ottinger, C. A. "Economic Trends and Higher Education." *Research Briefs* (American Council on Education), 1992, *3*(2).

Pennsylvania Department of Education. *Colleges and Universities Fall Enrollments 1991*. Harrisburg: Pennsylvania Department of Education, 1992.

Pennsylvania Federation of Community College Trustees and Commission for Community Colleges. *Funding Goals for 1992*. Harrisburg: Pennsylvania Federation of Community College Trustees and Commission for Community Colleges, 1991.

Rodriguez, R. "North Carolina CC System Considers Ending Open Enrollment." *Community College Week*, Dec. 23, 1991, pp. 1, 4.

Rodriguez, R. "Legislature Inaction Allows Merger of Minnesota's Higher Education System." *Community College Week*, May 11, 1992, p. 1.

"State Notes." *Chronicle of Higher Education*, May 6, 1992, p. A29.

Chapter 8

Management Perspectives at the State Level

Earl Hale

This chapter shows how the role of a state office of community, junior, or technical colleges differs from that of an administrative office at a college. These differences have significant implications for staffing, structure, and the functions to be performed. Management of a state office should flow from a clear idea of what role that office plays in the college system. A state office organized and managed with its role expectations clearly in mind provides a resource to a system of colleges that complements and focuses the collective strengths of the individual institutions.

Role of the State

Community, junior, or technical college systems are organized in a wide variety of ways around the country, with substantial variability in terms of local autonomy and the role of the state office. Role issues that should be considered include degree of system centralization, community responsiveness, functions, governmental relationships, and leadership.

141

Centralization

The various state systems fall along a continuum running from highly centralized to highly decentralized structures. The role of the state office will vary widely depending on how centralized the system is. Typically, the more centralized systems have a broader range of functions to perform, generally leading to larger staffs. If the system was created with the expectation that it would be centralized and the state office would perform many functions that could be performed at the local level, then to satisfy those expectations, a larger staff with a broader range of responsibilities is likely to follow. However, if the system places a premium on local autonomy with principal responsibilities largely decentralized, a much smaller office with a narrower set of staff functions is likely to be required. Comparing Washington with the neighboring states of Oregon and California reflects the differences that exist. The Washington state staff of about 50 compares to Oregon's staff of 15 and 200 in California. While these differences, to an extent, reflect system size, they also reflect the philosophy of the state leadership in place at the time the office was created and the degree to which the office performs various potentially college-level functions.

Obviously, it is important that a match be developed between the internal and external expectations of the central office and the size, structure, and skills of its staff. A state that expects to systematize the local institutions clearly must provide the resources for state-level coordination and planning to meet those expectations. To the extent that those resources are not provided, there is likely to be frustration among other elements of state government, both in the executive branch and the legislature, that the system is not performing and that the state office is not doing its job. Eventually a resolution must occur if the system is to interact effectively within the larger governmental environment.

Conversely, if a state clearly expects that the principal functions and responsibilities of the colleges will reside at the local level, it is important that a state office be constructed with that decentralization in mind. A large office, or an office staffed with people aspiring to greater degrees of control, will create continuing friction between the state and local levels, to the over-all detriment of the system. Internal and external expectations about who is doing what in the college system must be reflected in the size and composition of the state office.

Community Responsiveness

Closely related to the issue of centralization versus decentralization are the mechanisms that a state office can adopt to ensure that community responsiveness will be sustained at the college level. Put another way, what can a centralized state system do to ensure that "community" stays in the community colleges? Here again, the degre to which community responsiveness is valued at both the state and local level should influence the size, skills, and personal aspirations of the staff of the state office.

Resistance to overcentralizing operating procedures, program development, and policy formulation can go a long way toward freeing the local institutions to respond to changing needs in their communities. Examples include local setting of tuition and fee levels, local retention of the revenue, central purchasing procedures, and instructional course and program approvals. The state office, however, will be under conflicting pressures, often coming from other elements of state government, to systematize policies, to provide consistent approaches, and to ensure that a variety of operational controls are in place — all of which take their toll on local flexibility. The conflicting pressures of system management and local autonomy are resolved in a variety of ways in the various states. How they are resolved should be reflected in the organizational climate and staffing of the state office.

Functions of the State Office

What role is the state office expected to play in finance, policy development, data collection and analysis, monitoring, and advocacy? The answers to those questions should influence the way the state office is organized and staffed. Substantial variation

**Figure 8.1. Organization Chart,
Washington State Board for Community and Technical Colleges.**

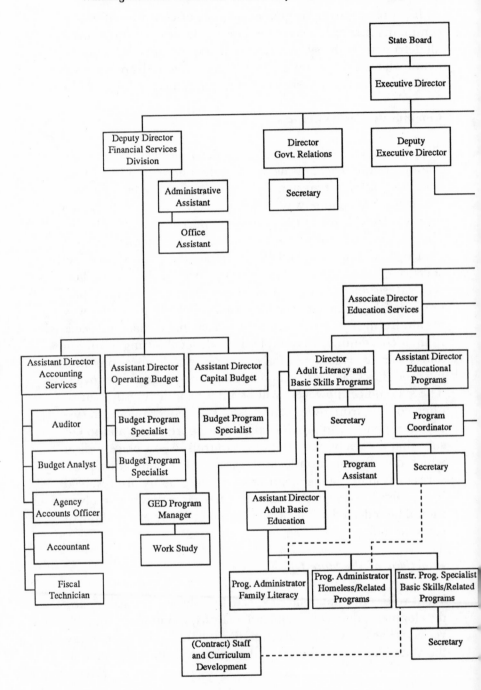

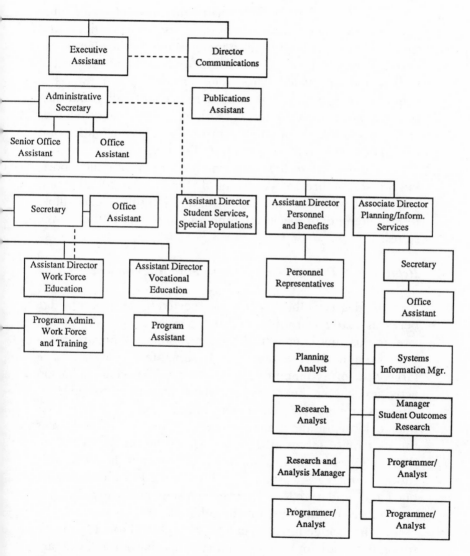

Source: Washington State Board for Community and Technical Colleges.

exists around the country. In many states, the state office is largely a finance staff that may include an advocacy function with the legislature and the governor's office but is mainly involved with distribution of funds and the monitoring of expenditures. In other instances, the office is expected to perform a much broader range of functions in the areas of educational policy, data collection and analysis, personnel practices, and so on. Again, it is important to match the roles the office is expected to perform with the way it is organized and the kind of staffing that is provided. These roles may change over time. For example, with the current interest in accountability and outcomes analysis, several states are under pressure to develop or broaden state-level capabilities in that area — capabilities that were not considered vital in an earlier era.

Figures 8.1 to 8.3 are summary organizational reports for the state offices of Washington, Oregon, and California, respectively. A review of staff, size, and job titles clearly illustrates different approaches to functions and roles in these three states.

Relationship Between Colleges and State Government

To what degree is the state office expected to serve as a bridge between state government and the local institutions? The answer to this question affects the organization, staffing, and capabilities required at the state level. In some states, the state office largely performs a monitoring function, while principal liaison activities between the colleges and the governor's office and legislature is provided by some other organization, often an association of local presidents and/or trustees. However, in most states the state office serves as the presence in the capital. It is continually expected to translate the aspirations of the local institutions to the various state agencies and the legislature, on the one hand, and to reflect and translate state policy expectations to the local institutions, on the other.

This bridge function can be very helpful to a local institution that does not have the luxury of specialized staff who are knowledgeable about state policies and rules and regulations.

Figure 8.2. Community College Organization,
Oregon Board of Education.

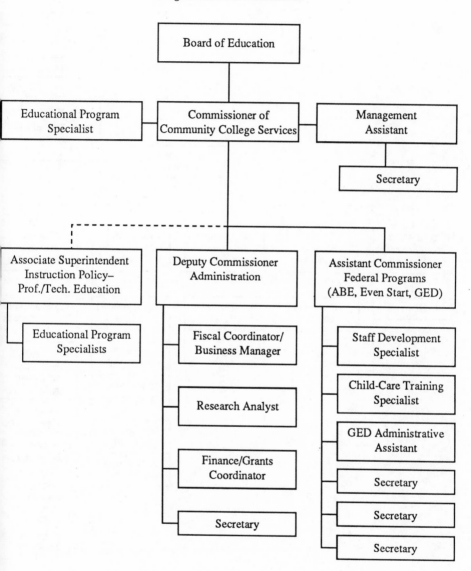

Source: Oregon Office of Community College Services.

Figure 8.3. Organization Chart, California Community Colleges.

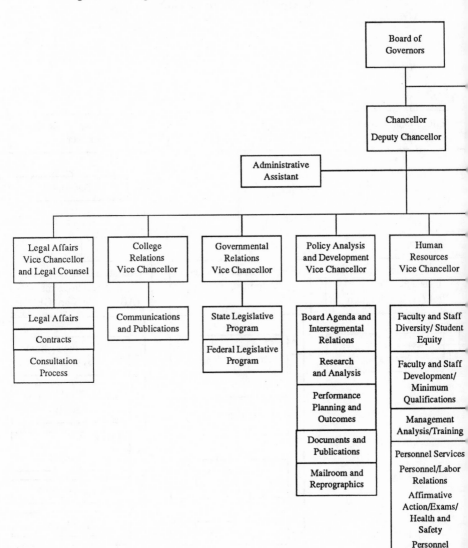

Figure 8.3. Organization Chart, California Community Colleges, Cont'd.

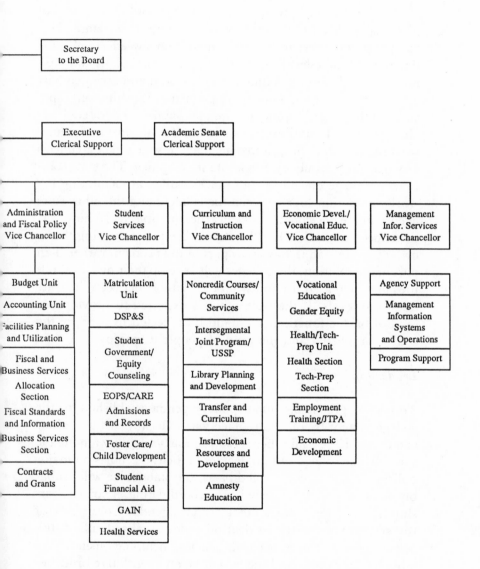

To the extent that the state office can serve as a buffer or provide a road map to state-level personnel policies, capital facility development, and the like, it can provide a real service to the local institutions by allowing them to avoid the expense of hiring specialized staff to deal with the state. If the state office can provide services to the local institutions by effectively cutting through state-level red tape to facilitate local plans and aspirations, it will become a much more integral and accepted part of the college system. This has happened in Washington, especially in the area of capital development and classified (civil service) personnel administration. In the former instance, functions ranging from project management to selection of architects are handled centrally by a separate state agency. The state community college office has staff that is skilled at facilitating the working relationships between the colleges and the other state agency in the development of construction projects. If, however, the expectations exist but the state office is not meeting them, or if the state staff is viewed as part of the problem rather than part of the solution, the colleges will develop their own capabilities and increased friction will be inevitable between the state and local levels. If the state office is expected to provide this kind of bridge function, it should be reflected in the way the staff is organized and the kind of people it employs.

Leadership

To what degree is the major policy agenda established for the college system by the state office versus locally at the various campuses? Here again there is substantial variability among the states. If the college system decides to focus its efforts on major policy initiatives on a unified basis, the state office will probably be expected to provide at least a coordinating, if not a leadership, role in the establishment of that agenda. Conversely, if the system is expected to deal on a decentralized college-by-college basis with outside constituencies, including business and labor organizations and the executive and legislative branches of state government, then the state office structure and staffing should reflect that expectation.

Again, problems arise when there is a mismatch between expectations and organization. If the colleges or state government decide that it is in the best interest of the system to speak with one voice on major policy initiatives, and if the state office is unprepared to offer either leadership or coordination in providing that voice, problems will ensue. Either the system will devise other mechanisms for developing a unified policy agenda, or it will continue to operate on an individual basis without taking advantage of the collective power of the institutions.

Clearly, then, the role expectations of the state office should affect its organizational structure, staffing patterns, and functions. The matching of expectations with organization and capabilities should not be left to chance. While a certain degree of tension will always exist between the colleges and the state office, it can be minimized. It is a responsibility of the leadership of the system and of state government to think through the degree of centralization that is desired and the appropriate division of labor between the state office and the local institutions. Only then can the office be organized in a manner that will allow it to effectively meet the expectations of both the system and its external audiences.

From a local college perspective, it is important to take state office functions and capabilities into account when developing local staff levels. Strong state-level organization and support in a particular area may raise the possibility of a reduced staffing commitment at the local level. Also, if a particular specialized area develops where it would be helpful to the colleges to have state-level support, that preference should be communicated to the state office. While such an occurrence may not be likely, there are times when it is easier for the colleges to rely on state-level expertise in areas that are not directly related to local operation. Expertise in federal Perkins Act vocational rules and regulations may be one example. State capital budget rules and procedures may be another.

Staffing

The development of a competent professional staff is one of the keys to a successful state office. The size of the staff is both a symbolic and a real statement about the role of the state office in the college system. The size and composition of the state office staff are keys to establishing the balance between state and local functions in achieving the overall mission of the system. Obviously, the depth and the number of staff members have a direct impact on office capabilities in the various functional areas included in its mission. Not only is there the direct connection between capacity for achieving work and the number of staff on the payroll, but the size of the staff also sends a philosophical message to audiences both within and outside the system. It can be a cause of considerable sensitivity within the system if the funding for the state office comes out of or competes with the resources that would normally be available to the colleges. The size of the office may also be viewed by the colleges as an indication of the state director's expectations about centralization and involvement in the operating affairs of the system. Consequently, local attitudes about the size of the staff should not be taken lightly, and the message it sends should not be underestimated.

Composition and Skills of Staff

The skills and experiences of the staff will vary depending on the areas of assignment and the constituencies to be served. For example, educational program and policy development staff members should have college experience. One of their principal constituencies is the instructional staff at the colleges, and it is important that state office personnel are sensitive to the pressures that exist at the local level. They must also understand instructional program administration (or at least be grounded in a clear understanding of the local implications of policy proposals) so that state office activities can be effective and supportive of local instructional activities. Development of statewide tuition and fee and fee waiver policies for individual instructional programs is an example of this point. Knowledge of the mechanics of local fee collection processes and of the impact different fees can have on individual programs and on the mission of the college is necessary if a state-level analyst is to develop recommendations that are realistic and do not have unanticipated outcomes.

On the other hand, because finance staff must effectively deal with other elements of state government on budget matters, that staff should have state-level experience in the budget and finance area as well as an understanding of the local situation. Here, the difference in responsibilities between the state and local levels is particularly crucial. Staff members who have their experience in an institutional budget office will not necessarily have the understanding of the legislative appropriations processes and the governor's budget office that will allow them to interact effectively with those two offices in their pursuit of resources on behalf of the system. A lack of understanding of how state budget processes work — and the frame of reference of the key staff people involved in that process — are major handicaps when dealing with state-level budget issues.

Because of the unique and sensitive nature of a state office in a system of essentially local institutions, the effectiveness of the office depends to a great extent on the skills, abilities, and diplomacy of the staff. Most positions, while having a technical dimension, require the maximum of interpersonal skills, communication skills, and organizational skills as well as the ability to read and analyze the environment. Often staff are placed in a position of dealing with pressures from conflicting, or at least quite different, constituencies. It is vital that they develop the ability to analyze those pressures and determine how best to operate the office so that it can achieve its goals. The fact that these staff often describe themselves as being in a fishbowl — being watched and second-guessed on most decisions they make — places a premium on these human relations skills.

State Director

The state director is not a super college president, but rather an administrator of a state agency who should understand the complexities of the office's role with both internal and external constituencies. The director must understand community, junior, and technical colleges, their missions, and how they operate.

But the director must also understand state government and how it operates. The director must know how government works, be able to understand and influence the state political process, and be able to relate to a broad array of external constituencies, including business, labor, four-year universities, and the K-12 system. The position requires the melding of state and local perspectives and the ability to compromise and accommodate to achieve the desired objectives. The absence of sensitivity and the ability to empathize with these perspectives can be a near fatal flaw to a state director trying to steer an office through a very complex and highly visible political environment.

Again, the skills and abilities of the state director must relate to the role the state office is expected to play in the college system. To the extent that programmatic leadership is vested in the state office, the director must have a vision, be able to articulate the vision both internally and externally, and be able to develop strategies to accomplish the desired results.

The state director should see priorities and pressures within the system and, at the same time, see statewide external trends and issues as they arise. The director is then uniquely positioned to see where the lines converge and can establish an agenda that will be supported both internally and externally. The director needs to be able to read state and local situations. Otherwise, there is the potential for erring either on the side of pushing an agenda that is too aggressive or at variance with the dominant values of the colleges on the one hand, or on the other hand, becoming caught up in the local institutional perspective and becoming oblivious to the role colleges can play in the larger policy setting. The opportunity to provide leadership and help set the agenda of the community college system can be productive and satisfying to the director—but it is a role that must be played with acute sensitivity to the needs and pressures both internal and external to the system.

Organizational Structure

While it is difficult to generalize about the type of organizational structure that best fits the needs of a state office, one must not ignore the fact that various organizational structures have a definite impact on the office's ability to perform effectively. An argument can be made for the value and benefit of a relatively flat organizational structure in terms of communication, productivity, and staff involvement in the affairs of the organization. While the state office structure usually reflects the style and preferences of the state director, a relatively flat structure rather than a more vertical hierarchy has clear benefits, given the unique roles that the state director and the state office are expected to perform.

Effective communication and the free flow of ideas from the various constituencies is important if the state office is to effectively carry out its responsibilities. The office and the state director must not become isolated and insulated from the forces at work both within the system and among the various external constituencies. While the state director should develop a style and method of operation that allows for accessibility and maintenance of a broad range of sources of advice and counsel, the balance of the state staff can also become sensors to the external environment. The internal structure should be flat enough so that the state director has access to those sensors within the staff. A more vertical or hierarchical structure tends to isolate the director from the people and system constituencies, thereby inhibiting communication that is vital to the overall success of the agency. Instances where the state director — and state office — become isolated are usually accompanied by reduced effectiveness and, at times, by a change in leadership!

Avoiding isolation and insulation are important enough to warrant the deliberate development of linkages of various key staff members to principal constituencies. These could include system groups such as the college presidents, trustees, and deans or outside groups such as business or labor organizations. If these linkages support the free flow of communication between the office and these various groups, they can be vital to the staff's efforts to read the organizational and political environment and achieve the office and system's goals within that environment.

Principal Functions

This chapter has offered in general terms a series of observations about staffing and organizational structure that contribute

to the effectiveness of a state office. It is now appropriate to turn
to more specific observations about functions that are often included in such an office. While the breadth and depth of functions performed by a state office should reflect the role the office
is expected to perform, the following five areas are likely to be
included to varying degrees under most circumstances: policy
development, finance, data collection and analysis, advocacy,
and monitoring and auditing.

Policy Development

Policy development includes subjects that run the gamut from
personnel and tuition to marketing, instructional program review, and the implementation or facilitation of new programs
initiated by the state legislature. Because the topics that are often
the subject of state-level policy development have direct operational impacts on the colleges, the staff that is involved in the
development of those policies needs to have a good understanding of community and technical college issues, problems, and
institutional capabilities. For example, tuition policies are often
set at the state level, and an understanding of changing student
behavior in response to the various tuition levels — and methods
of charging and/or waiving fees — is important to the development of sound policies and the avoidance of unanticipated impacts. College experience is usually vital if the staff is to be effective in the development of systemwide policies that gain the
respect and support of the institutions.

The staff also needs to develop good working relationships
with the rest of the educational system: the public schools, the
universities, and other training systems, including business, private industry councils, and apprenticeship councils. Often the
staff is the point of contact between the community, junior, or
technical college system and these other institutions — particularly
at the system or state level. Working relationships with the staff
of these other organizations and the ability to understand their
perspectives and the pressures they are under are essential if
partnerships are to be effectively developed, negotiations are to
be effectively conducted, or alliances are to be formed around

common issues and objectives. The system cannot achieve its ends independent of the rest of its environment, and interaction with these other organizations is often vital to achievement of its goals. A recent example in one state was the merger of vocational-technical institutes and community colleges into a combined adult education and training system. The merger could only have been accomplished because the state business organization and the state AFL-CIO Council worked closely with the college system and legislative leaders in the political activities leading to the change.

Staff involved in policy development in the state office needs the ability to synthesize input from a variety of groups, analyze policy implications, and make recommendations that recognize the differing perspectives and values of the various constituencies of the office. Again, the individual skills and capabilities of the staff can make — or break — an office policy initiative. Policies that are unrealistic and insensitive to the desires and capabilities of the system are doomed to failure — and with them will go the credibility of the office that put them forward.

Finance

The finance function depends on the structure of the individual state. It usually provides advocacy for state funding with the governor and the legislature. It also allocates state funds to the colleges. Thus, it includes both external and internal dimensions. As mentioned above, the staff needs a good understanding of both the state and local organizational and political environment to best represent the interests of the system. A former college business officer, even one who has been extremely successful at the institutional level, must bring to the state position a good understanding of how state decisions are made. Otherwise this person is doomed to fail as a contact and advocate in the interactions with the legislative ways and means committees and the governor's office.

The separation of the state office from the institutions places a premium on finance staff who have the ability to identify the instructional implications of funding decisions so that the educational business of the colleges can be integrated into budget priorities and unanticipated outcomes can be avoided. Here again, the state office differs from a local college, and the day-to-day interaction between the business office and the instructional staff of the institution to ensure that instructional implications are considered in financial decisions does not necessarily take place at the state level.

There are two ways that sensitivity can be built into financial decision making. The first way would be to ensure that the instructional and policy part of the state staff have close and ongoing interaction with the financial staff. A smoothly functioning team with representatives of a variety of perspectives will usually yield better analyses and decisions than those operating in isolation. The second way is to simply employ staff in the financial office who have some institutional experience or empathy and interest in the instructional process. Most state-level funding decisions have either direct or indirect impact on the local educational process, and the extent to which those impacts are anticipated and taken into consideration strengthens the overall effectiveness of the state office.

Internally, the process of allocating state appropriations to local colleges is one of the most time-consuming and sensitive areas with which state budget offices are concerned. It is easy to become consumed with the technical and financial implications of various allocation formula options without adequately considering the educational incentives and disincentives that are embedded in the various proposals. Examples of local decisions influenced by allocation formulas include the number of part-time faculty employed, program mix options (whether to start high-cost programs), and faculty salary administration options (size and characteristics of salary schedules, starting salary levels, and so on).

The state staff needs technical and analytical abilities to review financial and policy implications of budget proposals, allocation options, and other financial issues. The state office often is a focal point for a variety of funding proposals emanating either from the system or from the governor's office or legislature. The ability of the finance staff to quickly identify the advantages and disadvantages of the proposal and its implications for the individual institutions is crucial if it is to effectively advocate for the system.

It is often necessary that consistent and uniform financial data be available both for the system and for individual colleges to satisfy legal requirements and to support other state-level decisions. The office needs to develop leadership in the accounting area to ensure that accounting and financial reporting are done consistently — particularly to support internal analyses and decisions related to the allocation of resources to the colleges. The allocation of resources is often driven by data that originate at the college level. In order to have consistent and comparable information to ensure that these decisions are equitable, the data elements and the reporting system must be clearly defined and monitored on an ongoing basis. (Examples include information on faculty classifications and salaries, facility rentals, and other elements given specific treatment in the funding allocation formula.) While this area may not have the appeal of some of the more policy-oriented issues that involve the state office, it is crucial to undergird the decision processes with consistent data. The potential for divisions within the system and for the erosion of credibility at the state level with external audiences is considerable if this is not made a high priority.

Data Collection and Analysis

Consistent data that provide the basis for fair and equitable management and policy decisions by the state office are often a challenge in a system of local colleges. There are external expectations for data that can explain and describe the activities of the colleges (enrollment, staffing, and curriculum, for example). There are also internal expectations for data that can be used in advocating on behalf of the colleges to state government and other external constituencies, supporting state office decisions, and making institutional improvements. On this latter point, often colleges will make interinstitutional comparisons of such things as faculty and staff salaries, class sizes in various disciplines, and enrollment statistics, using data provided by the state system. This institutional use of the state data puts a premium on consistent definitions and collection of these data. (The Washington college system has taken this into account in the development of an integrated data system that combines a state and local management information system with finance, student registration, and instructional course management operating systems. This avoids the development of separate reports for the state at the individual colleges, but rather uses the operating systems as the basis of the reporting. The resultant data quality and reduction of extra time and effort devoted to state reports appear to warrant the integrated approach.)

Data analysis can be used in a couple of ways to support management and policy decisions. It can be used to illuminate the factors going into the decision and thereby lead to stronger and better considered decisions. On the other hand, if decisions are being made for other organizational or political reasons, the analysis can be used to help rationalize those decisions in policy terms. While that is a fairly cynical view of data analysis, it is obvious that both uses occur from time to time. In either event, analytical capabilities should be available to the state director and agency staff as they perform their administrative and leadership responsibilities. As noted before, state offices operate in a "fishbowl," and their decisions are often quite visible and sensitive to the various internal and external constituencies of the system. Having the office decision-making process firmly grounded on an analytical base will not only result in better decisions but also will strengthen the overall credibility of the office. Decisions that are not well thought out, and implications that have not been anticipated, will undercut the credibility of the office and erode its ability to lead. An example is the allocation of enrollment growth — often a principal driver in the allocation of operating dollars to the colleges. The extent to which enrollment allocations can be put on a policy basis — with predictable short- and long-term targets established on a solid analytical base — will dramatically affect the credibility of this sensitive state office decision.

As community, junior, and technical colleges become more active and visible players in the state's educational and economic policy arenas, there is an increasing expectation that the system identify the outcomes and impacts of its programs. Accountability for scarce resources often accompanies an increasingly competitive financial environment. To that end, the state office often finds it appropriate to develop, on systemwide terms, an outcomes reporting and analytical capability that furthers the policy and financial goals of the system.

Both public and private external audiences expect colleges to be able to identify what impact they have on public problems and to identify the results of specific appropriations or program initiatives. Given that expectation, the office needs to develop staff capabilities in this area. One note of caution, however: state-level outcomes assessment activities should be limited to broad general policy areas, and data should be summarized at the system level when they are used with external audiences. One should not confuse this system-level capability with institutional outcomes analysis that can be used locally for planning and evaluation purposes. If the institutions feel that detailed data about the effectiveness of the programs will be used at the state level in a punitive way, it will stifle initiative and enthusiasm for program improvement at the local level.

The state office should make clear to its state-level constituents the distinction between state and local outcomes assessment objectives and ensure that there are ironclad understandings that will avoid state-level scrutiny of individual campus programs in a manner that will completely frustrate local program improvement activities. In Washington, the state office has developed agreement about this difference with the Higher Education Coordinating Board and key legislative leaders and staff, and the result has been much greater institutional acceptance (particularly on the part of faculty) of outcomes assessment activities.

Advocacy

One of the principal reasons for most state offices to exist is to advocate on behalf of community, junior, and technical colleges to state government and other external constituencies such as statewide and regional business associations, labor organizations, and news media. To perform the advocacy function, the office must develop and coordinate effective public relations and legislative relations capabilities. Coordinated state-level communications are often targeted primarily at helping the system meet legislative or other state-level objectives. Local colleges need to be convinced of the importance of their participation in statewide programs even as they continue to carry out their traditional role of providing potential students with program and enrollment information.

The degree of coordination versus actual advocacy by the state staff will reflect the role expectations of the state office and of the local institutions. A balance must be reached between state-level leadership and coordination on the one hand and the basic recognition that much of the actual activity must occur locally if it is to be most effective on the other.

The development of a state-level advocacy role is increasingly important as the competition for adequate funding becomes intensified. The advent of more regional media and the increasing likelihood of regional or statewide policy initiatives by the colleges themselves also increases the need for state-level advocacy. The traditional assumption that each college will handle the local media must be modified to ensure that external leaders and policy makers receive a consistent message about the importance to the state of a healthy community, junior, and technical college system. In urban and suburban areas (where regional media coverage and college service areas overlap), it is particularly important that colleges coordinate their media strategies and priorities in a manner that will reinforce each other in the pursuit of common goals.

The role of the state office in that process will vary, but frequently some kind of coordination and focus will be its responsibility. That leadership needs to be exercised in a way that enhances the sense of ownership that local college information officers have in the systemwide information effort.

In the area of legislative relations, again it is vital that the legislative program reflects goals shared by the various institutions in the system and that the legislative process coordinates and focuses the collective political influence of those institutions to further those goals. Legislators are far more likely to have concern for the welfare of their home district's colleges than of the system. Yet unless all legislators are hearing similar messages about the local college, the legislative program will be ineffective.

Often the state office is asked to perform this coordination function. In both legislative and media relations, the coordinative and leadership role must be exercised with full sensitivity to the role of the local institution and recognition of the strength that local relationships, either with the media or with political leaders, bring to the total effort.

Monitoring and Auditing

This function, while often at odds with the advocacy function, usually cannot be avoided. Compliance with policies, development of common data definitions, and monitoring of reporting are often needed if the colleges are to be playing on a level field in a variety of financial and other areas. For example, fair and equitable treatment of colleges in the operating budget allocations assumes the availability of consistent financial, enrollment, and staffing data. This can only be assured if some degree of monitoring exists.

The monitoring and auditing function can be a source of tension between the state and local levels and can present the state office staff with conflicting role expectations. Most staff members prefer to be advocates for the colleges and would prefer to work with colleges on issues of common interest rather than to assume a monitoring — and often adversarial — role. This can create management problems within the state office. Staff members who have been employed at institutions — and want to go back to institutions at later points in their careers — may be unwilling to place themselves in an adversarial position with the institutions. However, if monitoring or auditing is vital to the effective conduct of the state office role, staff must be asked to perform the monitoring role even if it conflicts with their personal career aspirations. While most institutions recognize the

value of professional staff work in the state office (thus minimizing the long-term impact on careers by performing difficult assignments on a professional basis), the sensitivity of the role
conflict is clear, and the likelihood of the monitoring function
being underplayed by some staff exists.

The degree to which the state office becomes engaged in
monitoring activities should be a conscious decision, based on
its role within the system and the expectations of internal and
external organizations. The decision will have clear implications
for the kinds of skills needed by the staff and will influence the
overall relationship between the state office and the colleges.

Summary

This chapter has shown that the organizational structure and
the capabilities of a state office must be carefully tailored to meet
the role expectations of that office within the college system.
Staffing patterns and capabilities will vary depending on the organization of the system, the degree to which it is centralized,
and the manner in which it is funded. Basic to an understanding of the role of the state office is the recognition that it is not
simply a mirror of a local college but rather a unique organization with its own set of needs and requirements.

A state office organized and managed with its role expectations clearly in mind provides a resource to the system of community, junior, and technical colleges that complements and
focuses the collective strengths of the individual colleges. There
obviously will be tensions between the state and local levels, because the state office operates within a complex organizational
setting often dealing with conflicting constituencies, perspectives,
and values. This places a premium on the leadership of the office
and its ability to work with those constituencies to further the
policy goals and priorities of the system and of the state.

From the local perspective, it is important to clearly understand the role that the state office expects—and is expected—
to play in the overall governance of the college system. To the
extent that the state office can represent the colleges at the state
level, intervene on colleges' behalf with state agencies, and pro-

vide support on technical issues, the state's role can complement
the activities of the local college staff. This can reduce administrative staffing requirements at the local level and free up scarce
resources for instruction and student-related activities. On the
other hand, if there are serious disagreements about roles and
responsibilities between the state and local levels, friction can
develop. It is important from both perspectives that expectations are worked out and that an agreed-on division of labor
is developed.

PART TWO

ADMINISTRATIVE
AREAS

Part Two describes several of the administrative units in the contemporary community college: the president's office; business and finance; personnel; articulation and transfer units; instructional, community, and industry programs; student services; and campus planning.

In Chapter Nine, Daniel F. Moriarty describes the relations between the president and various college functions. Included here are sections on the president's responsibilities, delegation of duties and personnel, and direct involvement in college management. Moriarty also urges that presidents establish a standard of excellence and sustain a high ethical stance.

Colleges and universities are constantly being challenged to improve performance, contain costs, and demonstrate sound stewardship of their resources—challenges in which business and financial officers play a major role. In Chapter Ten, Albert L. Lorenzo focuses on the function of business and financial officers in terms of role expectations and contributions. Discussing emerging issues, Lorenzo points to some management practices designed to maximize personnel effectiveness.

167

Barbara E. Janzen argues in Chapter Eleven that a well-functioning personnel office is essential for college operations. Describing the functions and staffing of this office, she discusses major issues that confront it — affirmative action, the law, hiring and dismissing employees, and part-time faculty.

Can instructional programs be managed with effectiveness and efficiency as well as with creativity and harmony? In Chapter Twelve, Martha J. Kanter deals with issues relating to curriculum balance, shared governance, involvement in teaching and learning, intellectual exhaustion, and what she terms "self-actualized instruction."

In Chapter Thirteen — on administrative units — Trudy H. Bers holds that articulation and transfer offices are essential components of community colleges that seriously concern themselves with the transfer function. A number of articulation and transfer activities are described as useful tasks for assessing the effectiveness of this office.

In Chapter Fourteen, Geneva Waddell stresses the need for innovative programs to meet growing community and industry demands. Structures must exist to promote lifelong learning, community service, and workforce development.

Chapter Fifteen focuses on student services. Emphasizing the importance of active leadership in maintaining an effective student service program, Charles R. Dassance discusses the integration of these services into overall institutional planning. The student services' leader must be knowledgeable about all aspects of the program, understand theories of human and organizational development, be competent as a researcher and organizational effectiveness specialist, and value the goals of general education.

In Chapter Sixteen, John Losak takes a different perspective. He first provides a brief introduction to the history and nature of institutional research, then focuses more extensively on the many functions and interrelationships of an institutional research office.

Dan Angel and James Brader offer a general overview of campus planning and construction in Chapter Seventeen.

They detail procedures for addressing legislative requirements, financial constraints, environmental and energy concerns, and engineering concepts. A step-by-step process, from the initial planning stage through the completion of a construction project, is presented.

Chapter 9

The President's Office

Daniel F. Moriarty

Leadership literature challenges presidents to be masters of change, harbingers of innovation, dreamers of visions, shapers of culture, builders of consensus, and perhaps even movers of mountains — certainly movers of reluctant legislators. Beneath the rhetoric, presidents know they wear many hats, fill many roles, and are responsible to a variety of stakeholders. Fundamentally, boards and the public expect their chief administrators to provide leadership and manage their organizations, two tasks that have many subparts and require a variety of skills. Nowhere in this challenge does anyone say much about the management of the executive office. Yet to accomplish their many functions, all community college presidents must first be able to manage their office, and thereby earn the right to do the right thing.

Bennis (1989), fresh from his experience at the University of Cincinnati, reflected on the power of the trivial and routine to drive out the significant and important. Amplified, Bennis's observation serves as a salutary caution to all CEOs to take a proactive stand to avoid subservience to an imposed agenda and to manage for larger freedoms and a self-selected agenda.

Even in the best of times and with the most aggressive management, CEOs will not avoid time- and energy-consuming tyrannies. Without aggressive management that starts with the president's office, however, the instances of tyranny will multiply and the president's mode of conduct will become increasingly more reactive and always less effective. Managing the president's office is clearly one instance of doing things right. This chapter discusses management styles, responsibilities, perils, delegation, and standards that facilitate doing the right thing.

Office Organization

In a typical organizational scheme, a dean of instruction, a dean of students, a vice president of administration, and perhaps another senior officer responsible for planning and development will report directly to the president. In a multicampus or multicollege environment, unit presidents and senior officers of the central office staff will also report to the CEO. This organizational scheme basically allows the CEO to exercise operational responsibilities for instruction, student affairs, business services, and — in a multicampus environment — campus operations. With only modest variations, all community colleges' organizations resemble the above model in reliance on senior officers to carry out leadership and operational responsibilities for instruction, students, business affairs, and discrete campus units.

In addition to their responsibility for working with senior officers in achieving the college's goals, presidents have responsibilities that arise directly and uniquely out of their office, that are chosen for direct hands-on management, and that are fundamental to overall effectiveness. For example, the president manages demanding and complex relationships with individual board members and with the board as a whole. This relationship establishes the tone of the CEO's administration and sets its direction. As the organization's principal advocate and primary spokesperson, and as its symbolic leader, the CEO also manages a public affairs agenda that includes a dynamic set of internal and external constituencies. Both the board agenda and the public affairs agenda constitute essential job tasks and are unique to the president's office.

In recent years, CEOs have added to their office portfolio direct responsibility for implementing the college's affirmative action program. Understandably, constituencies feel that an effective affirmative action program can only be achieved when the CEO of the institution leads it personally. In addition to these discrete operational responsibilities, the CEO's office remains traditionally the final arbiter for grievances, both formal and informal. With the promulgation of affirmative action and American Disabilities Act policies and employee grievances, either through the union or without, the president's office can be a well-used court of last appeal.

In smaller colleges and, in some instances, because of a preferred operating style, CEOs choose to manage other functions and offices directly. These functions most often include the development office and less often staff development, labor relations, and institutional advancement. The latter term is defined narrowly to mean marketing but can also be defined to include public affairs, development, and planning as well as marketing.

Even as their portfolios build with line and staff responsibilities, the CEO continues to carry the overriding responsibility for exercising personal leadership. A critical part of this leadership includes articulating the organization's vision in its formative stage and continually educating the internal and external constituencies to this vision as it evolves from the mission of the college. Successful institutions are mission driven, as Drucker (1989) has noted, and the chief caretaker and driver of that mission must be the CEO. "Busy" presidents who choose not to take time for the larger, abstract issues, who take their pleasure from budget or legislative legerdemain, or who derive great satisfaction from running a tidy house steer their institutions into perilous waters for no clear purpose. Presidents also must take time to help establish and articulate the basic values and culture of the institution. Meaning and values do not spontaneously erupt, at least not meaning and values that inspire, unite, give purpose to, and build on and enhance the mission of the college. Presidents do not do it alone, but they need to be front and center in leading the charge. Leadership for vision and values takes time, effort, and commitment. Among all that presidents do, above all, they must exercise leadership.

Much closer to an integral part of the president's office are those who function as assistants, either as secretaries or as executive assistants. The tasks included in the immediate and elementary functions of the president's office include reception, correspondence, calendar, filing, social activity, and gatekeeping. All of these tasks require skill and discretion not only to do the job right but to do so in a manner that will greatly facilitate and increase effectiveness. In addition, the manner in which these tasks are carried out unequivocally communicates the CEO's style, values, and standards. If brusqueness and haughtiness emanate from an executive secretary, if phone messages are lost and letters or memos are at half-mast, it is not a big jump to imagine an arrogant or careless CEO. Conversely, a personable, responsive, and competent assistant at the very least raises the expectation that a like-minded person occupies the president's office. In the tasks managed by the CEO's immediate assistants, nothing should be taken for granted. Here, too, the president needs to exercise the care that will make good things happen purposefully.

If all the tasks within the president's portfolio were laid out end to end, then, one snapshot would look like this:

I. Leadership
    A. Articulation of college mission
    B. Formation and establishment of institutional values
    C. Development of college resources and priorities
II. Management
    A. Major line administrative units
        1. Dean, instruction
        2. Dean, student affairs
        3. Dean, administration
        4. Dean, campus units
    B. Major staff functions
        1. Director, development/institutional advancement
        2. Director, public affairs
        3. Assistant, board relations
        4. Director, labor relations
        5. Director/assistant, affirmative action

III.   Direct office functions
    A.   Personal schedule/calendar
    B.   Correspondence/record keeping
    C.   Access/reception
    D.   Social/ceremonial activity

In the face of these varied tasks and challenges, the CEO needs to do everything well, since all tasks are interdependent and constitute a whole. Although some presidents prefer one or the other task and indulge their previous passions for instruction or student affairs, they are not free to pick and choose without risk to their stewardship. Because of the importance of the CEO's office, the neglect of any one responsibility lets loose a cannon on the ship's deck that may eventually put a hole in the deck if not in the captain. The challenge to the CEO, then, is to exercise the organizational skills that make it possible to manage everything while avoiding the pitfalls that come from selective neglect or micromanagement.

Management Perils

Potential pitfalls are legion and cannot all be avoided, but clearly, some loom larger than others. One president of a small suburban college — a former student affairs dean — boasted that he personally reviewed the transcript of every applicant for graduation. A pleased look suggested that this action represented for him a telling sign of his commitment to students and to quality. Unfortunately, at the same time, he complained bitterly of his running battles with board members, with the faculty, and with key community leaders. While his relations with stakeholders may still have turned to dross, one cannot help wondering whether his time would have been better spent on stakeholder relations than on student transcripts, especially when a capable dean of students stood at the ready.

In another setting — a larger urban college — a seemingly competent and trusting CEO allowed his business officer full rein to carry out labor relations and personnel policies with little or no oversight while he focused on community relations.

Almost too late, the CEO discovered that his public words had an increasingly hollow ring, because at home the union leaders and their constituents had grown disenchanted with an administration they saw as hardnosed, unresponsive, and unsympathetic. Ironically, but not surprisingly, they excused the president but blasted his administration. This kind of distinction, as every president knows, offers little solace and suggests a CEO who is nice but incompetent. Somewhere along the line, the CEO had delegated authority without seeking accountability and ensuring that institutional standards and values were upheld.

The following examples are less dramatic but still revealing. A president spends weeks explaining the real meaning of an electronic memo sent under her name but issued by the finance officer, who was never known to have a soft touch. A new president finds his "out-of-control" calendar filled every day for weeks on end by a secretary who interprets his "open door" as a signal to pencil in everyone who asks for a meeting or delivers an invitation. Another president confronts the tension of her own staff meetings only to learn of the frustration arising from her own actionless marathon meetings at which agendas appear as if by magic thirty seconds before the call to order. A president earns the board's impatience for calling extra meetings to deal with critical resolutions that never quite hit the regularly scheduled meetings.

Presidents can avoid these perils of poor office management only if they adopt positive strategies that maximize their skills and talents and extend their effectiveness. On appointment to his first presidency, a CEO noted that he was not at all awed by the responsibility of leading a large institution because he had so many expert staff available to help do the job. For any CEO, the challenge is to use these resources well so that the job does get done. Too often, CEOs stumble and fall because they do not use the resources available to them.

Delegation

If presidents have acted wisely, they have assembled excellent, experienced talents in their deans or vice presidents and should use those skills accordingly. The dean of students does not need help in reading a college transcript; the dean does need help in keeping the college's mission, priorities, and values clearly focused. In working with their top line officers, presidents have an excellent opportunity, as Osborne and Gaebler (1992) have suggested, to steer the ship and allow the deans to row. Delegation to the executive officers can be quite extensive if accountability to college standards, priorities, and values is guaranteed.

In the case of other functions that the president chooses to manage — for example, development, labor relations, or affirmative action — delegation tends to be more specific and requires closer scrutiny. In these instances also, the directors need the room to do their jobs even if the range of responsibility is narrower and the CEO's involvement is more specific. In an effort to share specifics, the labor relations director in one college regularly parked himself on the new CEO's threshold to review the latest fast-breaking news on a developing grievance or to rehash a particularly Byzantine nuance of the faculty contract. The CEO, anxious not to be known as the labor president, abruptly reassigned the director to a new physical site and made any kind of regular contact or premature discussion of detail very difficult. There are less obvious ways to make the point, but even in the management of discrete functions within their offices, presidents need to delegate specific tasks, require accountability, and avoid the quicksand of detail.

Delegation for more discrete tasks of office support should also be definitive, but the steering hand of the president should be more obvious in the immediate vicinity of the office. If executive secretaries take charge of their presidents' calendars, they need to understand priorities and be advised regularly as these priorities shift. While mind reading and intuition are to be valued when all else fails, immediate office support staff need clear direction on tasks and continuing education on the priorities and values that inform office activities. There is some irony in situations where presidents direct their management and leadership skills to staff and stakeholders outside their office and neglect the support and development of the people who are alter egos within the office. Secretaries and assistants have no one else to lean on or work with other than their supervisor/president. That relationship should be consistent with other relationships the CEO develops.

Personal and Direct Involvement

Some tasks clearly cannot be accomplished through others. More presidents need to take charge personally and directly of relations with individual board members and with the board in general. While this responsibility does not include driving a board member to a weekly dry-cleaning pickup, it does include one-on-one meetings to explain the developmental education curriculum, the bid on bakery products, and the campus energy conservation project. It also includes work sessions with the full board on strategic planning, budget development, and administrative reorganization. To shift any of these responsibilities to staff invites disharmony and creates the impression that the president is aloof and disdainful. A president who habitually bumps board calls to staff and communicates with board members through secretaries should not be surprised to be labeled unresponsive and officious. Amazingly, some CEOs view the board's needs and requirements as ancillary to the real needs of the college, as if board members were somehow intrusive on the CEO's real job. Perhaps the greatest insight a president can have is that the board members really are the governing body of the college and that more than anyone else they can ensure the president's success. A CEO who does not work diligently and closely with the board is a president who does not understand the job.

The president must also take a direct role in certain areas of public affairs. For example, while the public affairs director can do much in legislative and state matters to till the ground, the president needs personally to build bridges with key legislators, with members of the executive branch, and with significant state officers. A basic insight into the way things work reveals that results depend on personal knowledge and interaction. Our leaders need to be seen as credible, competent, and ethical persons, not as bureaucratic shadows inhabiting the background.

This requirement also holds true in the community the college serves. No one can take the president's place in the development of strong bonds with the local elected officials, with the head of the Urban League, with the school superintendent, and with the president of the local Chamber of Commerce. Indeed, the CEO needs to be front and center for a variety of community calls, whether it is the neighborhood improvement association, the United Fund campaign, or the city planning commission. Again, staff work can set up and prepare for the personal contact, but only the president can carry out the contact.

The many instances in which the president alone must directly carry the message reinforces the importance of delegation where delegation is possible and reasonable. Not to delegate, for example, to the dean of students in the case of student affairs diminishes the time and energy that the president should devote to community affairs — a responsibility the dean of students clearly cannot assume. Drucker (1980) has described administration as the art of doing things through other people, an apt description of delegation. In the life of the president, certain activities and responsibilities lend themselves to delegation; others do not. A president must have the good sense to know when and what to delegate and the self-discipline to adhere to this judgment.

Organization

Despite the best efforts at delegation, the president's office will continue to be a place of intersecting lines, not unlike a transportation hub of a major airline. To make sure connections are made, timeliness met, and destination points reached, the president must organize in a manner to achieve maximum effectiveness without falling into a kind of mindless ridigity that destroys spontaneity, entrepreneurism, and responsiveness. The organization of the CEO's office invariably centers around the president's calendar and the use of resources immediately available to that office. No president can function well operating in a kind of ad hocracy and reactionism; the person in charge must take charge.

Calendar organization and hence activity and time organization can begin simply by plugging into the calendar on an annual basis such essential activities as board meetings, board workshops, key academic dates, regular and predictable meeting dates, travel dates, and decision points related to budget development. Together, the president will find, these key activities quickly outline and define the year. A next step or even a parallel step is to introduce into the calendar decision times related to new initiatives, whether they are targeted at constituencies within or outside the college community. Other examples could be cited, but all serve to illustrate the relative ease of organizing an entire year. It is important to understand that such an exercise also serves to identify conflicts and to raise important priority issues that compete for the president's time and energy. Calendar organization done well is planning by another name.

Obviously, calendar planning within the president's office can be and should be multiyeared. An accreditation visit scheduled for 1997 triggers a self-study in 1996 and other preparatory work in 1995. How do these dates tie in with a planned reclassification study or with an anticipated organization analysis or with a major fundraising effort? A state budget crisis projected for the 1997–1999 biennium should cause ripples in 1995–1997—perhaps a retirement incentive plan or a freeze on new hires. Nothing would be more embarrassing to the CEO and harmful to the college than to discover in 1997 that the tide has come in and the blanket is all wet, a blanket that could easily have been moved to higher ground. Organizing a CEO's calendar is more than saying the president is in or out. Planning for the office is frequently planning for the college; one should be a reflection of the other.

Who maintains that calendar, who answers phones, who receives visitors, who aids board communications, and who troubleshoots the office all are specific aspects of the routine operation of the president's office. Presidents need not mete out these tasks one by one, but they should work with assistants to identify the most effective manner to accomplish routine activities so that they are done well, predictably, and without confusion.

All those in the immediate area should clearly know their responsibilities and those of others as well as how to cover for each other. The president's office should never not be covered, even if the coverage in a small college is the telephone operator saying the president is off campus. A call from the chair of the board should directly interrupt a desultory conversation between the president and the academic dean, and a tardy president should deftly but firmly be reminded of the cross-town meeting with the local school superintendents. Mail should be screened and evaluated for importance and assembled in a priority order; correspondence should be put together immediately and posted after review. Staff should anticipate logistical problems, solve them, and keep the office flow in purposeful movement. The value of immediate office assistants is very measurable, as an experienced and successful president will testify. Not only will chief executives become more effective by this clear delineation of duties to staff, but those in the offices will have a reassuring sense of their contribution to the success of the office.

Establishing Standards

In managing their office, the CEOs have the opportunity to establish from the beginning clear expectations that influence direct reports and, even more important, send a loud and clear message about who they are and what their standards are. In one large community college district, the new president expressed his dismay that the formal invitations to celebrate the college's twenty-fifth anniversary were all addressed with white computer-generated labels that showed last name first, first name second. In response, the public affairs officer opined that people in that state did not care about such niceties as hand-addressed invitations. The CEO dissented and directed that all envelopes be readdressed personally and by hand. Respect for people and care in little things are standards that must begin in the CEO's office.

Whether an invitation, a memo, a letter, a phone call, a meeting, a report, or the reception of a visitor, every instance provides an opportunity for the president to insist that quality counts, that respect for every person is paramount, that proper decorum is always in style. A president's insistence on excellence in small things may strike some staff as persnickety but, in addition to being the right thing to do, it establishes a standard of behavior that extends into the organization and influences the actions of all. Presidents who overlook or ignore mishaps and carelessness in their own office operation may unwittingly stamp their styles as shoddy and disorganized.

Even more important than creating a standard of excellence, presidents also have the opportunity in the conduct of their office to put into practice the high ethical standards they wish for their entire organization. If a president talks openly with the staff about ways decisions can be kept from the board, the staff soon learns that this president tolerates or approves of deceit in certain instances. If the president talks disparagingly to one staff member about the other, that staff member may well wonder whether her turn will be next. Staff members who hear the president talk one way in public about the importance of key stakeholders and in the office hear him disparage these same groups necessarily must wonder about his sincerity in this or in any other matter. Presidents need to know that principles of honesty, truth telling, fairness, and respect can and must be practiced first in the executive office, with board members, deans, directors, and assistants. Then other staff will be more inclined to take the president's rhetoric seriously.

Managing Crises

What the president cannot anticipate and manage deliberately are the crises that erupt in any complex organization. Yet these spikes in the landscape of college life must be confronted and resolved if the life of the organization is to remain healthy. The disturbed student who bursts into the office unannounced, the sudden disruption of the day's calendar, the bomb threat, the screaming headline, the incipient protest, and the needed but temporarily lost files all provide vivid testimony as to how the president reacts in an extemporaneous setting. Detachment and steel nerves should not necessarily constitute the desired characteristics of presidential behavior. The super-hero approach to crisis management diminishes the important role that immediate staff can provide in contributing to the solution of unanticipated and urgent problems. The contribution can only be made when people know that crises do arise and have been schooled at least generally in the role they need to play. Fortunately, most colleges and most well-run CEO offices have established emergency procedures for bomb threats and other physical dangers, like personal threats, hazardous emissions, and ice storms. Other less defined procedures must exist so that deans know what the president expects, the secretaries understand their roles and options, and the public affairs director can respond appropriately to interested stakeholders. If the president's staff functions as a team, crises should certainly call forth team behavior. Every CEO has the responsibility for educating and preparing staff members to deal effectively as a team with any crisis.

Personal Style

In crises and in all aspects of office management, the president's personal behavior always commands attention and ultimately helps to describe the character of the president. No matter how prepared staff are to handle situations, they will still look to the president for their lead or at least will be conscious of the president's role and involvement. In all situations, CEOs should feel and act comfortably in the sense that they do not put on a face, act calculatingly, and generally play a role.

In another and more specific sense, however, presidents do play a role, and they should be comfortable with that role. People expect presidents to exhibit strength, judgment, control, and appropriate demeanor. While it is not sufficient, as one board member noted, that presidents dress, speak, and act presidentially, presidents help set the tone for their administration by their personal behavior within their offices. Courtesy, thoughtfulness, consistency, and a certain calmness and appropriate impatience all help to define the person. A sense of humor undoubtedly says that presidents understand their own mortality, see the paradoxes of life, and generally are good spirited. It is almost an axiom of management to recognize that much is forgiven those of light heart and good spirit, and, as we all know, presidents are in much need of forgiveness. The office rigors and demands are made more tolerable, even welcome, if the leader of that office exhibits a warm human touch.

To discuss the physical setting of the presidential office almost seems nitpicking in the extreme. Yet experienced presidents know that decisions about the presidential space can derail a presidency faster than a $5 million decision on a new computer system. Stakeholders in general seem to have little tolerance for the amenities of the presidential office, but this tolerance does vary from one part of the country to another. In a large urban community college on the East Coast, one president boasted a presidential suite replete with inner and outer offices, reception areas, a dining room, and a conference area. In the Northwest, very little would go unnoticed and less uncriticized in a place where the public insist their officials be humble. Presidents, wherever they are, must do their own assessment of the public's tolerance for amenities. In the larger scheme of operations, these amenities are not important, and some may prove embarrassing and even destructive. In choosing and molding a physical site, presidents should attend to more useful guidelines. First, the president's office should make sense in its location and function, and it should maximize the president's effectiveness. A reception area, a conference room, and an area for secure and confidential conversations all make sense. Second, appropriate decor should be established and maintained. While the public may wince at the oriental rug, they do expect the office to function and to look "right" for the president of the local community college. Stakeholders would like to take some pride in the office's appearance. For their part, the president's staff would very much appreciate an office location and layout that works well for them and the president.

Presidents need to make conscious, deliberate choices about the management of their offices. Such management cannot be left to custom or be taken for granted simply because the president is about "bigger" things. New presidents need to establish their styles and their values through the management of their offices; senior presidents need to evaluate whether their offices say what they want to say and whether they are constructed best to help achieve presidential goals. In the greater constellation of things, managing the president's office may be a small star. Without its light, however, the president may meander or even lose the way. We need to manage well in small things in order to be free to lead in big things.

Summary

Effective leadership and management begin in the president's office. Whether the organization is large or small, a single unit or a multicampus system, the president's responsibilities are similar in their variety and complexity. Lower-order and higher-order tasks compete for the president's time and energy. If the president is to successfully address the hierarchy of tasks, it is first necessary to attend to the organization of the president's office and to the predictable perils of poor office management.

Effective and clear delegation of responsibility to the talented officers of the organization ensures the accomplishment of tasks with appropriate accountability. Effective delegation leads in turn to the liberation of the president for those tasks that can be accomplished only by the CEO in a personal and direct manner. Within the immediate confines of the president's office itself, the president must attend to the organization of tasks, to the establishment of standards, and to the management of crisis.

References

Bennis, W. *Why Leaders Can't Lead: The Unconscious Conspiracy Continues.* San Francisco: Jossey-Bass, 1989.

Drucker, P. *Managing in Turbulent Times.* New York: Harper-Collins, 1980.

Drucker, P. "What Business Can Learn from Nonprofits." *Harvard Business Review,* 1989, *67,* 88–93.

Osborne, D., and Gaebler, T. *Reinventing Government.* New York: Addison-Wesley, 1992.

Chapter 10

Business and Financial Administration

Albert L. Lorenzo

Colleges and universities, like so many other organizations that serve the public good, are being challenged to improve performance, contain costs, and demonstrate sound stewardship of their resources. These challenges are confronting virtually all institutions of higher education and stem from the nation's need to extract greater outcomes from existing resource commitments.

Business and financial officers play a key role in meeting these challenges, since the functions under their control contribute so directly to the overall success of the institution. Moreover, business officers typically possess certain professional and technical skills not found in other educational administrators. They have also often had experience in nonacademic environments where performance standards and individual accountability are frequently more rigorous than in colleges and universities.

The primary contribution of a business administrator, however, should not be seen as simply providing technical expertise. The true test of effectiveness is how well that expertise is used in helping the institution achieve its purposes, planning for its future, and bringing about positive change.

Community colleges are complex organizations of considerable diversity in size, scope, and sources of funds. There is, however, a high degree of similarity in the way they are organized to carry out their business functions. Typically, a "cabinet-level" officer has the responsibility for all aspects of business, financial, and physical plant operations. In some larger or highly decentralized institutions, financial administration may be separated from the other aspects of business services. In either case, the senior business officer usually has direct access to and is a key adviser of the president or chancellor.

Reporting to the chief business officer will be other, somewhat specialized administrative personnel. The size and budget of the institution usually determine the overall size of the support staff and the degree of specialization each person possesses. Larger colleges not only have more staff, but evidence more specialization as well.

This chapter examines the function of community college business and financial administration. It discusses the role, expectations, and potential contributions of those individuals who choose this field as a career. It also suggests management practices designed to maximize personal effectiveness and identifies some emerging issues likely to have an impact on business officers and the colleges they serve in the decade ahead.

A Respect for Mission

Like their counterparts in other sectors, community colleges achieve their objectives by successfully combining three basic resources: human, physical, and financial. Since these resource groups are not discrete, ineffective practices in any one category will adversely affect the others and will ultimately restrict the ability of the organization to achieve its purpose. The critical interrelationship between sound business practices and the ability of an organization to fulfill its mission can be illustrated, in a somewhat humorous fashion, by recounting a conversation that occurred during a hospital board of directors' budget meeting.

A combination of restricted third-party payments and rapidly increasing operating costs had placed the budget forecast into a deficit situation. Still, the head of the religious order that owned the hospital expressed a strong desire to continue providing health care for the poor at no cost. To emphasize her point, she reminded members of the board that an essential component of the hospital's mission, for more than a century of service to the community, was to care for the indigent. She insisted that the pursuit of that mission had to continue regardless of the financial consequences. Finally, in an act of respect and desperation, the treasurer of the hospital countered by saying that everyone understood the importance of that mission but that there was another principle the board needed to remember — no margin, no mission!

Individuals who move into business and financial administration at institutions of higher education will have to continually strive to achieve a proper balance between margin and mission. To do that, business officers must be conversant with the organization's purposes. This knowledge is deemed so important that the introductory section of *College and University Business Administration*, published by the National Association of College and University Business Officers (1982, p. 1:1), states that a "clear understanding of the academic enterprise and a dedication to its mission are fundamental to service as an educational manager."

In most states, the mission of public community colleges was originally envisioned to be financed by a combination of funds coming from the state, the students, and the local community. In recent years, however, the trend has been for states to pick up an increasingly larger share of support. Considerable variation in support patterns within a state may also exist. In Michigan, for example, state aid to the twenty-nine public community colleges for 1989–90 accounted for as much as 64 percent of the total operating budget of one institution and as little as 21 percent at another. Tuition and fees were more uniform, contributing from 15 to 40 percent of operating funds. On the other hand, local property taxes had the widest variation, ranging from a high of 61 percent to a low of only 4 percent of general fund revenue (Michigan State Board of Education, 1991).

Variations in support patterns can cause the same event to have a dramatically different economic impact at different institutions. A 5 percent across-the-board reduction in state funding will translate into a loss of 3.2 percent in overall revenue for an institution receiving 64 percent of its funding from the state. For a college receiving only 21 percent of its support from the state, a 5 percent cut reduces total revenue by just 1.05 percent. Likewise, a 20 percent property tax rollback initiative would reduce operating revenue by 12.2 percent at one Michigan community college and eliminate only 0.8 percent at another. While business officers will need to be alert to potential changes in all sources of revenue, they need to be particularly sensitive to those issues affecting the largest component.

Evolution of the Profession

As critical as the role of collegiate business officers is today, business and financial management as a professional field is a relatively recent development. The accompanying professional literature is of similarly recent origins. Leslie (1987) points out that when the first edition of *College and University Business Administration* (CUBA) was published by the American Council on Education in 1952, the field of financial administration had not yet developed a separate identity. It was not until the third edition was published in 1974 that specialists in the field took charge of the process.

With regard to the recency of literature in the field, Leslie goes on to point out that the second edition of CUBA, published in 1955, listed fewer than a dozen references more than five years old in a bibliography of sixty pages. Since that time, the number of published works relating to senior institutions, but not to community colleges, has increased.

Few articles about business and financial practices in community colleges ever appear in higher education publications, and even fewer are written about business officials themselves. Palmer (1985, p. 117) notes that "of the thousands of documents processed by the ERIC Clearinghouse for Junior Colleges since 1966, fewer than twenty deal with these important members of the administrative team." Academics and practitioners alike should rectify this condition.

The mounting fiscal problems of the past decade have focused increased attention on campus business affairs and on the corresponding need to upgrade knowledge about business and financial management practices. There also is a growing tendency for colleges to recruit candidates with formal academic preparation and/or actual experience in business and financial areas. These two trends, coupled with a strengthening national association, have enhanced the professional status of community college business administrators. Campbell (1985) characterizes this transition as a shift from an independent record keeper to a valued member of an entrepreneurial team. In that new capacity, the professional business administrator is required to perform in two essential roles: as a highly skilled operational manager and as a strategic thinker and planner.

Managing the Basics

Noted management scientist Peter Drucker (1980) anticipated the turbulent times that would confront most American organizations. He cautioned that during this difficult period the fundamentals would have to be managed, and managed well. He also argued that the fundamentals themselves do not change, but the specifics to manage them can change as a result of changes in internal and external conditions.

Competent business and fiscal management has often been identified as a basic requirement for institutional success, and poor business practices almost always produce less than optimum results. Consequently, the first expectation of a collegiate business officer is to develop and maintain a sound underlying system of business and financial practices.

In a typical community college environment, basic business and financial functions include accounting and cash management; payroll; budgeting and financial planning; management information systems; purchasing and inventory control; safety, security, and law enforcement; audit and legal services; insurance and risk management; physical plant planning and operation; and auxiliary enterprises. Some structures may also include personnel and human resource administration.

Since the majority of these functions parallel those performed in private sector organizations, the question often arises as to whether private sector practices can be applied to nonprofit colleges and universities. The general consensus of both public and private sector experts is that, for the most part, they can.

Doescher (1986) contends that much like the managers of a private business, college administrators have to meet budgets, build and maintain a physical plant, and maintain a good working relationship with the people who work in the organization. Like leaders in industry, educators must develop enlightened policies and conform to many externally imposed regulatory requirements. He concludes that despite their differences, colleges must apply the management principles of successful businesses.

Morrell (1988) says that any argument that profit-driven business practices are not appropriate at not-for-profit institutions is invalid. Both are responsible for making effective use of assets, and both must find ways to reinvest in the organization. He also observes that many educational institutions have been forced to act more like commercial enterprises in recent years as resources have become tighter and as competition for students and outside funding has become more intense.

One notable difference between the public and private sectors is in the requirements of the accounting system. Public colleges and universities, like municipal corporations, are required by law to maintain a "fund accounting" system. The primary distinction is that a fund accounting system limits the use of resources and prohibits the commingling of funds.

A private corporation can use operating revenue, borrowed funds, or bonded debt quite freely. A college may not. Revenue raised from the sale of capital bonds can only be used for capital projects, and endowment contributions, like financial aid funds, can only be used for their stated purposes. People on campus sometimes do not realize this and do not understand that certain funds must be used only for certain projects.

Faculty, for example, may find it difficult to understand why there is no money to purchase equipment for existing classrooms when office furniture for a new building is being ordered. Worse yet, the entire staff well may question why an appropriate salary adjustment is out of the question when the college is in the process of remodeling a building or repaving a parking lot.

Financial administrators must work to achieve internal understanding of the limits that flow from a fund accounting system. If people are unable to comprehend the technical arguments, then understanding must flow from a broader level of personal trust. Sometimes it may be helpful to have someone from outside the organization present the explanation, such as a member of the college's auditing firm.

Among the functions routinely performed by business officers, by far the one most visible to the campus community is budgeting. This function impacts and involves every department of the institution. It is also the one that has the greatest potential to create controversy and disappointment, since opportunities generally outpace resources on the majority of college campuses.

All too often, budgeting is mistakenly used as a planning process. In reality, the budget should be a way to implement plans that have been formulated through the governance process. At a minimum, budget allocations should support the strategic goals of the institution (Lorenzo, 1983) and may go so far as to reflect the underlying values of the organization (McClenney and Chaffee, 1985).

Although developing a budget is a requirement for every institution, the techniques used to prepare the budget can vary considerably. Caruthers and Orwig (1979) provide a good description of the budgeting processes in the unique environment of higher education. They discuss five alternative techniques used by colleges and universities to build a budget, which are identified as incremental, formula, program planning budgeting system (PPBS), zero-based budgeting (ZBB), and performance budgeting.

Collegiate business administrators need to be familiar with the techniques and applications of alternative budgeting methods. Then, working with other members of the leadership team, they should select one (or aspects of more than one) that best fits the situation and culture of the organization. In the final analysis, however, people—not formulas or computers—will make decisions. As a result, such things as political considerations or personal biases are likely to impact even the most technical budgeting and financial forecasting system.

Strategic Dimensions

In most cases, the opportunity for business and financial administrators to make a strategic contribution to the organization will be determined by how well the basics are managed. For example, it will be difficult for campus colleagues to believe that strategic forecasts are accurate if the monthly expenditure reports they receive are frequently inaccurate. In short, strategic credibility will be influenced by operational competency. Given what is expected to affect community colleges in the decade of the 1990s and beyond, business and financial administrators are in a good position to make strategic contributions in the following areas.

Assessing Institutional Effectiveness

One of the major changes characterizing the decade of the 1980s in America was an intensified, almost obsessive concern for quality. As this concern spread to the educational system, administrators at all academic levels began to develop strategies for assessing and improving the quality of their institutions.

The quality improvement efforts at our nation's community colleges have been popularized under the heading of "institutional effectiveness." The term has become an umbrella that encompasses a host of related concepts, including accountability, student outcomes, assessment, and various measures of efficiency and vitality (Kreider, 1988).

Since the concept of institutional effectiveness is relatively new, there are very few well researched practices to use as guidelines. Furthermore, although organizational assessment is moving more in the direction of a requirement, individual institutions are generally permitted to determine their own methods for demonstrating effectiveness.

Efforts to determine institutional effectiveness are built on a foundation of quantitatively measuring outcomes. This is an area where business and financial administrators can lend their expertise. Even though their experience may be limited to business affairs, many of the principles involved in financial analysis can be adapted to assessing other aspects of institutional performance.

Since accurate and readily available data are critical to assessing effectiveness, those business officials who oversee the college's management information systems are even better positioned to help the effectiveness effort. One specific contribution is to ensure congruence between the indicators selected for measurement and the data elements that are maintained in the management information systems data base.

In the absence of a specific institutional assessment plan, the data base can be constructed around the general requirements of other effectiveness systems. For example, the Accountability Task Force (1990) created by the California Community College Assembly Bill 1725 developed a model to provide information that would facilitate the assessment of community colleges' educational and fiscal effectiveness.

The model contains five major components: (1) student access, measured in terms of actual student enrollment and participation rates as well as by programs that promote access; (2) student success, measured in terms of academic standards, course completions, and so on; (3) student satisfaction, assessed by surveys of students; (4) staff composition, reflective of the state's population diversity; and (5) fiscal condition, involving comprehensive reporting on revenues, expenditures, resource allocations, and various cost statistics.

Pursuing Alternative Funding

The restrictions now being experienced in the growth of traditional revenue will almost certainly continue in the years ahead. At the same time, the demand for services being placed on most community colleges continues to increase. If additional services are to be provided, some of the programmatic support will need to come from nontraditional sources.

One alternative is collaboration. Americans have historically prided themselves on their ability to "go it alone." That philosophy has carried over into the cultures of many American organizations. The result has often been an attempt to be a singular supplier of goods and services. But in the years ahead, as resource scarcity grows, independence will begin to give way to interdependence.

Collaborative efforts are not new to community colleges. There are countless examples of partnerships being formed with business, industry, labor, government, and other educational providers. But most of those partnerships have occurred at the periphery of the institution. In the years to come, collaboration will have to move closer to the core.

Business officers should look for opportunities to encourage collaborative efforts. Their many external contacts may put them in touch with potential partners for the institution. They should also look for opportunities to nurture internal partnerships. The budget process provides an overview of the entire institution and a way to identify similarities in programs and services that could be merged with synergistic results.

Encouraging Entrepreneurship

As not-for-profit organizations, the majority of community college programs are designed to function with financial subsidies. As a result, few activities are expected to earn their own way. But in reality, there are many services that have the potential to stand on their own in the marketplace.

For example, many colleges now offer customized learning experiences on a cost-recovery or cost-plus basis. Quality offerings that are fairly priced have strong market potential. The same is true for other specialty services. Another opportunity for entrepreneurship is in the sale of surplus capacity. This can range from rental of unused facilities and excess computer time to complicated land-lease arrangements. Unfortunately, the idea of generating a profit can run contrary to the culture of some institutions.

Brightman (1989) argues that the growth in entrepreneurial spirit in nonprofit organizations is a proper response to reduced public support for social services and the failure of private philanthropy to fill the void. He concedes that for-profit ventures can be risky, but if properly investigated they hold no less promise for community colleges than for other nonprofit organizations. A key to making wise choices is to remember that the purpose of the venture is to make a profit that will be used to help support educational activities; it is not an end in itself.

Reallocating Resources

If serving new needs cannot be financed by new increments of revenue, the institution can always fund the activities by reallocating existing dollars. In that way, the institution attempts to put all resources to their highest and best use. At most colleges, however, that is easier said than done.

Most mature community colleges have a well-defined and commonly understood governance process in place. Typically, that process is based on the principle of participation in decision making. While collegiality has proven to work quite well for approving new requests, it often breaks down when it comes to the need for retrenchment and reallocation. Individuals usually prefer to avoid being part of a process that may bring harm to a colleague.

Reallocation processes enjoy a better chance for internal support when they are based on sound data and analysis and are designed to move the institution forward, not simply to cut costs. Kotler and Fox (1985) suggest that successful redistribution efforts will cause the institution to focus its financial and other resources on programs that further its mission, build on its strengths, and meet identifiable target markets. They propose an "academic portfolio model" in which offerings are evaluated on (1) centrality to the school's mission, (2) the quality of the program, and (3) market viability. Programs are then ranked as high, medium, or low on each dimension.

Hyatt and Santiago (1984) studied retrenchment efforts of community colleges and universities under severe political, economic, and time pressures. They identified four components that characterized the most effective reallocation processes: some form of constituent involvement in the reallocation decision, preliminary reassessment of institutional role and mission, focusing on the quality of academic and support programs, and considering long-term versus short-term costs and benefits.

Shaping Public Policy

Experience shows that community college business administrators are second only to their chief executive officers in terms of their role in shaping public policy. This is probably due to the fact that the majority of state and federal legislative actions relate to funding.

Typically, state funding policies for higher education have two central themes: funding enrollment and equalizing revenue on a per-student basis. However, as the proportion of total funds coming from the state has increased, so has the complexity of funding practices. Wattenbarger and Starnes (1976) list four typical models for state support to higher education: negotiated budget, unit-rate formula, minimum foundation, and cost-based program funding. Of these, the most frequently used is formula funding. This is especially true for community colleges, where the formula approach is applied in more than two-thirds of the states (Wattenbarger and Mercer, 1985).

One drawback of the formula approach is the difficulty this method has in recognizing institutional differences. Community colleges were intended to reflect the communities they serve. As our nation's communities become more demographically, politically, economically, and ethnically diverse, so should the colleges that serve them. Funding formulas, however, typically reflect statewide averages or conditions, and as such, have difficulty supporting local situations.

As business officers work to influence public policy, they should view themselves as champions of the community college mission as well as representatives of a particular institution. They should also remember that, under ideal circumstances, the state funding process should result in all colleges being equally able to fulfill their mission and in all students being equally supported in their learning environment. Although this is a laudable goal, Cohen and Brawer (1989) point out that it is highly unlikely that absolute parity will ever be achieved.

Promoting Institutional Balance

It is not uncommon for organizations to simultaneously harbor a number of legitimate, yet somewhat contradictory, preferences. While operating toward either extreme may be acceptable, positions that strive for balance will generally result in greater harmony and overall effectiveness. Community college business and financial administrators, as part of the senior management team, should continually do their best to promote a strategic balance between a number of these competing alternatives.

Comprehensiveness and Quality

In times of limited resources, community colleges will have to choose between alternative strategies of getting bigger or getting better. There will likely be strong support for both. Pursuing comprehensiveness will steer the institution in the direction of stretching to serve unmet community needs. Advocating quality may require abandoning some things in order to do other things well.

The comprehensiveness-quality conflict becomes central whenever budget reductions are required. Across-the-board cuts usually favor comprehensiveness. Programmatic elimination tends to favor quality. During times of retrenchment, business and financial administrators can be extremely influential in striking a proper balance between the two.

Efficiency and Effectiveness

Closely related to the comprehensiveness-quality conflict is the issue of efficiency versus effectiveness. There is more than a semantic difference between these two terms. Efficiency calls for the organization to place lowest cost ahead of greatest outcome.

Effectiveness implies striving for maximum results regardless of cost. Clearly neither extreme is defensible in higher education.

Romano (1986) notes that in judging the appropriateness of public policy, economists employ the dual criteria of efficiency and equity. He states that, in their context, efficiency is not solely concerned with lowest cost but is interpreted by economists as a measure of how well society's scarce resources are allocated to achieve social benefit. Applying this concept to the community college would suggest that the institution should approve those options that produce the greatest mission-related benefits per unit of financial investment.

Service and Control

Empowerment is praised as a management virtue in most of today's organizational success literature. However, the same empowerment that can lead to high performance in one setting can bring chaos in another. The difference lies in the ability of the leadership team to create a sense of common purpose and to set limits that are not stifling.

Since business officers administer the final phases of critical institutional transactions, such as purchasing and payroll, they tend to feel as though they are in control of the actual decisions that initiated those processes. The fact that financial managers are subject to frequent internal and external audits enhances their feelings of ultimate responsibility and authority.

Business and financial administrators must learn to separate their true responsibility for adhering to formal policy and mandated practice from the valid authority of line managers to make their own operating decisions. Business officers need to strike the proper balance between service and control. Waterman (1987) urges organizations to treat facts as friends and financial controls as liberating. This is the kind of attitude that should be encouraged among all business office staff.

Tradition and Innovation

Tradition in an organization provides for stability. Innovation promotes vitality. Most organizations need both. Through their role in developing institutional budgets, business officers can help the college achieve a proper balance between the two.

The budget narrative can demonstrate a respect for tradition by emphasizing decisions that continue or increase support for past programs. It can also highlight areas of new investment and present ways they are helping the institution adapt to the changing environment. In the event that a traditional program is being eliminated or reduced while a new project is being funded, care should be taken to avoid the tendency to pair any unrelated decisions, making them appear to be trade-offs when, in fact, they are not.

Politics and Principle

Successful organizations will typically evidence a regard for fair and objective decision-making principles, and publicly supported institutions must also respect the political environment of which they are a part. Once again, the potential for conflict exists. In this case, how these two forces are reconciled will be strictly situational. It is likely that organizational culture and community attitudes will have a strong influence on the balance finally achieved.

The conflict between politics and principle in an organization may be a cause of great personal discomfort. Few people will find it easy to put politics ahead of their own personal beliefs, and ideally, no one should have to do so. At the same time, not all values are shared, and absent an illegal act, no one set of values has absolute primacy. Collegiate business officers will find their profession most rewarding in an environment where personal and organizational attitudes with respect to politics and principles are congruent.

Emerging Issues

Business and financial administrators at community colleges will increasingly be asked to assist their institutions as they confront some unfamiliar challenges. One of these challenges is aging infrastructure. Unlike their university counterparts, the majority of buildings on community college campuses are less than a quarter century old. As a result, most of the emphasis in physical plant planning has been on new construction. But as facilities age and enrollments stabilize, the focus of capital projects will shift to repair, remodeling, and renovation.

This change of emphasis will require rethinking many conventional strategies. For example, requests for capital funds, whether presented to the legislature for direct appropriations or to the community for an approval of a bond proposal, have traditionally been for new projects. It was easy to demonstrate how approving new money would result in new opportunity for students and the community. But in the future, new money will not as frequently produce something visibly new. Those colleges anticipating the need to shift the majority of capital spending to repairs and renovations should begin to plant the seeds of change early in the process.

Another issue likely to surface in the years ahead is a reassessment of the proportionate share of total cost to be borne by each of the community colleges' financial partners. It is fair to speculate that very few people in the 1960s anticipated the enrollment potential of community colleges, yet that is the era when most state financing plans were conceived. In three decades, the colleges have gone from serving about one million to enrolling nearly six million students. The question now is whether the colleges' financial partners are still willing and able to support this greatly expanded level of activity.

Most states were coping with serious budget deficits in fiscal 1992. Many of those were forced to restrict or reduce appropriations to community colleges. In Michigan, for example, enrollment growth has not been fully funded since the mid 1980s, and the current state allocation formula is over $40 million underfunded.

McPherson, Schapiro, and Winston (1989) concluded that changes in government funding levels have significant effects on tuition, expenditures, and resource allocations in higher education. Their study showed that colleges and universities appear to respond to reductions in government support by slowing their rates of growth and increasing the share of costs borne by tuition. The study also showed that increases in posted tuition charges have generally outpaced increases in consumer prices since the late 1970s.

A more recent trend has been increasing taxpayer unrest. Tax limitation proposals have appeared on the ballot in several states, and colleges that must seek voter approval for local tax support are experiencing higher failure rates. Taxpayers defend their decisions by expressing concern over their ability to meet their own needs, much less someone else's. They argue that those who will directly benefit from a college education should be asked to pay for it.

These shifts in attitudes, abilities, and policies will lead to a reexamination of how the costs of higher education should be shared. States will have to decide if they will continue to support the open-door philosophy of the community college. Communities must decide where their local college fits within their overall list of tax-supported priorities. And institutions will have to decide if there is an upper limit on the amount of tuition they can charge in light of their marketplace and their mission.

If resource pressures intensify, they likely will lead to a much broader reexamination of the role and purpose of community colleges themselves. Jacobson (1991) suggests that institutions faced with declining support will ultimately face trade-offs between student access and academic quality. He reports that even now, leaders at many institutions—both public and private—feel that they are headed for a probing reassessment and realignment of what they can or should be.

The Pew Higher Education Research Program (1991a) suggests any discussion of institutional redefinition should be preceded by asking three questions relative to role and purpose. These questions can be adapted for use by community colleges as follows:

1. What are community colleges expected to deliver and to whom?
2. What difference should a community college education make in the lives of its students who receive a degree or certificate?

3.　How much responsibility should community colleges have for maintaining social fabric, securing economic well-being, preserving history and culture, and strengthening social attitudes and beliefs?

Related to the issue of redefinition are the ongoing need for institutional renewal and the challenge of maintaining organizational vitality and viability. Bowen (1980) resolved that the costs of higher education are determined by a combination of both societal and institutional factors. The same factors will also contribute to other aspects of organizational climate. One element that serves as a foundation for continued internal and external support is clarity of purpose.

Those working within community colleges, as well as the people living in their service areas, must come to share a common understanding of why the institutions exist and how they are different from other educational providers. In times of resource scarcity, duplication and relevance will be key questions of common concern.

Quality is another area of public concern. Colleges must strive for continuous improvement so that their offerings will have continuing value. Institutions should not assume that quality improvement programs are incompatible with cost containment efforts. The Pew Higher Education Research Program (1991b) cites a report released by the University of Michigan in which a task force concluded that, in many areas of the university's operations, there is an inverse relationship between cost and quality. They became convinced that cost containment, and even cost reduction, can go hand in hand with quality improvement.

To remain viable, colleges must also demonstrate sound stewardship of their resources. Too many public figures have fallen from grace, and the level of trust in public institutions is declining. Business officers, in particular, will need to exhibit the highest ethical standards in performing their duties.

Finally, community colleges must strive for greater understanding of their contribution to society. Doucette and Roueche (1991) observe that community colleges are still struggling for respect in a world that too often provides only lip service to the democratic ideals of access and egalitarianism that these institutions represent. They point to an article in *U.S. News and World Report* that observed that policy decisions in several states were "pushing many economically disadvantaged students into the weakest four-year state schools and into community colleges, where it's often difficult to get a decent education" (Toch, 1991, p. 50). These perceptions must be changed if community colleges expect to benefit from public support in the years ahead.

Summary

Business and financial administrators perform a valuable role in community colleges and have the potential to make significant contributions to advancing the institutions they serve. Their unique skills and abilities round out the leadership team. They oversee the resource base of the college and maintain a network of contacts inside and outside the institution.

The most visible of the business officer's functions is budgeting, because it involves and impacts every department of the school. Often budgeting is mistakenly used as a planning process, instead of as a way to implement plans that have already been formulated through the governance process. Beyond mere funds allocation, however, the business administration has the opportunity to explore alternative funding sources, creatively redistribute existing funds, and determine when the most cost-effective methods should be discarded for methods that more effectively reach the goals of the college.

Though the financial administrators have a great impact on the community they serve, how much of a difference they make will be determined, to a large extent, by how well they understand and how deeply they are committed to the mission of the community college.

References

Accountability Task Force. *California Community College Accountability Model.* Sacramento: Office of the Chancellor, California Community Colleges, 1990.

Bowen, H. R. *The Costs of Higher Education: How Much Do Colleges and Universities Spend Per Student and How Much Should They Spend?* San Francisco: Jossey-Bass, 1980.

Brightman, R. W. "Entrepreneurship in the Community College: Revenue Diversification." In J. L. Catanzaro and A. Arnold (eds.), *Alternative Funding Sources.* New Directions for Community Colleges, no. 68. San Francisco: Jossey-Bass, 1989.

Campbell, D. F. (ed.). *Strengthening Financial Management.* New Directions for Community Colleges, no. 50. San Francisco: Jossey-Bass, 1985.

Caruthers, J., and Orwig, M. *Budgeting in Higher Education.* AAHE-ERIC Higher Education Research Report, no. 3. Washington, D.C.: American Association for Higher Education, 1979.

Cohen, A. M., and Brawer, F. B. *The American Community College.* (2nd ed.) San Francisco: Jossey-Bass, 1989.

Doescher, W. F. "Running a College Like a Business." *D & B Reports.* New York: Dunn & Bradstreet, 1986.

Doucette, D., and Roueche, J. "Arguments with Which to Combat Elitism and Ignorance About Community Colleges." *Leadership Abstracts,* 1991, *4*(13), 1-2.

Drucker, P. *Managing in Turbulent Times.* New York: Harper-Collins, 1980.

Hyatt, J. A., and Santiago, A. A. *Reallocation: Strategies for Effective Resource Management.* Washington, D.C.: National Association of Colleges and University Business Officers, 1984.

Jacobson, R. L. "Academic Leaders Predict Major Changes for Higher Education in Recession's Wake." *Chronicle of Higher Education,* Nov. 20, 1991, p. 1.

Kotler, P., and Fox, K. *Strategic Marketing for Educational Institutions.* Englewood Cliffs, N.J.: Prentice-Hall, 1985.

Kreider, P. E. "Institutional Learning and Effectiveness." *Leadership Abstracts,* 1988, *1*(19), 1-2.

Leslie, L. "Financial Management and Resource Allocation." In M. W. Peterson and L. A. Mets (eds.), *Key Resources on Higher Education Governance, Management, and Leadership: A Guide to the Literature.* San Francisco: Jossey-Bass, 1987.

Lorenzo, A. L. "Strategic Elements of Financial Management." In G. A. Myran (ed.), *Strategic Management in the Community College.* New Directions for Community Colleges, no. 44. San Francisco: Jossey-Bass, 1983.

McClenney, B., and Chaffee, E. "Integrating Academic Planning and Budgeting." In D. F. Campbell (ed.), *Strengthening Financial Management.* New Directions for Community Colleges, no. 50. San Francisco: Jossey-Bass, 1985.

McPherson, M. S., Schapiro, M. O., and Winston, G. C. "Recent Trends in U.S. Higher Education Costs and Prices." *American Economic Review,* 1989, *79*(2), 253–257.

Michigan State Board of Education. *Activity Classification Structure Data Book.* Lansing: Michigan Department of Education, 1991.

Morrell, L. R. "How Should a University Mind Its Business?" *Management Issues.* New York: Peat Marwick Main and Co., 1988.

National Association of College and University Business Officers. *College and University Business Administration.* (4th ed.) Washington, D.C.: National Association of College and University Business Officers, 1982.

Palmer, J. "Sources and Information: Financial Management at the Community College." In D. F. Campbell (ed.), *Strengthening Financial Management.* New Directions for Community Colleges, no. 50. San Francisco: Jossey-Bass, 1985.

Pew Higher Education Research Program. "An End to Sanctuary." *Policy Perspectives,* 1991a, *3*(4).

Pew Higher Education Research Program. "The Other Side of the Mountain." *Policy Perspectives,* 1991b, *3*(2).

Romano, R. M. "An Economic Perspective on Public Financing of the Community College." *Community College Review,* 1986, *14*(2), 8–13.

Toch, T. "The Great Tumble: Education Is Becoming More Stratified by Class." *U.S. News & World Report,* June 3, 1991, p. 50.

Waterman, R. H., Jr. *The Renewal Factor.* New York: Bantam Books, 1987.

Wattenbarger, J. L., and Mercer, S. L. *Financing Community Colleges.* Gainesville: Institute for Higher Education, University of Florida, 1985.

Wattenbarger, J. L., and Starnes, P. M. *Financial Support Patterns for Community Colleges.* Gainesville: University of Florida, 1976.

Chapter 11

The Personnel Office

Barbara E. Janzen

Although a well-functioning personnel office is essential for college operations, little has been written on the practical workings and issues of that office. This chapter focuses on the functions and staffing of the office, as well as on management issues that pertain to personnel.

Functions of a Community College Personnel Office

While the personnel office carries out various duties depending on the size and structure of the institution, most community college personnel offices are responsible for initiating and maintaining personnel records, supervising employee insurance, hiring nonfaculty (classified) employees, overseeing employee labor relations, and carrying out affirmative action procedures. Some also supervise payroll, but this is not standard procedure, since it is not considered good practice to have the department that initiates employment action also generate payment of salary.

Kathleen Alfano provided information about personnel offices that is pertinent to this chapter.

The following issues are important for every community college personnel office. Attention and diligence in these areas will help prevent problems with dissatisfied employees and legal complications.

Maintaining Personnel Files

Excellent recordkeeping is an important function of the personnel office. For legal reasons, it is imperative that records be accurate and current. Traditionally, individual file folders stuffed with applications, personal and educational profiles, documents on insurance coverage, performance evaluations, and other information have made up a personnel record. A newer approach, in use at many larger institutions, is an automated system of recordkeeping. In this system, the personnel record is just one of several kinds of data modules, linked via integrated computer software into a comprehensive management system (Midkiff and Come, 1988). This saves time, since office staff now press a computer key rather than riffle through drawers full of file folders to find a document. It also saves space usually taken up with filing cabinets.

Hiring Employees

The staff of the personnel office initiates and monitors the procedures for selecting a new employee. One dean of human resources said the most important thing in having a successful personnel program is choosing appropriate people for the job. Matching the best person with each open position should be a high priority. The individual departments will usually notify the personnel office of their need for a new employee and provide a job description. The staff will then place the job announcement in journals and newspapers and make it available by whatever other means is normal for reaching the pool of people that will be looking for that kind of job. When the job applications begin to come back, the office staff will process the applications, provide initial screening of applicants (such as administering basic skills tests for classified positions), and develop a list of qualified applicants to send to department supervisors for interviews and further testing.

For faculty hiring, the procedure is much the same, except that the decision to hire a new faculty member involves more people. Often the hiring committee is made up of existing faculty and some administrators, and often the president will take part in the interview process.

When screening applicants, it might also be a good idea to analyze their likes and dislikes. Would they rather work with paper or people? Figures or words? Do they like operating within fixed procedures or finding creative solutions? Are they motivated by filling the needs of other people, or by completing a task? Do they work better if constantly supervised or occasionally supervised? Do they work better under pressure, or do deadlines make them so nervous that they cannot do their work well? If the department issuing the request for an employee provided the screening personnel with a description of the job in these terms (simply describing the position as "assistant" is not much help), it would eliminate wasted time and paperwork in the selection process. Sometimes applicants for a particular job would be best directed to a different position for which they are equally qualified and better suited.

A labor pool community colleges do not often utilize is the student body. Consider the advantages: they already know their way around the school; they have flexible hours; they are willing to work part time and usually for lower wages; it gives the students a feeling of ownership in the school.

Carrying Out Affirmative Action Procedures

An important way to make sure that affirmative action principles are being carried out is to ensure that when a job position opens up, the position is evaluated to see how diverse the pool of available applicants is from which to draw. Are both genders and various ethnicities represented? Is this a job that someone with a disability could perform as well as someone without a disability? Is there a wide age span in the pool of possible applicants? If the answers to these questions are unsatisfactory, the office should broaden the range of people to whom it an-

nounces the job position. Whenever applicants are not chosen
for a position, it is imperative to keep their applications on file
and to document exactly why they were not chosen for the job.
This will be necessary if the college is ever charged with discrimination in a lawsuit.

But affirmative action goes far beyond regulating discrimination in employment. It includes whatever employers do to
ensure that current practices enhance the employment, upgrading, and retention of members of protected groups (Glueck,
1982). In large urban centers, community colleges have shown
strong commitment to this; rural schools have held to this philo-
sophically, but, according to Kaiser and Greer (1988), have
taken little action to recruit qualified women and minorities.
The personnel director must stay aware of the new legislation
and political climate surrounding affirmative action.

Keeping in Touch with Other Offices

While the communication between the personnel office and other
administrative offices is usually informal, it is an important way
for the personnel director to gather and disseminate information pertinent to personnel. The director is normally in daily
contact with the Instructional Office, Student Services, Public
Information, and Governmental Relations. Often there are also
weekly or biweekly meetings for all the department heads and
faculty leadership, which are also important sources of information on future staffing needs and other issues relating to personnel management, like recent board decisions that affect personnel, new laws, upcoming retirements, and matters of budget.

Handling Grievances

As someone once quipped, the only problem with personnel is
the people. Conflicts between people will arise, whether between
employer and employee or between two employees. Remedies
to handle these problems include the function of an ombuds-
man, college psychological services, or a mediation service. Some
schools also refer employees to outside consultants.

According to Lee (1989), grievance procedures do several

things. First, they are useful in identifying policies and practices that permit inconsistencies and biases toward employees. Forcing each level of the decision process to justify and document its recommendation generally improves the fairness of the outcome. Next, they allow complaining parties to blow off steam and have a group of people listen to their problems, which often deters litigation. Finally, the formal procedures remind administrators, faculty, and staff that their responsibilities must be taken seriously and approached professionally.

Biles and Tuckman (1986, p. 104) recommend the following as basic underlying philosophies for grievance procedures:

- The basic objective of a grievance procedure is to achieve fair and sound settlements. It should not be to set one side against the other with the attitude of winner take all, nor should the process be thought of as zero sum.
- Grievances should be considered as an aid in the process of discovering and removing causes of discontentment.
- The willingness of an institution to devote the necessary time and attention to handling disposition of grievances is crucial to the effective functioning of the process.

The grievance system implemented will vary depending on whether the cases involve classified employees or faculty and whether they belong to a union or not. The systems used will also need to take into account the institution's mission, goals, norms, and ways of operating.

Suggested evaluative questions for the grievance procedure include the following:

- What proportion of decisions are appealed? If it is substantial, does this suggest that whatever initial grievance mechanism exists is ineffective?
- Does the grievance procedure effectively identify weaknesses in the institution's decision-making practices? Have these weaknesses been resolved?

- Is every conflict resolved in the same way? If so, have the employees felt inappropriately dealt with in any situation? (adapted from Lee, 1989, p. 159)

Because laws and situations are constantly changing, grievance procedures should be periodically evaluated (perhaps yearly) to see if the process still reflects its underlying philosophies and to guarantee that the system is carrying out its function in the most efficient way. The astute personnel officer will respond to grievances promptly; disgruntled people are not placated when their complaints appear to be ignored.

Staffing a Personnel Office

A personnel program will be successful only if the staff in the personnel office are skilled, committed workers who have as their main concern the best interests of the employees. The staffing of a personnel office depends on which of the above functions the chancellor, superintendent, or board of trustees have assigned to the office and varies according to how many employees the office serves. The average community college personnel office has at least one management position, often called the director of personnel. This person will usually have a bachelor's degree in either public administration, human relations/resources, or business administration, and three to four years of personnel experience either as a personnel analyst or as a director of personnel.

If the personnel office must handle several hundred or more employees, there is often another manager, who may have a position higher than the director of personnel, such as dean of human resources. Both the affirmative action and labor relations function are considered specialist positions and are usually filled by professional-level employees whose background or degrees give them the ability to facilitate those functions.

Many governmental agency personnel offices have one or more personnel analyst positions, and some community colleges have begun to hire people for this position. This is a professional position requiring a bachelor's degree. The personnel analyst's duties include conducting salary surveys and classification studies as well as writing policy. Since many community colleges cannot afford a full-time analyst position, the directors of personnel will often delegate the data gathering part of an analyst's function to a personnel clerk and then do all the analysis and policy writing themselves. Clerks perform the rest of the functions of a personnel office, such as receiving applications and signing up new employees for benefits and payroll. They should have excellent clerical skills because of the volume of information they must handle. They should also be detail oriented and able to keep things confidential. The clerks should be good with people, since they will likely be the ones in the office who deal with the general public.

It is an advantage to have a staff that can do a good job in several areas of office operations. When things get busy in one area (like hiring, at the beginning of the year), more staff can be assigned to that task.

Legal Issues

In past years, the personnel director usually had a background in the humanities, and the functions of the office emphasized employee work conditions. Increasingly, however, legal issues have become important. Community college personnel managers usually spend at least 25 percent of their time on legal issues. They are usually the chief contact for the college with its attorneys. Within the college or district, the personnel manager must monitor all new and pending personnel actions. If an appeal of a personnel decision is initiated, the personnel manager will usually give the plaintiff a copy of the Education Code and the district or Title V procedure for filing an appeal. It is very important that the personnel manager is aware of the laws and precedents being set in personnel cases.

There are formal and informal ways in which the community college districts and their colleges are notified about pending or imminent legislation. Informal information sources include professional publications and organizations, like the regional meetings of community college personnel managers and the ties between the college and the district's administrators and lawyers. Also, some major law firms circulate a regular newsletter related to personnel law that community college personnel managers find useful.

Formal notification of a new law comes either from the state chancellor's office, from another stage agency, or from the appropriate federal agency. When formal notification is sent to the district's office of personnel, the supervisor evaluates the impact of the regulation on three areas:

1. *Contract implications.* Does this require a change in one or more union contracts? If so, notice of the new law is sent to the district's negotiating team members.
2. *Board of trustees notification.* The board of trustees are notified of the new legislation and any effects it may have on board policy. After board review, the personnel office then puts any new policy in the board policy manual.
3. *Review of general manual updating.* Whenever any new law takes effect, the head of personnel reviews and updates all personnel manuals, contracts, and personnel procedures. Updates are sent to each appropriate campus administrator who will be affected.

For example, recently a new federal law was enacted, granting employees the right to family leave. Personnel supervisors learned about the debate and approval on family leave informally through newspapers and immediately began reviewing what impact it would have in their districts. In the Ventura County Community College District in California, the new law required changes in all three union contracts (those of faculty, administrators, and classified employees), the board policy and managers' policy manuals had to be changed, and the regulations for the classified employees' merit system needed to be modified (P. Marchioni, personal communication, 1993).

Another legal issue to be considered is the problem of staff reductions; institutions should plan ahead to avoid the legal difficulties that can arise if financial or programmatic pressures necessitate staff reductions. Kaplin (1985, p. 200) suggests that the following questions should be considered in writing and reviewing employee contracts:

- Does the contract provide for termination due to financial crisis or program discontinuance?
- Does it specify the conditions that will constitute a financial crisis or justify the termination of a program and specify how it will be determined when those conditions exist?
- Does it require that other options be explored (such as transfer to another department) before job cancellation is permitted?
- Does it provide the released employee with any priority in rehiring when other openings arise or the financial stress eases?

Clear, precise answers to these questions can save the institution many long, expensive legal battles. In spite of careful planning, however, some termination decisions may still end up in court. For this reason, complete records and documentation of staff reduction policies, decisions, and internal review processes should be kept (Kaplin, 1985).

Part-Time Faculty

Part-time faculty, or adjunct professors, have been called the "homeless" of the academic world. Often they have no job security, no health insurance, no raises, no promotions, and no voice in decision making, and usually they earn one third of what their full-time counterparts earn (Twigg, 1989).

Part-timers are a concern for the personnel office because they present unusual legal problems caused by pay scales differing from those of regular faculty, have little or no job security, and could require irregular, specialized contracts. To minimize complications, Kobesky and Martorana (1987, p. 303) recommend that

- Colleges should maintain records and profiles of their part-time teaching staff. These should be cen-

tralized so they could be retrieved and reviewed
when needed for reporting to governmental agencies or policy formation.

- Pay scales should be carefully reviewed with the intent of avoiding gross discrepancies that could
foster situations of unequal pay for equal work. Instances where a part-timer may teach a course for
a flat rate while a full-time faculty member teaches
a different section of the same course for a much
higher rate based on rank should be scrutinized.

- Grievance mechanisms should be available to part-
timers, especially for questions of dismissal or non-
rehire. How the adjunct faculty member can access
these procedures should be stated in manuals or
publications for part-time hires.

For legal reasons, it is also suggested that equal opportunity and
affirmative action statements be specifically adapted to include
part-time faculty (Biles and Tuckman, 1986).

There are several things that the personnel office can do
to make part-time faculty feel at home in an environment where
they spend little time and have little input. One idea is to create a part-time faculty handbook, outlining the history and organizational structure of the institution, stating college goals and
objectives, including a map and a list of helpful phone numbers (audiovisual services, for example), and spelling out employee policies and regulations (Biles and Tuckman, 1986).
Another idea is to hold a one-day orientation seminar, complete with campus tour and a brunch with some of the college's
administrative staff. A program could also be set up where each
part-time faculty member is assigned a full-time faculty mentor, who could provide encouragement, advice, and a sense of
belonging to the campus community.

However, as with all programs, these should be subject
to periodic evaluation and revision. Some new professors have
found their orientation meetings extremely tedious and of little
help (Boice, 1992). One idea to help make the orientation successful is not to overload the new employees with detailed and
complex information such as parking permit applications and

legal complications in procuring grants. This information could be explained in handouts and then discussed in informal small groups. According to Boice, many new faculty who had a positive experience with orientations attributed it to their meeting and getting to know a few other faculty in a small-group setting (such as a table at the provided lunch).

Summary

This chapter has dealt with practical workings of the community college personnel office — its functions and staffing — as well as with some of the major issues that confront such an office. These may concern affirmative action, the law, hiring and dismissing employees, and part-time faculty. Careful, precise record keeping in dealing with all these areas is imperative, since American community colleges face legal complications on an unprecedented scale.

One of the most important attributes of personnel officers (and indeed, of every system the office employs in completing various tasks) is flexibility. A good rule is to keep all options open as long as possible and to always be ready to do things differently. Personnel is people, and people are different from each other. Policies that guide procedures must be implemented, but they should not be so unbending that there is no room to deviate from the norm. The best personnel officers can formulate multiple procedures to apply to diverse situations, without compromising on the principles behind the policies.

A smoothly running personnel office contributes to an effective institution. Except for its proactive programs, ideally most of the campus should not think about the office. It should do its job so well that employees rarely have to bring problems to the attention of the staff; when they do, things ought to be handled quickly and easily, so that the office is not viewed as a dark abyss of inefficiency, tardiness, and inconsistency.

References

Biles, G. E., and Tuckman, H. P. *Part-Time Faculty Personnel Management Policies.* New York: American Council on Education/Macmillan, 1986.

Boice, R. *The New Faculty Member: Supporting and Fostering Professional Development.* San Francisco: Jossey-Bass, 1992.

Glueck, W. *Personnel: A Diagnostic Approach.* Plano, Tex.: Business Publishers, 1982.

Kaiser, M. G., and Greer, D. "Legal Aspects of Personnel Management in Higher Education." In R. I. Miller and E. W. Holzapfel, Jr. (eds.), *Issues in Personnel Management.* New Directions for Community Colleges, no. 62. San Francisco: Jossey-Bass, 1988.

Kaplin, W. A. *The Law of Higher Education: A Comprehensive Guide to Legal Implications of Administrative Decision Making.* (2nd ed.) San Francisco: Jossey-Bass, 1985.

Kobesky, E. L., and Martorana, S. V. "Implications for Preventative Law in Development of Policies for Managing Part-Time Faculty in Community Colleges." *Community/Junior College Quarterly of Research and Practice,* 1987, *2*(4).

Lee, B. A. "Grievance Systems: Boon or Bane for Shared Governance?" In J. H. Schuster, L. H. Miller, and Associates, *Governing Tomorrow's Campus: Perspectives and Agendas.* New York: American Council on Education/Macmillan, 1989.

Midkiff, S. J., and Come, B. "Organization and Staffing." In R. I. Miller and E. W. Holzapfel, Jr. (eds.), *Issues in Personnel Management.* New Directions for Community Colleges, no. 62. San Francisco: Jossey-Bass, 1988.

Twigg, H. P. "Uses and Abuses of Adjunct Faculty in Higher Education." Paper presented at the conference of the Community College Humanities Association, Washington, D.C., Nov. 1989. (ED 311 984)

Chapter 12

Instructional Programs

Martha J. Kanter

From the boardroom to the boiler room, higher education, the *academy,* is a world in constant flux. Anyone attempting to describe the management of this world must first appreciate its random and seemingly chaotic nature. It is an environment that appears to be forever changing, redefining itself, and continually evolving toward something more (Maslow, 1943, 1968, 1970). Assuming responsibility for managing the affairs of the academy is a transformational process (Kanter, 1983). Coming to understand instructional management closely parallels the work of Tom Peters, who began his quest *In Search of Excellence* (1982) and quickly made a transition to *Thriving on Chaos* (1987).

The community college workforce is a potpourri. Some are visionaries — artists who create and impart differing perspectives and an appreciation of that which is beautiful. Others are scientists who investigate and share details of the world around us. Some are men and women of the trades who teach students the skills necessary to enter the community's workforce, while others are akin to assembly-line workers for whom higher education is *just a job.*

219

In the academy, some come to learn, others to teach, and finally, a few to facilitate a vision of something greater. These last individuals—the change agents of the community college academy—may themselves be teachers, students, administrators, or staff. Change can and does occur at every level of the organization (Covey, 1990; Drucker, 1973; Robbins, 1986). This chapter is intended for that final group, those with the vision and creativity to explore the world of managing instructional affairs in the community college academy.

The players in this world are uniquely idiosyncratic. For the most part, they are individuals who do not need, want, or value management. They serve as a fierce complement to the instructional deans and academic vice presidents who, for the most part, came up through the ranks to their positions of prominence within the community college. These former professors now find themselves thrust into a world of competing territories and values, in an environment dominated by the tenets of academic freedom and democracy, often divorced from responsibility or accountability. To the chagrin of management, a college academic senate, for example, voted to study the meaning of the term *insubordination,* finding the concept fundamentally at odds with their view of collegial organization (for instance, faculty are not, or ever could be, insubordinate to administrators under the terms of shared governance). They did not, however, consider that all players in the academy, whether managers or teachers, might themselves be subordinate to agreed-on principles of behavior that comprise a healthy institution of higher learning.

Can instructional programs be managed with effectiveness and efficiency on the one hand, and with creativity and harmony on the other? To answer this question, one must first understand who the participants on the playing field are, what they do, and how they contribute to the instructional enterprise (Covey, 1990; Drucker, 1973; Robbins, 1986).

The community college is an unconventional organism. In part, it is an abhorrent bureaucracy, responding to numerous state and federal mandates that have little or nothing to do with the college's fundamental, day-to-day mission of teaching and learning. These mandates, however, translate into dollars, which in turn translate into salaries of faculty and staff. With 85 percent of the college budget allotted to salaries, there are virtually no dollars to fund new, creative programs or innovations. How does this fit with a collegial environment that prides itself on continual reflection, change, and growth? Not very well. Because instructional affairs must be managed from the reality of limited resources (scarcity), creativity and innovation require careful planning and implementation using a variety of nontraditional sources.

Right now and into the foreseeable future, community colleges will be involved in exchanging their educational goods and services for improvements in the community at large (Rosenman, 1982; Stanton, 1989). To illustrate this point, students in accounting classes now assist elderly residents with their tax returns as part of the curriculum, and students in sociology classes conduct surveys of housing needs and resources for the homeless. Yet another example are small business courses that help companies in distress get back on their feet by conducting on-site audits, establishing inventory controls, and preparing new prospectuses based on market research done by students in marketing classes.

To fulfill the college's instructional potential, managers must develop and impart clear, direct educational goals that have at their foundation the academic achievement and betterment of students. Fundamental to the creation of these goals is a respect for and acknowledgment of the players along with a sincere willingness to share in their development. Faculty must own the instructional goals of the college. If faculty become alienated from these instructional goals, little real progress will be made. This chapter deals with accreditation, management of instructional programs, curriculum and instruction, shared governance, and teaching and learning—all as they affect academic administration.

Charting the Course: Accreditation

Whether instructional vice presidents or deans are promoted from within or hired from outside of the college, it is important to understand that they have assumed these leadership positions in midstream. It is very likely that the institution will already have well-established cultures and traditions, to say nothing of long-standing histories of allegiances and rivalries. A wise person once said: "That which is oldest is closest to truth — do what is right."

Accreditation standards for postsecondary institutions have served for decades as an external peer review of an institution's health and vitality for the purpose of accountability and institutional improvement. In the Western states, Standard 2 of each institution's self-study in preparation for accreditation is often a good place for managers to begin. The first provision of Standard 2 states: "The achievement and maintenance of high quality programs in an environment conducive to study and learning are the primary responsibilities of every accredited institution" (Berg, 1990, p. 16). From this provision, program quality, curriculum planning and evaluation, coherence of general education and major offerings, special programs, and articulation with high schools and universities are reviewed in depth. Using the self-study and report from the peer review as a guideline, instructional leaders can acknowledge where change must occur while respecting the traditions of the institution.

Academic visions that necessitate change or improvement should be implemented in such a way that they are understood and shared by all staff. Academic senates, instructional and student services support staff, student government, and other key college constituencies need to play a central role in the realization of a common vision and the achievement of shared goals (Theobald, 1992; Admire, 1992). This includes those who teach in a particular discipline or work in a specific division.

Conditions of Uncertainty

Managing instructional programs requires a delicate balance of ideals, ideas, and people. It is often difficult to tell whether a college is in a growth mode, building and strengthening academic programs, or in a decline mode, cutting classes, eliminating programs, and handling layoffs. Academic programs in community colleges are much like a hardy plant, accustomed to surviving in a harsh and changing environment. As demand increases and funding is available, the plant grows and expands. Witness the unprecedented growth in community colleges during the 1960s, synonymous with economic advances of that period. Programs and courses proliferated. When resources dry up and funding becomes scarce, the plant shrinks and withers. In the 1980s community colleges downsized, reigning in many programs and courses (Cortada, 1985).

Since colleges depend on state funding, and the state does not support education with any kind of long-range, base-budget funding mechanism, colleges are always on the edge, attempting to manage programs under extreme and varying conditions of uncertainty (Theobald, 1992). For example, since the early 1980s and well into the 1990s, the California state budget has been highly unstable. Past years have seen budget deficits and surpluses in the multibillion-dollar range. In spring 1992, a $10 billion shortfall was predicted, amounting to a proposed 10 percent budget cut to education in one year.

An instructional vice president or dean must engage in short- and long-range planning under these uncertain economic conditions. Many liken this scenario to an annual roulette game. In this context, decision making is difficult, with numerous variables to consider. As Tversky and Kahneman (1986, p. 53) point out, "The tendency to predict the outcome that best represents the data, with insufficient regard for prior probability, has been observed in the intuitive judgments of individuals who have had extensive training in statistics."

For the sake of sanity and survival, long-range strategic plans must be developed to identify areas of growth, maintenance, and decline. The question to be asked, then, is: What are the factors central to the academic health of this college? The answers to this question will provide a strategic long-term vision from which a practical and sustainable plan can be built.

Instructional programs lie at the heart of the institution's mission. As such, the programs and courses the college offers become its bread and budget. Given the predictability of the economic uncertainty that shrouds higher education instructional planning and budgeting, difficult questions must be asked and answered. Richard Goff (1990, p. 1), former chancellor of the San Jose/Evergreen Community College District in California, poses several questions:

> What is the *proper* percentage mix between vocational and transfer students? What should be the desired mix, in percents, between program takers and course takers? If you don't put an emphasis on *program takers* rather than *course takers,* will you ever offer a sufficient number of second year courses? How many students must transfer in order for your college to consider itself a *transfer* institution? At what point do high percentages of remedial courses radically redefine the definition of a college? How will the mission of the college be achieved if we fill our enrollment growth cap with second and third ring (from centrality of purpose) programs? What is it that we do that we want to be well known for? At present, we are trying to be well known for everything, but that isn't well known. What are our priorities? Everything cannot be tied for first. What percent of the institution's resources should be dedicated to off-campus credit instruction, especially when the state says we are obligated to do more in working cooperatively with private business? High school students tend to be more oriented to being full-time students than older students with jobs. Full-time students tend to be more directed to being program takers than course takers. Should we recruit more heavily for recent high school graduates? What kind of a percentage mix do we want between the traditionally aged college cohort and the older student? The point is, through management of enrollment and growth, we can shape what our college will become. The question is, will the faculty and staff of the college shape the college and curriculum, or will that be done by the happenstance of student enrollment?

Reflecting on questions of this type, academic deans and vice presidents will benefit from recognizing the uniqueness of the community they serve, the constituencies within the region seeking a community college education, the demographic sub-groups and attendant cultural, ethnic, and linguistic differences that exist in the community, and the diverse expectations of these education consumers. Similarly, differences in mission exist among community colleges. While transfer and occupational education are the primary missions of community colleges, the breadth and depth of what is offered varies, based on a cohesive understanding of the needs of local employers, university demands for specific lower-division sequences of courses, academic preparation of high school graduates, dropouts, immigrant students, the unemployed, older adults, and those simply seeking to enrich their lives through lifelong learning. All these groups put pressure on the community college to meet their needs.

Unfortunately, however, institutional resources are finite. Whether enrollment is expanding or declining, attention must be directed toward attracting the clientele appropriate to the particular institution, its mission and goals. An easy, if perhaps impractical, solution is to return to the early days of community colleges solely as junior universities or "transfer institutions." It would be equally simplistic for a community college to become an arm of a major corporation, providing occupational training on demand to meet the needs of industry for a highly trained workforce. Similarly, in communities where recent immigrants and underprepared students abound, a college could easily become a place largely devoted to basic skills education. Finding a way to balance these divergent needs must come from a holistic and shared understanding of "who we are" as a college, given our unique set of circumstances. Voices of faculty, staff, students, and community leaders can and do enrich this understanding as the institution evolves in a thoughtful and deliberate manner to improve itself in serving the educational needs of the community.

Economic uncertainties are the norm. Difficult questions arise in uncertain times. For that matter, can any administrator recall a time when uncertainty did not exist? Facing these conditions squarely through informed participation of stakeholders within the community will result in a strategic plan based on the clear educational priorities of the institution as it moves forward within the philosophical framework of service to the community. Considering these and related questions will help those engaged in the management of instructional programs formulate long-term, sustainable strategic plans. Such plans will guide the development and maintenance of the institution through conditions of economic uncertainty.

Curriculum Balance

Managing instructional programs depends on a clear understanding of the present balance of the college's curriculum. Comprehensive strategic plans are built on the curriculum. Available resources and curricular plans determine what the institution will offer in the future. One searches for the right mix of transfer (general education), occupational education, basic skills, English-as-a-second language, and contract/fee-based course offerings. Transfer (general education) courses must be synchronized with university lower-division requirements. This synchrony paves the way for students to obtain the baccalaureate degree unencumbered by superfluous departmental requirements.

Historically, in order to receive an associate degree with transfer to a four-year institution, community college students completed thirty units of general education and thirty units of courses in the major. Now, transfer to some universities requires students to complete thirty-nine units of lower-division general education coursework. High-unit majors have also become the norm, with requirements often exceeding thirty units, such as in engineering. Specialized single-course requirements — such as the California State University's demand that all students must have a course in critical thinking before their junior year — affects the curriculum in a system where 50,000 students transfer each year from community colleges. The net result is that students must deal with a host of specialized academic requirements, some of which, when scrutinized, add little value and lengthen the time to a degree.

Curriculum balance must be achieved continually through a dynamic strategic planning process. Setting realistic priorities — courses and requirements for the degree(s) — must be done in collaboration with the many idiosyncratic players in this lower-division world — those who believe that "the course that I teach is unequivocally essential to an education." A harmonious curriculum must build on the talents of the faculty within the framework of the academic mission and goals of the institution. Time and circumstances have a way of dimming our original academic visions. It is important in building and balancing the academic plan to periodically remind stakeholders of the stake that was initially created. Similarly, when the stake does not seem to be as new or as exciting as it once was, a willingness to reevaluate and change the stake is essential.

Academic administrators and faculty must carefully establish educational priorities that ensure a balanced curriculum. Courses must be offered with regularity and in proper sequence so students can complete their educational goals on time. During the past decade, time to the degree has increased because enrollment demand has exceeded the supply of courses and because of the irregular pattern of offerings. Students now often require one or more additional years to complete their intended educational goals. In taking the proper steps to balance the curriculum, institutions will be better able to provide access to the sequence of courses and programs to ensure graduation, transfer, and jobs for community college students.

In developing a balanced curriculum approach at San Jose City College (California), faculty and staff were asked to engage in a curricular planning process as follows: (1) analyze strengths and weaknesses of the curriculum in terms of the mission for community colleges (primary mission of transfer and occupational education and the secondary, important mission of basic skills and English as a second language); (2) identify fiscal parameters that affect the balance of offerings; (3) recommend ways in which courses required for the major can be offered with regularity, on a consistent schedule and within current fiscal resources; (4) determine appropriate percentages of the courses required for the A.A. or A.S. degree, the certificate only, entry level versus majors, general education, and so on; and (5) recommend an appropriate configuration of course offerings to ensure a balanced curriculum that assigns priorities within disciplines and divisions and with attention to future programs (Brobst and Kanter, 1992). Following these steps, improvements were made to develop a balanced curriculum designed for student success, based on the expertise of the appropriate college constituencies.

Shared Governance in Action?

Despite a compelling mission, comprehensive strategic plan, balanced curriculum, and an ideally suited faculty, the college may still be in crisis. Breakdowns may occur when an attempt is made to put ideas into practice. What creates an environment conducive to managing a healthy institution? The answer, perhaps, lies in the governance of an institution. Any discussion of governance must acknowledge its companions: accountability, authority, and responsibility. Authority and responsibility are, of course, "two horns on the same goat," as characterized by Zorba the Greek.

The next question we must ask, then, is: Who are the parties who must engage in a process that will be principally governed by the terms *authority* and *responsibility* and, perhaps most important, what do they understand these terms to mean? Formerly in community colleges, governance happened most often in a top-down, autocratic, and sometimes militaristic style. As the president went, so went the institution and all its parts. In recent years, faculty have called on institutions to recognize faculty expertise and, in fact, to delegate authority and responsibility in a more formal way for carrying out functions that are academic in nature (for example, curriculum matters, professional responsibilities, staff development).

Following the development of two Master Plans for California Higher Education (1960 and 1986), community colleges attempted to move toward a Yeshiva model of governance, introducing collegiality into the formal governance structure of the institutions (California Community Colleges, 1990; Clark, 1981; Kaplin, 1985, pp. 107–115; Lee, 1980; *NLRB* v. *Yeshiva University,* 1978, 1980). California community colleges' use of the term *shared governance* came into vogue in 1988 following the passage of reform legislation (Assembly Bill No. 1725; California Community Colleges, 1990).

Shared governance simply means collegial decision making. What was meant to be, in fact, collegial decision making and the concomitant empowerment of the faculty soon became an adversarial battle for power. In some colleges, faculty wanted the complete and final say over such institutional issues as budgeting and accreditation. The intent of the California legislation was to raise the standards of faculty expertise and to promote a sharing of perspectives in making academic decisions on behalf of students. Administrators were to work in harmony with faculty and staff to bring diverse views to issues that would, in turn, allow creative alternatives to come forth for discussion prior to decision making (California Community Colleges, 1990; Young, 1988). Unfortunately, the California experience demonstrates once again that when behavior is legislated, issues become polarized and often much more complicated than they were originally envisioned. The Tao says simply: "The fewer rules the better. Rules reduce freedom and responsibility. Enforcement of rules is coercive and manipulative, which diminishes spontaneity and absorbs group energy. The more coercive you are, the more resistant the group will become. Your manipulations will only breed evasions. Every law creates an outlaw. . . . When the leader practices silence, the group remains focused. When the leader does not impose rules, the group discovers its own goodness. When the leader acts unselfishly, the group simply does what is to be done" (Heider, 1985, p. 113).

Whether governance can truly be shared is yet to be seen (Young, 1988). Most conversations about shared governance continue to center around whether faculty, staff, and administrators have indeed been empowered in the decision-making process, or whether faculty and staff view shared governance as an opportunity to seize power from the administration. Some administrators, on the other hand, regard shared governance as an opportunity to hang on to power they never really had in the first place.

If the parties are unclear about who is doing what and

about who has responsibility and authority for the decisions that must be made within a shared governance framework, instructional decision making can become a nightmare. For example, at most community colleges, responsibility for developing courses and programs rests with the faculty. Curriculum committees are most often comprised of faculty and administrators who oversee what and how courses are taught. Similarly, administrators most often have the authority and responsibility to assign faculty to teach particular courses, to schedule courses, and to oversee program review—in short, to manage the aspects of the curriculum as a whole so the institution can maximize its resources.

The institutional challenge, then, is for administrators and faculty both—separately and then together—to identify specific areas of responsibility and authority *before* decisions are made and actions taken. Who has the responsibility? Who has the authority? To facilitate an orderly college, instructional administrators must work collegially with the academic senate, the classified staff, students, and the collective bargaining agents in an environment where the stakeholders of the institution clearly understand the scope of responsibility and authority of each of the constituent groups.

Instruction as Service

In building and managing the collegial environment, the stakeholders must also support a coherent philosophical framework based on the community college's mission. A cornerstone of this framework must be an understanding of service. Community college faculty, staff, and administrators are servants of the community. Instruction must be rooted in the commitment to service. Academic deans must keep before them a commitment to serving the communities both internal and external to the academy. This can be done in two ways: first, by linking instruction with student services, and second, by linking the content of the curriculum in a meaningful way to the larger environment.

Most often, academic deans and instructional managers have risen through the ranks from teacher to administrator. The majority come from a traditional classroom setting and have little understanding of the comprehensiveness of student services. Some have the attitude that counseling and special programs are outside the college's mission.

Student services are, in fact, the support structures binding students to the college, allowing them to enroll, persist, transfer, and/or get jobs. It is difficult to understand the scope of student services unless one has direct experience handling a student grievance, dealing with gangs on campus, providing support to an alcoholic or manic-depressive faculty member, doing downtown recruitment, or any of a host of activities that are essential to a well-run community college. Student services are further denigrated when they are funded in a categorical manner, raising the question, Are you truly part of the academic community?

Academic administrators must learn about student services and ask a variety of important questions in this regard: Would certain students be able to attend college if they did not have access to financial aid? If they did not have child care? If they were not selectively recruited from an insular community? Might some students fail were it not for a tutor or supplemental instruction? Would they transfer to a university without a transfer admissions agreement? Would these students have been hired if they had not visited the career/job placement center? Above all, instructional administrators must focus on what is best for students. Sometimes, student services becomes a separate entity in an institution, mysteriously funded, often taking what appear to be extraordinary measures for students, seemingly divorced from instruction.

To alleviate the artificial split between student services and instruction, steps must be taken to integrate student services with academic programs and courses. Academic deans should insist that counselors attend departmental meetings with faculty in a given discipline to promote coordination and identify student needs both within and outside the classroom. Many special programs exist in community colleges to serve a particular student constituency. These special programs must be clearly linked with the disciplines and must demonstrate how they are preparing students for mainstream college life.

For example, San Jose City College offers the Adelante program, targeting the preparation of Latino students for college-level English and mathematics through accelerated coursework. These students take advantage of a specially designed curriculum that builds on their cultural experiences and supports them to succeed in college. Mentors from the community are assigned to students in identified career areas, and students participate in numerous group activities to build their self-esteem and academic skills. The English and mathematics courses are crucial to Adelante's success, as are the counseling and mentoring provided with the coursework. Adelante integrally links student services and instruction. It is clear that, with its focus on student achievement, the program prepares students for college-level classes offered by the institution. The success of Adelante can be clearly seen when its students are mainstreamed into college life. After taking full advantage of the support base provided by the program's English and mathematics completion requirements, these same students compete and succeed in other transferable college courses on a par with their peers (Kangas, 1992).

Equally important is the linkage between the curriculum and the community. Academic deans should build and refine programs and courses that meet community needs within the context of a clearly defined mission. The closer the curriculum is aligned to the community, the greater the rewards to the institution in terms of community support, vitalization, and funding. Advisory committees are essential to the health of occupational programs, since partnerships with industry can bring state-of-the-art personnel, equipment, and new technologies to the college departments and disciplines. In return, the institution can deliver courses designed particularly for businesses and nonprofit community-based organizations. To bring various perspectives that strengthen the transfer function, articulation councils should be drawn from university and high school educators and those who serve on corporate boards.

Institutions can go one step further. They might consider joining the Campus Compact or a similar group that brings the college into the community in perhaps more dramatic ways. *Building communities* and *learning through service* are terms used to describe this approach (Eisenberg, 1990; Rosenman, 1982; Stanton, 1989). For example, community service can be built into individual courses. The anthropology department at UCLA offers a course called Introduction to Social Action Anthropology. Students do fieldwork six to eight hours per week, with a focus on domestic and international issues, such as poverty, discrimination, or public health.

Brevard Community College in Cocoa, Florida offers a seminar to teach faculty about service learning for infusion into courses they teach (Stanton, 1989). Community college students taking sociology might volunteer in a shelter for the homeless and write about what they learn. Students seeking careers in teaching could mentor elementary or high school students on a weekly basis. Students in a small business course might help a failing business get back on its feet by completing a prospectus for the company. An environmental studies course might include a beach clean-up project and offer to take elementary or high school students along. The Maricopa County Community College District in Arizona convenes an advisory committee to set district community service goals (Eisenberg, 1990). These, and a host of other ways to link the college and the community, should be brought into instruction as community needs are identified. The point is to stretch beyond the confines of a traditional lecture course mentality and bring some practical innovations into the educational arena.

Instruction can and should take place as service to the community. Following the lines of the Campus Compact and similar efforts, transfer and vocational education courses must link more closely with the community and address the dire social and economic issues facing it (for example child care, toxics, and so on) through appropriate curricular offerings. The college then emerges as a place where community problems can be considered and solutions found through instruction.

Involvement in Teaching and Learning

One effect of the instruction-as-service approach is that students get involved in what they are learning, faculty in what they teach, and everyone in making a unique contribution to the institution. Involvement is encouraged and reinforced. What underlies the success of a campus compact or advisory committee is, simply stated, an involvement in the life of the academy that goes beyond a fifty-minute lecture delivered three times each week. Involvement creates meaning in one's own life, both inside and outside the walls of the institution — for faculty, for students, for administrators, and for staff.

Young and others (1992) believe that passion for learning can be instilled in students and that once instilled, it becomes infectious, spreading to others who want to share in the joy of participating in an institution known for quality. Because students and faculty are involved, they become passionate about the institution. As a result, the community, students, faculty, staff, and administrators all take pride in the institution. This passion in promoting the idea that students should spend part of their time at college immersed in a culture different from their own, to broaden their understanding of the college as a microcosm of a global culture and to experience another culture firsthand, will be remembered for a lifetime.

Extensive studies conducted at Santa Barbara City College show that involvement in teaching and learning produces positive outcomes. Friedlander (1990a, 1990b), Friedlander and MacDougall (1991), and MacDougall, Friedlander, Ullom, and McLellan (1990) demonstrate that the more students use the library, the stronger they report their ability to learn independently. Similarly, the more students write, the more they report confidence in their writing abilities. The more contacts they have with faculty outside the classroom, the more involved they become with classroom and campus activities. They conclude by recommending that educators take steps to consciously involve faculty, students, and others in directed academic and social activities that bond these individuals to the institution while at the same time promoting greater independence and achievement.

The implications of this line of research for instructional management are enormous. Gains in the students' academic achievement and retention are in the forefront of the work plans of instructional deans and vice presidents. These same priorities serve the institution's viability as it delivers successful, involved graduates to its community. Any management of instruction must acknowledge the importance of involvement and, while these results may appear simplistic to some, perhaps a return to the simple things that work in the curriculum may return greater rewards to the partners of a college.

Elitism and Intellectual Exhaustion

At the other end of the spectrum, institutional apathy (often taking the form of deliberate and sometimes theatrical separation from the college community) continues to be a problem facing community colleges. Faculty and staff who seem apathetic and cynical often suffer from elitism, a feeling of social superiority that can lead to aloofness or intellectual exhaustion. These institutional plagues must be treated with powerful remedies, or they will quickly infect the instructional program. Instructional managers must pay particular attention to these institutional illnesses and take active steps to heal them whenever possible.

One remedy for elitism is to hire the best and the brightest faculty and staff—experts in their fields who are involved in their work and sensitive to the diverse, compelling needs of community college students. Elitists usually have a hard time with people who care, people who are involved, and in their cynicism, often see them as naive and unsophisticated. Direct and public confrontation also helps.

For intellectual exhaustion (sometimes called burnout), intensive staff revitalization is in order. A radical change in instructional environments or activities may be of great benefit. The promise of something new, such as designing a new course, targeted staff development, or coordinating a grant, sometimes reinvests individuals with their original enthusiasm for teaching and learning. Occasionally, the opportunity to mentor a new faculty member will have the same effect. In California, state-legislated staff development funds (Assembly Bill 1725) have been assigned to assist faculty in maintaining currency in their disciplines and to bring faculty and staff together in addressing instructional priorities.

Instructional managers should direct their energy to providing quality in academic and professional matters for the *involved* participants, though the elitists and intellectually exhausted may attempt to drain away that energy. If a sincere attempt to heal these institutional illnesses fails, a final strategy is to give minimal attention and little opportunity to these infections so they do not spread to others. Simply ignoring these troubled individuals sometimes works wonders. A sage once said: "That which you give your attention to grows stronger" (Maharishi Mahesh Yogi, 1966, p. 174). The time spent managing instruction is better invested in moving the institution forward; little or no attention should be given to those who are not similarly inclined. It is important, however, to read and carefully understand all collective bargaining agreements so that these agreements can be respected and acted on in the process of moving the institution forward.

Campus Climate and Instruction

In managing the academic affairs of a community college, deans and vice presidents must keep in the forefront an understanding and commitment to the ethnic, gender, and cultural diversity of the institution they serve (California Postsecondary Education Commission, 1990, 1992; Knutsen, 1987; Maslach and others, 1991; University of California, 1990). Do the curriculum, faculty development, support services, and other aspects of the college reflect this diversity? Do all students and staff feel welcome to take advantage of the educational opportunities afforded by the community colleges? Instructional managers must first know the students, faculty, and staff. What is the ethnic composition of the faculty? How many students speak English as a second language? Is there a preponderance of men teaching in the vocational programs? Are the cultural and ethnic backgrounds of support staff diverse? Do faculty and students of color feel supported by their peers? Are special instructional support programs available for underrepresented groups, and are they successful in preparing these students for the mainstream of college life? Are faculty working to build an inclusive curriculum

so that all constituencies of the college share and appreciate differing ethnic and cultural perspectives?

The report *California Faces California's Future* grappled with
such issues as part of a master planning effort for California
higher education, stating: "We regard it as axiomatic that a state
as diverse as California needs institutions whose faculty are
equally diverse . . . [students of] all races need to see adults of
all races in positions of authority and affection, welcoming them
and inspiring their allegiance and commitment. Consequently,
the quality for all students is enhanced by a more diverse faculty
and staff" (Joint Committee for Review of the Master Plan for
Higher Education, 1989, pp. 79–80). Relating these mandates
to the classroom, the Joint Committee recommended the expansion of international and multicultural education programs,
the requirement of a course in ethnic and multicultural studies,
competency in a second language for all students seeking the
baccalaureate degree, and the opportunity for voluntary public service (Joint Committee for Review of the Master Plan for
Higher Education, 1989, pp. 103–104).

Cultural pluralism across the curriculum, in teaching
strategies as well as course content, thus represents another demand that must be considered. The "Cultural Pluralism Program"
at Mission College in Santa Clara, California is one example
where courses have been modified according to the following
criteria: (1) deal comparatively with the value systems and subjective aspects of Western and non-Western cultures or the
dominant culture and minority cultures in the United States;
(2) introduce students to the interrelationships of the dominant
and minority cultures of the United States; (3) introduce students to the role and contributions of members of minority and
non-Western cultures in the discipline under consideration; (4)
give students insight into their own culture as well as that of
others; (5) approach the subject matter in a way that promotes
culturally pluralistic perspectives rather than monolithic or eth-
nocentric viewpoints; and (6) promote an understanding of the
universality of human needs and the diverse practices by which
these needs are met by a comparison of cross-cultural behavior
and values (Patton, 1990).

In addition to addressing course content, teaching styles of faculty, and learning styles of students, attention must also be given to the institution's academic climate. A landmark study "Assessing Campus Climate" led to the development of an instrument available to postsecondary institutions interested in conducting self-assessments. This tool may be used to assist community colleges in ensuring educational quality and in meeting educational equity goals. In this effort, colleges can "engage in a transformation of the total educational environment from a singular and dominant view of reality to a situation in which knowledge is seen as being more expansive and inclusive of alternate world views, and in which a multiplicity of views necessarily co-exist within a pluralistic society" (California Postsecondary Education Commission, 1992, p. 8).

Preliminary reports from institutions that have already conducted such assessments (UCLA, Berkeley, and Stanford) illustrate that perceived differential treatment of students, faculty, and staff from particular underrepresented groups "often negatively affects institutions' retention and graduation rates" (California Postsecondary Education Commission, 1992, p. 20). Analyzing the results of such studies in curricular and other academic decisions can have a direct and beneficial effect on instruction (Maslach and others, 1991; Stanford University, 1989; University of California, 1990). The effect of the campus climate on teaching and learning is central to the success of academic programs (transfer and occupational offerings leading to the degree), especially as it pertains to curriculum content and related pedagogical approaches in the classroom. Every academic vice president and instructional dean must actively seek out ways to diversify the curriculum and the faculty through self-examinations of this type that continually impact institutional effectiveness.

Cutting Edge Versus Ragged Edge

Any chapter about managing instruction would not be complete without some words about innovation and technology. Just as involvement and diversity in instruction must be consciously addressed, so must innovation and technology. Instructional deans and vice presidents are hired because the institution and its people want to become something more than what they already are (Maslow, 1943, 1968, 1970). Academic leaders are brought into the community college for a variety of purposes. These individuals must bring to the institution their unique visions of the academy along with programs and methods for realizing these visions. Equally important, academic deans must recognize and nurture the creativity and visions of those with whom they work (Admire, 1992). One hallmark of a successful instructional leader is the capacity to engage the energies and enthusiasm of persons with the skills to get the job done. Even the most innovative concepts will fail if the right people are not selected to implement them. Along with the content of a good idea must come the wherewithal to execute it in a simple way.

When good ideas become complex programs, bureaucracy takes over in ways often unanticipated at the start. So, when planning for innovation and/or technology, the first rule is to take small, direct, simple steps. Methods for realizing such innovations abound—campus minigrant programs, classroom-based assessment programs, blocked classes such as afternoon colleges or middle schools, accelerated programs, the use of cohort groups that target a specific student clientele, and college-within-a-college designs built around central themes such as the environment or the arts, to name a few (Cohen and Brawer, 1989, pp. 336–340). The trick is to keep ideas generating, to produce easily seen results that are beneficial to students, and to keep it simple so that it can be managed efficiently. The visionary dean will periodically revisit the instructional mission of the institution as innovations are put into place, recognizing along the way that the college is changing and maturing—becoming a better place to be. Supporting innovation is a procedure to spark faculty to strengthen their academic commitments in ways that perhaps they had not considered previously. It is also a way to emphasize and reward creativity.

Instructional managers must ask all constituents of the college—the faculty, students, staff, and community members—what education will look like in the next century. Managers must be ahead of the game, anticipating some of the answers and searching for new answers collaboratively. It is critically important that innovation be incorporated into the lifeblood of the institution (Theobald, 1992).

Right now, for example, academic deans know that technology is, and will be, a central conduit for teaching and learning. Colleges must keep pace with automation while keeping the use of technology practical. This cannot be underscored enough. Quality instructional planning depends on the availability of reliable information in formats that academic deans can access and use. It takes time to plan an electronic classroom or lab. The next century will incorporate virtual reality into the educational process. Students as explorers will take advantage of real-time education. Someday soon students may visit the Louvre from the classroom or experience the Battle of Lexington and Concord, playing the fife while marching toward the enemy. Students will use other technologies with which we are not now familiar. What we do know is that they will have access to vast amounts of information through distance learning, computers, television, media, and other technological pipelines (Anandam, 1989). Academic deans must understand that community college students need to learn how to access information. In a world in which information is available at one's fingertips, memorization becomes less important than knowledge navigation.

In the future, learning will take place in small groups and teams (Kanter, 1983). Content will be more easily internalized and remembered because learning experiences will take place in real time. Learning traditional course material will be supported by structured study groups that take place outside the classroom. Enabled through technology, learning will take place everywhere (Anandam, 1989; Leonard, 1968; McLuhan and Powers, 1989; Naisbitt, 1982; Young and others, 1992).

Traditional classrooms will continue to exist alongside nontraditional classrooms where students' experience of the world will be informed by technology. International perspectives will be emphasized. At the same time, industry will be on campus and the campus will also exist within industry so that students (employees) can receive current course content that makes them immediately employable. Because most students will need to work while attending college, community college relationships with industry will be strengthened so that work and education are integrated. Business will become more intricately involved in supporting students who are their employees with incentives such as instructional equipment and mentorships. Learning will occur at work, at home, and at the campus (Young and others, 1992).

Academic leaders will prepare community colleges to provide basic skills in new and expanded ways. Basic skills as we know them now (reading, writing, and mathematics below college level) will be redefined and expanded to include the teaching of leadership skills, self-esteem, information literacy, problem solving, working as a member of a team, development of a work ethic, and investing students with a passion for learning (Young and others, 1992). Anticipating the future is a mandatory objective for instructional deans and vice presidents.

Self-Actualized Instruction

This chapter has offered a sincere look at managing the heart of the community college enterprise — instructional programs. It is an enterprise that requires a "serious" person, serious in the best sense of the word. Every language has a word that describes such a person. In Yiddish, the word is *mensch*. It means a person with integrity, energy, dedication, commitment, intelligence, vision, compassion, and no small amount of patience and humor. Academic deans and vice presidents must keep in the forefront of their effort a seriousness about teaching and learning; a seriousness about the vision and the mission of the college; a seriousness about every course, program, certificate, and degree the institution offers; a seriousness about innovation, technology, campus climate, diversity, and governance; a seriousness about strategic planning and quality; a seriousness about involvement; and above all, a seriousness about service.

When President Del Anderson hires new faculty for San Jose City College, she looks for missionaries because, as she says, community college students need faculty who believe in them. It is equally true and equally important that community college instructional managers must believe as strongly in their faculty, staff, and colleges. Believing in the ability, intelligence, and commitment of faculty and staff creates an academic climate that cannot be falsified or synthesized. This fundamental trust is the foundation on which an institution is constructed and through which its potential is actualized. In the midst of the change, uncertainty, and transformation that are the very nature of the academic institution (Kanter, 1983), an abiding constant must be this essential belief in the potential of faculty, staff, and the institution as a whole.

Summary

Instructional programs must be managed with effectiveness and efficiency, as well as with creativity and harmony. This balance can only be achieved when the curriculum is built on the talents of the faculty within the framework of the academic mission and goals of the institution.

The administration must have a strong sense of clearly defined mission and a comprehensive strategic plan if it is to manage the instructional programs at the institution effectively. Administrators must work with the faculty in shared governance to bring diverse views to issues so as to allow creative alternatives to be developed before any final decisions are reached. They must see the institution, and also themselves, as servants of the community and of the students.

At the core of community college instructional development in the years ahead will be the actualization of the human potential of students, faculty, and staff. An unshakable belief in the ability of these persons and institutions to grow, change, and improve will be the hallmark of education and its management into the twenty-first century. Administrators at all levels must exercise their beliefs, attend to the needs of both faculty and students, and recognize the importance of renewal.

References

Admire, N. "Visionary Planning—A Consensus Process." *Trustee Quarterly*, Winter 1992, 5, 9–10.

Anandam, K. (ed.). *Transforming Teaching with Technology: Perspectives from Two-Year Colleges.* EDUCOM Strategy Series on Information Technology. McKinney, Tex.: EDUCOM Academic Computing Publications, 1989.

Assembly Bill no. 1725. *California Community Colleges* (Vasconcellos). Sacramento: California State Assembly, 1987.

Berg, E. H. *Handbook of Accreditation and Policy Manual.* Aptos, Calif.: Accrediting Commission for Community and Junior Colleges, Western Association of Schools and Colleges, 1990.

Brobst, D., and Kanter, M. J. *Charge to the Instructional Policies/Curriculum Committee's Subcommittee on Curriculum Balance.* San Jose, Calif.: Office of Instruction, San Jose City College, 1992.

California Community Colleges. *Shared Governance in the California Community Colleges.* Sacramento, Calif.: Board of Governors, 1990.

California Postsecondary Education Commission. *Toward an Understanding of Campus Climate: A Report to the Legislature in Response to Assembly Bill 4071.* Report no. 90-19. Sacramento: California Postsecondary Education Commission, 1990.

California Postsecondary Education Commission. *Assessing Campus Climate: Feasibility of Developing an Educational Equity Assessment System.* Report no. 92-2. Sacramento: California Postsecondary Education Commission, 1992.

Clark, C. A. "The Yeshiva Case: An Analysis and an Assessment of Its Potential Impact on Public Universities." *Journal of Higher Education,* 1981, *52,* 449–469.

Cohen, A. M., and Brawer, F. B. *The American Community College.* (2nd ed.) San Francisco: Jossey-Bass, 1989.

Cortada, R. L. "Change Without Growth: The Access Dilemma of the Community College in the 1980's." *Proceedings of the 1984 Educational Testing Service Invitational Conference: Educational Standards, Testing, and Access.* Princeton, N.J.: Educational Testing Service, 1985.

Covey, S. R. *Principle-Centered Leadership.* New York: Simon & Schuster, 1990.

Drucker, P. F. *Management: Tasks, Responsibilities, Practices.* New York: HarperCollins, 1973.

Eisenberg, J. "Campus Compact's 1990–91 National Members' Survey and Resource Guide." *A Report of the Campus Compact: The Project for Public and Community Service.* Denver, Colo.: Education Commission of the States, 1990.

Friedlander, J. "Approaches for Promoting Student Involvement in Existing Out-of-Class Campus Activities." Unpublished manuscript, Santa Barbara City College, Santa Barbara, Calif., 1990a.

Friedlander, J. "The Role of the Student and the College in Promoting Student Achievement." Unpublished manuscript, Santa Barbara City College, Santa Barbara, Calif., 1990b.

Friedlander, J., and MacDougall, P. *Achieving Student Success Through Student Involvement.* Unpublished manuscript, 1991. (ED 329 310)

Goff, R. W. Unpublished manuscript, San Jose City College Administrators' Retreat, Carmel Valley, Calif., 1990.

Heider, J. *The Tao of Leadership.* New York: Bantam, 1985.

Joint Committee for Review of the Master Plan for Higher Education. *California Faces California's Future.* Sacramento: Joint Committee for Review of the Master Plan for Higher Education, California State Legislature, 1989.

Kangas, J. *The Academic Performance of Adelante Students at San Jose City College.* San Jose, Calif.: San Jose/Evergreen Community College District, 1992.

Kanter, R. M. *The Change Masters.* New York: Simon & Schuster, 1983.

Kaplin, W. A. "Bargaining Unit Eligibility of Full-Time Faculty." In W. A. Kaplin, *The Law of Higher Education: A Comprehensive Guide to Legal Implications of Administrative Decision Making.* (2nd ed.) San Francisco: Jossey-Bass, 1985.

Knutsen, K. L. *Differential Treatment: A Prospectus for Legislative Action.* Sacramento: University of California Student Association, 1987.

Lee, B. A. "Faculty Role in Academic Governance and the Managerial Exclusion: Impact of the Yeshiva University Decision." *Journal of College and University Law,* 1980, 7(3–4), 222–266.

Leonard, G. B. *Education and Ecstasy.* New York: Delacorte Press, 1968.

MacDougall, P., Friedlander, J., Ullom, J., and McLellan, K.

Approaches for Increasing Students' Involvement in Their Learning. Paper presented at the annual convention of the Community College League of California, Los Angeles, Nov. 1990.

McLuhan, M., and Powers, B. R. *The Global Village: Transformations in World Life and Media in the 21st Century.* New York: Oxford University Press, 1989.

Maharishi Mahesh Yogi. *The Science of Being and the Art of Living.* Rev. ed. London: International SRM Publications, 1966.

Maslach, C., and others. *Report of the Commission on Responses to a Changing Student Body.* Berkeley, Calif.: Commission on Responses to a Changing Student Body, University of California, 1991.

Maslow, A. H. "A Theory of Human Motivation." *Psychological Review,* 1943, *50,* 370–396.

Maslow, A. H. *Toward a Psychology of Being.* (2nd ed.) New York: Van Nostrand Reinhold, 1968.

Maslow, A. H. *Motivation and Personality.* Rev. ed. New York: HarperCollins, 1970.

Naisbitt, J. *Megatrends.* New York: Warner Books, 1982.

NLRB v. *Yeshiva University,* 582 F.2d 686 (2d Cir. 1978).

NLRB v. *Yeshiva University,* 100 S. Ct. 856 (1980).

Patton, J. *The Cultural Pluralism Program at Mission College.* Santa Clara, Calif.: 1990.

Peters, T. J. *Thriving on Chaos: Handbook for a Management Revolution.* New York: Knopf, 1987.

Peters, T. J., and Waterman, R. H. *In Search of Excellence: Lessons from America's Best-Run Companies.* New York: HarperCollins, 1982.

Robbins, S. P. *Organizational Behavior.* (3rd ed.) Englewood Cliffs, N.J.: Prentice-Hall, 1986.

Rosenman, M. "Colleges and Social Change: Partnerships with Community-Based Organizations." In E. Greenberg (ed.), *New Partnerships — Higher Education and the Nonprofit Sector.* New Directions for Experiential Learning, no. 18. San Francisco: Jossey-Bass, 1982.

Stanford University. *Building a Multiracial, Multicultural University Community: Final Report of the University Committee on Minority Issues.* Palo Alto, Calif.: Stanford University, 1989.

Stanton, T. K. "Integrating Public Service with Academic Study:

The Faculty Role." *A Report of the Campus Compact: The Project for Public and Community Service.* Denver, Colo.: Education Commission of the States, 1989.

Theobald, R. "Community Colleges as Catalysts." *Trustee Quarterly,* Winter 1992, 5–8.

Tversky, A., and Kahneman, D. "Judgment Under Uncertainty: Heuristics and Biases." In H. R. Arkes and K. R. Hammond (eds.), *Judgment and Decision Making: An Interdisciplinary Reader.* Cambridge, Eng.: Cambridge University Press, 1986.

University of California. *The Diversity Project: An Interim Report to the Chancellor.* Berkeley, Calif.: Institute for the Study of Social Change, University of California, 1990.

Young, D., and others. *The Future of Community Colleges.* Paper presented at the annual meeting of the Commission on the Future, Community College League of California, Los Angeles, Nov. 1992.

Young, J. W. *California Community College Governance.* Rancho Cucamonga, Calif.: Chaffey Community College District, 1988.

Chapter 13

Articulation
and Transfer

Trudy H. Bers

Maintaining and disseminating accurate information about articulation and transfer to senior institutions are more intricate than almost anyone realizes, but they are absolutely essential for fostering and effecting smooth transfers between community colleges and four-year colleges and universities. The complexities and challenges of developing and implementing transfer policies and executing essential operational tasks are exacerbated by continual changes in courses, curricula, and personnel at both the two-year and four-year college levels. However, often it seems to be assumed that providing articulation and transfer services is an easy job that a single person or small staff can handle, often as an add-on to an already packed portfolio of responsibilities.

Most literature about articulation and transfer focuses either on attributes of programs and projects designed to enhance transfer, often targeted at minority and disadvantaged students; on alternative models for defining transfer rates; or on empirical or normative studies of transfer patterns. This chapter is somewhat different. Assuming that readers understand and accept that transfer is a key component in a community

247

college's mission and are generally familiar with the problems inherent in fulfilling this purpose, I focus instead on some structural and organizational concerns related to facilitating transfer through discussing a hypothetical articulation and transfer office (ATO). A key contention is that articulation requires constant vigilance by professional staff, that neglect breeds rapid decay in the value of information, and that students will suffer if sufficient resources are not attached to the articulation and transfer services of a community college.

ATO Functions

For the purposes of this chapter, I have adapted the general definitions of articulation and transfer suggested by Bender (1990). *Articulation* refers to "systematic efforts, processes, or services intended to ensure educational continuity and to facilitate orderly, unobstructed progress between levels of segments of institutions on a statewide, regional, or institution-to-institution basis" (p. viii). *Transfer* is the movement of a student from one institution to another with credit recognition for coursework successfully completed and treatment equitable to other students; transfer is also the compilation of mechanisms and processes used to facilitate admissions, recognition of credit, and related services.

Models for Facilitating Transfer

The literature on transfer suggests three broad approaches for fostering transfer from community colleges to senior institutions: the student development model, the documents model, and the academic model (National Center for Academic Achievement and Transfer, 1990). The student development approach concentrates on efforts such as helping students identify their criteria for selecting potential transfer institutions, advising and counseling students about transfer opportunities and appropriate course selections, arranging for campus visits by students to senior institutions and by representatives of senior institutions to the community college, and ascertaining probable costs and financial aid benefits. A natural organizational home for this combination of activities is the student affairs area.

The documents approach emphasizes the development and ongoing maintenance of formal or official agreements related to course equivalencies, articulated 2 + 2 programs, legislative or state agency policies related to transfer, and perhaps statistical reports about student transfer, persistence, and academic performance. Equally strong arguments can be made for vesting these responsibilities within student affairs or within the academic side of the institution.

The third approach, exemplified especially in the work of Judith S. Eaton and her associates at the Ford Foundation–funded National Center for Academic Achievement and Transfer, is the academic approach. Here the accent is on faculty-to-faculty collaborative efforts to align courses and programs, to reach common understandings within disciplines about accepted and expected content and rigor at the lower-division level, and to erode walls of misunderstanding and misperception between two- and four-year institutions.

Each approach has merit, and none is sufficient by itself to facilitate transfer. The balance among approaches will vary from institution to institution and even state to state depending on a variety of factors.

General Observations

Regardless of the approach or locus within the community college for articulation and transfer efforts, several observations apply.

1. *ATOs are boundary spanners within the college as well as externally.* ATO personnel both support and depend on administrators and faculty in student services and academic affairs with respect to giving and receiving information, working with students, and preparing materials about articulation and transfer for use by students directly and by staff. Externally, ATO personnel serve as liaisons between their own colleges and other organizations: colleges and universities to which and from which transfer occurs; state agencies that govern or coordinate higher education; legislators, many of whom receive questions or complaints from constituents about the transfer process and the sometimes mysterious or arcane reasons why students cannot trans-

fer credits from one college to another; and high school personnel seeking information to convey to their students during the
college choice process.

2. *ATOs work both with people and with paper.* Without documents that confirm the transferability or equivalency of courses
and/or programs and associated materials related to more general policies regarding transfer, core data that must be transmitted to students and advisors will be unavailable. As institutions and states move more to electronic sharing of information
and computer data bases to replace hard-copy files—a process
that allows data to be more readily updated—paper as we know
it may be reduced or displaced, but the basic need for data and
information remains. And people are essential, because ultimately it is people—faculty, staff, students—who make decisions about articulation and transfer.

3. *The specific tasks assigned to an ATO as well as the relative
complexity of these tasks and the time consumed in executing them are influenced by a variety of factors external to the office itself and even external
to the institution.* For example, in a state such as Florida, with
its common course numbering system and rules mandating
course transferability, communicating among colleges is simpler than in states such as New Jersey, where institutions negotiate directly with each other about course equivalencies and transferability and where course prefixes, numbers, and titles are
assigned at the institutional level. Where a college sends the vast
majority of its transfers to a single university, as does Kishwau-
kee College in Illinois—where some 80 percent of transfers move
to Northern Illinois University—tasks may be simpler than in
colleges like Oakton in Illinois, from which students transfer
to literally hundreds of different institutions, no one being dominant. However, even where only a small percentage of students
want to go to other places beyond the dominant school, it is
incumbent on the community college to keep abreast of changes
elsewhere.

In communities where parents have high educational expectations for their children, facilitating transfer is likely to be
of higher priority than will be the case in areas where expectations for higher education are lower. In addition, high-socio-

economic-status communities are more likely to perceive flagship state universities and a selected set of independent colleges and universities as the primary schools to which transfer ought to be possible, even if the actual number of students moving to these institutions is relatively small. Thus, for political and symbolic reasons, certain senior institutions will be more salient to an ATO than the incidence of transfer might suggest.

4. *Many discrete activities fall under the broad rubric of articulation and transfer. Most of these activities* must *be executed, though they need not all be assigned to the same office within the institution.* Factors such as institutional history, ad hominem interests and talents, and availability of staff and even of space will shape the actual distribution of responsibility and authority for these activities. In the next section, a variety of articulation and transfer activities are described. The list indicates the array of tasks that comprise the articulation and transfer function writ broadly and can be a useful tool for assessing the extent to which a college is organized and staffed to support articulation and transfer.

Articulation and Transfer Activities

Key articulation and transfer activities are described below. The list, while extensive, is not exhaustive.

Articulating Courses and Programs. This includes communicating and documenting the equivalency of at least all transfer courses to all applicable senior institutions, the substitutability of specific courses from one institution to another, and the alignment of associate degree curricula or prescribed patterns of coursework. The goal is to ensure the transfer of credits as a bloc from one institution to another, ideally to satisfy general education or other specified lower-division work required at the receiving institution in its entirety. Continual revisions in course contents and in general education and major requirements make articulation a never-ending process. Changes in course/curriculum contents or in the acceptability of work are not always communicated clearly or in a timely fashion from one college to another, so that information thought to be accurate may in fact be outdated. General education requirements differ among institutions and sometimes even among colleges within the same university, exacerbating the acquisition and communication of accurate information. Sometimes articulation information that senior institutions provide is inconsistent or inaccurate, requiring clarification. Most frustrating, community colleges may be asked to provide course syllabus information about their courses that does not exist comparably at the senior institution because they do not require faculty teaching the same course to adhere to a common outline or set of assignments and may not even have copies of syllabi to send to the community college.

Researching Transfer. Researching transfer includes tracking students' transfer behavior among institutions; calculating transfer rates using alternative models; examining academic performance and achievements after transfer; and assessing the experiences of students who transfer through surveys, on-campus visits, and other means. This is among the most sensitive areas for the ATO given, for example, widespread misunderstanding about the nature of community college students and the fact that for many, transferring is not a desired goal. Other obstacles include the reluctance of many institutions to share student-specific data such as grade-point averages; the absence of shared datafiles that permit tracking students among public and private, two- and four-year institutions in and out of state; and debate about alternative formulas for measuring transfer.

Preparing Advising Information. Compiling accurate, pertinent information about topics such as program articulation agreements, recommended courses and course equivalencies, and admissions policies is essential. Determining how much detailed information students need at various stages in their college careers and presenting the information in an understandable format are key parts of the process. The advent of computers, especially PC data base programs, networks, voice mail and bulletin boards, and touch screens has opened new and exciting opportunities for maintaining and conveying data and information. At the same time, the influx of students with limited English proficiency into community colleges, many from nations that have no equivalents to community colleges and that do not enable transfer among colleges, has brought another new, challenging dimension to explaining transfer and helping students make wise choices about their courses and programs of study.

Monitoring Changes, Trends, and Opportunities. Through formal and informal means, community colleges should stay abreast of developments such as budgetary constraints that limit or reduce spaces available for transfer students at senior institutions. They should also track changes in the economic environment likely to affect families' or students' abilities to finance college, especially at residential, higher-priced institutions. Other factors that should be monitored include changes in external accrediting agency criteria affecting course acceptability or the prescribed level at which certain subjects are to be taught, shifts in federal and state student financial aid policies or appropriations, and labor market restructurings that enhance or diminish the attractiveness of certain fields. This type of activity necessitates moving beyond the specifics of courses and curricula, into the world of environmental scanning and strategic thinking. The ATO that can conceptualize and synthesize information about topics such as these will be invaluable in helping the college position itself to be able to respond to changing needs and dynamics associated with articulation and transfer.

Troubleshooting Specific Problems. Troubleshooting may involve intervening on behalf of a specific student or program that is experiencing difficulty in obtaining information about transfer or receiving credit for courses. While the ATO cannot always resolve problems satisfactorily, a direct telephone call or letter written to the appropriate person at another school can untangle bureaucratic red tape or confusion that would otherwise impede or even prevent articulation and transfer.

Establishing Connections with Other Institutions. Developing positive working relationships to enhance credibility and foster candid, timely exchanges of information is crucial. This is one of the most important characteristics of an effective ATO, because it provides the foundation on which both formal and informal articulation and transfer activities are based.

Identifying Problems in Courses and Programs. Using feedback from other institutions about course and program transferability and student performance, the ATO is in a unique position to flag problems or desired shifts in content in courses and programs and to alert faculty within the community college about these. Requests from senior institutions for specific information about writing assignments in courses other than composition send clear signals that community college faculty need to incorporate required writing assignments. Sometimes the embarrassment of sending a general syllabus dated ten years earlier is a prompt to revisit the course outline. The senior institution is not always "correct," however. For example, community colleges were ahead of most colleges of businesses in understanding that business majors were better served in their required business computer courses by learning to use software application programs than by learning a programming language. For several years, then, the content of transferable business computer courses lagged behind what business and industry wanted from their employees.

Implementing Educational Guarantees. Compliance with provisions of educational guarantees related to courses or programs must be ensured, and cases where the guarantee is invoked need to be monitored. Educational guarantees are relative newcomers to the portfolio of mechanisms by which community colleges are measuring and demonstrating accountability and quality. Greeted with enthusiasm in some quarters and with skepticism in others, the guarantee process can provide important cues about transfer.

Organizing and Publicizing Campus Visits. Campus visits are useful activities for enhancing person-to-person contacts and for expanding knowledge about transfer among students, faculty, and staff. Examples include bringing representatives of senior institutions to the community college campus to meet with potential students or with faculty and staff, encouraging students to visit campuses to which they are considering transfer, and arranging for community college faculty and staff to meet with colleagues on site at transfer institutions.

Arranging Special Programs. This activity encompasses a large variety of special events that can be targeted to specific groups. Examples include group field trips (students or faculty) to visit several institutions in one itinerary; financial aid workshops conducted by representatives from several institutions; and college fairs that include schools within commuting distance, targeted especially to place-bound students nearing the end of their community college programs. Special programs launched on a pilot or one-time-only basis encourage innovation and risk taking without locking the college into long-term commitments.

Collaborating on Tech Prep, 2 + 2 + 2 Programs. This entails helping high school personnel understand issues pertinent to the transfer of vocational coursework and helping four-year college and university personnel understand the structure and content of community college associate in applied science degrees in order to build 2 + 2 + 2 articulation agreements. Tech Prep is a fairly new but rapidly growing approach to vocational education that comprises a variety of initiatives. These initiatives are designed to improve the technological and workforce skills of high school students and young adults; to modernize and revitalize what used to be called vocational education, practical arts, or industrial education; and to bolster the academic credibility and strength of vocational education at the high school level. One concept that is particularly attractive in areas where parents are intent on their children earning baccalaureate degrees is the development of agreed-on courses of study whereby a student begins taking vocational courses in high school, moves to the community college in a related program and places immediately into courses that begin where the high school courses left off, and ultimately transfers at the junior level to a senior institution that gives full credit for the associate in applied science degree. Very attractive in theory, 2 + 2 + 2 agreements can be exceedingly difficult to negotiate, partly because of ingrained skepticism that university faculty have for high school and even community college vocational education.

Developing Novel Approaches to Creating Programs. Developing creative approaches to structuring and delivering programs can involve putting together what is heard from students about programs they need; synthesizing information about actual course-taking and transfer patterns; and working with other institutions to establish and promote innovative academic programs. One example of a novel approach is the offering of joint degrees in collaboration among several institutions. A second example might include guaranteed admissions, whereby students entering the community college are guaranteed admission and full credit at a participating senior institution, provided they meet certain standards such as a minimum grade-point average or completion of sixty hours within a given time frame. A final example would be concurrent enrollments, through which students register at several colleges simultaneously, each institution having given prior approval to coursework taken at the others.

Communicating with Receiving Institutions. Communicating with key receiving institutions and asking their probable response to proposed changes at the community college can identify and prompt reconsideration of policies and practices that make sense internally but do not work well for students beyond the immediate institution. For example, a community college might be pressured to give proficiency credit for coursework taken in high school. But if most students plan to transfer these credits to senior institutions and if senior institutions will not accept the credits, a short-term benefit to students will be converted to a long-term disadvantage. Sometimes community college faculty want to revise a course that is crucial for transfer, not realizing the newer version will not articulate well.

Feeding Back Information from Senior Institutions. This activity involves communicating internally changes occurring at senior institutions in areas such as general education, contents of specific course and programs, policies related to transfer, and even deadlines for application. Designating an office to receive this type of information from senior institutions increases the likelihood that it will be received and disseminated and simplifies getting answers to questions or resolving problems. Formation and active participation in statewide groups comprising transfer representatives from both two- and four-year institutions, such as the Illinois Transfer Coordinators Group, can promote feedback as well.

Issues Requiring Special Tact and Sensitivity

The activities outlined above are relatively straightforward, though their complexity and the vast amount of detail involved cannot be minimized. Other issues are much more sensitive in nature; handling them requires the ATO to exercise tact and to be familiar with the politics of institutions as well as with unique relationships or goals. These issues need to be dealt with on a case-by-case basis because circumstances, stakeholders, and other influences vary.

Saying No to Formal Agreements. Sometimes well-intentioned representatives from senior institutions seek to establish formal articulation agreements with community colleges without understanding the time-consuming nature of the process if curricula do not align well. If few students transfer to that senior institution currently, the establishment of an articulation agreement will be unlikely to prompt a spurt in transfer numbers, while curriculum revisions at either school will trigger even more time-consuming labor to refine the agreement.

Put another way, it is sometimes not worth the effort to develop a formal articulation agreement. But an outright no is hardly politic. One alternative approach to suggest would be to develop general principles of articulation—for example, whereby the senior institution would accept the student's associate degree work in its entirety and give the student junior status. Alternatively, arrangements could be worked out on a student-by-student basis (which can actually take little or no time if the number of transfer students is small). Another proposal might be to increase the visibility of information about the senior institution to encourage students to consider transferring there.

Encouraging Faculty-to-Faculty Interactions. There is universal agreement that articulation and transfer improve where faculty from two- and four-year institutions work together, where mutual respect exists, and where problems are resolved amicably. A danger, however, is that faculty will reach "agreements" that reside in their heads, in scribbled notes filed in bottom drawers, even in formal letters not copied to ATOs. There is also a risk that in their enthusiasm to conclude articulation agreements for a specific program, faculty may not appreciate the narrowness of the agreement and begin promoting it as being more comprehensive than it is. A challenge for the ATO is both to foster faculty involvement in articulation and transfer and to maintain an active role so that agreements reach whatever official status is needed. This will ensure that they last beyond the tenure of those directly involved in negotiating them. Establishing the ATO as the funnel through which communications and agreements pass is one method for accomplishing this.

Balancing the Needs of Minority and Other Students. National concern about the relatively small number of minority and disadvantaged students earning baccalaureate degrees and targeted funding support for transfer centers designed to promote minority transfer have prompted substantial efforts to help these students transfer. In some institutions, transfer centers were established for minority students that duplicated activities already carried out elsewhere in the institution. This led to confusion about what office was responsible for what, redundant actions to gather and distribute information, and a sense among majority students that the institution was less interested in their academic progress. Clearly many minority students face special challenges in transferring, but all students might be better served by differentiating articulation and transfer activities that serve the needs of all students from those needed by minority students, and efficiently allocating resources to avoid repetition and redundancy.

Providing Appropriate Information About Transfer Options. Students easily become overwhelmed by the details of transfer and the difficulty of assessing their options; thus, they tend to limit the range of schools to which they consider transferring. ATOs may also unintentionally guide students to institutions with which the ATO regularly works and that provide the clearest information about transfer. The ATO needs to remain alert to these tendencies so as to expose students to multiple transfer opportunities.

Pressing for Internal Changes in Courses and Curricula. An extension of the activity of feeding back information, pressing for change requires the ATO to be proactive with faculty, sometimes in the face of resistance to change. Strong relationships with academic deans and faculty and being perceived as credible standard-bearers for academic quality and currency are essential ATO attributes for this process to be effective. Arguing the college's case requires the same attributes, along with strong relationships and respect at the senior institution.

Engaging in Boundary Spanning Versus Territorial Aggression. It is highly unlikely that all articulation and transfer activities listed above will be housed within the same office at a college. Executing tasks that rub against the authority and responsibilities claimed by other offices can be challenging. Periodic "audits" of ATO activities can be useful to determine who within an institution is taking care of various articulation and transfer tasks, to clarify assignments, and to reorganize processes. However, there probably will always be incidents where two areas assert authority over the same activity, and/or other areas where no one accepts responsibility and a task is left undone.

Staffing and Support for the ATO

No single way to organize an effective ATO is preferable. As should be clear from the discussion above, the range of tasks associated with facilitating articulation and transfer is wide, and a variety of offices may appropriately be assigned a given responsibility. Good internal communications among various departments involved in the articulation and transfer process and a willingness to collaborate and listen to each other are more relevant attributes for a high-quality process than a prescribed organizational structure.

There are, however, certain characteristics of an ATO—whatever its formal name, organization, or task agenda—that are crucial to its success. One is that the ATO be headed by an individual with sound academic credentials who is high enough in the organization to command respect through both position and abilities. Whether because of this person's title, personality, or both, the ATO needs to have access to faculty. The

ATO administrator has to be able to represent the institution with faculty and staff elsewhere, to have internal credibility, to be knowledgeable about and sensitive to the kinds of intra- and interdisciplinary conflicts that drive decisions about articulation and transfer, to have the insight and tact to address sensitive issues such as those outlined above, and to be able to organize and monitor never-ending details. ATO leaders will need the talent to interact, often directly, with a host of constituencies, including faculty and staff from their home and other institutions, students and advisers, state agencies, boards and advisory committees, high schools, foundations, and even the press.

The effective ATO will also have competent staff and technology to manage the day-to-day activities of the office and to build and maintain data bases related to course equivalency, articulation agreements, and so on. Among the most exciting possibilities is the construction of regional or statewide on-line data bases that allow data to be updated and shared efficiently and on a real-time basis. This will facilitate direct student access to on-line articulation and transfer information.

Summary

ATOs are essential components in community colleges that take seriously their transfer purpose. Often, however, the many duties associated with facilitating articulation and transfer are assigned willy-nilly, with minimal regard for how they correlate or whether the sum of assignments leads to optimum practices and policies.

The articulation and transfer activities described above can be useful tools for assessing the effectiveness of the ATO. Many of the activities deal with information — gathering it, disseminating it, and using it to plan future directions and programs. Others have to do with developing new programs and stimulating creative change in existing ones. Since the activities of the ATO will vary according to the surrounding environment at the individual school, the administration must be sure that none of these important areas of concern are overlooked, even though they might be the responsibility of another department. Community college leaders committed to articulation and transfer must recognize the importance of the ATO and the barriers to transfer that can evolve in the absence of an effective office.

References

Bender, L. W. (ed.). *Spotlight on the Transfer Function: National Study of State Policies and Practices.* Washington, D.C.: American Association of Community and Junior Colleges, 1990.

National Center for Academic Achievement and Transfer. *An Academic Model of Transfer Education.* Working papers, vol. 1, no. 1. Washington, D.C.: American Council on Education, 1990.

Chapter 14

Community and Industry Programs

Geneva Waddell

Innovative programs are urgently needed in most communities to meet growing community and industry demands. Reframing existing programs can lead to innovations in program development. Keeping good programs healthy by making them more viable in the community must be a top priority in the 1990s and beyond.

Program Types and Needs

This chapter reviews the types of programs that have been or should be designed for off-campus agencies. Ways of organizing, funding, and categorizing such programs are also discussed.

Several questions frame the area of programs designed for the external community. Who needs new programs? What organizations would be interested in these programs? How can they be exhibited best? How can we keep the recipients' needs in mind at all times? How can the programs be self-supporting? Other questions arise as well. How can we get and keep people excited about the programs? Who can help with development,

262

implementation, or marketing? How can we build in acceptance and ownership? How can we share the benefits?

Specific answers to these questions must be incorporated into the structure, planning, implementation, and evaluation processes for community and industry programs in order for them to be most successful in meeting community needs. Added efforts to solve problems and foster growth in our communities are vital to our changing economy.

Types of programs that should be developed include the following: Allied Health, adult literacy, technical training, and cooperative education. Providing practitioners who function well in health-care settings is an important step in meeting community health care needs. Developing programs "specific to the needs of a community will positively affect the supply of health care in the area and provide a stable work force, since graduates of community colleges often remain in the geographic area, and increase accountability in program development" (Turkeltaub, 1991, p. 55).

As we move through the information economy into a bio-economy, we see astounding technological changes in health care and other industries. Innovations, such as smart toilets, for example, can generate information on blood pressure, pulse, temperature, urine, and weight (Davis and Davidson, 1991). This technology allows for "storage of up to 130 days of readings, prints them out, transfers them to a personal computer or transmits them via modem to a medical service for further analysis" (p. 16). Likewise, smart refrigerators could, in the future, "guide our health by monitoring our intake, in much the same way that smart toilets can now guard our health while monitoring our outtake" (p. 195). Can community colleges afford to be less innovative than this in reframing and rethinking their programs? Will community colleges still be in business in the twenty-first century if they fail to redefine their business based on these and other technological advances?

Concurrently, the substance of technical education programs must be improved. National studies regularly report growing shortages of people in technical careers. More fundamental than the lack of employees in these fields, however, is a heightened level of skill and sophistication needed to enter and be successful in certain technical fields. According to Parilla (1991, p. 1) revolutionary thinking will be required to create the programs we need: "Employers have been clear in defining skills that they require from employees and educators must now reassess their natural conservatism and become catalysts of change. Joining forces with private and public sector employers in our communities to provide students with technical education which focuses on development of the whole person is urgently needed in most communities to keep pace with technological and economic changes."

One example of this type of cooperative effort is evident at a Maryland community college through an institute for technical education. This institute was made possible through an innovative partnership between private and public sectors. A single private contribution of about $1.5 million brought private donations in cash and equipment to about $3 million, which the county government matched. Over 200 additional gifts in scholarships, instructional supplies, equipment, and funds were also received. The institute houses facilities for the apprenticeship/ technical trades, automotive technology, building trades technology, and printing management programs. As employment opportunities in these fields continue to grow in the community and as technology becomes increasingly more sophisticated, the institute is providing hands-on training to meet employer and employee needs. The board of directors of the College Foundation, the chief administrative officer, and the appropriate instructional dean provide fiscal management of this institute. Programs are managed on a day-to-day basis by program coordinators. The institute is organized to accommodate both credit and noncredit programs in technical education.

Further, deficiencies in basic skills have created a "literacy crisis" across our nation that may be directly related to lagging productivity and may endanger future American economic competitiveness (Rothwell and Brandenburg, 1990). Rudimentary abilities to read, write, and compute as well as abilities to demonstrate productive work attitudes and behaviors need improvement. Communities, industries, and community colleges must be a part of the solution. Partnerships with public school systems must also be strengthened to provide solutions to adult literacy problems (Waddell, 1991).

The American Association of Community and Junior Colleges' Commission on the Future of Community Colleges urges colleges to coalesce around the concept of community education to solve literacy problems and meet other related needs. In its 1988 report, the commission suggests that "the community college, at its best, can be a center for problem-solving in adult illiteracy or the education of the disabled. . . . It can also be the place where education and business leaders meet to talk about the problems of displaced workers. . . . The community college can take the lead in long-range planning for community development. And it can serve as the focal point for improving the quality of life in the inner city" (American Association of Community and Junior Colleges, 1988, p. 35).

Invaluable to achieving employment objectives in our communities are cooperative education programs. However, many community colleges may be shortchanging their students and communities by underutilizing co-op potential (Rheams and Saint, 1991). For example, many policies are restrictive and do not address the need for attracting and retaining at-risk students. Rheams and Saint suggest that "cooperative education programs be strengthened in community colleges by working cooperatively with local unemployment and social services agencies to provide basic skills training through existing developmental programs and by providing employment and life skills training through a pre co-op work experience" (p. 52). Cooperative education is an investment that can yield immediate dividends through taxes and pays a continuing annuity through self-sufficient citizens in the community (p. 53).

In the concluding thoughts of a report titled *The Way We Are: The Community College as American Thermometer* (1992, p. 32), Adelman points out that "the time we typically allow for schooling does not permit depth. So we grasp for something particular, something we perceive as related to current or future work. The result is that we may know more about what we do for a living, but are less adaptable to changes in the conditions or opportunities of work." Rethinking some of our community and industry programs to help employees and employers adapt to changes in conditions and opportunities of work is urgently needed.

Structures and infrastructures must exist that promote lifelong learning, community service, and workforce development. While standardization and the "one size fits all" approaches cannot be applied to structure, some common threads do exist. These threads are interwoven throughout the fabric of the institution. They link providers of programs and services with community and industry groups who need them. They are not credit/noncredit sensitive. They share a common goal of meeting the needs of employees and employers in the community.

Structures and Infrastructures

A wide array of structures exists in community colleges for meeting community and industry needs. Structure, or the lack of it, is generally determined by such factors as community need, financing, level of state or local control, or institutional needs. For example, Myran (1969) lists traditional college structures, including five patterns for community service programs: (1) Departmental Extension Pattern — community service programs are located in and generated through traditional departmental structures, (2) College Centralized Pattern — professional community service staff members divide their time between assessing community needs and coordinating programs and are located in a separate department or division, (3) Community Specialist Pattern — specialists are located in the community rather than on campus, (4) Community Advisory Group Pattern — ad hoc committees deal with critical issues, and (5) College Affiliate Pattern — individuals have direct responsibility to organizations in the community and an affiliate relationship with the college (pp. 23–27). Whatever the structure for meeting community and industry needs, however, faculty and administrators must be committed to, and be a part of, the plan to address these needs.

An infrastructure is also key to successful community and industry programs that relate to economic development efforts. According to Kopecek (1991, p. 46), "A broad-based organization that brings together the leadership of the community is an absolute necessity. It must enjoy the endorsement and involvement of key political and business leaders, including representatives of major banks. The specific function or objective of the organization should be to plan and market and to provide a one-stop information service. Its more important task, however, is to be the integrating force that gives continuity to efforts to provide a favorable climate in which economic growth and expansion can occur." Kopecek asserts that "when an organization of this type exists, the community college president should join it. If it does not exist, then he or she should work to establish it" (p. 46). He says that the president who wishes to become a leader in the community among other things must be concerned with the expansion of infrastructure, competitive tax structures, provision of competitive financing packages, and active ongoing regional marketing programs that clearly demonstrate why the targeted communities are good places to live, work, and raise a family (p. 41).

Funding

No best plan for funding community programs is apparent. According to Cohen and Brawer (1989), ways community programs are funded reflect both their growth and variety. They point out that "some community education activities receive no direct aid; all expenses are borne by the participants themselves or by an agency with which the institution has a contract. Others are funded by enrollment formulas that tend to be lower than the formulas used for the career and collegiate courses. Funding for the recreational and avocational activities within the community education definition is the most difficult to obtain because those activities seem least justifiable for support at taxpayer expense" (p. 271). Maryland, for example, funds continuing education courses meeting specific criteria related to occupational, developmental, and consumer education, but recreational courses are not eligible for reimbursement (Maryland State Board for Community Colleges, 1988).

Funding by local taxes and participants' fees are most typical. However, such funding practices tend to vary among states. For example, some states fund adult basic education programs at the same rate as career or collegiate programs, while other states fund them under different formulas (Cohen and Brawer, 1989). Oregon and Florida reimburse colleges for remedial and continuing education courses at the same level as career programs, while continuing education courses in Iowa are not eligible for state reimbursement (p. 272).

Funding questions that require specific answers include the following: What level of funds currently comes from the local community? How is the college financed? Should community and industry programs be funded privately, publicly, or both? What funding alternatives can we provide decision makers? What does the budget for the first year look like? What support for community programs is available from civic, social, and political organizations? What social and political sensitivities relate to existing or new programs? What effect will past or present social or political behavior have on promotion of new services or programs?

Newly Emergent Programs

The years ahead will no doubt bring strategic alignment of community colleges and state economic development policy, according to Melville and Chmura (1991). They suggest that in the 1980s, "the most common approach at the state level was to create new programs that made special monies available outside the traditional higher education funding process which enabled state policy makers to earmark funds for specific purposes" and that "some states have begun the process of 'strategic alignment' of their community colleges with economic development policy" (p. 8).

Examples of programs and activities highlighted by Melville and Chmura include: Oregon — taking responsibility for small business assistance; Arizona — actively anticipating community needs; Illinois—building a foundation and rewarding innovation; Ohio—making technology transfer a community college priority; South Carolina—investing in comprehensive flexibility; North Carolina—creating the climate for collaboration; and California—using intermediary organizations as catalysts (pp. 8–14).

Nespoli (1991, p. 21) further highlights state support of community programs through support of activities such as 2 + 2 programs across America, the California Employment Training Panel, the Florida Sunshine State Skills Corporation, the Iowa Industrial New Jobs Training Program, and the Maryland Partnership Through Workforce Quality.

According to Zeiss (personal communication, Dec. 1991), types of programs and services need to include *at least* technical training, employee retention services, literacy training, management development, and assessment services based on specific, documented needs. Parilla (1991, p. 1) adds that community colleges "need to expand the concept of technical education to encompass not only acquisition of skills but also the development of the whole person. Curricula and programs must be reevaluated and revised to provide the broad general background needed to achieve these goals. Partnerships must be developed between industry and education to obtain the sources and support required for the task of reframing technical training within the context of higher education." According to Parilla, "The first and most essential step is a joint institutional and public commitment to a fresh interpretation of the nature of technical education" (p. 1).

Exhibit 14.1 gives examples and sources of some *community* programs provided by community colleges. Exhibit 14.2 furnishes examples and sources of some *industry programs* provided. These exhibits are not intended to be representative of all community colleges or programs or to be all-inclusive.

Questions of Vision, Mission, and Purpose

As we move into the twenty-first century and as the "information economy" becomes the "bioeconomy" (Davidson and Davis,

Exhibit 14.1. Community Programs.

Example	Source
Career	Cohen and Brawer, 1989
Occupational upgrade or relicensure, such as nurse practitioner, insurance, and real estate	Hirshberg, 1991
Compensatory	Cohen and Brawer, 1989
Credit by exam; co-op	Rheams and Saint, 1991
Adult literacy	Zeiss, 1991; American Association of Community and Junior Colleges, 1988
Collegiate	Cohen and Brawer, 1989
2 + 2 Tech Prep	Nespoli, 1991
2 + 2 + 2	Parnell, 1990
Combined	American Association of Community and Junior Colleges, 1988
Prison inmate, day care, displaced worker, and so forth	

1991, p. 21), how must our visions change? Does the president's vision include community and industry programs and services? In an environment of "smart toilets," how will communities and industries differ? How will community college students differ? What is the college's mission today? How will it change? Who can change it? What does the college do best? Do the faculty members react to social entities or are they proactive in offering services?

It is helpful when colleges include community and industry services as an integral part of their vision and mission statements (Zeiss, personal communication, Dec. 1991). Carmichael (1991, p. 25) further adds, for example, that the practice of hosting quasi-independent entities, such as small business development centers, requires clarification of Small Business Administration and college goals.

Exhibit 14.2. Industry Programs and Services.

Example	*Source*
Small business	
Development centers	Carmichael, 1991
Business incubators	Weinberg and Burnier, 1991
Economic development	Katsinas and Lacey, 1990
Importing and exporting	Gell and Crupi, 1991
Apprenticeship and technical training	Parilla, 1991
Industry-specific training	
Health care	Turkeltaub, 1991
Retail, automotive, construction	Palmer, 1990
Contract training	Wuertele, 1990
Management development	
Operations research	
Total Quality Management	
Technical writing	
Computer and other skill building	
Assessment services	Zeiss, 1989; personal communication, Dec. 1991
Employee retention	Zeiss, 1990; personal communication, Dec. 1991
Partnerships	Carnevale, Gainer, Villet, and Holland, 1990
Other services	Hirshberg, 1991

Conceptualization

Knowing how programs will meet specific needs most effectively is the key to conceptualizing community and industry programs. Zeiss (1991) suggests beginning with an idea and a concept paper, having knowledgeable people review the concept paper, then researching and preparing a technical paper that can be used as a vehicle to focus on essentials. It is important to communicate the idea energetically.

According to Zeiss, a concept paper should identify a specific need, list objectives to meet this need, describe program benefits, and provide technical data for program evaluation. Questions to be answered in the conceptualization stage include the following: Does this concept fit within the college mission, the president's or trustees' vision, and college objectives? Are we willing to provide for extra work and energy to see the concept developed and the program implemented through evaluation and needed revision?

Principles

Some basic principles for successful community and industry programs relate to: (1) knowing the college and community, (2) identifying and specifying a clear need, (3) developing the idea fully, (4) identifying alternative funding sources, (5) selling to publics regularly, (6) implementing programs with enthusiasm, and (7) evaluating and publicizing results internally and externally (Zeiss, 1989). These rules apply consistently across communities, their colleges and industries. Deviation from, or elimination of, any one of these rules can place both programs and the college image in jeopardy. Zeiss (1989) suggests that a strong need exists to deliver on commitments, ask advice, and send thanks frequently.

Skills

The ability to communicate with diverse groups is a primary skill and must include wit, clarity, and profundity of expression. Marketing skills are essential at all levels, and the ability to develop a sound marketing plan is a must.

Strategic decision-making skills by key administrators can determine success or failure of programs, since timely decisions based on pertinent and reliable research data are required. Planning and organizing skills can make or break a much-needed program or service. Sensitivity to and knowledge of political and social implications of programs are essential, too.

MacDougall and Friedlander (1989, p. 259) suggest that "many business representatives still do not believe that an academic person is willing to work on business or governmental problems not directly related to education. As with all groups, these initial concerns dissipate quickly when the individual does a competent job." As one college president discovered, "You have to deliver on what you say and promise. Otherwise, you lose your credibility. Once you lose your credibility, staff are reluctant to put out energy to follow in other categories" (p. 259).

Managers of community education programs "must be curriculum and instructional designers" and be able to "interact with community advisory committees, find agencies to bear the cost of their programs, advertise for students, employ part-time staff members continually, produce varieties of new instructional media, and resolve jurisdictional disputes with other agencies (Cohen and Brawer, 1989, p. 270).

Community programs, which include such endeavors as business incubators, require individuals who have had experience in both real estate management and the provision of assistance to entrepreneurial start-ups. According to Weinberg and Burnier (1991, pp. 37–38), "When the community college lacks experience in these areas, it may be more appropriate to pursue alternative entrepreneurial development programs that provide business development services to community entrepreneurs or to develop an entrepreneurial outreach program or an incubation system."

A basic knowledge of financing methods and tools is essential to cost-effective community and industry programs. For example, Cohen and Brawer (1989, p. 274) point out that

> Much of community education transfers the cost of certain programs from one public agency to another. The training programs conducted by community colleges on behalf of police and fire departments that are too small to operate their own academies offer an example. Where the departments pay the college to do the training, little changes except that the college coordinates the training. But in some instances law enforcement programs are converted to degree-

or certificate-credit programs, thus qualifying them for support through the state's educational funds. The cost of these programs is therefore transferred from the local to the state government budget. Similarly, some industries contract with community colleges to train their workers, paying for the services. But in numerous instances such specifically targeted training programs are given for credit, thus shifting the cost from the industrial concern to the state budget.

Future Trends, Issues, and Challenges

Community and industry programs will continue to grow in the 1990s and beyond. In this and the next decade, however, these programs will require added efforts by community college administrators and faculty as well as community and industry leaders. For example, community colleges will need to go the extra ten miles to understand the workforce training needs of business and industry (Waddell, 1990).

Among trends affecting workforce training needs are (1) the growing complexity of many jobs, (2) a drop in the number of entry-level employees available, (3) a decline in the quality of basic skills of entry-level employees, and (4) the need for constant retraining as whole classes of jobs are made obsolete because of changing technology or organizational restructuring (U.S. Department of Labor, 1989). Further, trends related to the "graying of America" and increased use of technology in health-care settings, for example, have important curricular implications (Turkeltaub, 1991, p. 55). Community colleges not only need to take proactive steps to address community and industry needs created by these and other trends but must make additional efforts to encompass renovations in existing programs.

Issues and challenges community colleges will face in this and future decades center around funding, keeping pace with technology, and keeping two steps ahead of changes in community and industrial needs in order to provide rapid response and program flexibility.

According to Cohen and Brawer (1989, p. 82), continuing questions are:

How can an institution funded predominantly by the state respond appropriately to local needs? How can noncredit courses that may be every bit as valuable as credit courses be funded equitably? Can cultural presentations be offered as part of the regular humanities programs and thus absorbed into their funding packages? Should colleges expand their efforts at educational brokering? Who benefits? Who should pay? Should colleges seek additional contracts to provide educational services to industries and government agencies? How can the costs of these services be distributed equitably? How can quality be controlled in community education programs that do not come under scrutiny of any outside agency or under internal curriculum review?

Community leaders must be catalysts for change, and employers must be clear about the skills they require and training and services their employees need.

Forecasts

Difficulties in forecasting the need for community and industry programs become obvious when we examine global changes. While changing technology is reshaping the American economy, even more profound changes are occurring in the global economy that have a rippling effect on local economies. Parnell (1990, p. 69) points out, for example, that "stock market traders and farmers speculate in global financial markets that never sleep."

Among the forecasts Parnell offers that have implications for community and industry programs are the following:

- Many colleges and universities will reexamine their mission statements as related to community service, updating that mission to match the economic development needs of their service region or constituency. [p. 62]
- More cooperative efforts will be developed among research universities, state and private colleges, community colleges, and the employer community

in each state with an eye toward developing a more
effective system to support technology transfer
efforts. [p. 62]

- New and strengthened partnerships will be developed between the employer community, schools,
and colleges. It will be a rare community college or
state college that will not have established some
kind of special employer-college liaison office.
[p. 62]

- Colleges and universities will increasingly examine
internal institutional policies and procedures as to
flexibility and responsiveness. If community service
is a part of the institutional mission, then flexibility
and response time become important operational issues. [p. 62]

- An increasing number of colleges and universities
will reach out to help the eleven million or so small
business owners of the country. Such help will take
many forms (small business incubators, consultants, and worker training or retraining). [p. 63]

- A new and integrated 2 + 2 + 2 tech prep/associate
degree/bachelor of technology degree program will
become commonplace in schools and colleges. This
will be an applied academic program combining
the liberal arts with technical education, requiring
interdisciplinary and multidisciplinary teaching approaches. [p. 63]

- The associate degree will become an increasingly
important credential in helping to meet the emerging technical workforce needs of the employer community. [p. 62]

Recommendations

Emerging issues, forecasts, trends, and challenges lead to these
recommendations:

- Reframe technical training to focus on development of
the whole person.

- Develop partnerships that solve problems and meet needs (especially as they relate to health care, adult literacy, technical training).
- Build infrastructures that contribute to economic development and community service.
- Develop small business development centers and/or business incubators to meet community small business needs.
- Strengthen 2 + 2 + 2 programs to prepare students for technical careers.
- Provide employment and life skills training through precooperative education work experiences.
- Expand the vision and mission to include community and industry programs specifically.
- Examine institutional policies and procedures to operationally facilitate flexibility and responsiveness.
- Grow "imagineers" who can envision what needs to be done and engineer it through completion.
- Ask, ask, ask the right questions, know, know, know the best answers, and deliver, deliver, deliver as promised.
- Develop a sound marketing plan for community and industry programs based on documented needs.

Summary

Community and industry programs in the 1990s and beyond must be innovative, responsive, and flexible. They will require creative and knowledgeable people who are willing to take appropriate risks. The community college can be a leader in problem solving as academics and industry leaders work together to find solutions that are mutually helpful.

To develop effective community- and industry-based programs, planning must be done carefully, grounded in research done on demographics, current and developing career trends, budget constraints, and student interest. As the culture around us changes from an information economy to a bioeconomy, programs in health care and social services should be included in the curricula. The growing complexity of many jobs is a basis for new, high-quality technical programs. Faculty will play a key role in the success or failure of the program, so they should be chosen prudently.

Other important factors that require careful forethought are the issues of structure and funding. While the types chosen will vary depending on the location of the institution and the community's needs, the faculty and administration must be committed to these methods of meeting the needs. Reframing and rethinking existing programs must be a top priority in order to continue to meet community and industry needs.

References

Adelman, C. *The Way We Are: The Community College as American Thermometer*. Washington, D.C.: Office of Educational Research and Improvement, U.S. Department of Education, 1992.

American Association of Community and Junior Colleges. *Building Communities: A Vision for a New Century*. Report of the Commission on the Future of Community Colleges. Washington, D.C.: American Association of Community and Junior Colleges, 1988. (ED 293 578)

Carmichael, J. "Meeting Small Business Needs Through Small Business Development Centers." In G. Waddell (ed.), *Economic and Work Force Development*. New Directions for Community Colleges, no. 75. San Francisco: Jossey-Bass, 1991.

Carnevale, A. P., Gainer, L. J., Villet, J., and Holland, S. L. *Training Partnerships: Linking Employers and Providers*. Alexandria, Va.: American Society for Training and Development, 1990. (ED 319 925)

Cohen, A. M., and Brawer, F. B. *The American Community College*. (2nd ed.) San Francisco: Jossey-Bass, 1989.

Davis, S., and Davidson, B. *2020 Vision*. New York: Simon & Schuster, 1991.

Gell, R. L., and Crupi, J. A. "Trading in a Global Economy: Obstacles and Opportunities." In G. Waddell (ed.), *Economic and Work Force Development*. New Directions for Community Colleges, no. 75. San Francisco: Jossey-Bass, 1991.

Hirshberg, D. "Sources and Information: Community Colleges and Economic Development." In G. Waddell (ed.), *Economic and Work Force Development.* New Directions for Community Colleges, no. 75. San Francisco: Jossey-Bass, 1991.

Katsinas, S. G., and Lacey, V. A. "Community Colleges and Economic Development." *Community Services Catalyst,* 1990, *20*(1), 6–14.

Kopecek, R. "Assuming a Leadership Role in Community Economic Development." In G. Waddell (ed.), *Economic and Work Force Development.* New Directions for Community Colleges, no. 75. San Francisco: Jossey-Bass, 1991.

MacDougall, P. R., and Friedlander, J. H. "The Costs of Innovation." In T. O'Banion (ed.), *Innovation in the Community College.* New York: American Council on Education/Macmillan, 1989. (ED 305 981)

Maryland State Board for Community Colleges. *Maryland Community Colleges Continuing Education Manual.* Annapolis: Maryland State Board for Community Colleges, 1988. (ED 295 700)

Melville, J., and Chmura, T. "Strategic Alignment of Community Colleges and State Economic Policy." In G. Waddell (ed.), *Economic and Work Force Development.* New Directions for Community Colleges, no. 75. San Francisco: Jossey-Bass, 1991.

Myran, G. A. *Community Services in the Community College.* Washington, D.C.: American Association of Junior Colleges, 1969. (ED 037 202)

Nespoli, L. A. "Investing in Human Capital: State Strategies for Economic Development." In G. Waddell (ed.), *Economic and Work Force Development.* New Directions for Community Colleges, no. 75. San Francisco: Jossey-Bass, 1991.

Palmer, J. "How Do Community Colleges Serve Business and Industry? A Review of Issues Discussed in the Literature." Washington, D.C.: American Association of Community and Junior Colleges, 1990. (ED 319 443)

Parilla, R. E. Preface to G. Waddell (ed.), *Economic and Work Force Development.* New Directions for Community Colleges, no. 75. San Francisco: Jossey-Bass, 1991.

Parnell, D. *Dateline 2000: The New Higher Education Agenda.* Washington, D.C.: American Association of Community and Junior Colleges, 1990.

Rheams, P., and Saint, F. "Renovating Cooperative Education Programs." In G. Waddell (ed.), *Economic and Work Force Development*. New Directions for Community Colleges, no. 75. San Francisco: Jossey-Bass, 1991.

Rothwell, W. J., and Brandenburg, D. C. *The Workplace Literacy Primer: An Action Manual for Training and Development*. Amherst, Mass.: Human Resource Development Press, 1990.

Turkeltaub, M. K. "Meeting Health Care Credentialing Needs." In G. Waddell (ed.), *Economic and Work Force Development*. New Directions for Community Colleges, no. 75. San Francisco: Jossey-Bass, 1991.

U.S. Department of Labor. "Center for Advanced Learning Systems for the Employment and Training Administration." *CALS Bulletin*, 1989, *4*, 1.

Waddell, G. "Tips for Training a World-Class Work Force." *Community, Technical, and Junior College Journal*, 1990, *60*(4), 21–27.

Waddell, G. (ed.). *Economic and Work Force Development*. New Directions for Community Colleges, no. 75. San Francisco: Jossey-Bass, 1991.

Weinberg, M. L., and Burnier, D. L. "Developing Rural Business Incubators." In G. Waddell (ed.), *Economic and Work Force Development*. New Directions for Community Colleges, no. 75. San Francisco: Jossey-Bass, 1991.

Wuertele, P. "The Business and Industry Liaison as Consultant." *Community, Technical, and Junior College Journal*, 1990, *60*(4), 26–27.

Zeiss, T. "Employee Retention: A Challenge of the Nineties." *Community, Technical, and Junior College Journal*, 1990, *60*(4), 35–37.

Zeiss, T. *Creating a Literate Society*. Washington, D.C.: American Association of Community and Junior Colleges Press, 1991.

Zeiss, T. (ed.). *Economic Development: A Viewpoint from Business*. Washington, D.C.: American Association of Community and Junior Colleges and the Association of Community College Trustees, 1989.

Chapter 15

Student Services

Charles R. Dassance

Every two-year college in the United States has some form of student services program. How the program is organized and managed and what its goals are, however, vary considerably from college to college. There is also considerable variation in terms of what the program of student support services is called. *Student affairs, student personnel services,* and *student development services* are among the terms most frequently used to describe the student support services function. The term *student services,* as used throughout this chapter, means that functional area within the community college with the primary purpose of providing support services for students while they attend college.

While the nature of the student services programs varies among colleges, community college leaders generally recognize the need for a function dedicated to providing student-oriented services. These may include academic and personal counseling, financial aid, tutoring, and other academic assistance. According to Matson (1983), nearly all major community college writers have included guidance and counseling in lists of purposes of the two-year college. Tillery and Deegan (1985) found that while counseling and student support services were minor functions during the early years of the community college (1900–1930), those functions blossomed during the 1930s and 1940s in concert with the development of the field of student personnel, moved toward professionalization in the 1950–1970 period, and expanded greatly and became more fragmented between 1970 and the mid 1980s.

In a recent comprehensive review of the literature on student services in the community college, Creamer (1993) concluded that while student services has historically been important to the achievement of the goals of the community college, the function of student services has never been as critically important to community college education as some have claimed it should be. Creamer also drew the following compelling conclusion about the historical role of student services in the two-year college: "The review revealed an historical portrait of professional educators who are assigned responsibilities that are vital to student and institutional success, but who are struggling under chronic conditions of inadequate resources and colleague support for achieving their assigned duties" (pp. 449–450).

Creamer's conclusion may well characterize the current state of the student services function. Assuming the role of student services is vital to the achievement of the goals of students and the community college, community college leaders need to find a way to correct actual or perceived inadequacies of the function. This chapter addresses questions important to organizing and delivering an effective program of student services in the community college.

What Role for Student Services?

Many in the student personnel profession trace their roots to an American Council on Education report, issued in 1937, titled *The Student Personnel Point of View* (Saddlemire and Rentz, [1937] 1986). This report outlined the philosophy, services, and coordination for the emerging field of student affairs. In unequivocal terms, the report stressed the importance of educating the whole person, not just the intellect. The statement also listed twenty-three services that were deemed to be a part of a student services program, including admissions, orientation, advising, job placement, and housing.

The American Council on Education statement was updated in 1949 (Saddlemire and Rentz, [1949] 1986) but remained essentially the same, especially in regard to a philosophical commitment to educating the whole person. Student services has traditionally been based on humanistic, democratic principles, and a commitment to caring and concern for students remains a hallmark of the function.

What has also remained fairly constant is role confusion for student services. Offering an assessment of student services that reverberated throughout the profession, Elsner and Ames (1983, p. 139) stated that "no general consensus exists about the nature of, need for, or direction of community college student services programs. A model for change seems to elude most leaders. . . . Leaders of community colleges and student personnel staffs agree on one point: student services needs to be redesigned."

Should student services focus inclusively on its traditional role of being a provider of such specialized services as counseling, financial aid, job placement, and academic advising? Or should student services have the more esoteric goal of "developing the whole person"? Or should there be some completely new role for student services?

A related but critical question is who should determine the role student services should play within the college. In many cases, the student services division has defined its own role. All too often, such decisions have been made without consultation or concurrence from other segments of the college. Community college presidents, most of whom come from the ranks of academic deans, often have not had a clear understanding of the student services function or how it fits into the overall institutional program. As a result, many presidents have not focused much of their attention on the student services function.

Chief student affairs officers too often have been willing to accept the benign neglect of presidents as a blessing rather than viewing it as a matter of concern. Moreover, student services personnel have not been particularly articulate about their program goals or the need to integrate the student services function into the institutional fabric. Since many critics of student services have questioned the adequacy of its leadership function, one has to also ask if presidents have contributed to that perceived problem by the student services leadership appointments they have made. The combination of a president's ignorance of student services and inadequate student services leadership will certainly contribute to the ineffectiveness of a student services program.

While these points may be somewhat overstated, the fact remains that the role of student services has not been clear in many community colleges. With such lack of clarity as a beginning point, it has been particularly difficult to judge the effectiveness of student services or to judge the effect of budget reductions. If effectiveness is defined as attainment of intended goals, student services has often been in trouble from the start of the process, since goals frequently have been unclear or not stated at all.

The following sections will address administrative issues in student services relative to leadership organization, institutional and program planning, and assessment. The chapter also offers suggestions for further reading on program models and standards for student services.

Leadership

The success of any program, and certainly for the student services program, depends to a significant extent on leadership. Creamer (1989, p. 38) stated that leadership is "the greatest single deficiency in student affairs today." In planning for an effective program of student services, the issue of leadership must be addressed. The president is ultimately responsible for ensuring that proper leadership is provided. Too often in the past, choosing leaders has been a process of finding an individual who "gets along well with students" or "has done a good job as a counselor." Such a basis for the selection of a student services leader sets the stage for an ineffective student services program.

What then should be the basis for choosing leaders in student affairs? Creamer (1986) has suggested those things that he believes characterize an effective leader for student services. His list serves as the basis for the following recommended characteristics of an effective student services leader.

1. *Knowledgeable about student services, including the historical aspects.* Of course the leader should be knowledgeable about student services, but having a historical perspective is also important. A solid understanding of how student services has developed and changed within the community college provides a substantive basis from which to develop an effective program of student services and also adds to the leader's credibility as a well-grounded professional.

2. *Knowledgeable about human development theory and organizational development.* The explosion of human development theory in the past thirty-five years offers a wealth of information that can be used to theoretically ground student services programs. A thorough knowledge of human development theory also provides a basis from which the student affairs leader can contribute to the improvement of the teaching/learning facets. Knowledge of organizational development is important for planning and implementing change, and appropriate change is a requirement for the long-term health of any program.

3. *Competence as a researcher.* This skill is important so that the leader can formulate important questions to be addressed about students, accurately describe the reality of the institution, and contribute to the development of effective methods of assessment.

4. *Competence as a planner and organizational effectiveness specialist.* These skills are a key for an effective student services leader and programmer. While the ability to plan for student services is important, it is equally important for the student services leader to be concerned with the overall effectiveness of the college. This broader perspective is critical if student services is to be a significant factor in the total educational program. A focus on effectiveness also means a focus on outcomes, and that focus should be the ultimate guidepost for the leader.

5. *Value the goals of general education.* A case has been made elsewhere (Kuh, Shedd, Whitt, and Associates, 1987) that the goals of student services and the liberal arts are similar. The student affairs leader should be an educator who understands the broad goals of general education and can articulate student services support for those goals.

6. *Have vision.* The student services leader needs to provide a vision for what the student services program should be.

The vision will flow from personal beliefs about education and from knowledge and experience. Providing the vision is so important that it might be considered the most critical skill of an effective leader of student services, especially if the president's strength is not in student services.

These are not all of the competencies a president would want in a student services leader. Experience in budgeting, conflict resolution, and communication skills, to name a few, are also important skills. The point is that if student services is to achieve success, effective leadership is required. In choosing a leader for student services, a president must use criteria directly related to the desired outcome: an effective student services program.

Organizational Issues

How student services is organized is an important matter and has been the subject of some debate. In many cases, a major question has been the status of the student services function, especially in relation to academic affairs. This issue — a frequent topic of discussion among student services professionals — may obscure more important organizational considerations.

In his monograph on managing student affairs program, Deegan (1982) presented four organizational models for student services described in the literature. Three of the models were variations of traditional line-staff structures, and the fourth was a *hub-spoke* model. The hub-spoke model was designed to help integrate the student services and academic departments. Traditional models for organizing student services, which were not particularly effective, were nonetheless the norm. One of Deegan's recommendations, based on his review of organizational models, was that community colleges experiment with more flexible systems of organizing student services.

In a more recent article, Deegan (1984) again stressed the need to use models that integrate student services and academic affairs. He presented a *team organization model,* which was essentially a matrix management model designed to ensure the integration of academics and student affairs.

No one correct organizational mode for all student services programs exist. A number of factors, however, should be considered when deciding on an organization model. Among these factors are:

1. *Effectiveness.* The question of effectiveness should have top priority. What organizational structure is preferable for achieving institutional and student goals? While this may seem an obvious question, the norm is a line-staff organization perpetuated more by tradition than any other considerations. Educators are still learning to focus on outcomes and are often caught up in processes and procedures rather than concentrating on the desired goals. The president should be oriented toward the outcomes desired, and the organizational model for student services should evolve from that consideration.

2. *Integration with other college functions.* As has been emphasized, student services should be fully integrated with the other college functions, especially academic affairs. Cohen and Brawer (1989, p. 196) recognized this as an issue when they stated that "the challenge for college leaders has been to maintain a balance among all services and coordinate them with the formal instructional program."

While the organizational mode selected can certainly facilitate the integration of student services with the instructional program, so can an organizational culture that favors such integration. One way to achieve this integration has been recommended by Creamer (1987, p. 14), who suggests the establishment of an organizational standard requiring that the student services program "is planned, implemented, and evaluated by interunit, collaborative strategies." Any proposed new program or change of an existing one would only be considered if appropriate units outside student services have been involved in the planning for the program or change.

3. *Clear line of communication.* Student services leaders, if they are effective, should be representing a unique institutional perspective. With their knowledge of human development theory, grasp of student and institutional profile information, and awareness of the effects of institutional environmental factors on student learning and development, they should be in a position

organizationally to clearly present the student services perspective to the institution. Deegan (1982, p. 29) recommended that the chief student affairs officer "be at the highest level of management and report directly to the president." That recommendation appears to deal more with the issue of status than with the issue of effectiveness. The president needs to hear the student services voice, as do other key personnel in the institution, but the lines of authority and communication should be guided by whatever effectively achieves that end, not by a preconceived notion of appropriate organizational status. If the president understands the value of having the student services perspective clearly articulated, the issue of organizational placement for student services will be clear.

4. *Flexibility/experimentation.* The importance of being open to creating student affairs organizational structures that are flexible has been discussed. Achieving this goal will require experimenting with new structures, but such experimentation is appropriate. If student services programs have been criticized as ineffective, as has often been the case, it is logical to at least consider whether a radically different organizational structure might help improve effectiveness.

Experimenting is also likely to raise an issue that plagues student services: status. As discussed elsewhere (Dassance, 1988), student services has not been well served by fretting about its status and identity. How student services is perceived will be based on its effectiveness, not on organizational structure. Student affairs leaders should lead the charge to focus the program on an effectiveness model; the issues of identity and professionalism will be resolved naturally.

Partner in Institutional Planning

The recent focus on institutional effectiveness offers an opportunity for the development of more accepted, supported, and potent programs of student services. While the concept of institutional effectiveness is not new, the emphasis on the concept can be a catalyst for focusing attention on student services. Using the general definition of effectiveness as "comparing goals

achieved to results intended," the starting point for student services must involve stating goals.

In considering goals, student services leaders need to address two major questions:

- What are the college's goals, including its goals for students?
- How does student services contribute to the achievement
of college and student goals?

It cannot be emphasized too strongly that student services
must operate within the context of the purposes of the institution. However, this seemingly obvious point is frequently not
observed in practice, and both student services leaders and presidents need to share responsibility for ensuring that the student
services program is fully integrated into the institution's plan
for institutional effectiveness.

In terms of institutional goal setting, student services
should be a partner with other segments of the institution in
establishing the college's goals. Student services personnel should
bring to the goal-setting process a unique perspective on students, certainly including ideas for supporting student goal
achievement in college settings other than the classroom. Theories on the powerful learning results that can be achieved from
student involvement (Astin, 1985; Kuh, Schuh, Whitt, and Associates, 1991), as well as recent theories dealing with the importance of the interaction of the student and the environment
(Banning and Hughes, 1986), offer learning possibilities for student development. They also highlight learning that might not
be considered if student services leaders do not articulate these
perspectives. Since student services personnel should also be in
a position to articulate what students say about their experiences
at the college, this "customer satisfaction" perspective is one that
needs to be constantly considered.

While the major purpose of educational institutions is intellectual development, many colleges, as they wrestle with the
question about student outcomes, are recognizing the need to
state affective outcomes for students. As changes in the needs

of the workforce are recognized, outcomes such as critical thinking, self-direction, and interpersonal effectiveness are receiving more attention. Student services can help support these outcomes through out-of-class programming and through the way services are structured. Failing to recognize and use the student services program to support the college's plans for outcomes is to miss an important opportunity.

Perhaps most important, involving student services in the establishment of college goals sends two messages: first, student services is recognized within the college as having a legitimate role to play in contributing to the attainment of college goals, and second, student services receives the message that it must operate to support the overall institutional purposes.

Planning for Effectiveness

One key function for a successful student services program is planning. It is equally important that planning be conducted in a manner that fosters assessment of the effectiveness of the program. Because student services plays an important role in institutional planning, when the mission and goals of the institution are clearly established, student services must plan its program in a way that meshes with the institutional plan. Too often, student services planning has failed to relate to the institutional plan or has tried to do more than resources would permit. Drucker (1990) has pointed out that deciding what functions an organization should give up is the most important and difficult decision managers must make; such "giving up" seems to be particularly difficult for student services.

In the planning process for student services, consideration needs to be given to both long-term (that is, five-year) goals and annual objectives designed to achieve those goals. One useful approach to the longer term is to state "planning directions" for the program. The process of determining planning directions can be valuable for student services as well as for gaining support from other segments of the college for the general direction of the student services program. Statements of planning direction would provide parameters for the planning process by establishing intentions of the short-term planning process. Examples of planning direction would be:

Collaboration. Planning, implementing, and evaluating programs and services *only* in collaboration with other college departments, especially instructional affairs. (This establishes a standard for the way planning will occur.)

Student involvement. Increasing opportunities for student involvement on campus and reorienting cocurricular activities to directly support the mission and goals of the college. (This states a focus on programs that promote student involvement in the institution.)

Customer service. Standardizing the delivery of high-quality programs and services with a focus on quality in customer services. (This establishes a focus on quality services for students.)

These planning directions, which should be reviewed and updated annually, are important in establishing the focus of the student services department. The desire to collaborate with other departments within the college can be initiated by developing these planning directives in collaboration with other segments of the college, principally the academic division and the president.

The student affairs department at Florida Community College at Jacksonville (1989) used this "planning directions" approach to focus its planning activities. A large, multicampus institution, Florida Community College at Jacksonville has a large and complex student affairs program. To establish parameters for the planning process, the administrative leadership team established, and updated annually, a set of planning directions. As annual objectives were established, planning directions were used as one of the standards to determine if the objectives were appropriately focused.

The next step in the "planning for effectiveness" process for student services is to establish annual priority objectives to support the college's goals, with the planning directions providing

Exhibit 15.1. Objectives and
Measurement Criteria for Job Placement Services.

Objectives/outcomes	Effectiveness indicators
1. Students who need assistance obtaining full-time employment will learn job-seeking skills.	1a. At least 90 percent of the graduates who needed job placement assistance indicate on a survey that they know of the availability of the job placement services and have the skills necessary to obtain employment. 1b. Students participating in a "job-seeking assistance class" will achieve 90 percent mastery of the course objectives.
2. Students who use the job placement services will be satisfied with the services they receive.	2a. At least 90 percent of the students completing an opinion survey will rate the job placement services as satisfactory or better.

the general guidelines. At the same time that the objectives are agreed on, a method for assessing the degree to which the objectives are achieved should also be stated. This can be done in a variety of ways. Assuming that job placement services is offered as part of the student services program and that the availability of such services is part of the college mission, some examples of priority objectives for job placement services, and the criteria for their measurement, are listed in Exhibit 15.1.

We can make several points about the examples in the exhibit. First, the objectives/outcomes can address both developmental needs and the need for a service. If the college states in its goals an outcome for students to achieve "self-direction" (that is, assume responsibility for leading a life based on competent choices), that is a developmental goal. In the first objectives/outcomes in the exhibit, it is stated that students will gain the skills necessary to obtain a job (how to look for and interview for a job, how to prepare a résumé, and so on), rather than simply finding help with finding a job. Thus, the effectiveness indicator attempts to measure the degree to which students become self-directed with respect to obtaining employment. Second, the assessment of effectiveness should be based on multiple measures. In the first effectiveness indicator, both an opinion survey (1a) and a skills assessment (1b) are stated. The opinion survey measures an affective outcome, while the skills assessment measures a cognitive outcome.

This example can be expanded to every program and service that student services and the college offer. Nichols (1989) has proposed a similar process that links the college's mission statement, intended outcomes, and assessment criteria and procedures. Regardless of the process used, it is critical that a clear connection be made between institutional goals and student services plans. Demonstrating the degree to which plans are carried out, by stating effectiveness indicators and assessing the degree of successful objective attainment, will go a long way toward strengthening the credibility of student services.

Ashland Community College (1991) has used Nichols's approach in developing what are being called *institutional effectiveness plans*. From its statement of purpose, Ashland Community College developed program objectives for all areas of the college and also specified criteria for determining the degree to which the objects were met. The program is still in the developmental stage but has great promise for program accountability and improvement. For student affairs, effectiveness plans were established for admissions, registration and records, counseling, veterans services, testing, job placement, student activities, financial aid, and disabled student services.

Assessment

This chapter has emphasized the need to assess the effectiveness of student services objectives. Some other matters related to assessment are also important in the administration of student services.

It is generally agreed that the only two reasons to conduct assessment are accountability and program improvement. Linking objectives/outcomes and effectiveness, as already described, addresses the issue of accountability. Measuring student satisfaction is one powerful, direct, and fairly simple way to address the issue of program improvement.

Astin (1991, p. 6) says that student satisfaction is "perhaps the single most important affective . . . psychological area for outcomes assessment." The degree to which students are satisfied with the various programs and services offered provides a rich source of information for educators who are serious about providing the best possible educational experience for students. Information gathered directly from students provides an indirect way for educators to improve the learning process. Banta (1985) has demonstrated that satisfaction data can be powerful enough to result in significant change in college policies. If, for example, student satisfaction with the tutoring service is low, that is a clear signal for us as decision makers to direct attention to that area. Subsequent surveys also allow for indications of whether the actions taken to improve areas of low student satisfaction are successful.

The good news is that student satisfaction is easy to measure. Standardized instruments are readily available and easy to administer. It is also simple to develop a college-specific instrument for conducting an institutional student opinion survey. Astin suggests two approaches. The first approach simply asks that students indicate, on a scale from "very satisfied" to "very dissatisfied," the degree of satisfaction with various aspects of the college experience. The second approach is to pose hypothetical situations ("If you need help choosing a major, would you use the college counseling service?") and have the students respond on a scale from "definitely yes" to "definitely no."

Using a standardized opinion survey has the advantage of allowing comparison with national norms. This provides a useful point of reference and can also be helpful in establishing targets. For example, the overall goal of a student services program could be that student satisfaction with programs and services will be above the national norm. Regardless of the target, if resources permit only one form of student assessment, the assessment of student satisfaction is a good choice.

Another issue related to assessment is how to measure development changes in students in the affective domain. While a thorough discussion of that important question falls outside the domain of this chapter, those wishing to pursue this area can find guidance in Erwin (1991), Hanson (1989), and Kuh (1988).

Program Direction: External Validation

In considering altering a program of student services, it is often useful to validate one's plans with external resources. Within the past several years, a number of initiatives on the national level have addressed programmatic issues related to student services. The "Traverse City Statement" (Keyser, 1984) was the earliest of a series of position papers developed during the 1980s to point the direction for a revitalization of student services. This statement contained a number of recommendations for action for student services at both the national and local levels. This initial report was followed by a series of reports dealing with leadership strategies for student success (Floyd, 1987), a reassessment of the original Traverse City Statement (Keys, 1989), and a report on the issues and challenges facing student services in the 1990s (Floyd, 1990).

During the same period, the League for Innovation in the Community College (1987) developed a statement focusing on strategies to foster student success. A more recent paper outlines the major challenges facing student services in the 1990s (National Council on Student Development, 1990). All of these reports and statements provide recommendations for strengthening student services, but few deal with administrative or organizational matters.

There are also several useful resources on the management of student services programs. Barr and Albright (1990) offer a useful perspective on its organizational role, and Miller, Winston, and Mendenhall (1983) have edited a book dealing with administrative issues in student services. Deegan (1982) has addressed management issues for these programs, and Carroll and Tarasuk (1991) offer an organizational model drawn from a public school perspective.

A brief synopsis of models for student services has been

developed by Hernandez (1989). Creamer (1993) also provides an overview on models of practices found in the literature. Several state manuals for student services have been developed as well (Washington State Student Services Commission, 1989; Slowinski, 1984; Michigan Association of Community College Student Personnel Administrators, n.d.).

Another important recent development for the student services profession was the establishment of a set of national standards for student services. First published in 1986 (Council for the Advancement of Standards for Student Services/Development Programs, 1986), the standards provide a basis for self-study of student services programs. Suggestions for using the standards have also been recommended (Bryan, Winston, and Miller, 1991).

Summary

Although student services has traditionally been considered an important function in the community college, this function has also frequently been criticized as inadequate. The inadequacy of student services has been blamed on many factors, the most consistent of which has probably been inadequate support. As a "non-FTE-generating unit," student services has often been a target for budget reductions. Yet almost no one denies that student services plays an important part in the educational process.

It has been a central thesis of this chapter that presidents play a critical role in determining the effectiveness of the student services program. By the student services leader they choose, by the placement of student services within the institutional organizational structure, and by the expectations they establish for the role student services plays in planning and assessment, presidents are in a position to redefine the future for student services. How they meet that challenge depends on their willingness to learn more about the possibilities for student services and to establish the same level of expectations for student services as for academic and other programs.

Student services professionals have an equally important responsibility for the future of the student services program.

Leaders in student services must be responsible for the vision for the program and for demonstrating the effectiveness of the program. To do less is to jeopardize the potential for student services to support students in their educational development.

References

Ashland Community College. *Planning an Evaluation Handbook: 1991–1992 Academic Year.* Ashland, Ky.: Ashland Community College, 1991.

Astin, A. W. *Achieving Educational Excellence: A Critical Assessment of Priorities and Practices in Higher Education.* San Francisco: Jossey-Bass, 1985.

Astin, A. W. *Assessment for Excellence: The Philosophy and Practice of Assessment and Evaluation in Higher Education.* New York: American Council on Education/Macmillan, 1991.

Banning, J. H., and Hughes, B. M. "Designing the Campus Environment with Commuter Students." *NASPA Journal,* 1986, *24,* 17–24.

Banta, T. W. "Use of Outcomes Information at the University of Tennessee, Knoxville." In P. T. Ewell (ed.), *Assessing Educational Outcomes.* New Directions for Institutional Research, no. 47. San Francisco: Jossey-Bass, 1985.

Barr, M. J., and Albright, R. L. "Rethinking the Organizational Role of Student Affairs." In M. J. Barr, M. L. Upcraft, and Associates, *New Futures for Student Affairs: Building a Vision for Professional Leadership and Practice.* San Francisco: Jossey-Bass, 1990.

Bryan, W. A., Winston, R. B., Jr., and Miller, T. K. (eds.). *Using Professional Standards in Student Affairs.* New Directions for Student Services, no. 53. San Francisco: Jossey-Bass, 1991.

Carroll, B. W., and Tarasuk, P. E. "A New Vision for Student Development Services in the 90's." *Community College Review,* 1991, *19*(2), 32–42.

Cohen, A. M., and Brawer, F. B. *The American Community College.* (2nd ed.) San Francisco: Jossey-Bass, 1989.

Council for the Advancement of Standards for Student Services/Development Programs. *CAS Standards and Guidelines for Student Services/Development Programs.* Iowa City, Iowa: American College Testing Program, 1986.

Creamer, D. G. "Opportunities in the Future." D. G. Creamer and C. R. Dassance (eds.), *Opportunities for Student Development in Two-Year Colleges,* NASPA Monograph Services, 1986.

Creamer, D. G. "Excellence in the Practice of Student Affairs in the Two-Year College." Paper presented at the annual meeting of the Student Development Commission of the Florida Association of Community Colleges, Gainesville, Fla., May 1987.

Creamer, D. G. "Changing Internal Conditions: Impact on Student Development." In W. L. Deegan and T. O'Banion (eds.), *Perspectives on Student Development.* New Directions for Community Colleges, no. 67. San Francisco: Jossey-Bass, 1989.

Creamer, D. G. "Synthesis of Literature Related to Historical and Current Functions of Student Services." In G. A. Baker (ed.), *Handbook of Community Colleges in America.* Westport, Conn.: Greenwood Press, 1993.

Dassance, C. R. *Student Success in the Community College: A Renaissance Opportunity for Student Affairs.* Occasional papers, no. 6. Greenwood, S.C.: Southern Association of Community, Junior, and Technical Colleges, 1988.

Deegan, W. L. *The Management of Student Affairs Programs in Community Colleges: Revamping Process and Structure.* Washington, D.C.: American Association of Community and Junior Colleges, 1982.

Deegan, W. L. "Alternatives for Revitalizing Student Services Programs." *Community and Junior College Journal,* 1984, *54,* 14–17.

Drucker, P. F. *Managing the Nonprofit Organization.* New York: HarperCollins, 1990.

Elsner, P. A., and Ames, W. C. "Redirecting Student Services." In G. B. Vaughan and Associates, *Issues for Community College Leaders in a New Era.* San Francisco: Jossey-Bass, 1983.

Erwin, T. D. *Assessing Student Learning and Development: A Guide to the Principles, Goals, and Methods of Determining College Outcomes.* San Francisco: Jossey-Bass, 1991.

Florida Community College at Jacksonville. *Department of Student Affairs Annual Plan: 1989–90.* Jacksonville: Department of Student Affairs, Florida Community College, 1989.

Floyd, D. L. *Toward Mastery Leadership: Strategies for Student Success.*

Summary report of the National Council on Student Development colloquium in Columbia, Md. Iowa City, Iowa: American College Testing Program, 1987.

Floyd, D. L. *Toward Mastery Leadership: Issues and Challenges for the 1990s.* Summary report of the National Council on Student Development colloquium at Hilton Head, S.C. Iowa City, Iowa: American College Testing Program, 1990.

Hanson, G. R. "The Assessment of Student Development Outcomes: A Review and Critique of Assessment Instruments." Unpublished manuscript prepared for the College Outcomes Evaluation Program. Trenton: New Jersey Department of Higher Education, 1989.

Hernandez, K. R. "Are New Models of Student Development Needed?" (ERIC Clearinghouse for Junior Colleges, Los Angeles), Dec. 1989, pp. 1–2.

Keys, R. C. (ed.). *Toward the Future Vitality of Student Development Services: Traverse City — Five Years Later.* Iowa City, Iowa: American College Testing Program, 1989.

Keyser, J. S. (ed.). *Toward the Future Vitality of Student Development Services.* Summary report of the National Council on Student Development colloquium at Traverse City, Mich. Iowa City, Iowa: American College Testing Program, 1984.

Kuh, G. D. *Personal Development and the College Student Experience: A Review of the Literature.* Prepared for the College Outcomes Evaluation Program. Trenton: New Jersey Department of Higher Education, 1988.

Kuh, G. D., Schuh, J. H., Whitt, E. J., and Associates. *Involving Colleges: Successful Approaches to Fostering Student Learning and Development Outside the Classroom.* San Francisco: Jossey-Bass, 1991.

Kuh, G. D., Shedd, J. D., Whitt, E. J., and Associates. "Student Affairs and Liberal Education: Unrecognized (and Unappreciated) Common Law Partners." *Journal of College Student Personnel,* 1987, *28,* 252–260.

League for Innovation in the Community College. *Assuring Student Success in the Community College: The Role of Student Development Professionals.* Los Angeles: League for Innovation in the Community College, 1987.

Matson, J. E. "Primary Roles for Community College Counselors." In A. S. Thurston and W. A. Robbins (eds.), *Counseling: A Crucial Function for the 1980s*. New Directions for Community Colleges, no. 43. San Francisco: Jossey-Bass, 1983.

Michigan Association of Community College Student Personnel Administrators. *A Guidebook for Student Services*. Traverse City, Mich.: Northwestern Michigan College, n.d.

Miller, T. K., Winston, R. B., Jr., and Mendenhall, W. R. *Administration and Leadership in Student Affairs: Actualizing Student Development in Higher Education*. Muncie, Ind.: Accelerated Development, Inc., 1983.

National Council on Student Development. *Student Affairs Professionals in Two-Year Colleges: Priorities for the 1990s*. Joint statement of the National Council on Student Development of the American Association of Community and Junior Colleges, Commission XI of the American College Personnel Association, and the Community College Network of the National Association for Student Personnel Administration. Washington, D.C.: National Council on Student Development, 1990.

Nichols, J. O. *Institutional Effectiveness and Outcomes Assessment on Campus: A Practitioner's Handbook*. New York: Agathon Press, 1989.

Saddlemire, G. L., and Rentz, A. L. (eds.). *The Student Personnel Point of View*. Alexandria, Va.: American College Personnel Association, 1986. (Originally published 1937.)

Saddlemire, G. L., and Rentz, A. L. (eds.). *The Student Personnel Point of View*. (Rev. ed.) Alexandria, Va.: American College Personnel Association, 1986. (Originally published 1949.)

Slowinski, D. J. (ed.). *A Guide for Effective Student Services in Maryland Community Colleges*. Monograph prepared by the deans of students of the Maryland Community Colleges. Baltimore, Md.: Essex Community College, 1984.

Tillery, D., and Deegan, W. L. "The Evolution of Two-Year Colleges Through Four Generations." In W. L. Deegan, D. Tillery, and Associates, *Renewing the American Community College: Priorities and Strategies for Effective Leadership*. San Francisco: Jossey-Bass, 1985.

Washington State Student Services Commission. *A Manual for Student Services: Directions and Challenges*. Des Moines, Wash.: Highline Community College, 1989.

Chapter 16

Institutional Research

John Losak

Institutional research in community colleges shows enormous variation from state to state, college to college, and director to director. No more than three-fourths of all two-year colleges even have an institutional research office (Rowh, 1990), and, in those that do, an office consisting solely of a director and a secretary is not an uncommon arrangement. While acknowledging this variation in practice, this chapter presents information from the perspective of an office staffed with six professionals, two para-professionals, and two secretaries.

The chapter provides a brief introduction to the history and nature of institutional research and focuses more extensively on the various functions and interrelationships of an institutional research office. It concludes with brief observations concerning quality control and other forecasts for the future.

History

The evolution of institutional research within two-year colleges in the United States over the last half century has occurred in a less cohesive and structurally integrated manner than in four-

301

year colleges and universities (Neave, 1989). It would be surprising if this were not the case, given the anathema with which the term *research* has traditionally been viewed at the two-year college. Two-year colleges emerged, developed, and grew as teaching institutions with extremely little focus on research of any kind, including institutional research.

A major factor contributing to the growth of institutional research was the emergence of state and federal reporting requirements for all institutions of higher education under the rubric of accountability. In the early 1950s — as the burgeoning two-year college movement took shape — the reporting of student enrollment and graduation data by registrars or admissions offices satisfied the generally low-level interest or demand for such information. However, the emergence in the 1960s of state and federal reporting requirements associated with civil rights guidelines, along with accountability for financial aid and vocational program funding, created opportunities for interpretation of the new data beyond the "counting" activities initially carried out by registrars. The data generated for these external requirements provided an opportunity for internal program evaluation, analysis, and interpretation not hitherto available.

In those colleges where the administration valued research based on the analyses of these data, the activities served as justification for initiation or expansion of the responsibilities assigned to offices of institutional research. Within the organizational structure of the community college, the institutional research staff may exist as a unit combined with planning, assessment, budget, or grants. More frequently, institutional research stands alone as a separate functional office. In the past decade, institutional research functions have further evolved at some colleges to become an integral aspect of the college's preparation for accreditation. This is especially so in those accrediting regions where institutional effectiveness measures have been specified as minimal expectations.

A number of two-year colleges have developed into institutions of enormous complexity and diversification. Their programs reflect the myriad political forces seeking representation in both the formal missions set forth by governing boards and the more frequent informal commitments of daily decision making. Their student populations exhibit increasing diversity as nontraditional groups gain access denied to earlier generations. The task of helping the community understand if the colleges are carrying out their stated missions requires information on the extent to which graduates are achieving employment opportunities, succeeding at transfer institutions, or are generally satisfied with their educational experiences.

In recounting the relatively brief history of institutional research in two-year colleges, several authors have found common patterns: (1) institutional research has undergone remarkable growth from 1960 through 1990, (2) institutional research functions are often dominated by reporting activities to state and federal agencies, (3) few people holding the title of director of institutional research are specifically trained in their graduate work for the field of institutional research, and (4) many two-year colleges continue to operate with minimal resources committed for the express purpose of institutional research (Endo, 1990; Pace, 1990; Rowh, 1990). In a recent survey of 326 institutions within the region of the Southern Association of Colleges and Schools, only 134 of the 301 responding institutions reported having an institutional researcher assigned on a half-time or greater basis (Rowh, 1990). However, it is clear that demands for institutional accountability and demonstrated effectiveness will continue, creating an expanding role for institutional research personnel. A recent national survey of community college presidents concerning their use of management concepts found a significant increase in the level of activity in the general areas of research and evaluation and more emphasis on using data to provide feedback to faculty, staff, and students (Deegan, 1992).

Nature of Institutional Research

Even though institutional research is a widespread function among two-year colleges, it has a relatively short history and virtually no systematic theory underpinning its operations. Institutional research activities may be viewed as an introspective process, analogous to personal introspection in many important ways. On a personal level, most people engage in introspection at some time, but there are extremely wide variations with respect to how thoroughly they look at themselves, how honestly they do it, and how effectively they report their "findings" to both their own levels of consciousness and to others. Institutional research as an introspective function may be viewed along the same dimensions. Some institutions continually engage in the process of self-study and analysis and are extremely open about their findings, both within the institution and to their various publics. Other institutions scarcely engage in any introspection except as may be required by outside agencies, legal impositions, or accreditation. Likewise, they fail to share information with others in the institution and certainly do not distribute their introspective findings beyond the confines of the college.

As with personal introspection, institutional research as an introspective process should enhance our learning about the various components of the institution under study. Pace's (1990) position that institutional research is learning calls to our attention established relationships between research and learning that are useful in the framing of questions, analysis and interpretation of data, and gaining acceptance of findings.

Finally, as with individuals, the strongest institutions are those that are most open and intellectually honest regarding the outcomes of their operations and that present a willingness to acknowledge the failures as well as the accomplishments that may be uncovered during the institutional research processes. Dressel (1971) encouraged this approach by suggesting that systematic research will focus on institutional weaknesses rather than strengths. The regular identification of areas that need improvement permits and encourages faculty and administrators to engage in more informed and objective decision making as they plan for curricular or administrative changes.

In what ways has institutional research moved beyond the traditional responsibilities for reporting and program evaluation? In the last decade, we have witnessed the appearance of quasi-experimental studies that address causal issues. These efforts to conduct educational research projects represent one area of expansion for institutional research activities. Another arises from the fact that most community college faculty do not have the doctorate at the time of their initial employment. When they subsequently reach the stage of working on dissertations, institutional research can offer a supporting or guiding role. This assistance is particularly appropriate in the case of faculty whose dissertations address issues or problems at the institutions where they are employed. Assessment of institutional effectiveness provides another arena for expansion of institutional research functions.

What purpose is served by the primary activities that operationally define institutional research, other than the compulsory compliance implied by state and federally mandated reports? The objective for virtually all activities beyond the reporting function is to learn more about the institution, to broadcast this learning as widely as possible, and to have the information lead to more objectively informed decision making than would be the case without such information.

Several definitions of institutional research have been offered (Maasen, 1986; Muffo and McLaughlin, 1987; Peterson, 1985), but as McKinney and Hindera (1992, p. 19) note, the definitions "fail to address the process and structure of the research part of institutional research." Middaugh (1990, p. 36) provided one useful definition: "Institutional research is the sum total of all activities directed at empirically describing the full spectrum of functions (educational, administrative, and support) at a college or university. Institutional research activities examine those functions in their broadest definitions and, in the context of both internal and external environments, embrace data collection and analytical strategies in support of decision making at the institution."

A simpler definition sees institutional research as the systematic documentation and interpretation of the activities of a particular institution. While most colleges from their inception have counted graduates and faculty, the documented and systematic approach distinguishes institutional research functions from either mere counting or from impressions, intuitions, or hearsay.

Internal and External Relationships

A model institutional research office exhibits a proactive philosophy with respect to reaching out beyond the physical confines of the office. In determining criteria for a model office, the emphasis is primarily on function and philosophy rather than structure. It is created initially by a college president who demands accurate, timely data, provides opportunity for written analysis, allocates sufficient resources, and appoints a professional educator to direct the operation. Each of the internal and external relationships described in this chapter represents opportunities for direct involvement with others — the college president, faculty, students, and groups external to the college.

Role of the College President

At most colleges, functions carried out by institutional research beyond the required state and federal reporting are derived from the basic philosophy of the college president. Probably the single philosophical orientation that drives the nature of daily activities for an institutional research office is the emphasis the college president places on acquiring data along with the openness permitted for sharing such information. Clearly these values exist on a continuum rather than being either totally present or absent. The effectiveness of institutional research activities can be enhanced if the institutional research office works with a college president who values data as a basis for administrative decision making and to provide insights into the operation of the college. It is also preferable if the president uses the research results in an open and direct manner.

It is not always comfortable for the college president to encourage data gathering and analysis, if the results continually focus on exposure of problems, weak points, and otherwise embarrassing information. Since few of us can deal with a constant onslaught of nothing but negative reports, institutional research benefits from efforts to balance positive and negative findings where possible. The president's commitment to research is usually enhanced if the institutional research director keeps in mind that both the strengths and weaknesses of the institution need to be systematically documented.

An obvious technique for helping the president avoid embarrassment is to present accurate and straightforward information. A president who discovers, following a presentation at a national meeting, that the institutional research director had made serious errors in the data used in the presentation may decide to look for a new director. Job saving is not necessarily the name of the game, but accuracy certainly is. Accuracy cannot guarantee continuation on the job, but lack of accuracy devalues everything associated with the institutional research office.

How close a relationship should exist between the institutional research office and the college president? The institutional research director ought to be close enough to the college president to know of plans, directions, and major philosophical orientations but far enough away so as to be viewed as impartial and objective in the gathering, analysis, and reporting of data. In a recent advertisement for an institutional research director, one of the described functions was to write speeches for the college president. That is likely too close a relationship for objective research. On the other hand, if the institutional research director does not have the opportunity for substantial conversations with the college president throughout the year, such lack of access or knowledge will diminish the ability of the institutional research office to provide useful support.

Key administrators other than the college president should also play a major role in the definition of institutional research functions, especially for multicampus colleges. If the president provides sufficient latitude for interaction with other areas of the college, those relationships will enhance the credibility of institutional research throughout the college. One technique is to use other college administrators as a sounding board both for ideas and for initial drafts of reports. Their comments are usually invaluable in keeping a project on track with regard to current activities and for avoiding misinformation or misinterpretation. A steering committee of college administrators can provide assistance or guidance in establishing a research agenda and in prioritizing resources.

Getting to Know Faculty

The relationship between institutional research staff and faculty remains tenuous and varies more among institutions than any of the other relationships mentioned. At some two-year colleges, interaction with faculty is negligible, while at others, faculty play a major role in establishing goals, priorities, and work assignments for institutional research. Faculty support is essential for the viability of an institutional research office that seeks to move beyond reporting functions. Few college presidents could stand the pressure of a full-fledged faculty effort to withdraw financial support for a broad institutional research effort. This suggests that faculty, at least at some level, need to be convinced that institutional research contributes to instruction. An uninformed attitude views institutional research as simply a bureaucratic burden subtracting from the resources that would otherwise be available to directly support the instructional program.

The institutional research office has many opportunities for working directly with faculty. Often they are in the process of conducting their own research, whether for personal or professional satisfaction or because they are enrolled in a graduate seminar or working on a dissertation. For the faculty member, the persons most familiar with the conduct of research in an educational setting outside of the dissertation advisory committee, and often the most accessible, are the institutional research staff. Benefits accrue exponentially to the institutional research office that engages in frequent interaction with faculty. Faculty provide a perspective on their lives and the lives of their students that is simply not obtainable elsewhere. They frequently engage in research activities involving the college where they teach. Insight provided through discussions and through careful review of research questions that a faculty member may be exploring often leads to spin-off pieces of research that are important for the institution. The cumulative benefits of their work represent a significant resource to the institutional research office and the college administration.

One of the first reactions from people who listen to ideas about interacting with faculty is to conclude that the institutional research office will be overwhelmed by faculty seeking assistance. Actually, this is not the case for several reasons. First, many graduate dissertations have little to do with the college as such or with institutional research. For example, virtually none of the research conducted by faculty in the natural sciences would go through institutional research. Only faculty from those areas in which the use of students or the educational environment could be a topic of study would seek interaction with the institutional research office. Next, many participants in various programs or graduate seminars will not need any further guidance than they already receive from their advisory committee. When those defined groups of faculty are eliminated, it leaves a manageable number of individuals who are exploring questions that will entail research on students at the institution.

Finally, support can be offered without requiring a formal research design or formal request for a meeting to discuss these topics. The faculty member may come by the office, or pick up the telephone, or set up an appointment time for a discussion. Whichever approach the faculty member initiates, the bureaucracy of the process should be kept to an absolute minimum. Unnecessary structure wastes time and will only serve as a barrier to keep faculty away. A steady level of interaction between institutional research personnel and teaching faculty yields positive benefits for the faculty and contributes to the professional development of the institutional research office as they receive front-line perspectives on both the problems faculty find most difficult to address and the practices that lead to student success.

Remembering Students

When people ask what qualities or characteristics an institutional research person should possess, the first quality coming to mind is that the person should be someone who is trained and knowledgeable about human behavior. Someone with a degree in behavioral sciences is preferable, or at the very least someone who has moved from another discipline to the behavioral sciences but who has clearly demonstrated an appreciation of the study of human behavior. The behavior that we observe, comment on, and write about is that of students. On occasion, we write about administrators or faculty, but the sine qua non of institutional research is the contribution toward understanding and predicting student behavior. In an atmosphere in which deadlines constantly appear, vice presidents and presidents request data for their next public appearance, and state offices seek specific information for inquiring legislators, the institutional research office must act vigilantly to keep the student as the primary focus of institutional research efforts.

The need to understand student behavior in a changing educational context cannot be overemphasized. The college attendance behavior of students has changed over the years, but researchers' conceptualization of that process has tended to remain the same. Studies of student performance often conceptualize college-going behavior as continuous attendance for four years, followed by receipt of the bachelor's degree. In fact, student behavior has radically differed from this model for at least a decade. Most students are part-time and drop in and out successively. At most two-year colleges, the modal year for reaching graduation is now three, and at four-year colleges and universities, the modal year is five. It is not at all unusual for students to take four years to get their associate in arts degree and another three or four years to get the baccalaureate. When colleges fail to recognize significant changes in student behavior, the subsequent evaluation of student performance imposes a false notion of student success. In his detailed analysis of student behavior derived from reviewing transcripts, Adelman (1992) has made the same point using a broad-based sample.

Experience has demonstrated that students are extremely cooperative in research efforts when they are in class and are also inclined to return surveys given to them during class for return at the next class meeting. The use of surveys calls for a great deal of sensitivity to not only the nature and structure of the questions, but also with respect to the level of language to be used and the assumptions made concerning information students may or may not have available. Some researchers are inclined to write surveys that use the simplest language and that are extremely brief, implying (or even stating explicitly) that students are unwilling or unable to read material of any length or complexity. With this approach, the researcher risks being perceived as condescending. Students should receive a literate survey from a college or university; they are shortchanged if the college sends them anything less.

All staff in the office who are involved in research projects should be expected to read and follow ethical guidelines for research with humans as adopted by the American Psychological Association. But beyond this, wherever possible students should be apprised of the findings of studies, even if the only medium available happens to be student newspapers. Most researchers would agree that those who contribute to studies should be informed of the findings, but we often leave students out of this feedback loop.

Forming a Partnership with the Public Relations Office

The images of a college held by its various constituencies contribute to both short-term acceptance and long-term viability. Although the exact nature of the images presented by the college will certainly differ depending on whether we ask the community at large, the students, or employers about certain aspects of the college, the commonly shared goal is to have those responses be positive. No college deliberately seeks a negative image. A natural function of a public relations office is to develop, preserve, and protect a positive public image of the institution. This is an important function of the public relations office and should not be denigrated or undervalued.

The clear distinctions between the functions of the public relations office and the institutional research office can ordinarily be mutually accommodated in a professional manner. However, difficulty naturally occurs when the public relations office is asked to behave as though it were the institutional research office, or the institutional research office is asked to function as a public relations office. The most common examples occur when the public relations office receives requests for facts, information, or data that deserve precise and carefully stated responses. Likewise, institutional research offices frequently receive calls that should be handled with emphasis on the image or political message. The two offices can work cooperatively and complement each other's perspective by acknowledging that responses from institutional research tend to be straightforward and to provide the not-always-positive facts of the matter, while the public relations office is expected to put on the best "spin" for the most positive college image.

Reaching Out to the Community

Community contacts from institutional research occur at several points, one of the most frequent contact points being the news media. Generally speaking, the news media are strong allies of community colleges. Reporters ordinarily prefer to print something positive about their local community college. Occasionally, misquotes occur or figures appear in the wrong place or in the wrong context, but positive reporting about community colleges is the rule rather than the exception. Nevertheless, the college representative from institutional research who interacts with reporters should be cognizant of several factors to be addressed with each and every interview.

First, questions from reporters should always be clarified as closely and as intently as possible. Keeping in mind that reporters often have little factual knowledge or little overall conceptualization of the mission and goals of the two-year college, gentle questioning can often formulate for the reporter more concisely and precisely what is being sought and lead to more accurate conveying of information. Second, reporters are rarely conversant with either statistical analysis or with education jargon. As an example, when reporters are inquiring regarding growth at a college, neither they nor the public have much interest in knowing about FTE or credit hour increases. Their primary focus is on the number of students. For the institutional research office to answer in terms of FTEs tends merely to confuse. Yet we know that giving a simple clarification of the number of students enrolled is no easy task.

One question reporters frequently ask is along the following lines: Of those students who begin at your college, how many graduate? Staff sessions should review how this question can be answered, or how to clarify the reporter's questions so as to convey to the reporter and subsequently to the public facts known to virtually all community college professionals but rarely to the public. In particular, many students who enroll in a two-year college already have associate and bachelor's degrees, and many students who enroll in occupational programs or in courses for their own personal advancement have no intention of graduating. With these qualifications in mind, we should present graduation data based on full-time first-time in college degree-seeking students who graduate three years later. My experience has been that the perception from reporters when this brief explanation is provided has virtually always been positive. Information conveyed to the public in a reasonable manner provides a more satisfactory and accurate description of the ratio of graduates to enrollees.

Other points of encounter with the community include surveys of employers and surveys of community members at large. When the image of the college is strong and positive, a letter from the local community college is typically well received and response rates tend to be high. Success in conducting surveys of employers can be enhanced by indicating in the letter that they will receive a follow-up phone call to give the information on the telephone. This is simultaneously a more personal approach and also somewhat of a time-saver. The personal interaction further permits the employer to provide side comments, which are often quite illuminating, beyond the specific information asked for in the survey.

In a more general sense, few items are more critical to the functioning of institutional research than a sound knowledge of community demography, politics, and economics. These contextual references must continue to guide and shape questions asked by institutional research and provide a framework within which research endeavors are undertaken. Such basic items as enrollment projections are tied quite closely to the community factors mentioned above, and the predictions are strengthened to the extent that the knowledge of the community is accurate and current.

The role of the community college as catalyst for interventions on local community issues, particularly with providing the expertise to address issues confronting the community in which the college is located, is likely to grow in the next few decades. A current leading-edge example of this type of endeavor is the ACCLAIM Project at North Carolina State University, funded by the W. K. Kellogg Foundation. The project will establish six pilot community colleges as catalysts for community development and provide graduate courses emphasizing the role of the community college in community development activities. The Miami-Dade Community College Neighborhoods Project is another example of the community college as coordinator of relationships and connections among social service agencies. Institutional research functions in these projects range from gathering data for the initial planning to guiding the flow of resources and eventually to providing evaluation of the efficacy of the efforts.

Articulation with the Public Schools

Ties between local secondary schools and community colleges have been stronger in the past than they are today. Some early writers envisioned the two-year college as the thirteenth and fourteenth grades, and many colleges began operation under the control of public school boards. Despite the emergence of the community college as an independent and vastly different institution, the remaining ties with the local secondary schools provide several opportunities for institutional research activities. One common research question shared by the secondary schools administration and the community college addresses the relationship between the secondary curriculum and subsequent success at the two-year college. Another research question often studied is the relationship between test performance in the secondary schools and success in the two-year college. Finally, while recent high school graduates represent a smaller proportion of the total college enrollment, they represent a major factor in predicting enrollment and long-term planning at most two-year colleges.

Formal reports and informal feedback to the secondary schools about research studies conducted at the two-year college that directly relate to high school performance set the stage for ongoing discussions. In large systems, it is no easy task to ensure that the information reaches people who are most affected. If you ask students what they thought of their high school preparation as it relates to their current functioning in freshmen remedial classes, every effort should be made to get the results of such a study to the high school principals and, where possible, to the high school mathematics and English faculty. Annual reports describing initial test performance of recent high school graduates should also be distributed widely within the secondary schools. Follow-up meetings of top-level administrators, as well as curriculum articulation between discipline faculty and teachers, can be arranged to further clarify, analyze, and interpret the information. These measures can also form the basis for interventions that might improve performance of future students during their first year of collegiate work.

Another research question of shared interest for public institutions committed to programs of equal opportunity has been the extent to which members of each ethnic group are proportionately represented in the population of entering freshmen. If a particular group is found to be underrepresented, arrangements can be made with the public schools administration to explore the reasons for this decline through focus-group interviews at local high schools. One obvious explanation might be the intense competition for minority students from major colleges and universities. The focus-group interviews may identify other factors that can receive appropriate attention from both the public schools and the community college.

Cooperative Research Projects

Shortly after the Florida community college system was organized in the late 1950s, the Inter-Institutional Research Council (IRC) for cooperative research among community colleges was established (Wattenbarger, 1990). The purpose of the cooperative effort among community colleges has been to conduct research on a statewide basis that would not be feasible for a particular college to undertake. For example, working with the voluntary member colleges (which number between twelve and fourteen each year) in the early 1980s, the IRC established a system for following graduates that has permitted Florida to generate a great deal more information about the students transferring from the two-year to the four-year college than can be found in most other states.

Another example of research conducted in a cooperative manner is the University of Florida's predictive analysis of students who wrote the College Level Academic Skills Test (CLAST) as college sophomores and who then enrolled in the university system. It was possible to determine performance level and relate that performance level in the university to a series of passing score levels on the CLAST. These are but two examples of many that over the years have generated a great deal of information helpful in the analysis of two-year college functions in Florida.

With the continuing improvement in computerization of student records, it should eventually become easier for colleges to do follow-up of their own students with only minimal cooperation from the computer services at each of the state universities to which most of the graduates transfer. It is extremely important in this regard that the two-year colleges participate in the conceptualization as well as the conduct of the research, so that criteria and variables can be developed in light of the objectives of the students and missions of the two-year colleges. University personnel are rather far removed from the two-year college setting and may not be able to provide the perspective and context necessary to reasonably interpret the data. On the other hand, some two-year college personnel become so defensive when the outcomes may not appear to be as satisfactory as they would like that their own perspective tends to be too narrow and not sufficiently objective. Therefore, cooperative interaction between university and two-year college personnel in initiating, conceptualizing, conducting, interpreting, and writing offers the best circumstances for undertaking research of this type.

Probably the most common kind of cooperative research occurs when university personnel, often doctoral students, routinely ask two-year colleges to participate in a study. Each college should have a policy for determining when and with whom to cooperate in these endeavors and to have a process by which each of the requests received is reviewed. A collegewide committee charged with this responsibility offers one approach that permits not only consistency but also review by persons who are reasonably knowledgeable about the nature of the request. Since most of the requests coming forward are from doctoral students, occasions arise when the resource requirements placed on the college to participate are extremely heavy. In those cases, the review committee may be wise to decline, particularly if the research is extensively intrusive of classroom time.

Professional Preparation and Autonomy

Professional preparation of the institutional research staff varies widely. While the majority of directors have come out of the behavioral sciences, many have degrees in English, other humanities fields, and a variety of other areas. The institutional research director provides vision, context, and perspective in the analysis of the issues, not only for a college but also as they relate to the field of higher education.

The most important attributes the institutional research staff can have are a sound understanding of human behavior, a desire to write, and intellectual integrity. Whether that understanding of human behavior derives from formal academic study or from practical experience is not of critical importance. What is needed are disciplined thinkers who view their work as significant and who continually strive for intellectual integrity as questions are framed, questionnaires are developed, data are analyzed, and findings are reported. Professional staff members in institutional research should not function simply as skilled technicians but should be able to analyze, interpret, and write reports. They should be expected to collate the data, think about the implications of the findings, and write a report that recognizes both the historical context and the implications of their findings.

As a primary operating premise, an office of institutional research must strive to have a clear and unblemished reputation for presenting findings in a manner that is as free from "administrative spins" or "public relations spins" as it is possible to achieve. For this reason, it is preferable that the institutional research office not report directly to the campus or college president. Such a direct relationship may well elicit from faculty and others a perception that the president "owns" the institutional research office and its findings. While it is true that no institutional research office can function with absolute autonomy, each director needs to achieve as much independence as can realistically be obtained.

Each report generated from the institutional research office should have no required review except by peers in institutional research. The publications (in the form of either full-length research reports or two- or three-page information capsules) should be distributed simultaneously to administrators, faculty, and the board of trustees. That level of autonomy sends a message to those who look at the process that the material is not rewritten for publication in order to provide a particular slant. This is not to say that politics do not play a role in inquiry or in publication: they always do to some extent. Nonetheless, one strives not for perfection in this area but for as much autonomy and integrity as can be achieved.

Data from institutional research are gathered primarily by persons who are well trained in the technology of computer skills and are prepared for review by our research staff. The data are then analyzed, interpreted, published, and disseminated to a very wide audience. People new to the area of institutional research frequently believe that once the material is disseminated, future decisions will be guided by findings that seem clear to the researcher and appear to point in a particular direction. However, one of the first lessons in the practice of institutional research is that we strive to provide information and increase the general understanding about the institution for those who take the time to read the material, but we cannot control what use, if any, they make of the findings or results of our work. On some issues, research information never affects decision making; on other issues, such information is used extensively. Economics and politics remain the primary influences for decision making, far ahead of educational considerations and certainly light years ahead of information institutional researchers provide.

Future Role

All noninstructional areas experience increased pressure to justify their expenditures when budget growth fails to keep pace with enrollment, as has been the case in recent years. This pervasive atmosphere of competition for resources will require careful monitoring of research functions and priorities, since institutional research will undoubtedly continue to compete for scarce college resources. As in the past, if the flow of information from institutional research openly contributes to problem solving and decision making, the commitment of resources generates less criticism and debate.

Paradigms for addressing institutional effectiveness will continue to be much sought after and used by institutional research. Some accrediting regions now require institutional effectiveness measures as part of the accreditation process, and other regions are moving in that direction. Most colleges will turn to the institutional research staff for help in this area. Institutional effectiveness requirements have led several colleges (and universities) in the Southern region to establish institutional research offices where none formerly existed.

Another event that will affect institutional research functioning is the likely increase in federal involvement with student assessment. At the state level, assessment requirements imposed on colleges have already created enormous data resources that many institutional research offices are using to generate information about student progress not previously available. Should federal demands for assessment continue, the impact for institutional research will be significant.

Evaluation of program efficacy will probably increase in the future as a major function of institutional research. Clearly the need for remediation of students in the open-door two-year college will remain a major mission, and research related to the entire remedial effort will be a major agenda item for the foreseeable future.

Each of these forecast events individually has the potential to broaden institutional research activities and responsibilities. In combination, they will undoubtedly move institutional research to a more prominent role in the community college within the next decade.

Summary

Institutional research has undergone remarkable growth from 1960 to 1990. Though it is now a widespread function among two-year colleges, it has practically no systematic theory supporting its operations. While some institutions rarely engage in introspection, the strongest institutions continually engage in the process of self-study and analysis and are open about their findings. Institutional research involves the systematic documentation and interpretation of the activities of the school.

The institutional research office must pay attention to its relationships with the president, the faculty, the students, the surrounding community, local secondary schools, and other community colleges. The staff must have a solid understanding of human behavior, a desire to write, and intellectual integrity. Accuracy is perhaps the single most important characteristic of a research office. For the sake of the reputation of the school and because of ethical considerations, great care must be taken to be precise in all information handled.

Institutional research is, and will continue to be, an important part of the assessment of various institutional programs. Since government agencies want student assessments and the schools themselves want to evaluate their own policies and practices, the research office will continue to be an important part of the community college.

References

Adelman, C. *The Way We Are: The Community College as American Thermometer.* Washington, D.C.: Office of Educational Research and Improvement, U.S. Department of Education, 1992.

Deegan, W. L. "Proven Techniques: The Use and Impact of

Major Management Concepts in Community Colleges." *Community, Technical, and Junior College Journal,* 1992, *62*(5), 26–30.

Dressel, P. L., and Associates. *Institutional Research in the University: A Handbook.* San Francisco: Jossey-Bass, 1971.

Endo, J. J. (ed.). "Institutional Research: Coming of Age." General session presentation at the thirtieth annual forum of the Association of Institutional Research, Louisville, Ky., May 1990. (ED 328 184)

Maasen, P. "Institutional Research and Organizational Adaptation." Paper presented at the Eighth European Association for Institutional Research Forum, Loughborough, Eng., Aug. 1986.

McKinney, E. B., and Hindera, J. J. "Science and Institutional Research: The Links." *Research in Higher Education,* 1992, *33*(1), 19–29.

Middaugh, M. F. "The Nature and Scope of Institutional Research." In J. B. Presley (ed.), *Organizing Effective Institutional Research Offices.* New Directions for Institutional Research, no. 66. San Francisco: Jossey-Bass, 1990.

Muffo, J., and McLaughlin, G. *A Primer on Institutional Research.* Tallahassee, Fla.: Association for Institutional Research, 1987.

Neave, G. "Foundation or Roof? The Quantitative, Structural, and Institutional Dimensions in the Study of Higher Education." *European Journal of Education,* 1989, *24*(3), 211–222.

Pace, C. R. *A Personal Retrospective on the Development of Institutional Research.* Presentation at the thirtieth annual forum of the Association for Institutional Research, Louisville, Ky., May 1990.

Peterson, M. "Institutional Research: An Evolutionary Perspective." In M. W. Peterson and M. Corcoran (eds.), *Institutional Research in Transition.* New Directions for Institutional Research, no. 46. San Francisco: Jossey-Bass, 1985.

Rowh, M. C. "Job Duties of Institutional Researchers in Southern Two-Year Colleges." *Community/Junior College Quarterly of Research and Practice,* 1990, *14*(1), 35–44.

Wattenbarger, J. L. *The Florida Community Junior College Inter-Institutional Research Council: Past, Present, and Future.* Gainesville, Fla.: Inter-Institutional Research Council, 1990 (Photocopied).

Chapter 17

Campus Planning and Construction

Dan Angel, James Brader

This chapter describes the process of developing facilities. It should prove beneficial to those interested in creating timely, economical, cost-effective, and energy-efficient solutions to their current and projected space needs. It should also assist facility planners and managers in addressing legislative requirements (such as the stipulations of the Americans with Disabilities Act), financial constraints, environmental and energy concerns, and updated design and engineering concepts. Here is a step-by-step process, from the initial planning stage through the completion of a construction project, based on information compiled from various internal facilities planning documents and reports.

Planning the Facility

Planning for a new facility involves a great deal of preparation. The process begins with an identified need for space and/or additional programs. It is important to understand that there must be a balance between the needs and the available resources. In some instances, the plans must be altered to match the available resources. Initially a budget should be estimated so that limits may be established. In planning the facility, it must be determined that the resources are available to finance the needs of the college. Normally, funds will be acquired from the sale of revenue or general obligation bonds, a college building fee, or a cash reserve. Approximately *two years* should be allotted for the planning, design, and construction of the project. This allows the architect six months to design and write the specifications for bidding, twelve to fifteen months for the actual construction, and three months for internal needs asessment. The internal needs process continues throughout the life of the project.

Next, a time line or project schedule should also be devised. Educational institutions are unique, and projects should be arranged around the college calendar. For example, smaller refurbishing projects should be scheduled for the periods in which there is limited disruption to students and classes, such as over Christmas or spring break. During this preliminary period, the academic area must determine specifically which programs will be housed in the new facility. To avoid costly revisions and modifications to the plans, it is imperative that all decisions are finalized prior to the selection of an architect. Prior to any student demographic studies, there should already be a clear understanding as to the basic programs that will be offered at the proposed site.

Area population studies should be conducted to project the potential student population. The state education agency, which oversees K–12, can provide the most comprehensive information on current and past high school graduates. The state health department or water/wastewater commission provides population projections by gender, ethnicity, age, and county.

The city planning department also provides population information in various formats. One format involves census tract data. Another format is more specifically geared toward traffic counts. The information is particularly useful in planning a campus location.

Other sources of information for obtaining population data are telephone, power, and water connections, various marketing reports, and public libraries. The local newspaper also has a research file that will provide an excellent demographic depiction of the site and the surrounding market area with a targeted neighborhood of one to five miles.

These studies provide information on education, buying power, and age eighteen and older separated by group: baby boomers, full and part-time students, and working women. Specific information such as a breakdown of credit card usage and types of people who shop at a particular store is also included.

It is very important to research the surrounding area for potential growth. It is also wise to be aware of competing educational institutions and their demographics, which can be obtained from the institution or the state education agency that oversees postsecondary education.

The state employment agency should provide a good representation of the regional economic condition, and the state comptroller's office should have some statistics on projected jobs and needed skills. Also, public four-year colleges or universities should have a planning component that provides the demographics for the area market.

After compiling all the documents and assessing the need for a facility, the college administration presents the plan to the board of trustees for approval.

Site Analysis and Evaluation

Based on information derived from demographic studies and research, the approximate locale of the facility is determined. At this point, the college may prepare a public notice in search of a parcel of land. Exhibit 17.1 provides an example of a public notice used by Austin Community College during its search for a southwest Austin site.

To receive several qualified responses, it is generally a good idea to run the public notice in three to four different publications.

Once all proposals have been submitted, a data checklist should be used to analyze whether the property satisfies the necessary requirements (Exhibit 17.2). Special attention should

Exhibit 17.1. Public Notice Inviting Proposals for a Parcel of Land.

Public Notice

Request for Proposals — Austin Community College is inviting proposals for a parcel of land as described below:

Southwest Site: 30 +/- acres located within the Austin Community College District, bounded on the north by highway 71 and highway 290; on the south by the southern boundary of Austin Community College District; on the east by Congress Avenue; and on the west by the Austin Community College District. On this particular tract, previously submitted proposals should be updated. The Austin Community College Board of Trustees will also consider the lease purchase of an existing building with a minimum of 30,000 square feet and the capability to expand to 60,000 square feet. The site must have adequate parking for a college campus.

The Board of Trustees will consider various financing options for the site and/or building purchases. Information documents and forms for submitting proposals may be obtained between the hours of 8:00 A.M. and 5:00 P.M., Monday through Friday, at 205 East 5th Street, Room 209, Austin, Texas, in the office of James Brader (512) 483-7611.

Proposals will be accepted until April 30, 1992. Proposals received after 4:00 on April 30th will be returned to sender unopened.

Proposers shall not undertake any activities, actions, or contacts to promote or advertise their proposals to the Board of Trustees of Austin Community College except in the case of College sponsored briefings, interviews or presentations or in the form of general comments made to the public at large. Violations of this provision will be grounds for rejection of the proposal.

---

be paid to *parking needs, zoning, future expansion needs,* and *access* to and from the site.

Obviously, as much land as possible should be purchased without jeopardizing the construction budget. Some states have regulations regarding the amount of land needed for postsecondary institutions.

The list of parcels submitted should be carefully analyzed and evaluated to determine which sites would best serve the college. A *feasibility study* should be performed on the sites in order to address the scope of work, adequacy of the location, road network, and needed public transportation (Exhibit 17.3). The study will also consider population trends in the area and site characteristics such as the availability of utilities.

Exhibit 17.2. Data Checklist for Undeveloped Land.

Size and Description

1. Number of Acres _____

2. Price per Acre   _____   Total Purchase Price _____

3. Location   _____

Physical Characteristics and Utilities
1. Indicate which best describes the land:
   ☐ Farm   ☐ Ranch   ☐ Timberland
   ☐ Industrial ☐ Commercial ☐ Residential
2. Give a general description of the topography of the land.

3. Describe floodplain designation and watershed ordinance impact.

4. Soil and subsoil description, if available.

5. Identify and plot the following on a general location map:
   • Existing easements — size and purpose
   • Sanitary sewer lines and size, if applicable
   • Storm sewer line and size, if applicable
   • Water service and size, if applicable
   • Gas service and size, if applicable

Local Regulations
1. Zoning; existing
2. Describe any building restrictions
3. Describe any use restrictions

Restrictions and Obligations
1. Describe any special assessments that may be required of the owner of the property, i.e. water district tax, street assessments

Financing Options
1. If this property is purchased, what financing options are available?
2. Is your proposed price cash only?   ☐ yes   ☐ no
3. Would you consider financing? If so, please state terms.

The following exhibits must be included with your proposal:
1. Area map with property plotted.
2. Survey, if available.
3. Aerial photograph (if aerial is not available, please include photos of property).
4. List any improvements on the property.

**Exhibit 17.3. Outline for Feasibility Study
to Be Prepared by Land Planner and Engineer.**

1. Letter of transmittal
2. Table of contents
3. Summary of conclusions
4. Scope of work
   a. Physical inspection of the subject and surrounding area
   b. Study of past and current economic and demographic data related to the area
   c. Land use intensity related to floor area and density
   d. Analysis of all data and tentative conclusions
5. Site location — maps and photographs
   a. Relationship to population trends and urbanization
   b. Adjoining land uses
   c. Proximity to major commercial centers, residential development, and industrial facilities
   d. Proximity to recreational and cultural amenities
   e. Availability of utilities
   f. Living unit equivalencies' availability
6. Site characteristics
   a. Physical characteristics
   b. Topography
   c. Subsurface conditions (foundation requirements)
   d. Natural amenities
   e. Zoning
   f. Quality water zone
7. Highways and road networks
   a. Existing network
   b. Circulation in the vicinity of the subject
   c. Traffic counts at the subject
   d. Planned and proposed construction improvements
8. Transportation
   a. Public transportation
   b. Planned improvements
9. School district in which site is located
10. Delineation of study area
    a. Neighborhood association
    b. Population
    c. Income
    d. Employment
11. Study area's development potential
12. Conclusion of feasibility

Retaining the Services of a Construction Manager

Depending on the size and experience of the college's physical plant staff, it may be advantageous to employ a construction manager to help guide the college through the construction process. Construction managers' responsibilities should include the following:

1. Consult with, advise, assist, and make recommendations to the owner and architect/engineer on all aspects of planning for the project construction
2. Review the architectural, civil, mechanical, electrical, and structural plans and specifications as they are being developed, and advise and make recommendations with respect to such factors as construction feasibility, value engineering, availability of materials and labor, time requirements for procurement and construction, and projected costs
3. Review and refine budget estimates as the development of the plans and specifications proceeds and advise the owner and the architect/engineer if it appears that the budgeted targets for the project cost and/or completion will not be met
4. Recommend for purchase and expedite the procurement of long-lead items to ensure their delivery by the required dates
5. Make recommendations to the owner and the architect/ engineer regarding the division of work in the plans and specifications to facilitate the bidding and awarding of trade contracts, taking into consideration such factors as time of performance, availability of labor, overlapping trade jurisdictions, provisions for temporary facilities, and so forth
6. Review plans and specifications with the architect/ engineer to eliminate areas of conflict and overlap in the work to be performed by the various trade contractors
7. Monitor the schedule closely during both the design and construction phases of the project and be respon-

sible for giving the owner periodic reports on the status of the work with respect to the project schedule
8. Inspect the work as it is being performed, until final
completion and acceptance by the owner, to ensure
that the materials furnished and work performed are
in accordance with working drawings and specifications
9. Make recommendations for and process requests for
changes in the work
10. Attend job-site meetings

These ten items should be done in-house or by a construction
manager.

Architectural Services

When considering architectural services, the college must be
clear in its goals. One of the major goals is to define the building in terms of how it will be utilized. For instance, the college
should decide which courses will be offered in the building in
terms of lectures and/or labs and also support services that will
be provided.

Another consideration is whether there is a policy on space
requirements of the classroom and within the classroom. For
instance, a standard classroom is 500–600 square feet, with an
average of 16–20 square feet per student station. The college
policy manual and state agency that oversees postsecondary education should be consulted in addition to regional or national
accrediting agencies.

The college must determine precisely which services the
architectural firm will be providing. Exhibit 17.4 provides an
example of a request for proposals (RFP) or public notice that
specifies the services required from the architect.

An architecture/engineering (A/E) questionnaire has
proven successful as an evaluation tool to select the best-suited
bidder (Exhibit 17.5). This instrument may be helpful in determining which firm is most experienced in the design of educational facilities and thus best qualified for the project. The
board of trustees should be presented with a list of all architec-

Exhibit 17.4. Public Notice Specifying Architectural Requirements.

Public Notice

Austin Community College invites proposals for Architectural/Engineering Services to design a building of approximately 40,000 square feet at the Northridge Campus located at 11928 Stonehollow Drive. The site has been master planned, therefore the location of the building is determined. The building must be compatible with the existing buildings with regard to color, format, style, etc.

The proposed building will contain approximately 6,000 square feet for a telecommunication production studio, approximately 2,000 square feet for a bookstore, plus general classroom and office space.

Information documents and forms for submitting proposals may be obtained between the hours of 8:30 A.M. and 4:30 P.M., Monday through Friday, at 5930 Middle Fiskville Road, Room 512, Austin, Texas, in the office of James Brader (512) 483-7611 beginning Monday, August 6, 1990.

Proposals will be accepted until 12:00 noon, Monday August 13, 1990. Proposals received after 12:00 noon, August 13th will be returned to the sender unopened. Proposers shall not undertake any activities, actions, or contacts to promote or advertise their proposals to the Board of Trustees of Austin Community College except in the case of College sponsored briefings, interviews or presentations or in the form of general comments made to the public at large. Violations of this provision will be grounds for rejection of the proposal.

---

tural firms that submitted proposals and asked to narrow the list to two or three firms.

During this selection process, the board should evaluate the proposals based on responses to the questionnaire *and reference checks* made by the administration. The authority should then be given to the college administration to negotiate an architectural contract specifying *fees* and *timetables.*

Architects' fees are based on services provided. Basic fees will normally be a percentage of the building cost and will include the following:

1. Plans and specifications, consultations, estimates, and engineering studies
2. Overall supervision of construction and general administration of the project
3. Approving payment vouchers and change orders
4. Acceptance of the completed project at the end of construction

Exhibit 17.5. A/E Questionnaire, Austin Community College.

1. Firm Summary
   List each firm or consultant proposed on this project; architect, structural, mechanical, electrical, civil, landscape, other. Please include the following information: a) name of firm, b) indication of prime, consultant, or joint venture relationship and discipline(s) provided for this project, c) local office address, d) telephone. A simple graphic organizational chart in 8½ × 11 format may also be included.
2. Background and Organization of the Firm
   This information shall be completed separately for each firm involved in your proposal.
   Firm Data: Firm name, disciplines provided this project, prime, JV or consultant, project contact/title, office address, city, state, zip code, telephone number, year local office established, form of organization.
   Key staff members of this firm to be involved in the project: name and responsibility.
   Relevant Experience: List five recent projects where this firm provided services of a scope and complexity similar to that proposed on this project. ACC is interested only in community colleges, colleges, and secondary school vocational/technical facilities. Include project/owner, square footage, total cost and date completed.
3. Qualifications of Proposed Key Staff Members
   Provide for all Key Staff Members listed by all firms in question 2. Include name, responsibility, firm, education, registration, years with this firm, total years experience, qualifications.
4. Summary of Five Recent Projects Comparable in Scope
   To be completed by the prime firm only. Include project name, location, date construction completed, square footage, construction cost, description, original budget, owner, owner's representative, title, telephone, address.
5. Summarize the techniques and methods used by your firm in controlling construction costs (budgets, estimates, change order control).
6. Summarize your firm's approach to project management (communications/scheduling, construction administration).
7. Describe the energy conservation techniques your firm could employ in the design of this facility.
8. Describe the success of the Equal Employment Opportunity (EEO) program of your firm. Identify any MBE and WBE business participation in your proposal.
9. Professional Liability Insurance Coverage
   Does your firm currently have professional liability insurance? Please list carrier, amount, comments.
10. Describe any recent litigation relative to professional performance.
11. Provide an outline of your proposed schedule for project development, from design through construction, to achieve the desired completion date.
12. Provide any additional relevant information and discuss any special qualifications.

In addition to the basic fees, multipliers are used for print-ing and reproduction of plans and specifications. Fees gener-ally do not include furniture design, building layouts for equip-ment, or detailed special items. To avoid pitfalls later, a detailed agreement for architectural services is extremely important.

Employing the Contractor

Once the architect has completed the drawings and specifica-tion manual, the next step is employing the contractor. Again a public notice is used to draw responses. An example is provided in Exhibit 17.6.

One primary difference between hiring an architect and hiring a contractor is that the general contractor should be *pre-qualified*. To avoid any confusion, this should be clearly expressed in the public notice.

To become prequalified, the contractor should submit an AIA 305 form along with any other information that might as-sist the administration with its decision. The administrative de-cision should be based on relevant experience and references. The architect should make the project specifications and plans available to interested contractors either at their office or in a plan room. At the discretion of the owner, the architect may furnish the plans at no charge, may require a refundable deposit, or may require a nonrefundable deposit. The plans and speci-fications should also be made available through a plan room for prospective contractors to review the plans at no cost and evaluate the feasibility of the project for bid purposes.

A prebid conference should be held at the job site to review the project requirements by the architect and owner. This pro-vides an opportunity for contractors to ask questions and to avoid any discrepancies regarding the project. The public notice should note whether attendance at the prebid conference is mandatory.

Prospective contractors must then submit their bid within the time line specified by the college. In addition, a *bid security* or *bid bond*, such as the one in Exhibit 17.7, should be required as a guarantee of the sincerity of the proposal. Bid security may also be furnished as a certified check.

Exhibit 17.6. Public Notice Soliciting Bids from Contractors.

Notice to Prospective Bidders

Austin Community College proposes to construct a new building at our Northridge Campus, 11928 Stonehollow Drive, Austin, Texas. The two story building will contain approximately 53,600 square feet with a steel frame structure, singleply roofing system and brick veneer facing. Bid documents will be released on approximately May 28, 1991 from the project architect, BLGY, Inc., Jefferson Building, 1600 West 38th Street, Suite 100, Austin, Texas 78731. No firm will be allowed to bid or to receive plans and specifications until the firm has been determined to be qualified by Austin Community College. Application forms for prequalification may be obtained from James Brader, Vice President for Planning and Development, Austin Community College, 5930 Middle Fiskville, Room 512, Austin, Texas, 78752, (512) 483-7611, between the hours of 9:00 A.M. and 4:00 P.M., Monday, May 13 through Friday, May 24, 1991. The deadline for submitting prequalification forms is 4:00 P.M., Friday, May 31, 1991.

Bids must be received by 2:00 P.M., Tuesday, June 18, 1991 at the ACC District Administrative Offices, Board Room (Room 233), 5930 Middle Fiskville, Austin, Texas. The bids will be publicly opened and read aloud. Evaluation of Qualifications will be based on the following minimum criteria:

1. Contractor has completed within the last five (5) years, three (3) or more projects of similar size (53,600 square feet), scope (2 story metal frame) and dollar amount.
2. Previous educational/institutional facilities experience, including vocational educational facilities.
3. Current commitments on other projects and ability to perform work, including identity and experience of project superintendent and key employees.
4. Performance, references and evaluation of former projects.
5. Evaluation of all information requested in AIA form A305.
6. Bid security in the amount of 5% of the total bid amount will be required at the submission of bids.
7. Consideration of ACC MBE/WBE goals.

Proposers shall not undertake any activities, actions or contacts to promote or advertise their bids to the Board of Trustees of Austin Community College except in the case of College sponsored briefings, interviews or presentations or in the form of general comments made to the public at large. Violations of this provision will be grounds for rejection of the bid. The acceptance of bids is subject to the discretionary approval by the ACC Board of Trustees.

Bid security protects the owner's right to accept a bidder's offer. If the bidder does not enter into a contract, the bid security is forfeited to the district.

At the bid opening, bids are opened publicly and read aloud by the architect and owner. The architect and owner then evaluate and review the lowest bids to verify the accuracy of

Exhibit 17.7. Bid Security or Bid Bond.

Bid Bond

KNOW ALL MEN BY THESE PRESENTS: That the undersigned Principal and Surety are firmly bound to Austin Community College ("ACC") in the principal sum of _____ Dollars ($ _____).
Now the condition of this bond is this: That whereas the undersigned Principal has submitted to ACC a Proposal to enter into a certain Contract whereunder Principal would undertake to perform the following described work of construction, alteration or repair:

NOW, THEREFORE, if the Principal shall, within ten (10) days following acceptance by the Board of Trustees of ACC of such Proposal and award by said Board to said Principal of said Contract, execute and return such further Contract Documents, together with such bonds as may be required by the terms of the Proposal as accepted, then this obligation shall be null and void; otherwise, it shall remain in full force and effect and the amount hereof shall be paid to and retained by ACC as liquidated damages for principal's failure to do so.

PRINCIPAL   SURETY

_____   _____

By: _____   By: _____

Title: _____   Title: _____

Date: _____   Date: _____

---

all documentation. The college administration recommends the "best and lowest" bid to the board of trustees for its approval.

Once the board of trustees has employed the contractor, an *Agreement for Construction Contract* must be executed. A clearly worded agreement is an essential element of the construction process. The contract should include the following: (1) statement of work specifying that the contractor shall furnish all materials, supplies, labor, services, and equipment for the construction job, (2) time for completion, (3) contract documents such as the agreement, schedule of special conditions, exhibits identified in the schedule of special conditions, the general conditions, schedule of hourly wage rates, specifications and drawings, special instructions to bidders, and advertisement for bids, (4) pricing schedule, (5) payment bond, and (6) performance bond. Construction may begin once the contract is executed. Early in the project, the college could introduce the *partnering* approach. Partnering is a new concept in the construction industry. It allows a "team" consisting of the architect, engineer, general contractor, and owner to develop a positive approach to the project through regular and open communication.

The team establishes goals and commits to achieving those goals through cooperation, trust, and excellence within the project. Topics for discussion may include job safety, value engineering, cost-saving measures, ways of minimizing paperwork, techniques for maintaining open and effective communication throughout all levels of the project, and suggestions for completing the facility in a more efficient, productive manner. Initially, supervisors and management meet to discuss preliminary concerns. Then they convey the information to their employees. Everyone involved with the project should be provided with partnering information and given an opportunity to voice their concerns and ideas. Meetings may be held as often as participants feel necessary; too many meetings may become burdensome, but too few meetings may not give participants time to express their concerns. Partnering is a beneficial tool used to create a positive working environment.

Another means of conveying concerns and maintaining constant communication between the architect and contractor is through weekly and monthly project meetings. During the initial stages of the project, weekly progress meetings should be held. As the project progresses, the meetings may be held less frequently. To avoid potential construction problems, it is a good practice to hold monthly meetings between the construction manager, project architects, and the owner to discuss project updates and review the site.

Likewise, the board of trustees typically likes to be informed on construction projects, but due to time constraints it is not always able to visit the site. One excellent method for keeping the board informed is to provide short videos of the progress during regularly scheduled board meetings. Normally the contractor attends the board meetings and, when necessary, acts as narrator for the video.

Since plans or specifications are rarely 100 percent correct and complete, *change orders* are inevitable during the con-

struction or refurbishing of a building. Change orders are similar
to addenda; they may affect corrections, add or delete work from
the original contract, change conditions, or extend finish times.
Since change orders increase and/or decrease the construction
contract total, board approval may be needed for change orders
exceeding predetermined dollar amounts. Change orders require
close supervision, and close attention should be given in order to
clearly determine legitimate need. Before beginning the project,
the architect and contractor should be informed if the board or
owner has established any limits.

Contractors are normally paid monthly as the construction work progresses. They should submit an application and
certificate for payment to the architect, who certifies and submits
the certificate for payment to the owner. The college internal
audit staff should review the certificate for payment, keeping
an eye on labor and material percentages.

Depending on college purchasing procedures, furniture
and equipment for the facility should be requisitioned *midway*
through the project, contingent on the delivery schedule. It is
imperative that the delivery schedule and the project completion date are coordinated in order to avoid problems that could
conceivably delay the opening of the facility.

On completion of the project, the owner, architect, and
contractor should schedule a walk-through and make a *punch
list.* The list should include items that need cosmetic attention—
for example, doing touch-up painting, replacing ceiling tiles,
and repairing mislaid carpet.

A well-written contract requires the contractor to provide
the owner with *warranties* and *operating* manuals at the completion of construction. The owner should request all warranties
and guarantees for the building as well as for furnishings and
equipment supplied by the contractor (for example, hot water
heaters, building products and materials used in the construction process that were installed by the contractor). After the walk-
through has been completed and the owner is satisfied with the
project, the contractor should obtain a *certificate of occupancy* from
the proper authority. If good construction practices have pre-
vailed and regular inspections by certifying authorities have been
obtained, this certificate of occupancy is easily secured.

Summary

The steps outlined in this chapter should provide the college with a general overview of campus planning and construction procedures. The many sample public notices and worksheets in the chapter will give helpful direction in planning these kinds of documents. A well-planned project contributes to a healthier and more effective learning and working environment.

Demographic studies, site analysis and evaluation, and feasibility studies are important groundwork for the development of the facility. Next, the selection of architects, contractors, and construction managers will be an integral part of the success or failure of the project. Finally, putting the timetable, fees, and guarantees in writing ensures that the building will be completed within chronological and budgetary guidelines. The planning and construction of a facility can be a satisfying experience for the college, with many years of benefits being derived from building utilization.

PART THREE

ROLES AND RESPONSIBILITIES

Part Three of this handbook deals with college functions, including staff recruitment, selection, evaluation, and dismissal; community relations; goal development; futures forecasting; and the plotting of indicators. These functions are broad responsibilities that transcend the workings of a single administrative office.

In Chapter Eighteen, Michael H. Parsons discusses budgeting, resource allocation, and instructional renewal.

Edwin E. Vineyard addresses recruitment policies, the selection process, and personnel policy systems as well as tenure and dismissal in Chapter Nineteen.

In Chapter Twenty, Albert B. Smith and Jacquelyn A. Barber focus on evaluation and performance appraisal for faculty.

Hans A. Andrews — in Chapter Twenty-One — stresses the importance of board policies as a way for college boards to communicate with college administration and faculty on issues of personnel management, tenure, faculty, students, and peer and administrative evaluations.

Alfredo G. de los Santos, Jr., and Scott Finger include a discussion of strategic goals, general objectives, action plans, assessment, and multi- and single-unit operations in Chapter Twenty-Two.

In Chapter Twenty-Three, Billie Wright Dziech argues that in a period of limited resources, unprecedented change, and ever-accelerating technology, colleges must examine relationships with their communities. Topics the chapter touches on include consultations with local businesses and industry, credit and credit-free programs, heterogeneous groups, and external evaluations.

In Chapter Twenty-Four, we return to institutional mission and goals. In this chapter, James C. Palmer discusses the criteria for measurable indicators of student progress and points out several imperatives of educational goal assessment.

In the concluding piece of this handbook—Chapter Twenty-Five—Arthur M. Cohen and Florence B. Brawer point to a few trends that will affect college options as we move into the twenty-first century.

Chapter 18

Budgeting and Resource Allocation

Michael H. Parsons

Growth has been the hallmark of American culture in the twentieth century, but the last decade of the century is reflecting a change in attitude on the part of the public. Americans no longer are enamored of uncontrolled expansion. Questions regarding quality, productivity, and value received characterize public response to all sectors of society. How does this change in focus relate to community colleges in general and to their budgeting practices specifically?

The environment that encompasses the community college of the 1990s is far different from that of a decade ago. The world has become tough, competitive, and entrepreneurial. Community college educators are no longer able to depend on the traditional sources of funding to provide for growth, development, and the replacement of equipment, facilities, and personnel.

Hauptman (1991, pp. 8–10) indicates that there are four variables that combine to influence budgeting in the 1990s. First, there is a continuing demographic shift away from the traditional seventeen- to twenty-year-old recent high school graduate who plans to attend college full time. However, there is no shortage of students. Community colleges are serving increasing numbers of part-time students from the age cadre of twenty-five to forty-five. These customers are more quality conscious, require more attention because of their lengthy absence from school, and, although attending part time, cost at least as much as their full-time cohorts to educate.

The second variable is the unstable economy. The repeating recessions of the past half decade are interacting with rapid technological change and slow but steady inflation to create a continuing shortage of resources at a time when retooling is essential and available funds have declining buying power.

Third, all public higher education institutions are experiencing increased competition for public funds. The state of the economy, mentioned above, has expanded the need among agencies that serve the disadvantaged, particularly in the areas of unemployment, health care, welfare, and aid to dependent children.

Finally, there is a two-pronged decrease in public support for education. Initially the recession devastated state budgets. Angel and DeVault (1991, p. 27) quantify the problem: "Vermont — $200 million shortfall; New Jersey — $600 million; Ohio — $1.5 billion; Texas — $4 billion; New York — $6 billion; and California — $14 billion." Fiscal 1992 did not fare any better. Concurrently, the nation is faced with a taxpayers' revolt. Wherever possible, voters reject new taxes. Also, they are increasingly critical of the performance of all aspects of education.

In essence, the 1990s are not emerging as a "user-friendly" decade for community college personnel — boards of trustees, administrators, faculty, or students. All constituents will be expected to do more with less under closer scrutiny from the taxpaying public. At the same time, society is placing greater demands on higher education. The next generation of professionals must be prepared; workforce 2000 must be retrained to meet the technology needs of a rapidly changing business and industry sector. Hauptman (1991, p. 13) presents the case precisely: "Shifting fortunes can be viewed as a curse or an opportunity. Adversity often provides an impetus for innovation and change that would not occur in its absence. . . . The challenge for higher education in the 1990s is to use revenue restrictions as a force for reform rather than as an excuse for failure." Budget development strategies must be designed to be cognizant of these variables while operating in an internal environment that produces teamwork and psychological commitment to change.

This chapter explores the factors influencing budget making and presents guidelines for developing the budget documents. The nature of revenue enhancement, decision making, and productivity improvement as they relate to budget development is also considered.

Factors Influencing the Budget

In what has become a minor classic — *Management: Tasks, Responsibilities, Practices* (1974, p. 144) — Drucker suggests that before budgeting is undertaken, the organization must decide what its mission is and how it will be effected: "Nothing is ever accomplished unless [a plan is developed to] concentrate scarce resources on a small number of priorities." The importance of mission definition and planning in providing a foundation for budget development is the essence of the change emerging during the 1990s.

In "creating our future," DeHart (1992) calls for a commitment to planning — "long-term strategic planning and annual operational planning." He considers it essential to provide the college with the direction needed to realize mission. Further, he suggests that planning enables institutions "to avoid the bad . . . and capitalize on the good . . . even when, and maybe especially when, conditions look their worst" (p. 25). It seems that without a clear articulation of mission and a fully operational and integrated planning process, budgeting becomes a frustrating and nonproductive activity.

Budgeting as a component of mission definition and planning is a relatively new phenomenon. It is the result of financial hard times. The last decade has seen changes in the clientele of higher education along with increased competition for limited, and often shrinking, resources. Recent analyses of the financial universe of higher education present a new assessment of the budgeting process (Deegan, 1992; Hauptman, 1991; Vaughan, 1991).

The budget document is increasingly being described as a plan written in financial and statistical terms that makes an institution's goals and objectives achievable. The budget process provides development along two axes. The first is a long-range document projecting institutional development over a three- to five-year period. This dimension is linked closely to the strategic plan. The process of development calls for annual assessment and revision of both components. Ideally, the result is orderly implementation of institutional goals and the management of change.

The second axis is the annual operating budget. This dimension is linked even more closely with the institution's operational plan. The purposes of the operating budget are quite precise: it serves as a benchmark for measuring institutional performance within the context of the operational plan, it acts as a vehicle for transmitting awareness of performance throughout the institution, it provides a procedure for allocating resources among competing units within the institution, and it promotes a disciplined strategy for solving problems.

Is the operating budget always used in such an efficient manner? Unlikely! Deegan (1992) surveyed the problem areas that community college presidents consider most vexing. Three of the top four relate to budget development, implementation, and monitoring. Horton (1991), former chief executive officer of the American Management Association, suggests that the budget is one of the most underused tools available to managers. How can the gap between theory and practice be bridged?

An important beginning point is the identification of the resources to be used in implementing the institutional planning process. Ideally, there would be sufficient resources to implement all of the primary objectives of the institution. But the world is not ideal; no institution has all the resources it needs. In fact, many are losing resources when comparisons are made with their resource base of a decade ago. Minter's (1991, p. 22) assessment sets the tone: "Faced with slower revenue growth and steadily increasing operating costs, institutions will have to make tough choices. Creative institutional leaders seeking to continue to address the expectations of both the institution and its clients must take a hard look at ways to balance operating costs and increase productivity in order to offset the declining income growth."

The increasing pressure being brought to bear on the academic community by external variables makes mobilizing and sustaining institutionwide participation in planning and budget development difficult. Yet community colleges have historically practiced a participatory form of budget development. The demand to continue this collegial decision making is growing.

Alfred and Kreider (1991, pp. 37–38) identify five factors found in those community colleges that are effective at promoting broad-based budget development. First, these colleges' planning process reflected widespread support and acceptance of the planning/budgeting system among diverse constituencies. Second, the colleges' environmental scanning processes promoted institutionwide understanding of the future enrollment and economic trends affecting the institutions. Third, the internal problems facing the institutions were recognized and action was under way to engage them. Fourth, an ethic of cooperation permeated the institutions, leading to a recognition of the interdependency among organizational divisions. Finally, faculty attitudes toward budget development, planning, and governance were generally positive. The development and maintenance of these factors make cooperative budget development possible.

Further, Angel and DeVault (1991, p. 28) present an eleven-dimension model of proactive planning. They suggest that four dimensions are essential to budget development in times of declining financial resources. They are "conceptual, adaptive, anticipatory, and action oriented" factors. The educational leader seeking to enhance institutional involvement in and commitment to a budget development process designed to meet the requirements of the decade ahead will use proactive planning to ensure that these factors characterize the process.

Budget Design, Development, and Implementation

All budgets begin with a design. Following is a set of minimal budget development guidelines.

1. Operational planning and budget development
   Needs assessment
   Feasibility analysis
   Cost estimation
   Budget design
2. Resource procurement
   State parameters
   Local parameters
   Tuition/fees determination
   Special projects contribution
3. Resource allocation/fiscal monitoring
   Internal resource distribution
   Establishment of restricted accounts
   Operations monitoring
   Cost control
4. Performance audit
   Financial audit
   Program/project evaluation
   Institutional accountability reporting
   Cost-benefit analysis
5. Repeat of the process

In previous decades, budget development in higher education was largely a process of maintaining the status quo. This decade is emerging as an era of change. Often the process begins with the current operating budget as a base, then planning models are applied to align available resources with institutional objectives for the fiscal year. Information regarding resources is more accessible, if not more positive.

In Maryland, for example, the state's contribution to the operating budget is predetermined. It is based on a flat grant/enrollment formula using a data base from two fiscal years past. Also, the county political jurisdiction, which plays a major role in college financing, provides funding parameters early in the budget development process. The most flexible component of the budget is tuition. Careful attention to economic conditions, student financial aid data, and the enrollment niche that the college needs to fill are contributing factors in the tuition-setting process.

Clearly these conditions mandate the development of guidelines for budget preparation. Capone and colleagues (1991, p. 2) suggest that the planning phase of the budget is the most critical. Input to the development process needs to be solicited across the college community. Faculty, department/division chairpersons, mid-managers, and deans need to develop an action plan supported empirically. The plan is a projection in financial terms of the goals and objectives of the program, division, function, or area for the appropriate fiscal period. Pohlman (1990) and Garner (1991) present similar models. In their opinion, the draft document should include the following elements:

1. Program or division overview and description
2. Accomplishments of the program, division, and so on during the preceding year, including a cost-benefit analysis
3. Specific measurable objectives and goals for the coming year, in priority order with cost-benefit data
4. Resource requirements in financial terms for the coming year by cost center or line item
5. Projected revenues for the coming year directly attributable to the program, division, and so on

The design presents a comprehensive yet easily understood analysis of the purpose, plan, and financial resource base of the area.

Budget presentations should use appendixes to provide supporting data. Usually included are any evaluation studies of the area completed during the previous year, explanatory material regarding "out-of-the-ordinary" expenditure requests, and justification for any special deviations from institutional budgeting practices. Overall, the document should be as brief as possible and conform to the format in general use by the college.

Most colleges separate personnel and capital equipment budgets from the general operating budget. In presenting personnel requests, a rationale regarding the "value-added" aspect of the new hire is useful. Such elements as what new services will be available to clients, how many part-time personnel will no longer be needed, and how the new individual will strengthen accountability practices are relevant. Further, a relationship to the program's or division's strategic plan is essential.

The capital equipment budget is developed using the following structure.

1. A description of the item and its relationship to the operational plan is needed.
2. The item must have a minimum useful life of more than one year. (Actual minimum parameters will be set by the institution.)
3. It must have a minimum dollar-value threshold. (Actual minimum dollar value will be set by the institution.)
4. It is acquired to continue a function that is essential to the continued operation of the program, division, and so on or to implement an approved element in the operational plan.

Capone and colleagues (1991, p. 10) present a useful five-step process in organizing a capital equipment budget.

1. Identify equipment needs and categorize them as "new" or "replacement."
2. Within each category, identify a priority ranking system.
   a. *Urgent* — (specify "cost of nonprocurement")
   b. *Essential* — (first priority in the operational plan)
   c. *Economically desirable* — (will permit entrepreneurial venture resulting in enhanced revenue)
   d. *Enrichment* — (will allow area to implement a strategy or tactic ahead of schedule)
3. For each equipment request, identify any associated costs that accompany the purchase (wiring, facility modification, and so on).
4. Determine the associated noncapital expenditures for each equipment request. For example, are there training costs, supply costs, service contracts, and so forth?
5. For each replacement equipment request, identify any

trade-in or net salvage value of items being replaced that will lower the net cost of the request.

These steps help develop a cost/budget scenario for capital equipment requests.

Garner (1991), Mallory (1989), and Vandament (1989) present the elements of a process for developing linkages between operational planning and budget development. College planning/budgeting systems should be uniquely suited to the institution's culture and integrate participation, accountability, and outcomes. Critical elements include:

1. Implementing annual academic operating plans containing unit goals as planning and budget development tools
2. Developing and providing access to a common data base that is used by all within the institution to make academic planning and budget decisions
3. Decentralizing the budget development process to the lowest administrative level possible, integrating from the bottom up
4. Providing planning and budget development training for all personnel within the institution and relying on them to provide input to both the budget and planning process
5. Developing a planning/budgeting environment in which accountability is expected at all levels of faculty and administrative decision making

Application of the aforementioned strategies will help develop psychological ownership of the planning/budgeting process among faculty, staff, and administrators. The result will be a more realistic response to the shifting financial realities of the years ahead.

Institutional Advancement/Special Projects

The operating and capital equipment budgets are two legs of the college financial triangle. A third leg, the institutional advancement or special project budget, will be of increasing importance in the future.

Projects are one-year to multiyear programs funded by external sources designed to implement a specific aspect of the institution's strategic plan. Project budgets differ from operating budgets in that they usually extend over more than one year. They rely, however, on the annual operating plan for implementation. In developing the budget for the project, college personnel must include procedures for monitoring progress, assessing the degree of relationship to planning objectives, and evaluating the quality of project outcomes.

Such diverse project areas as the Perkins Career and Technology Education Act; Title III, Developing Institutions, of the Higher Education Act; and Fund for the Improvement of Postsecondary Education grants share several common practices.

1. The project director must develop a master schedule designed to provide benchmarks for completing specific tasks.
2. The institution must identify an implementation structure that integrates the project into the operational life of the college. An example is a project director who has complete responsibility for a team charged with implementation. In contrast, the director may be a facilitator/evaluator with responsibility for project tasks residing with division or department heads.
3. In projection operation, time is of the essence. A project calendar with critical target dates provides the director with visual reinforcement of the importance of completing tasks at the expected quality standard within the projected time parameter.
4. Financial expenditures are charged to restricted accounts for a time period specified in the project document. All costs must be accrued by the end of the appropriate time period, with project reports usually including an audit component.
5. Project evaluation is an integral element in the implementation process. Most projects require both for-

mative and summative assessment. Various designs, both empirical and qualitative, are used regularly. In multiyear projects, the results of the evaluation are directly related to funding for project continuation.

Given resource scarcity, specially funded projects are assuming increasing importance. How do they influence the mission and operational life of the college?

Thompson (1992, p. 38) presents an interesting perspective using an ethical frame of reference. He suggests that fundraising via projects or solicitation is a core function of the college and not a peripheral activity. Therefore, it must be integrated into and governed by the same ethical principles as the rest of the institution.

The significance of this perspective is threefold. First, the college must take care to avoid involvement in any project or fund source that would inhibit the institution from making academic decisions using academic criteria. Second, the college cannot become the captive of any special interest(s). Academic autonomy depends on careful assessment of the implications accompanying the resources being sought. The college's project development staff must serve as a litmus test for projects presenting threats to institutional mission, ethics, or autonomy. Finally, resource scarcity forces institutional personnel to confront difficult ethical choices. The process of clarifying the college's ethical stance requires broad-based communication. A consensus must be reached regarding the institution's guiding principles. The essential dimension, therefore, of resource development is the clarification and reinforcement of the college's mission, goals, and ethical stance.

Developing and Applying
Financial Management Expertise

All members of the college community who have financial decision-making responsibility must use monitoring techniques to ensure that actual performance and planned performance are consistent. Any divergence between the two must be investigated, explained, and corrected. The most commonly used technique to effect the procedure is *variance analysis*.

Capone and colleagues (1991, p. 20) define *variance* as the difference between the actual income or expenditure and the budgeted income or expenditure. Variances are most commonly assessed in terms of one or two indicators: actual dollars and/or percentages. The most thorough design examines both categories.

College personnel at all levels must decide which variances are large enough to merit investigation. A practical assessment system usually combines both dollar and percentage variance analysis in the following manner: assess all variances of 15 percent or larger where the actual dollar variance exceeds $500. Capone and colleagues (1991, p. 20) call this tactic the *materiality factor*. The frequency of variance analysis is influenced by the degree of control that the institution has over its financial data. Highly automated systems allow monitoring on a daily basis, if desired. Realistically, quarterly assessment seems consistent with the nature of college operations. If a written variance report is required, the following outline is useful.

1. Identify the divergent factor and explore only significant variances.
2. Explain the causes or sources of variance from both a financial and a planning perspective.
3. Where possible, use projective techniques to predict future directions if the variance is not corrected.
4. Provide recommendations for corrective action. Include the impact of the correction on the college's operational plan.

Variance analysis is valuable in two ways. First, as a control procedure it allows college personnel to keep the institution within the parameters of available resources. Second, the variance analysis reports are important inputs to future budget estimation and development.

Expertise in budget management is essential if colleges are to meet the financial challenges of the future. Commitment to the institution's planning process and its financial expression, the budget, is directly related to the manager's sense of autonomy and control. Messmer (1992, pp. 26–27) recognizes that managers have a core of expertise that is essential to the institution's mission. He suggests that cross-discipline training is a strategy for understanding the relationship of their primary function to others within the college. Careful attention to cross training in fiscal areas will contribute, materially, to the operation of a cost-effective, accountable institution.

Developing and revising a budget along with integrating it into the college's operational plan is a process essential to successful management. The growing automation of American higher education has increased the sophistication of the process.

The adoption of management information systems for the colleges' mainframe computers was the first step. By the mid 1980s, the increased availability and sophistication of microcomputers expanded access to automated budget management procedures. Today, first-line administrators can access their budgets, update or change data, monitor variance analysis, and initiate integration activity with the college's operating plan using a desktop system. Software production companies are able to develop customized programs that are individually tailored to the needs of specific colleges (Pohlman, 1990).

The "spreadsheet" revolution is another significant application of technology to budget development. The spreadsheet program basically duplicates the forms used to prepare the budget. The user calls up the form, puts headings on the rows and columns, and adds budget data. The spreadsheet program performs the basic arithmetic calculations needed to compile the budget. Further, as changes are required, the program will sequentially compute modifications. The most important advantage of spreadsheet construction of the budget is the speed of compilation and revision. The time saved can be used to apply "what if" analysis. The initial assumptions on which the budget was constructed can be changed, and the subsequent impact on the budget can be determined. Further, budget revision and planning for future budget development can be quickly initiated through the inclusion of variance analysis data and information resulting from changing financial conditions.

While the application of technology to budgeting has increased efficiency and speed, it is important to remember that automation merely provides tools. They are only as accurate and helpful as the understanding of the operator and the accuracy of data entry. Without understanding the concepts of budget development and access to accurate data, the application of technology will only hinder the budget development process.

Budgeting, Planning, and Resource Allocation: State of the Art

The foregoing pages sketched the essential changes in planning and budgeting practices that have recently emerged. How accurate are the perceptions? Three recent empirical studies help answer the question. Ashworth and Vogler (1991, pp. 22–26) report on a study of the congruence between forty members of the Virginia State Senate and the twenty-three presidents of the state's community colleges regarding funding goals. The results are encouraging. Planning and budget allocation seem to be "on target" when the opinions of the senators are assessed. There is little variance between presidential decisions and senatorial rankings. The authors suggest that the congruence between the two groups indicates "strong lines of communication and a willingness to discuss issues openly" (p. 26). The congruence underscores the importance of environmental scanning and integration of resource allocation with the needs of the service area.

Deegan (1992, pp. 26–30) surveyed 311 community college presidents in the spring of 1990. Fifty-four percent responded. The focus of the survey was the implementation of modern management concepts in community colleges. The issues of planning and budgeting were studied, and the results are revealing. Eighty-nine percent of the respondents report using the concept of strategic planning, yet only 34 percent note the tactic as very successful. Only 39 percent report that planning has been decentralized to the department level. Further, only 29 percent consider it very successful. If these findings are representative of the nation's community colleges, much work remains to be done. Institutionwide strategic planning is considered to be the driving force behind budget development. Only through more attention to planning will the budgeting process become truly reflective of the needs of the college's internal and external customers.

The questions related to budgeting are equally interesting. Fifty-nine percent of the respondents report using traditional line item or incremental budgeting. Only 13 percent rate the approach as very successful. Fifty-four percent report using program- or project-based budgeting. A larger number, 31 percent, consider this approach to be highly successful. This comparison suggests that the planning required to produce a program budget seems to result in a higher degree of satisfaction with the process.

Three categories studied reflect the fiscal changes required to meet the challenges of the 1990s. First, 74 percent of the respondents report using the college's foundation to raise funds. The satisfaction (very successful) rating is 45 percent. Second, 69 percent report beginning or expanding the use of business/industry contract training. The very successful rating is 52 percent. Finally, 45 percent of the respondents report using special funds for internal innovations. The success rating is 47 percent. These categories indicate that college presidents are becoming increasingly aware that their institutions must seek out new sources of funding to augment traditional practices. The planning/budgeting process must change to accommodate these nontraditional strategies.

Deegan's (1992) interpretation of the data mirrors the preceding interpretation. He questions whether strategic planning can become effective until it has reached the entire college. Further, he indicates that a serious inadequacy of resources is observable throughout the survey and that an entrepreneurial spirit is "increasing in both internal and external activities" as a result. He concludes that there is no simple solution to the issues facing community colleges in the immediate future. He hopes that the adoption of contemporary management techniques will serve as "a focus for analysis and change" (pp. 28–30). Planning and budgeting practices are likely to benefit from the changes chronicled by the study.

Gardner (1992, pp. 28–29) reports on the outcomes of the 1992 American Association of Community and Junior Colleges convention. She indicates that the decline in traditional funding sources continues to plague community colleges. Participants reject significant modification in the colleges' mission. There is no viable rationale for reducing services to those who display the greatest need. "Speakers challenged attendees to find a way. Dig deeper . . . rearrange priorities. The needs are too great to ignore" (p. 28). Her statements are a fitting endorsement of the position that institutionwide integrated planning and budgeting are an essential response to the challenge community colleges face.

All three studies reinforce the importance of implementing new strategies so that community colleges will remain the agent of social equalization in American society. How will planning and budgeting contribute to keeping community colleges on the cutting edge of change in the 1990s?

Understanding the Challenge

DeHart (1992, p. 27) suggests that community colleges must have "a true sense of community among ourselves. We need a community in which all members feel valuable and in which administration, faculty, and staff are not only concerned about students, but also about each other." The process of planning and budget development can contribute significantly to realizing this goal.

The focus of planning and budget development needs to be redirected to meet changing circumstances. Eaton (1991, p. 38) notes that along with being "the least well financed sector of higher education," community colleges are "funded to the extent that they *enroll* students; funding is not tied to student *achievement*. Yet both factors deserve consideration." Along with these elements, cost containment will receive extensive attention. Parnell (1990, p. 285) provides a valid perspective: "Cost containment will be a motivational force in the decade ahead for colleges and universities of all kinds. Cost containment discussions will not be limited to college presidents, but will involve the entire college community." Where will the discussion begin; what will be the issues?

The case has been made that planning drives and is integrated with budgeting. What gives direction to strategic and operational planning? Vaughan (1991) suggests that the college mission is the moving force behind all aspects of institutional operation. He indicates that there are four dangers besetting the college's mission in the 1990s. All of them have budget implications. The dangers are:

1. *The colleges are too avant garde.* If too much effort and too many resources are dedicated to innovation, the core of higher education services will wither. Vaughan notes, "Once this happens, the community college has trouble justifying funding from the sources that normally finance higher education."

2. *The colleges are in danger of losing their sense of purpose.* If colleges continue their attempt to be all things to all people, their mission will lack focus. Legislators are likely to be troubled by the request for continuing increases in funding for activities that they and, too often, the colleges' personnel do not understand.

3. *The colleges risk losing their membership in the higher education community.* With increasing emphasis on nontraditional activities, colleges are being questioned about their commitment to traditional higher education values and activities. The most traditional members of the higher education community view with alarm the increasing number of cutting-edge activities conducted by community colleges.

4. *The colleges must develop a process for institutionalizing change.* The rate of change experienced by society today is unprecedented in the nation's history. What were cutting-edge programs and activities a decade ago are becoming obsolete. Yet they have advocates who seek to keep resources flowing to them. These individuals must be prepared for career modification as programs and activities are phased out and new opportunities emerge. These dangers appear to be a valid agenda for community college renewal in the 1990s. Is there a paradigm available around which to structure the renewal?

In the preceding pages, I have argued for three interrelated processes in budget development. In essence, they are planning, both strategic and operational, integrated with budget development and resource allocation, which draws on all levels of the college — administrators, faculty, staff, and students. Perhaps the elements themselves are sufficiently realigning that the institution will need no further impetus; however, this does not appear likely. Covey (1991) presents a seven-step paradigm for institutional renewal. The elements seem uniquely suited to facilitating change in America's community colleges.

1. *Develop a shared vision.* All members of the college community will be involved in restating the college's mission, integrating the result into each college's unique organizational culture, and participating in a process of budget development that allocates resources by priority to the operation of the revised vision.

2. *Design an integrated strategic/operational plan that helps institutionalize the shared vision.* The planning process must include all institutional constituencies, flow from the mission statement to the operational realities of the institution, and be based on environmental realities. The budgeting/resource allocation process is a monitoring effort to assure that the alignment between the ideal and real remains productive.

3. *Effect an organizational system that is structured for security yet flexible enough to adapt to ever-occurring change.* No design for the day-to-day operation of an institution can remain rigid. Regulations and procedures need constant modification to adapt to change. Carefully articulated values regarding employees and clients will provide sufficient structure so that change can be the hallmark. Budgeting procedures and resource allocations are the blueprint for change management.

4. *Inculcate a principle-centered management style that is simultaneously fluid, flexible, yet value centered.* The quality revolution that is sweeping the nation currently is well suited to the reformation of community college management. A management style that is based on articulated values and not wedded to a single operational design will survive into the twenty-first century. If all of the institution's personnel recognize the commitment to quality, are encouraged to contribute to its achievement, and are recognized for their accomplishments, they will "buy into"

the process. Budget development will become a process of affirming the institution's values and vision.

5. *Instill an institutionwide training program that will align vision, values, and skills.* Quality management requires a modified repertoire of skills from all institutional personnel. The institution's commitment to quality demands that all levels of staff be given the opportunity to develop the required repertoire. As suggested above, cross training in budget development/resource allocation/budget management pays dividends through individual ownership and innovation.

6. *Build a system of institutional assessment, problem management, and trust development.* The lack of trust at any level of an institution threatens the success of institutional renewal. A monitoring process designed to identify and solve problems where psosible, improve communication, and allow all personnel a voice in institutional management will enhance trust. Inclusion of all personnel in budget development and continuing communication regarding budget management is an integral part of the process.

7. *Ensure that the pronouncements and behaviors of the institution's leaders are congruent.* If the college's leaders do not display integrity, the entire process is doomed. Periodic review of operational plans, budget allocations, and institutional goals involving all personnel will reinforce the importance of integrity development.

This paradigm will not emerge overnight. Yet if constant effort is applied, change will be internalized and renewal will occur. Is the result worth the effort? In discussing the expansion of the British electorate, nineteenth-century Prime Minister Benjamin Disraeli stated: "All power is a trust; . . . we are accountable for its exercise; . . . from the people, and for the people, all springs and all must exist" (quoted in Drucker, 1985, p. 194). We deliver our service through a people-to-people process. The clients, internal and external, deserve our best effort.

Summary

The biggest influence on developing a college's budget is the expressed mission of the institution. The budget must be compatible with and even help to advance the goals of the school. A budget is actually a plan written in financial and statistical terms that makes an institution's goals and objectives achievable. It must take into account both financial and legal parameters and the need for both faculty and administrators to feel that their ideas and concerns are being listened to. Developing a successful budget also requires a system of evaluation and review. Variance analysis is valuable both as a check for keeping college spending within resource limitations and as a guideline for future budget planning.

There are three interrelated processes in budget development: planning, integrated with budget development and resource allocation, drawing on all levels of the college, from students to administration. To ensure the success of any budget, those who direct the institution must do so with a shared vision, a structure that is principle based and balanced between flexibility and security, and personal integrity.

Community colleges of the twenty-first century will be required to serve an ever-changing clientele with scarce resources. Effective planning, budgeting, and resource allocation processes that can meet the challenge require a new paradigm. Our clients deserve quality and cost-effective service. What better strategy exists than for the peoples' college to base the new paradigm on the perceived needs of the people—those employed and those served.

References

Alfred, R. L., and Kreider, P. "Creating a Culture for Institutional Effectiveness." *Community, Technical, and Junior College Journal,* 1991, *61,* 34–39.

Angel, D., and DeVault, M. "Managing 'McLean': Proactive Planning." *Community, Technical, and Junior College Journal,* 1991, *62,* 26–29.

Ashworth, P. C., and Vogler, D. E. "Community College Funding Goals: Senate and Presidential Comparison." *Community Services Catalyst,* 1991, *31,* 22–26.

Capone, F., Hendricks, W., and Pohlman, R. *Building Budgeting Skills*. (Rev. ed.) Shawnee Mission, Kans.: National Press Publications, 1991.

Covey, S. R. *Principle-Centered Leadership*. New York: Simon & Schuster, 1990.

Deegan, W. L. "Proven Techniques: The Use and Impact of Major Management Concepts in Community Colleges." *Community, Technical, and Junior College Journal*, 1992, *62*(5), 26–30.

DeHart, A. R. "Creating Our Future." *Community, Technical, and Junior College Journal*, 1992, *62*, 24–27.

Drucker, P. F. *Management: Tasks, Responsibilities, Practices*. New York: HarperCollins, 1974.

Drucker, P. F. *Innovation and Entrepreneurship: Practice and Principles*. New York: HarperCollins, 1985.

Eaton, J. S. "Encouraging Transfer: The Impact on Community Colleges." *Educational Record: The Magazine of Higher Education*, 1991, *72*, 34–38.

Gardner, B. "72nd Annual AACJC Convention Wrap-Up Expanding the Vision: Leadership into the 21st Century." *Community, Technical, and Junior College Journal*, 1992, *62*, 28–29.

Garner, C. W. *Accounting and Budgeting in Public and Nonprofit Organizations: A Manager's Guide*. San Francisco: Jossey-Bass, 1991.

Hauptman, A. M. "Meeting the Challenge: Doing More with Less in the 1990s." *Educational Record: The Magazine of Higher Education*, 1991, *72*, 6–13.

Horton, T. R., and Reid, P. C. "What Fate for Middle Managers?" *Management Review*, 1991, *80*, 22–23.

Mallory, C. *Team Building*. Shawnee Mission, Kans.: National Press Publications, 1989.

Messmer, M. "Cross-Discipline Training: A Strategic Method to Do More with Less." *Management Review*, 1992, *81*, 26–28.

Minter, J. "Fiscal Facts, Trends, and Forecasts." *Educational Record: The Magazine of Higher Education*, 1991, *72*, 19–22.

Parnell, D. *Dateline 2000: The New Higher Education Agenda*. Washington, D.C.: American Association of Community and Junior Colleges, 1990.

Pohlman, R. *Understanding the Bottom Line: Finance for Non-Financial Managers and Supervisors.* Shawnee Mission, Kans.: National Press Publications, 1990.

Thompson, D. F. "Ethics and Fundraising: An Educational Process." *Educational Record: The Magazine of Higher Education,* 1992, *73*, 38–43.

Vandament, W. E. *Managing Money in Higher Education: A Guide to the Financial Process and Effective Participation Within It.* San Francisco: Jossey-Bass, 1989.

Vaughan, G. B. "Institutions on the Edge: America's Community Colleges." *Educational Record: The Magazine of Higher Education,* 1991, *72*, 30–33.

Chapter 19

The Administrator's Role in Staff Management

Edwin E. Vineyard

Personnel administration in community colleges has become an increasingly complex facet of general leadership, so much so that it has emerged as a specialty of its own. This has also become an area laden with pitfalls and potential controversy that may involve liabilities in resources, risks to professional careers, and threats to institutional reputations. It nevertheless offers great opportunity for the college leader who seeks to make substantive changes and improvements in the most basic services related to the institutional mission.

No endeavor is more significant to building institutional excellence than hiring, developing, and retaining quality professional personnel. Larger institutions have developed self-contained personnel offices staffed with trained administrators; smaller ones have continued to place responsibilities for personnel matters within the principal administrative offices. But in either case, well-operated colleges clarify these assignments and specify persons to tend to the considerable procedural details.

While this chapter deals primarily with personnel management as it pertains to faculty and other professional academic personnel, first- and second-echelon administrative staff should not be neglected. And while it assumes the existence of a collegial environment within the institution, it does not ignore the fact that throughout the nation a large number of colleges operate under formal contracts reached through collective bargaining. These will, of course, affect the applicability of some suggestions made in the chapter.

Staff Recruitment

Certain criteria pertain to all staff recruitment efforts, and each step in the process stems from them.

Credentials

The master's degree is usually considered the basic degree for community college faculty, though exceptions are sometimes made in the case of certain occupational programs. For faculty who do not possess the necessary credentials, the college should have policies requiring the completion of the appropriate degrees as well as programs that assist instructors in accomplishing this.

Experience is usually considered desirable for new faculty or other professional candidates. At one time, the principal recruiting ground for new academic faculty was the secondary school, and this continues to be a major source of employees. However, community colleges have increasingly tended to look toward university sources, particularly for staff in academic transfer disciplines, and to practicing professionals from the private arena. As examples, attorneys teach political science, accountants teach accounting, and engineers teach mathematics, often on a part-time or adjunct basis. Early retirees from the military services, as well as from business and industry, also constitute a rich pool of academic talent that is often overlooked.

Recruitment Procedures

The obvious first steps in the recruitment of staff are writing the job definition and preparing the position description for circulation. In many instances, these may be one and the same, but for administrative posts and related assignments, a length-ier definition of the position may be in order. The position description for circulation tends to be succinct, and descriptions normally originate with academic supervisory personnel, such as the department chair, and pass through the chief academic officer. Personnel specialists may refine the descriptions (Midkiff and Come, 1988). Preparation of position descriptions for ad-vertisement and circulation should not be undertaken without serious thought and some caution, since both the assignment specifications and the description of required and preferred char-acteristics could become significant in case of legal challenge.

All institutions normally advertise upper-echelon adminis-trative posts nationally. Vineyard (1993) provides extensive guidelines for the recruitment and selection of presidents as well as advice for presidential aspirants. A broad applicant pool is desirable. But some institutions are too cautious in trying to meet affirmative action requirements and go overboard in terms of extensive advertising of positions. This is unnecessary. What is important is circulating announcements widely enough to reach qualified minority candidates. Even so, special strategies are often necessary to reach minority groups. One institution, located away from any urban center and minority population base, obtained the cooperation of a friendly urban peer college in mailing announcements to candidates in its applicant files. Another institution ran a regular follow-up program of its own minority graduates, seeking to recruit into their applicant pools those who completed advanced degrees. Some colleges adver-tise in area or regional publications that have a large reader-ship among minority groups. Personal visits, as well as posted materials, in secondary schools with concentrations of minority faculty may prove fruitful.

The announcements are distributed broadly, but seldom nationally, for faculty recruiting. Usually the college will have a standard listing of graduate university placement offices in the region to whom these are sent. Announcements are also often sent to the appropriate academic departments in these same universities. It is a good idea to include baccalaureate-level col-leges in this procedure, especially those with substantial proportions of minority graduates. Few community colleges utilize the services of placement agencies operated for profit in seeking academic instructional staff. However, colleges must adapt strategies to the characteristics of the job market and the particular field in question.

Selection Process

Selecting potential employees involves processing the applications and screening and selecting the candidates.

Paperwork

Advertisements and circulars will have specified the format of the application and desired attachments, if any, and the office to which these are to be sent. Normally a résumé, perhaps with certain specified elements, constitutes the application. This avoids any legal problems that might arise through items on a standard form. One principal use of the official application form is to provide the basis of the personnel file of new hires. Colleges that collect only the résumé from applicants may still utilize a standard personnel information form for these new hires. Normally, job reference letters are neither solicited nor sent with résumés of academic applicants.

The office responsible should create a search file for each position vacancy, normally retained for at least five years. This file should contain appropriate documentation of all search and selection actions.

Screening

In small community colleges, academic personnel operations will normally be centered in the office of the academic dean or vice president, sometimes in the office of the president. In institutions large enough to support a separate personnel office, the process will be coordinated there. Personnel offices are administrative service centers and therefore not appropriately involved in the evaluation and selection of academic staff on any basis other than to ensure that applications meet basic procedural requirements.

Systems for screening and selecting academic and other professional staff vary considerably from institution to institution, but normally these involve participation and input from both the administrative and the faculty sector. Cooper and Garmon (1990) discuss a "holistic" approach to personnel selection. In some larger colleges, staff selection may be delegated to the academic division head with provision for participation by a staff committee. Sometimes the academic dean (or vice president) takes the lead and organizes a committee involving the chair or other lead staff in the process. In some smaller institutions, a "committee" consisting of the president, chief academic officer, and department or division head performs this function. Other small or medium-sized colleges have a personnel committee performing at least the initial screening, and sometimes the interviewing and recommending, of new staff. While some presidents, or even chief academic officers, prefer to remain aloof from the selection process except for some final approval role, this practice is questionable.

However a college conducts the screening and selection processes, the procedure involved should be clearly spelled out in the college's policies and procedures manual (and its faculty handbook). Development of such a policy statement forces the institution to examine critically, to clarify, and to standardize its procedures. Careful adherence to a well-conceived and well-written policy statement not only contributes to a better and more reliable process but also protects both individual rights and institutional vulnerability.

Selection

Once a group of semifinalists is selected, references are asked to provide further information or insights. However, in today's legal climate, most people accustomed to writing letters of recommendation are extremely cautious about negative comments. Those supplying recommendations tend to be much more candid in face-to-face discussions and unrecorded telephone conversations than in letters. It is also desirable to contact people not listed in an application who may have knowledge of a candidate.

There is no magic number of candidates to interview. In some instances, one candidate appears clearly the best, and this person should be interviewed and selected if found worthy. In other instances there may be three possibilities, but it is usually an inefficient use of staff and administrative time to interview a list of candidates longer than this. Sometimes the decision seems clear to all after the first interview with an impressive person, but once a commitment has been made to interview a certain number of candidates and appointments have been set up, this must be carried through. Some institutions establish a hierarchy of leading candidates and work from the top down until a suitable person is found, then stop the process.

The interview represents an extremely significant portion of the selection process. While individual interviews may be scheduled with everyone involved in the process, it is more efficient for the committee as a group to interview the candidate. Each member of the team will have the same opportunity to hear and observe the candidate.

A few enterprising committees devise lists of selection criteria by which to judge candidates. This does indeed introduce more system to the process, but the committee must be careful not to establish additional "requirements" for the position not covered in the vacancy announcement. Similarly, any such criteria should mesh with the college's own policy statements defining faculty role performance.

Sometimes a committee follows an advance agenda or script to ensure proper coverage of the areas of significant interest and to allow different members to take the lead on different topics. These scripts introduce greater commonality of coverage when several candidates are considered.

The interview is also an opportunity to orient the candidate to the college environment, its professional climate, the societal setting, and the policy milieu within which services are to be rendered. The college representatives should be honest with the candidate in presenting the assignment and the institutional working environment in a realistic light.

How then is selection made once the interviewing is over? Again, this depends somewhat on the individual committee. If the committee is a departmental one, perhaps under the department chair, the committee makes a recommendation that the chair can support and recommend upward through the chain of academic command. At each link in that chain, there remains the right to reject a recommendation and to refer the matter back for further deliberation.

When the academic vice president and perhaps the president serve with the department chair on the selection team, the deliberations may become a bit more delicate. In these cases, the ultimate decision must be acceptable to each of the titular leaders involved.

Administrators who desire to be leaders rather than mere managers and who have a vision that they are trying to bring to fruition for the institution must view the faculty selection process as an important means of reaching these goals. It is only through the work of the professional corps that goals are accomplished, visions are fulfilled, and dreams are realized for the college.

Personnel Policy System

Without becoming excessively rigid, the college must have a comprehensive set of personnel policies governing its relations with its academic and professional staff and its other employees. These policies serve to define the professional environment and conditions of service and to regulate the interpersonal and interprofessional dynamics of the college. Not only does the personnel policy system regulate, it also protects. Personnel policies define the obligations of the staff to the institution and the obligations of the institution to its staff. Kaiser and Greer (1988) discuss the various legal entanglements of personnel practices and policies and offer certain cautions.

The long list of topics that these policies may cover includes equal opportunity and affirmative action; employment processes and procedures; role definitions and position descriptions; leaves and absences; tenure and dismissal; guidelines for workloads and assignments; fringe benefits; evaluation principles and system; compensation system; retirement; academic freedom; professional development and improvement; extra-institutional commitments (outside work); interpersonal relations (including sexual harassment); institutional professional participative system (internal governance, committee work, and so on); retrenchment of staff; grievances; time obligations; vacations; internal communications channels; drug-free workplace; political actions and freedoms; guidelines pertaining to AIDS; and extensions of protected rights, such as those relating to sexual orientation.

Faculty Development

Recruitment and selection are processes through which the cadre of professionals is built and strengthened. What happens after the group has been assembled is of extreme significance to institutional performance. Most readers will have observed colleges that appear to stagnate. Other colleges take tangential courses as staff fall victim to some new educational fad.

Some plotted course of improvement rather than either stagnation or mere change for its own sake is desirable. Leadership seeks to stimulate progress, which is change toward carefully considered institutional goals. Progress is accomplished through group efforts and group processes, as well as through individual growth and development on the part of the staff.

Seminars and consultant units can be highly stimulating for academic and professional staff. The cost-effectiveness of these activities, however, must be evaluated in terms of the difference between them and the cost of sending delegations to regional or consortium workshops on the same subject.

A few colleges offer university graduate courses on campus and pay fees for staff to receive credit for enrollment, usually in teaching technologies, measurement and assessment, or curriculum organization courses. Some progressive colleges have linked faculty development with evaluation outcomes, individually tailoring in-service growth to a faculty member's perceived needs.

Other institutions have development programs that go beyond the ordinary—for example, research grants or released time for faculty interested in doing educational or "classroom research" geared toward professional interests. Summer grants, or released time during the academic year, for faculty to work on special projects related to instruction normally do not place great stress on the institutional budget, especially if the summer grant approach is taken rather than released time. These measures may lead to distinctive improvements in the affected areas of endeavor. In 1982, Northern Oklahoma College initiated an unusual grant program for staff development titled Renewal and Revitalization (affectionately abbreviated by faculty as "R and R"). This program provides financial assistance to professional staff who desired to improve or broaden their credentials through part-time or summer study, covering expenses to attend special workshops and seminars, as contrasted with meetings or conventions for which the traditional travel budget was available. Travel related to the faculty member's academic assignment and site visits to other institutions with exemplary programs are special features of the program.

Wherever possible, programs designed for faculty should have features that will allow other professional staff to participate. Adams (1983) discusses applications to technical as well as academic staff. It is important that appropriate opportunities for professional growth be available to all.

Compensation Systems

While compensation levels are probably no more significant to academic staff than other psychological and social factors, these are still highly important to these front-line servants of the college and its students. The most important considerations regarding compensation revolve around the general level of compensation of the profession related to its value and position in the larger society; the comparative level with other tiers in education, other peer institutions, and peers within the institution; the perceived fairness of methods utilized to arrive at compensation levels; and the priority given to faculty compensation within the college budget. While most institutions employ salary schedules based on academic qualifications and experience, Vineyard (1993) presents a unique system utilizing these elements plus merit factors.

Faculty Evaluation

Every system for evaluation of faculty service should be based on a definite rationale. Most are, even if this rationale is informal. The problem with systems that have no formal rationale is that these tend to be unclear to the raters and to the rated and thus inconsistently administered in an atmosphere that can easily become antagonistic. Vineyard (1993) illustrates the conversion of a comprehensive role rationale to an evaluative instrument utilizing behavioral criteria.

Holloway (1988) reviews various considerations in evaluation of different professionals in community colleges, even relating these to merit pay concepts. Holleman (1983) gives special attention to the evaluation of college librarians. Smith (1983a) discusses staff evaluation from a historical perspective, describing conceptual frameworks, while Palmer (1988) reviews evaluation systems historically through the 1970s. Perhaps the best basis for an evaluation system is a clearly stated definition of role expectations from the perspective of the institution itself.

Seldin (1988) provides a rich source of evaluation materials and ideas. While these are directed primarily toward the evaluation of administrators and nonteaching personnel, many of the concepts and techniques described are generally applicable. Romanik (1986) describes a personnel evaluation system on one of the Miami-Dade campuses encompassing all personnel. Smith (1983b) makes predictions about the future of staff evaluation, some of which have been borne out in practice, and Vineyard (1993) offers an evaluation system applied to college presidents.

The evaluation instrument is only one dimension of the process. Who does the evaluation, how it is to be done, how the results are to be utilized, and outcomes assessment must also be considered.

Far more controversial than the development of the evaluation criteria or instrument has been the question of who evaluates. There are strong objections to every known suggestion regarding just how this should be accomplished. The evaluation process is psychologically threatening to any except the most self-confident. When career decisions are involved, in addition to mere judgments and critical suggestions, the process may become even more threatening. For these reasons, the participative process is essential to defining the process in its entirety.

Any designation of raters and evaluators — the use of the department head or division chair and others in the academic chain of command; the use of peers within the department, or from other academic sectors, or students; self-evaluations — will have detractors. Much depends on the professional rapport, and the structured relationships within the college, as to the acceptance of authority ratings. Where mutual trust exists between faculty and administration, and where antagonisms are minimally disruptive, these ratings may not only be acceptable but may be preferred to other systems. Many faculty simply do not want to be judged by peers, especially those outside the disciplinary field, and few want to engage in "popularity contests" for students.

In collegial situations, the evaluative process might well begin with the faculty member doing a self-rating and the immediate academic supervisor doing an independent rating of the faculty person. These are followed by a conference of the faculty member with the immediate supervisor, which serves as an opportunity for professional counseling as well as for possible alteration of the supervisor's ratings in areas where further information and insights are gained. Both the immediate supervisor and the faculty member then take copies of their respective ratings for a three-way conference with the individual next in line upward, normally the academic dean. After this free and open discussion, the academic dean prepares an evaluation checksheet with his or her own impressions and writes a narrative paragraph to attach to the record, along with the other two instruments received. From these, the dean makes, supports, and documents any recommendations regarding the individual's employment status. If any form of merit salary provisions exists within the college, these results may also support recommendations regarding merit factors. While this process is indeed authority centered, it is difficult for an evaluation system to be otherwise if it is geared not only toward professional improvement but also toward weeding out nonperformers and improving academic quality (Duncan, 1988).

Controversies over student evaluations tend to center mostly around their purpose and the utilization of outcomes. The use of student evaluations in influencing employment status or merit decisions is objectionable to faculty and is likely inappropriate for other reasons. Accordingly, many colleges encourage (or require) the use of student evaluations for the purpose of the instructor's own information, providing clues for professional growth. In such circumstances, the sharing of student evaluation results with supervisors is optional.

The use of outcomes measures as evaluation indicators raises innumerable problems. Outcomes testing tends to concentrate on general fields and general competencies rather than on learning in any specific course. While these may reflect on the college's curriculum and instructional effectiveness, many cautions must be inserted into any judgmental considerations that might be forthcoming from such assessments. The movement of accrediting associations and sometimes governing authorities into this realm has enhanced its significance to community college leaders, but it remains laden with potential misconceptions, pitfalls, and abuses because of the complexity of the issues.

Tenure and Dismissal

Several topics related to tenure and dismissal merit attention.

Need for Policies

The achievement of tenure is a significant milestone in an instructor's professional career. For the community college instructor whose destiny is that of teaching throughout the service career and who cannot attain promotions in rank as do cousins in universities, this is perhaps the most rewarding official honor the institution can bestow. The granting of tenure to a faculty member should be an action decision, based on performance and evaluations, not merely default status accorded as a result of longevity.

Further, it is preferable that the tenure action come as a result of a process, rather than representing a purely arbitrary act of someone in authority. It should be noted that nonaction is not quite the same as a denial action, particularly when policies are clear that tenure is not automatic but is "granted" as a positive action from a deliberative process. If policies or statutes define the action differently, denial of tenure may become an act for which there must be a defense rationale (Smith, 1983a).

Dismissal of staff tends to be governed under several different types of law: contract law, labor relations law, constitutional law, and state statutes and regulations pertaining to public employment (Kaplin, 1985). One might hasten to add another body of "law": governing board policies properly drawn in conformity with applicable legal constraints. As an example, the Florida State Board of Community Colleges (1987) has provided college trustees with guidelines pertaining to the personnel realm.

Dismissal

It is important that policies clearly spell out the contract nature of employment at the institution. If the college has a probationary period and if it is not constrained by statutes, the policy should state that all faculty are employed for a specified period, usually one academic year, and that there is no obligation for the person or the institution past the limited period of the existing contract. It should define the meaning of the probationary period, of "temporary" or similar faculty status, in terms that clearly state that continuance each year is a separate decision as to whether to offer another one-year contract.

These policies should also state that nonrenewal of a contract of a temporary or probationary staff person is without stated cause. This nonaction is not deemed to be subject to due process since no "property" interest is involved in nonrenewal (failure to issue a new contract), and no "liberty" interest is at stake, since no reasons are made public that adversely affect the faculty member's pursuit of life or career (*Board of Regents* v. *Roth,* 1972; *Perry* v. *Sindermann,* 1972).

In the *Perry* decision, the significance of policy is resoundingly clear. This case involved the dismissal of a faculty member with lengthy service from an institution that declared that it had no tenure policy but through its practices and in written communications *implied* that continuing employment was customary for faculty who performed creditably. In a sense, the court held that a condition of de facto tenure existed and that this "property" interest required due process. The same finding was true in *Ferguson,* which speaks to "expectation" of continuing employment (*Ferguson* v. *Thomas,* 1970). In *Roth,* which concerned an institution's failure to renew a contract during the probationary period without a stated cause or hearing, the court held that no stated cause or hearing was required because no "liberty" or "property" interests were involved.

While no one is suggesting that arbitrariness is appropriate in decisions regarding continuance of faculty or other personnel, it is clearly to the institution's advantage to retain as much control over hiring and tenure matters as possible. This is necessary to rectify shortcomings in the screening and selection process.

In public institutions, tenure, once granted or attained by policy default, is protected under constitutional law. This protection includes the right of due process. Essentially, due process involves: (1) notice and a statement of applicable cause, (2) information as to the basis of the infraction of cause, and (3) a hearing before a body in which the affected person has the right to dispute evidence and offer defense (Alexander and Solomon, 1972; Kaplin, 1985). Again, this is an area that should be covered in institutional policies governing tenure and dismissal. Such policies, drawn up with the legal framework in mind, define the rights of the individual and the rights of the college and its administration. The college leadership acts in the context of these carefully formulated but not excessively legalistic policies.

Dismissal of any employee within the term of a valid contract requires due process as well. Further, it is appropriate that reference to college policies, as stated in the policies and procedures manual or in the faculty handbook, should be made in the employment contract or letter, although such inclusion is not obligatory in order to be applicable (*Skehan* v. *Board of Trustees of Bloomsburg State College*, 1976).

The terms of tenure for administrators tend to be different. Tenure may be retained *as a faculty member* by administrators who are moved from faculty status to an administrative assignment, but not in the administrative position itself. New administrators employed directly into their positions from outside may or may not have tenure of any kind unless it is specifically granted by governing board action of record. Nevertheless, administrators are public employees with implied property interests in continued employment, although not necessarily in their current position. Termination must be for cause and due process provided. Reassignment to another position, when there is a substantial pay differential, should also be accompanied by due process rights. Of course, college personnel policies should cover these matters.

Cause

What about permissible causes? Alexander and Solomon (1972) discuss the more common causes as provided for in the legal regulatory climate. The most commonly stated cause, according to these authors, was "incompetency." Yet this, they said, is one of the more difficult ones to define or to prove. Others were "immorality," "insubordination," "neglect of duty," and "other good cause." Perhaps because each of these terms has a history in law and each has a body of relevant case law, they have tended to persist in statutory language where public employment protection exists at the state level. College policies have also tended to utilize such language, perhaps as a result of legal advice and/or modeling practices.

A cursory review of the case law precedents will surprise most as to just how well, and how broadly, the courts have defined each of the above causes. "Good cause," for instance, has been held to be any ground put forth by the governing authority that is not "arbitrary, irrational, unreasonable, or irrelevant" to the operations of the educational institution (*Renaldo* v. *Dreyer,* 1936). Nevertheless, within the limitations of any applicable statutes, college policies should define causes for dismissal. Wherever feasible and advised by counsel, these more general causes should be defined in behavioral terms. Kaplin (1985, p. 166) advises that "since incompetency, insubordination, immorality, unethical conduct, and medical disability are the most commonly asserted grounds for cause dismissals, institutions may wish to include in their dismissal policies definitions of these concepts and criteria for applying them to particular cases. Such definitions of these concepts or criteria should be sufficiently clear to guide the decision makers who will apply them and to forewarn the faculty members who will be subject to them."

It appears that the task of policy writers is to make the causes for dismissal sufficiently clear as to avoid challenge on constitutional grounds of *vagueness,* but not so specific as to limit applicability to unique situations that arise and merit action. Such definitions of cause may include:

- Permanent, chronic, or protracted physical or mental illness
- Personal misconduct or unethical or unprofessional conduct
- Professional incompetence or unfitness
- Failure to obey the law in areas that adversely affect the staff member's value or usefulness to the college
- Insubordination or noncooperation affecting professional effectiveness or working relationships within the institution
- Inability or unwillingness to adjust to changes in the college program, philosophy, or purposes
- Bona fide lack of need for one's full-time services, reductions or changes in courses or curriculum, or changes in student enrollment patterns
- Bona fide necessity for financial retrenchment

- Failure to meet the standards and requirements for professional improvement as defined in college policies and/or failure to respond satisfactorily to evaluational shortcomings

A considerable body of case law limits the interpretation and application of certain causes. Perhaps the most extensive treatment surrounds the First Amendment rights of employees. There is also case law defining the limits of academic freedom, as well as other causes. Administrators would do well to familiarize themselves with precedents, and to seek legal counsel, should cases arise that fall into questionable areas.

Summary

The mission of academic personnel administration and governance is, of course, the procurement and retention of highly qualified and competent faculty and other professional personnel. A comprehensive set of personnel policies defines the professional environment and conditions of service for the college. Of necessity, this involves not only selection processes designed and conducted in a manner compatible with the goal, but also the continuous professional development and growth of staff once hired. Sadly, this mission also includes the necessary purging of those who are unwilling or unable to perform satisfactorily. While faculty evaluation is never problem free, it yields beneficial results both to the instructors, who can gain valuable insights to improve their teaching, and to the school as a whole, as students learn more and the institution becomes a center for quality education.

Faculty are the front-line forces, interacting directly with students in the teaching and learning processes. All other college services are in a sense supportive of this academic thrust. It is essential that administrative and other services focus on creating an institutional climate conducive to effective instruction. Such an environment provides for needed freedoms, but also for needed system, order, and quality control. This is the challenge to leadership.

References

Adams, F. G. "A Personnel Model: Hiring, Developing, and Promoting Community and Technical College Employees." *Journal of Studies in Technical Careers*, 1983, *5*(2), 100–110.

Alexander, K., and Solomon, E. S. *College and University Law.* Charlottesville, Va.: Michie Co., 1972.

Board of Regents v. *Roth*, 408 U.S. 564 (1972).

Cooper, J. F., and Garmon, J. F. *Personnel Selection: The Holistic Approach.* Los Angeles: ERIC Clearinghouse, 1990.

Duncan, D. S. "Performance Appraisal: Reducing Errors at Pensacola Junior College." *CUPA Journal*, 1988, *39*(4), 40–54.

Ferguson v. *Thomas*, 430 F.2d 852 (5th Cir. 1970).

Florida State Board of Community Colleges. *Personnel Responsibilities: Issues and Perspectives.* Trustee monograph. Tallahassee: Florida State Board of Community Colleges, 1987.

Holleman, P. "Evaluating Community College Faculty Librarians." *Community and Junior College Libraries*, 1983, *2*(1), 63–72.

Holloway, M. L. "Performance Appraised." In R. I. Miller and E. W. Holzapfel, Jr. (eds.), *Issues in Personnel Management.* New Directions for Community Colleges, no. 62. San Francisco: Jossey-Bass, 1988.

Kaiser, M. G., and Greer, D. "Legal Aspects of Personnel Management in Higher Education." In R. L. Miller and E. W. Holzapfel, Jr. (eds.), *Issues in Personnel Management.* New Directions for Community Colleges, no. 62. San Francisco: Jossey-Bass, 1988.

Kalinos, K. D. "Changes in Employment Placement." In R. I. Miller and E. W. Holzapfel, Jr. (eds.), *Issues in Personnel Management.* New Directions for Community Colleges, no. 62. San Francisco: Jossey-Bass, 1988.

Kaplin, W. A. *The Law of Higher Education: A Comprehensive Guide to Legal Implications of Administrative Decision Making.* (2nd ed.) San Francisco: Jossey-Bass, 1985.

Midkiff, S. J., and Come, B. "Organization and Staffing." In R. I. Miller and E. W. Holzapfel, Jr. (eds.), *Issues in Personnel Management.* New Directions for Community Colleges, no. 62. San Francisco: Jossey-Bass, 1988.

Palmer, J. "Sources and Information: Faculty and Administrative Evaluation." In R. I. Miller and E. W. Holzapfel, Jr. (eds.), *Issues in Personnel Management.* New Directions for Community Colleges, no. 62. San Francisco: Jossey-Bass, 1988.

Perry v. *Sindermann,* 408 U.S. 593 (1972).

Renaldo v. *Dryer,* 294 Mass. 167, 1 N.E. 2d 37 (1936).

Romanik, K. O. *Staff Evaluation: Commitment to Excellence.* Miami, Fla.: Mitchell Wolfson New World Center Campus, Miami-Dade Community College, 1986.

St. Petersburg Junior College. *Toward 2001: An Odyssey of Excellence.* FACET Report. St. Petersburg, Fla.: St. Petersburg Junior College, 1990.

Seldin, P. *Evaluating and Developing Administrative Performance: A Practical Guide for Academic Leaders.* San Francisco: Jossey-Bass, 1988.

Skehan v. *Board of Trustees of Bloomsburg State College,* 501 F.2d 31 (3rd Cir. 1976).

Smith, A. B. "A Conceptual Framework for Staff Evaluation." In A. B. Smith (ed.), *Evaluating Faculty and Staff.* New Directions for Community Colleges, no. 41. San Francisco: Jossey-Bass, 1983a.

Smith, A. B. "Concluding Comments." In A. B. Smith (ed.), *Evaluating Faculty and Staff.* New Directions for Community Colleges, no. 41. San Francisco: Jossey-Bass, 1983b.

Vineyard, E. E. *The Pragmatic Presidency: Effective Leadership in the Two-Year College Setting.* Bolton, Mass.: Anker, 1993.

Chapter 20

Faculty Evaluation and Performance Appraisal

Albert B. Smith, Jacquelyn A. Barber

In 1986, the board of directors of the American Association of Community and Junior Colleges (AACJC) appointed nineteen distinguished educators to a commission charged with a study of the future of community, technical, and junior colleges. The commission was to study the history, assess the current status, and develop recommendations for the directions these institutions should take. The commissioners spent eighteen months in intensive study and made a comprehensive report centered around the theme "Building Communities." To emphasize the major point of the study, they made the following statements: "At the center of building community there is teaching. Teaching is the heartbeat of the educational enterprise and, when it is successful, energy is pumped into the community, continuously renewing and revitalizing the institution" (Commission on the Future of Community Colleges, 1988, pp. 7–8).

Echoing the conclusions of numerous studies dating back to the 1930s, the 1988 commission recommended that each college should set its priorities for defining and implementing programs to improve teaching. The commission strongly urged that colleges take action by starting with clear goals and criteria for evaluating successful teaching. Once successful teaching was defined and evaluated, it was hoped that exemplary programs could be developed that would showcase effective teaching. The commission further pointed out that good teaching requires active learning in the classroom, calls for a climate in which students are encouraged to collaborate rather than compete, builds community, and can only be improved if the teacher is willing and able to improve teaching. Therefore, the teacher must be receptive to performance evaluation, constructive feedback, and behavioral change focused on continuous improvement and innovation.

Professional management of the faculty to accomplish good teaching has been the topic of many books, articles, and research papers (Smith, 1983, 1988; Andrews, 1985, 1989; Cashin, 1989; Boyer, 1990). Other publications show that teaching is an art that can be taught and that can be developed through inquiry into one's own teaching (McKeachie, 1986; Lowman, 1984). When faculty are asked to become involved in collecting data about how they and their students learn, they become engaged in learning about learning (Cross and Angelo, 1988). Therefore, to enhance and monitor these faculty resources, community college administrators must regularly assess programs that contribute to the continuous growth and development of their faculties (Jennings, Barlar, and Bartling, 1991).

One of these programs — probably the most significant — is faculty evaluation and performance appraisal, which become the basis for faculty development programs. This chapter describes the administrators' role in furthering such programs.

Why Evaluate and Assess Performance?

Performance appraisals serve a variety of purposes. They provide feedback to faculty on their performance; serve as a basis for improving performance; provide data for making decisions on pay, tenure, transfer, promotions, or discipline; and force supervisors to relate faculty behavior to actual results (that is, good teaching). Appraisals are usually performed by the supervisor, but there are situations in which faculty rate themselves or each other (peer ratings) or their supervisors.

A wide variety of appraisals are currently in use; however, no "best" appraisal system exists (Aleamoni, 1987; Andrews, 1987). A viable appraisal will be systems oriented and will contain validated rating methods, have evaluations based on hard criteria, provide for consistency in ratings among appraisers, and be resistant to rater-error tendencies (Arreola, 1987). Regardless of the system employed, its effectiveness will be enhanced if appraisers are trained in the underlying philosophy of the system, techniques of rating and forms completion, and the basic skills of appraisal interviewing (Centra, 1979; Crane, 1979). Key to performance appraisal effectiveness is the interaction of the faculty member and supervisor. Here faculty and supervisor mutually evaluate the faculty member's performance, analyze strengths and weaknesses against set criteria, plan for professional development, and discuss how the faculty member's goals and objectives coincide with those of the institution. These appraisal activities are the basis for career development and help to achieve good teaching.

Instituting a results-oriented performance appraisal program in a community college requires care to ensure the success of the program. Because evaluating faculty is such a sensitive issue, it is easy to make mistakes in the initial stages. An orderly, systematic approach can minimize these potential problems. However, the administrator must first decide whether to extend the goal-setting and monitoring efforts down to the level of the individual faculty member. The decision requires a major administrative commitment, since detailed documentation, standardized forms, and periodic follow-up are necessary for each individual to be appraised. The burden of appraisal must be considered, not just the expected benefits.

It is through the evaluation and assessment of performance that an effective appraisal of the faculty member can be made. However, the evaluation or assessment instrument must be criterion based, measurable, and equitable. It must measure performance against established goals and objectives, be development oriented, and be user friendly or easy to use. Collecting data, assessing the current status, skills, and abilities, and establishing performance goals and objectives are the initial steps in the process.

Once the staff decide to appraise faculty, they must determine what they want to accomplish in the first year or two. Will evaluations be used for short-term purposes such as awarding salary increases or tenure, for obtaining information for planning professional development programs, for reviewing and clarifying job requirements, for assisting in the retention of faculty, or for the improvement of performance and good teaching in the classroom? Qualified faculty are a limited resource, and every effort should be made to train and develop them toward success. Turnover is costly and unproductive in the long term, and the appraisal process must fit into the selection, appraisal, and retention system.

Administrators themselves should be trained in performance appraisal procedures. The commitment to training requires an acceptance of purpose, acceptance of methods, skill in appraisal, and an administrative network to maintain a faculty appraisal system (Nash, 1983). Steps to be considered in the development of an evaluation and appraisal program include the assessment, planning, development, implementation, and evaluation and redesign of the program.

Evaluating Administrative Performance

Performance evaluation for college administrative personnel is based on similar theory and basic models used for general performance appraisal (Seldin, 1988). It should be data driven, well planned, comprehensively developed, effectively implemented, and periodically reviewed. The administrative personnel's accountability for the fiscal operations, the management and administration of the institution and its departments and units, the success of the academic programs in general, and the overall direction and performance of the staff will be measured and evaluated. The evaluation results will be used to assign funding and budgetary parameters; assess the retention, promotion, developments, and salary status of administrative personnel; and inform the public, faculty, and student body of the level and degree of success of the institution's administration in regard to predetermined goals and objectives (Genova, Madoff, Chin, and Thomas, 1976).

The evaluation process should include the systematic collection of data in an organized manner, a comprehensive evaluation of all major responsibilities, written policies and procedures, and goals and objectives, and enough flexibility to fit the varying circumstances of different administrative and academic units (Seldin, 1988). In this way, the outcomes of the administrative performance evaluation will provide data to be used for diagnosis for improvements in, and effective decision making for, the operations and management of the community college as well as its educational divisions and departments. Administrative requirements for faculty should also be evaluated in context with the faculty performance appraisal and should consider the administrative requirements of the faculty member's position (that is, book orders, library reserve, syllabi on file, attendance, grade reports, and so on).

In contrast, the administrative performance evaluation program for administrative staff is more institutional in nature. For administrative personnel, considerably more emphasis should be placed on the managerial, administrative, operational, and economic conditions of the institution. A final difference that should distinguish the administrative appraisal is that the governing body must also consider the external legal, financial, and political conditions that influence the community college's success in its service community (Austin and Gamson, 1983).

Conducting a Successful Faculty Evaluation Program

Smith (1987) has identified a three-year strategy for the implementation of a successful faculty/staff evaluation or appraisal system in two-year colleges. The first step in his approach is planning. This planning should be data driven and should be based on a firm assessment of the current skills, abilities, educational levels, and experience of the faculty. It has been stated that because of community colleges' roots in the lower schools, evaluations were often conducted by administrators who visited classrooms and recorded their perceptions of instructors' performances. As colleges broke away from the lower schools, evaluations became more complex, faculty gained more power, and students and peers were brought into the planning process

(Cohen and Brawer, 1989). Involving the users and the providers in the evaluation system greatly enhances the program. Relevant data can be gathered from these populations that will facilitate planning, add quality to the teaching, focus on the needs of the curriculum at the current place and time, and assist in the development of the teacher to be evaluated.

One of the fourteen steps in Smith's (1987) strategy for implementing a new or revised faculty or staff evaluation system entails the identification of faculty roles and the characteristics of effective community college teachers. Additional background and data can be found in the literature to identify the characteristics of effective two-year college instructors. For example, Baker, Roueche, and Gillett-Karam (1990) identify six exemplary community college teacher behaviors. They are:

- Exemplary teachers see themselves as facilitators of a student's own active learning rather than as experts transmitting information; in a word, they are student-centered.
- Exemplary teachers look for and commend their students for enhanced self-esteem, realization of new possibilities, and signs of having gained new perspectives; they see value in learning.
- Exemplary teachers understand that adult learners are unique and that experiential learning is a part of adult learning theory.
- Exemplary teachers understand students' needs, concerns, and interests and integrate them in their teaching; they assume a directive and influential role in facilitating learning.
- Exemplary teachers create situations through a variety of strategies to keep students actively involved in the learning process.
- Exemplary teachers are actively involved as leaders in the classroom through motivational, interpersonal, and cognitive skills. [p. 57]

As successful teachers and their behaviors are analyzed, the college planners can determine whether these behaviors and characteristics are reflected in the college's current evaluation instruments, particularly the student rating instruments. It should also be determined early on if the evaluators are able to, or can be trained to, recognize these behaviors. Then it can be determined how a systematic evaluation process that uses these exemplary behaviors as indicators of quality teaching is to be developed for the specific department or institution. Flexibility in adapting these behaviors to the reality of the institutional and departmental environments is essential to success (Cashin, 1990).

The most successful community college faculty evaluation and performance appraisal systems are those that have included data from a wide range of sources in the evaluation process. In the 1960s, if a college had an evaluation system for faculty, it consisted primarily of a student rating system. Today, most community college administrators have implemented faculty evaluation systems that make use of data collected from the faculty member's peers, supervisor, the faculty member himself or herself (self-reports), and the faculty member's students. This trend in the direction of a more comprehensive approach to faculty evaluation is likely to continue. If implemented effectively, it provides for the most complete assessment of both full-time and part-time faculty members' performance.

Some two-year colleges have successfully developed, planned, and integrated an appraisal system designed to help faculty improve professionally and, at the same time, to assess the performance of faculty based on established job descriptions and standards (Smith, 1983, 1987). For example, Arizona Western College, with mandates from the North Central Association of Colleges and Schools and its district governing board, began developing an institutionwide employee appraisal system in 1989. A faculty task force, comprised of twelve individuals representing a cross section of the teaching population, agreed to develop a system based on established job descriptions and job standards. The task force worked to develop an appraisal system that would both help faculty improve professionally and assess their performance. It was expected that the results of this appraisal would be used as one factor in determining continued employment.

The task force administered surveys to the faculty to assist in the development of the system. These surveys asked faculty to define the various components of their jobs, to rank each component in terms of its importance, and to identify sources of appraisal information. With the survey results from this job analysis, student evaluation forms and faculty self-evaluation forms were developed. These two rating forms were designed to be scanned for computer processing. The output of this processing is a printout for division chairs that includes both student mean scores and faculty self-evaluation scores for each statement on the appraisal.

The newly developed appraisal system at Arizona Western College was piloted in the spring of 1991 with a randomly selected group of faculty representing each division. The goal of the pilot was to test the system, not evaluate faculty. In this manner, the survey form instructions, data collection procedures, and data analysis techniques were validated. This validation test produced significant information used by the task force to make system revisions, changes in specific wording of evaluation forms, and the elimination of redundancies. The result was a faculty-tested, standardized, criterion-based appraisal system ready for implementation (Olp, Watson, and Valek, 1991).

The Milwaukee Area Technical College system is also a good example of planning and effective implementation. Known for its well-established and stable faculty, this college system used a different approach in the planning, development, and implementation of its systematic faculty evaluation process and faculty coaching system. Since no formal evaluation mechanism existed, the faculty, administration, and union joined together to develop the coaching system in which the faculty members are expected to plan, implement, and evaluate their professional growth, while their immediate supervisors/administrators act as coaches. The coaches ask a series of open-ended questions to help the faculty define, establish, and then achieve their respective goals (Slicker, 1988).

The faculty coaching system operates on two tracks, with procedures and purposes differing for tenured and nontenured members. The coaching supervisors and administrators use a guidebook for the evaluation. The comprehensive guidebook includes an introduction to the faculty coaching system; coaching guidelines with criteria for evaluation of the faculty with regard to contact with students, class preparation, instructional effectiveness, and professional development; information and forms for ensuring the professional growth of tenured, Track I faculty; a summary of Track II procedures and forms to be used to make decisions regarding the continued employment of nontenured faculty; a coaching verification form; procedures for the faculty coaching system; and a glossary. This system represents a dynamic effort by the faculty, administration, and union to formulate an effective, performance-based appraisal system.

The Teaching and Learning Project at Miami-Dade Community College is another excellent model for review. The goals set for the project were to improve the quality of teaching and learning, to make teaching a professionally rewarding career, and to make teaching and learning the focal point of college activities and decision-making processes. The new faculty were required to research specific topics essential to the teaching and learning of the specialty of their respective departments. Research materials were then developed to facilitate the faculty's skills and abilities to teach the materials. These courses were modularized and used in faculty workshops and training programs.

Videotapes exploring classroom feedback and cultural differences in learning styles were produced for faculty use and training. Statements of faculty excellence provided a common understanding of what it means to perform in an excellent manner at Miami-Dade Community College. Courses in Classroom Research and Effective Teaching and Learning are taught by University of Miami faculty from curriculum developed collaboratively with two Miami-Dade Teaching and Learning Project subcommittees, with the community college assuming the tuition cost (Baker, Roueche, and Gillett-Karam, 1990). Without this kind of commitment to good teaching, educators at community colleges will continue to fail to understand why students are not learning as effectively as possible. This can be easily demonstrated by considering evaluation and development procedures and instruments often used for appraisal and assessment.

Planning, implementing, managing, and evaluating an effective faculty evaluation program can be time consuming and require a great deal of preparation and training. To succeed, the administrator must make sure the system is participative in nature. There have been some excellent examples of how this process can work with positive results (Romanik, 1986). Well defined goals and objectives coupled with a commitment to effective teaching are of the utmost importance if success is to be realized. If the institution decides that good teaching is the expected and desired outcome, the investment of time and effort in measuring, assessing, and developing an effective appraisal program are warranted. In addition, the administrator must take steps to ensure that faculty members are adequately supported by the institution's staff, so that barriers to good teaching can be removed. In this way, the faculty can focus on their goals and objectives.

The development of a comprehensive, systematic evaluation program is a difficult process. It should include faculty observation, quantitative measures of student achievement of specific goals and objectives, measurement of the faculty member's use of instructional methodologies, control and direction of classroom behaviors, and other measures specific to the college's demographics and environment. Data collected in such a manner will provide important information for evaluating good teaching as well as the end product—learning.

Ensuring a Sound Legal Basis for Evaluation Activities

Performance appraisal systems are beginning to enjoy extensive application in community colleges for a multitude of purposes. They may serve as a basis for deciding tenure or evaluating teaching, serve as a criterion in performance goal setting and salary rewards (including merit pay), be used in developing retention programs (Genova, Madoff, Chin, and Thomas, 1976; Smith, 1987), and provide a basis for the promotion and/or discipline of faculty and staff (Andrews, 1985, 1987). In recent years, serious legal questions have been raised concerning their use. A significant number of Equal Employment Opportunity

Commission (EEOC) and labor law cases brought to the courts involving performance evaluations have found them to be in violation of equal employment guidelines. Given the widespread use of these methods, the purposes for which they are used, and results of recent court cases, administrators and supervisors utilizing such data for personnel decisions may be in a precarious position. Thus, much research remains to be undertaken on the applicability of performance evaluation for faculty and administrators in the junior and community college environment (Smith, 1983; Seldin, 1988).

A first step in this direction must be in terms of the validation of the methods, criteria, and ratings used in performance appraisal of faculty and staff. Documenting the processes used for training evaluators as well as the evaluations given and the remedial or developmental programs assessed is also of prime importance. Establishing empirical, concurrent, or predictive validity of ratings is likely to be difficult and, in some cases, impossible. Content validity, on the other hand, seems to be a reasonable step toward a validation effort. In addition, behavioral expectancy rating scales using specific job behaviors related to good teaching—rather than relying on subjective traits—must be developed. The scales must be job specific, criterion based, and defensible in a court of law and/or an EEOC hearing. Regardless of the methods employed, the evaluation techniques must be centered on research of the viability and effectiveness of the methods and conducted within the framework of EEOC and court requirements. Good job analysis, goal setting, participation by all parties in the planning and development stages, fair and equitable implementation, and the use of "due process" will provide a firm base for maintaining and ensuring a sound legal basis for the appraisal system.

Finally, to maintain a proactive, legally defensible, and action-oriented program, the administrator, working with and through the staff supervisors and department chairs, must continuously monitor the entire faculty and support staff employment process (Strike and Bull, 1981). This includes the job evaluation process and the hiring, retention, and dismissal practices. The administrator must staff the personnel office with qualified professionals and verify that the appropriate procedures are being followed (Hendrickson and Lee, 1983). These may include:

- Encouragement of minority faculty and staff to participate in career days and similar activities designed to educate and motivate young people to pursue their academic training at the community college.
- Participation in and recruitment of minority candidates for vacant staff and faculty positions.
- Special employment programs focused on hiring minorities in areas where they are underutilized in the institution, including the setting and periodic evaluation of hiring goals.
- A job-posting system that announces all staff and faculty promotional opportunities and encourages applications.
- Remedial job training programs and upward mobility programs for staff; professional development programs and tenure opportunities for faculty.
- Appropriate implementation and control of a performance evaluation, as discussed in this chapter.
- Review of job descriptions and qualification standards to ensure job relatedness.
- Requirements that chairs and supervisors provide written justification for decisions to pass over apparently qualified candidates for tenure and promotion.
- The use of success indicators with regard to legal issues as criteria for performance evaluation of supervisors and department chairs.
- Periodic and consistent review of seniority and tenure practices to ensure nondiscrimination.

It is important to remember that affirmative action goals need to be set only in areas where underrepresentation exists. The administrator must know where adverse legal issues are and where the problems concerning the performance evaluation process may impact the institution (Seldin, 1988). A written evaluation of the system that describes the methods developed to monitor and record the progress of the institution's formal and informal programs is essential. Integration with the other legal, regulatory, governance, and political programs of the institution is also imperative. If all these procedures are followed, the community college will have a model program in place to address the future growth and development of the campus.

Summary

Good teaching attests to the effectiveness of faculty members. Evaluating faculty is one of the many roles of the college administrator, particularly the department or divisional head (Tucker, 1984). This role has two focuses. One is to define good teaching with specific regard to the faculty and their respective courses and then to provide for the improvement of instruction and curriculum to achieve good teaching. The other is that of performance evaluation for reasons of promotion, tenure, retention, and pay.

The keys to effective performance appraisal are the skills and abilities of the evaluator and the quality and comprehensiveness of the evaluation instrument. If the evaluator is responsible for appraisal of both performance and good teaching, it is convenient to combine the roles. The most sensible way to begin is by referring to the current faculty member and student outcomes—what is being accomplished and what fails to be accomplished in the present classroom. In other words, to decide rationally what to do to develop goals and objectives for tomorrow, it is imperative to know what level of success one's faculty and students are having in the classroom today. This is the purpose of data collection and evaluation, planning and development, and careful evaluation of programs.

The administrator/evaluator should also know other, more complex things about how faculty members learn and work in their individual classrooms. As leaders, department chairs must define teaching activities and curriculum programs that will help faculty improve and that will influence individual instructors or groups of faculty in efforts toward goal achievement in a given situation (Hersey and Blanchard, 1984).

The specific evaluation of teaching is a difficult task and is rarely performed with measurable success. It is more than administering a performance appraisal instrument or simply observing the faculty member in the classroom environment and having an informal chat about how things are going. It is accurately assessing the outcomes of the teaching/learning process and comparing these outcomes to expected or desired outcomes. It is then preparing an appropriate structured plan for the individual to enhance future teaching and good teaching outcomes. The evaluator's role is extremely difficult, because he or she must maintain a professional environment, create equilibrium in the curriculum, and be the agent of change toward performance improvement (Alfonso, Firth, and Neville, 1981).

Significant questions to be addressed in the appraisal of faculty teaching are whether the faculty are qualified as teachers, and whether the individual faculty member is doing the job. Agreement on a quantitative standard against which teaching can be measured has been elusive (McNeal, 1987). Academic degrees and achievement do not necessarily equal qualification. Once a faculty member is degreed and academically prepared in a specialty, it is essential to monitor performance in the classroom to determine if the job of good teaching is getting done. Therefore, administrators, particularly department chairs, need to evaluate their faculty members using a procedure that encompasses many measures.

It is obvious that the chair as evaluator must be well equipped in clinical supervision skills, in quantitative evaluation strategies, techniques, and constructs, and in the development of curriculum to correct or enhance classroom teaching. Armed with this training and knowledge, the chair, as consultant and evaluator, can help faculty evaluate their classroom performance, assess their own strengths and weaknesses, and select means of overcoming deficiencies in the achievement of mutually agreed-on and defined teaching goals. In this manner, the development of future instruction will be firmly based in an appropriate evaluation of past and current classroom teaching (Geis and Stahelski, 1991). It will be designed for the individual faculty member as well as the departmental teaching team and will be focused on the improvement of actual skills and abilities in order to improve positive outcomes in the classroom. It will be targeted at teaching as an art that can be taught and that can be developed through inquiry into one's own teaching (Katz and Henry, 1988). Systematic evaluation and inquiry can enhance student learning and student development, which are the positive outcomes desired in the community college classroom.

A final key for successful evaluation is evaluator/faculty commitment to the performance appraisal process. Part of this commitment is recognition of the difficulty of matching the perceptions of the professionals with the specific goals and objectives of the institution. Many educational professionals are reluctant to be subjected to strong measurement and control mechanisms for ensuring levels of productivity. From classroom behavior, to community service, to involvement with students, to basic research, educational professionals generally believe they are responsible and should not be monitored (Gray and Brown, 1989). These beliefs make it difficult to establish a goal-directed, quantitative measurement-based program of teaching and instructor/faculty evaluation. It is essential that a constructive relationship exist between faculty members and evaluators (chairs) if anything beyond evaluation is to occur. This requires that both view the evaluation process as positive professional development.

How do administrators, evaluators, and faculty acquire the necessary training and knowledge? Are they willing and able to utilize this background? How skilled are they in the evaluation of training for good teaching for their faculty and instructors? There are many questions and topics for continued research and study of evaluation and performance appraisal. This chapter has summarized some of these in presenting an overview of the current process and a focus for future studies.

References

Aleamoni, L. M. *Techniques for Evaluating and Improving Instruction.* New Directions for Teaching and Learning, no. 31. San Francisco: Jossey-Bass, 1987.

Alfonso, R. J., Firth, G. R., and Neville, R. F. *Instructional Supervision.* Needham Heights, Mass.: Allyn & Bacon, 1981.

American Association of Community and Junior Colleges. *Information Brief 1991*. Washington, D.C.: American Association of Community and Junior Colleges, 1991.

Andrews, H. A. *Evaluating for Excellence: Addressing the Need for Responsible and Effective Faculty Evaluation*. Stillwater, Okla.: New Forums Press, 1985.

Andrews, H. A. *Merit in Education: Assessing Merit Pay as the Catalyst to Pay and Evaluation Reforms*. Stillwater, Okla.: New Forums Press, 1987.

Andrews, H. A., and Licata, C. M. *The State of Faculty Evaluation in Community, Technical, and Junior Colleges Within the North Central Region, 1988–89: A Research Study*. Council of North Central Community and Junior Colleges, 1989.

Arreola, R. A. "A Faculty Evaluation Model for Community and Junior Colleges." In L. M. Aleamoni (ed.), *Techniques for Evaluating and Improving Instruction*. New Directions for Teaching and Learning, no. 31. San Francisco: Jossey-Bass, 1987.

Austin, A. E., and Gamson, Z. F. *Academic Workplace: New Demands, Heightened Tensions*. ASHE-ERIC Higher Education Research Report No. 10. Washington, D.C.: Association for the Study of Higher Education, 1983.

Baker, G. III, Roueche, J. E., and Gillett-Karam, R. *Teaching as Leading: Profiles of Excellence in the Open-Door College*. Washington, D.C.: Community College Press, 1990.

Boyer, E. L. *Scholarship Reconsidered: Priorities of the Professoriate*. Princeton, N.J.: Carnegie Foundation for the Advancement of Teaching, 1990.

Cashin, W. E. *Defining and Evaluating College Teaching*. Idea paper no. 21. Manhattan: Center for Faculty Evaluation and Development, Kansas State University, 1989.

Cashin, W. E. "Assessing Teaching Effectiveness." In P. Seldin and Associates, *How Administrators Can Improve Teaching: Moving from Talk to Action in Higher Education*. San Francisco: Jossey-Bass, 1990.

Centra, J. A. *Determining Faculty Effectiveness: Assessing Teaching, Research, and Service for Personnel Decisions and Improvement*. San Francisco: Jossey-Bass, 1979.

Cohen, A. M., and Brawer, F. B. *The American Community College*. (2nd ed.) San Francisco: Jossey-Bass, 1989.

Commission on the Future of Community Colleges. *Building Communities: A Vision for a New Century.* Washington, D.C.: American Association of Community and Junior Colleges, 1988.

Crane, D. P. *Personnel: The Management of Human Resources.* Belmont, Calif.: Wadsworth, 1979.

Cross, K. P., and Angelo, T. A. *Classroom Assessment Techniques: A Handbook for Faculty.* Ann Arbor, Mich.: National Center for Research to Improve Postsecondary Teaching and Learning, 1988.

Geis, L., and Stahelski, A. "An Evaluation of a Community College Supervisor Training Program." *Journal of Staff, Program, and Organization Development,* 1991, *9*, 132–140.

Genova, W. J., Madoff, M., Chin, R., and Thomas, G. *Mutual Benefit Evaluation of Faculty and Administrators in Higher Education.* New York: Ballinger, 1976.

Gilbert, T. F. *Human Competence: Engineering Worthy Performance.* New York: McGraw-Hill, 1978.

Gray, G., and Brown, D. "Pay for Performance in Academia: A Viable Concept?" *Educational Research Quarterly,* 1989, *13*(4), 45–52.

Hendrickson, R. M., and Lee, B. A. *Academic Employment and Retrenchment: Judicial Review and Administrative Action.* ASHE-ERIC Higher Education Research Report No. 8. Washington, D.C.: Association for the Study of Higher Education, 1983. (ED 240 975)

Hersey, P., and Blanchard, K. H. *Management of Organizational Behavior: Utilizing Human Resources.* Englewood Cliffs, N.J.: Prentice-Hall, 1984.

Institute for Future Studies, Macomb Community College. *The Top Ten Issues Facing America's Community Colleges.* Macomb, Mich.: Institute for Future Studies, Macomb Community College, 1991.

Jennings, C. M., Barlar, A. D., and Bartling, C. A. "Trends in Colleges' and Universities' Faculty Development Programs." *Journal of Staff, Program, and Organizational Development,* 1991, *9*(3), 147–154.

Katz, J., and Henry, M. *Turning Professors into Teachers: A New Approach to Faculty Development and Student Learning.* New York: American Council on Education/Macmillan, 1988.

Lowman, J. *Mastering the Techniques of Teaching.* San Francisco: Jossey-Bass, 1984.

McKeachie, W. J. *Teaching Tips: A Guidebook for the Beginning College Teacher.* Lexington, Mass.: Heath, 1986.

McNeal, J. P. "Teacher Evaluation." *Science Teacher,* 1987, *54*(8), 40–41.

Nash, M. *Managing Organizational Performance.* San Francisco: Jossey-Bass, 1983.

Olp, M., Watson, K., and Valek, M. *Appraisal of Faculty: Encouragement and Improvement in the Classroom.* Yuma, Ariz.: Arizona Western College, 1991.

Romanik, K. O. *Staff Evaluation: Commitment to Excellence.* Miami, Fla.: Mitchell Wolfson New World Center Campus, Miami-Dade Community College, 1986.

Seldin, P. *Evaluating and Developing Administrative Performance: A Practical Guide for Academic Leaders.* San Francisco: Jossey-Bass, 1988.

Slicker, R. "Team Building Through Faculty Coaching and Faculty Coaching System Guidebook." Paper presented at the sixty-eighth annual convention of the American Association of Community and Junior Colleges, Las Vegas, Nev., Apr. 1988.

Smith, A. B. (ed.). *Evaluating Faculty and Staff.* New Directions for Community Colleges, no. 41. San Francisco: Jossey-Bass, 1983.

Smith, A. B. "A Conceptual Framework and Change Strategy for Improving Faculty Evaluation Programs." In D. Grieve (ed.), *Higher Education: Significant and Contemporary Concerns.* Cleveland, Ohio: Info-Tec, Inc., 1987.

Smith, A. B. "Innovations in Staff Development." In T. O'Banion (ed.), *A Renaissance of Innovation in the Community College.* New York: Macmillan, 1988.

Strike, K., and Bull, B. "Fairness and the Legal Context of Teacher Evaluation." In J. Millman (ed.), *Handbook of Teacher Evaluation.* Newbury Park, Calif.: Sage, 1981.

Tucker, A. *Chairing the Academic Department: Leadership Among Peers.* New York: American Council on Education/Macmillan, 1984.

Chapter 21

Involving the Board in Personnel Management

Hans A. Andrews

New trustees quickly learn that the personnel functions of the college make up the lion's share of the college budget, programs, and reputation. By the same token, these trustees make or break the reputation of the college by their contributions to its administration and to the quality of its instructional personnel and programs.

There are many quality issues involved in running an outstanding college; most of these center on how well the personnel who are hired perform. The board of trustees is in a position to help determine the quality of the college for its students and taxpayers. This chapter discusses the board's role in developing and monitoring personnel policies.

Personnel Policy Needs

Jasiek, Wisgoski, and Andrews (1985, p. 87) suggested that "there is no greater responsibility of a board of trustees than personnel management." They went on to say that "the board's role in hiring and firing is an issue that is so sensitive and misunderstood that no one wants to mention it." They listed the

400

important ingredients of a college's effective recruitment, retention, or dismissal of college personnel to be a strong governing board, a strong president and staff, mutual support, and clearly defined personnel policies and procedures. They pointed out that a personnel system is doomed to fail if any one of these essential ingredients is lacking.

McGrath (1977) saw the basic functions of a board as setting the basic policies of the college, monitoring how these policies are carried out, keeping informed on all significant aspects of the institution's operation, and ensuring that the chief executive has integrity and enjoys the board's confidence. Kauffman (1983) regarded the board-president relationship as the most important in determining the successful functioning of the president in implementing board policy. He viewed the authority of a president as being enhanced by a board that insists on approving major policy and fiscal matters, including tenure. He also saw board policies as key to providing the president with a means of resisting pressures for a questionable action, thereby, "making it difficult for special interests to precipitate unwise actions" (p. 19).

Board's Legal Base in Personnel Management

The powers and duties of boards of trustees are assigned by state laws. Piele (1980, p. 8), in determining the level of powers of individual boards, found "it is a well settled rule of law that boards of education have only those powers that are expressly granted or reasonably inferred to them by the legislature of the state or that have been granted to the board of education through the state board of education by rule or regulation." He went on to say that such power or authority cannot and should not be delegated. Piele also found that powers and duties of a board are often better known in law and in courts than by individual board members.

Courts have found board of education policies to carry "the same weight of authority as state law within the confines of the school district. Policies that are unreasonable, arbitrary, or capricious must be found so by the courts" (Piele, 1979,

p. 14). Piele (1980) suggested that, in most states, the boards of education are the only bodies that can hire or fire employees. He noted that "the board's use of discretion in hiring personnel usually is not qualified or successfully challenged by anyone as long as the letter of the law is not violated" (p. 12).

Nason (1982) noted that trustees possess final legal authority for the policies that are developed for their school district. He pointed out that "only the courts or the legislature can legally challenge a board's decisions" (p. 23). While individual faculty or other personnel may not like board action, it stands as final unless it is challenged and taken to court. Faculty negotiations come under the same rule. Board action becomes the determining action in the approval process in the settlement of a contract.

Rebell (1990) pointed to the federal Constitution as providing no explicit right to education and showed that "the Tenth Amendment to the Constitution operates to reserve educational issues to the states." His research found that most of the evaluation issues regarding teachers that come before the court system involve "questions of interpretation of the specific requirements of state statutes or state board regulations" (p. 341). The courts watch very closely how the cases have been related to *specific procedural requirements* that state law, common law, or due process require. Rebell saw these as much more important than professional "psychometric standards."

Legislative Mandates

Continually changing federal and state laws affect personnel policies. There are both informal and formal ways in which the community college districts and their colleges are notified about pending or imminent legislation. Usually a community college head of personnel is first alerted informally that personnel-related legislation is coming. Informal methods utilized by personnel heads include professional organizations and publications, especially the regional meetings of personnel heads of community college districts. Other informal information comes from the organizational ties of the college and district's administrators and the district's lawyers.

Formal notification comes either from the state chancellor's office, from another state agency, or from the appropriate federal agency. When formal notification is sent to the district's office of personnel, the head of personnel evaluates the impact of the regulations on three areas:

1. *Contract implications.* Does this require a change in one or more union contracts? If so, notice of the new law is sent to the district's negotiating team members.
2. *Board of trustees notification.* The board of trustees is notified of new legislation and any effects it may have on board policy. After board review, any new policy is then put in the board policy manual by the office of personnel.
3. *Review of general manual updating.* All personnel manuals, contracts, and personnel procedures are reviewed and updated by the head of personnel whenever any new law takes effect. Updates are sent to each appropriate campus administrator who will be affected.

For example, a federal law was enacted granting employees rights to family leave. Personnel supervisors learned about the debate and approval on family leave informally, from the newspapers and elsewhere, and immediately began reviewing the impact it would have in their districts. In some districts, the new law required changes in all three union contracts (those of faculty, classified employees, and administrators); the board policy and managers' policy manual had to be changed; and the regulations for the classified employees' merit system needed to be modified.

Tenure and Dismissal

Murrell and Crawford (1987) discussed how tenure has been a center of controversy since its introduction to the United States during the early 1900s. They stated that tenure is not a precise "well-defined, universally accepted concept, but rather is an amorphous idea, the parameters of which are shaped by the nature of the institution controlling and bestowing it" (p. 34). They

presented a number of "tenure myths" administrators and boards
believe in due to a lack of information on the extent to which
courts have *restricted* administrative decisions regarding tenure
awards (p. 34). Some of these myths are listed below, together
with facts they see as contradicting them:

1. *Myth.* If faculty members are hired in tenure track positions, they have a right to tenure.
   Fact. Award of tenure is not a right for anyone.
   Nontenured employees have neither a property right
   nor a liberty right in tenure. (See *Katz* v. *Board of
   Trustees of Gloucester County College,* 1972.)
2. *Myth.* If faculty members get good evaluations from
   their department chairs, they have a right to be
   awarded tenure.
   Fact. Good evaluations do not create a right to receive
   tenure. And nonaward of tenure is not an indication
   that evaluations were not good.
3. *Myth.* If faculty members are part of a protected class
   under Title VII of the Civil Rights Act of 1964, Title
   IX of the Education Amendments of 1972, or the
   Vocational Rehabilitation Act of 1973, they have a
   greater claim to tenure than other faculty members.
   Fact. While faculty members in protected classes under
   such legislation may not be denied tenure because of
   their status, this status does not create any right to
   receive tenure.
4. *Myth.* If faculty members are denied tenure, the reasons given for denial must be proven.
   Fact. The institution's burden of proof, even where the
   employee has proven a prima facie case of discrimination, is merely to explain clearly the nondiscriminatory
   reasons for not awarding tenure.
5. *Myth.* If there is a procedural flaw in adherence to locally established procedures, the institution must award
   tenure.
   Fact. Unless the procedural flaw is of sufficient magnitude
   as to deprive the faculty member of substantive due process,
   it seems likely that the flaw would not be actionable.

Murrell and Crawford concluded that the courts have "not significantly eroded" administrative procedures in the properly applied denial of tenure. They cautioned boards to pay close attention to details and procedures when making tenure decisions.

Tenure (or continuing contract in some states) is one of the concepts college administrators and board members most often misunderstand. Board members and administrators frequently complain that tenure gives faculty members a secure job for life. The literature on university faculty seems to support this assumption, since there are few documented cases of incompetent university faculty being removed. The literature on community colleges, however, indicates that tenure is not necessarily a sinecure for faculty who do not perform at those institutions.

Jenkins and others (1977) suggested that administrators and governing boards were at fault if faculty felt they had "guaranteed lifetime employment" once they received tenure. They criticized administrators and boards for being unaware of the legalities concerning tenure and for being unsure of the process involved in discharging unsatisfactory faculty members. They also noted that the real problem may be the lack of an adequate evaluation process, not the tenure system as such.

In a landmark decision — *Board of Regents* v. *Roth* (1972) — it was determined that no property interest rights exist for nontenured teachers. The decision further showed that it is not necessary to provide formal dismissal proceedings in the dismissal of a nontenured teacher.

In a New Jersey case, a faculty member challenged a board's dismissal decision (Knowles and Wedlock, 1973, p. 205): "The instructor claimed that his nonretention was based upon his exercise of lawful union activities and thus violated his First Amendment rights. The court, in holding against the instructor, felt that to hold otherwise would be tantamount to abolishing the tenure system." The decision further stated that "inherent in our legislatively enacted tenure policy is the existence of a probationary period during which the board will have a chance to evaluate a teacher with no commitments to re-employ him. . . . We hold that it is the prerogative of the board of trustees to discontinue the employment of a non-tenured teacher at the end of his teaching contract with or without reason" (*Katz* v. *Board of Trustees of Gloucester County College,* 1972).

Andrews (1985) found that the Third District Appellate Court of Illinois reaffirmed the power invested in the governing board in *Krizek* v. *Board of Trustees of Community College District No. 513* (1983). The court clearly supported the governing board's ultimate authority on tenure questions, stating that "there can be no dilution of the board's authority whether the evaluation of teachers is mandated by contract or by statute" (*Krizek* v. *Board . . . ,* 1983, p. 76).

Piele (1980) presented a Michigan case which came down to the court to determine if *reasons,* or *causes,* needed to be given the faculty member when denying tenure: "The state supreme court was evenly divided in a previous hearing of the case. In this instance, one of the justices changed his vote, and the majority now held that reasons need not be stated. Citing Roth, the court concluded that there was no entitlement under the state tenure act" (*Lipka* v. *Brown City Community Schools,* 1978, p. 84).

The year 1972 also produced a landmark decision relative to a board's decision not to renew a faculty member's continuing contract (tenure). In *Perry* v. *Sindermann* (1972), the court found a "constitutionally protected" property interest in a teacher's job that had been held for the past ten years: "The contract renewal practice in effect in the college system (Texas) implicitly conferred upon long-term employees a legitimate expectation of future employment, which constituted a property interest sufficient to require formal procedures." This case has often been wrongly interpreted to mean it is supportive of tenure and the nonremoval of tenured faculty members. In fact, however, tenured faculty can be removed for *cause* in four areas: (1) incompetence, (2) immorality, (3) neglect of duty, and (4) insubordination. Exhibit 21.1 lists examples of court cases focusing on these areas.

Tenure is a term used to recognize faculty members who have achieved a satisfactory degree of competence in their employment at a college during a specified period of probation. The board has the final authority to accept or to reject a recommendation for tenure.

Exhibit 21.1. Cases Involving Removal of Tenured Faculty.

---

1. *Incompetence.* A tenured teacher was dismissed for poor preparation and poor relations with his students in *Jawa* v. *Fayetteville University* (1976). A civil rights challenge was rejected by the court in this case.

In a second case decided by the Missouri Supreme Court — *Saunders* v. *Reorganized School District No. 2 of Osage County* (1975) — the court upheld a decision of dismissal of a tenured junior college professor for incompetency, inefficiency, and insubordination. The court found the charge of inefficiency was given sufficient support by the evidence presented to show the plaintiff's manner of teaching to be unsatisfactory.

In *Chung* v. *Park* (1974), a tenured professor was dismissed on grounds of intransigence in dealing with his supervisors, especially because of poor teaching. The federal district court held that the allegations were supported by substantial evidence.

2. *Immorality.* The courts have held dishonesty, sexual harassment, and extreme vulgarity to constitute immoral behavior in a number of cases. In the case of *Lehman* v. *Board of Trustees of Whitman College* (1978), sexual advances toward female students, faculty, and others were considered sexual harassment and adequate cause in Lehman's dismissal.

3. *Neglect of duty.* Violation of the terms of the teacher's employment contract was found in *Shaw* v. *Board of Trustees of Frederick Community College* (1976). In this case, the court upheld the dismissal of two professors — one tenured and the other on a continuing appointment — for boycotting a faculty workshop and commencement exercises in their protest of the college's plan to abolish tenure at the college.

In *Jawa* v. *Fayetteville University* (1976), the court cited the plaintiff's failure to keep office hours and properly advise his students as well as his unwillingness to follow proper procedures as valid grounds for his discharge.

In *Bates* v. *Sponberg* (1976), a tenured professor was dismissed in part for failing to submit required reports on the project he directed.

4. *Insubordination.* Writers in this area of dismissal point to the challenges by teachers that their "academic freedom" and "free speech," constitutionally guaranteed, have been denied. The courts, however, found this not to be the case in a number of court challenges by teachers.

In Kentucky, a vocational education teacher from a state school was dismissed for "friction" between her and her superior (*Wagner* v. *Department of Educ. State Personnel Bd.*, 1977). The supreme court rejected her claim of statutory and constitutional violations and observed that sufficient evidence showed that she was indeed uncooperative and insubordinate to her superiors.

A case involving an unapproved leave of absence led the court to conclude that "academic freedom is not a license for activity at variance with job related procedures and requirements" (*Stasny* v. *Board of Trustees of Central Washington University*, 1982).

Academic Freedom

Some faculty and administrators have felt that implementation of administrative evaluation procedures is in conflict with academic freedom. Olswang and Lee (1984) answered this concern directly when they pointed out that academic freedom and tenure, while providing some important protections, do not provide unlimited protections. They went on to say that "evaluating the continued competence of faculty does not infringe on faculty freedoms as competence is a condition of tenure" (p. 3).

In 1916, the American Association of University Professors described the conditions that should exist for academic freedom. It proclaimed that academic freedom should allow for "fairness and honesty in conducting and reporting research, the maintenance of professional standards, the importance of avoiding indoctrination or its appearance, and temperance in extramural utterances" (Olswang and Lee, 1984, p. 8).

Those who drafted this academic freedom statement made "a special effort to disassociate academic freedom from the protection of incompetence" (Olswang and Lee, 1984, p. 8), as the following passage shows: "If this profession should prove itself unwilling to purge its ranks of the incompetent and the unworthy, or to prevent the freedom which it claims in the name of science from being used as a shelter for inefficiency, for superficiality, or for uncritical and intemperate partisanship, it is certain that the task will be performed by others" (Olswang and Lee, 1984, p. 8).

Evaluation of Faculty

Possibly the number one quality control any college board can provide for itself and the college is that of an effective faculty evaluation system. This section will present some of the key elements in establishing a legally defendable and procedurally effective faculty evaluation system.

Evaluating faculty begins with the hiring process. The North Orange County Community College District (1992, p. 1) in California approved an academic hiring policy for new faculty that reflects both careful preparation for the position and sensitivity to the changing demographics of its college district: "The selection of new faculty is one of the most important functions of an educational institution. The implementation of the following policies and procedures governing the hiring process is intended to ensure that the faculty and administrators that are hired and retained are people who are sympathetic and sensitive to the racial and cultural diversity in the district, are themselves representative of that diversity, and are well prepared by training and temperament to respond effectively to the educational needs of all the special populations served by the community college."

Board policies that allow for "open searches" to hire for new positions or to replace personnel help ensure that nepotism and other political pressures will not usurp the opportunity for a college to seek and hire the best persons available. Many colleges conduct a national search to obtain a hiring pool that guarantees a high-quality staff.

Student Evaluations

Many college board and staff members believe that student and peer evaluation processes should be preeminent in setting up evaluation systems. Representatives of senior colleges and universities who have dominated the field of faculty evaluation have imposed this concept on two-year colleges for many years. But Andrews (1985) and Licata and Andrews (1990) have found many gaps in the student and peer evaluation models. Andrews, in his search of *The Yearbook of School Law* over a nineteen-year period, did not find a single case in which a poor instructor was removed from a teaching position based on student and/or peer evaluation models. But he found numerous cases where administrative supervisors removed incompetent faculty.

Centra (1979) found that students were much too generous in their evaluations of faculty members. His conclusion was based on a summary of the best research then available on student evaluation. He further concluded that a poor instructor who is a lenient grader may be rated higher than a good instructor who is not lenient. In addition, poor instructors often do not realize their weaknesses and continue to make the same mistakes rather than working to improve or remediate them.

Hocutt (1987–88) presented a scathing review of what he feels has happened to lower the quality of education in the American higher education system since it has moved to accept student evaluation as a means of assisting in tenure and merit pay decisions on a large scale. Twenty-five to thirty years ago, only a few schools relied on student evaluation for these purposes. But Hocutt found that 87 percent of public institutions recently professed to use student evaluation in determining pay raises. He defined a good teacher as "simply someone from whom students learn." He also saw Student Poll of Teaching (SPOT) as checking to see how *satisfied* are the customers, in this case the students. The following summary points from Hocutt's indictment of SPOT highlight problems with student evaluation:

1. It does not matter what the student learns, or even whether he learns anything; what matters is whether he is satisfied with the process. If the student likes the service he is getting, his teacher is good; otherwise not.

2. There is a debate between (a) those who think that the teacher's business is to see that pupils are satisfied and (b) those who think that the teacher's business is to induce students to learn.

3. More people are attending college and liking it better while learning less. Students are not our customers; they are our products.

4. The SPOT yields not an objective measure of teacher's performance but a subjective index of the student's satisfaction.

5. The research on grades has been even worse. Cynical professors have long suspected that they can buy ratings with grades. [p. 56]

For Hocutt, it is no coincidence that, at the same time that we see mass acceptance of student evaluation processes, we also have the most pronounced grade inflation in the history of American education. He says that "we are giving better grades to worse students" (p. 61).

The arbitration case of *Sever* v. *Board of Trustees, Illinois Valley Community College District No. 513* (1984) shed further light on these problems. In this case,

The arbitrator took note of the student evaluations, the letters from students on behalf of the Respondent, the positive evaluations of two teachers who visited her classes, and the favorable testimony of those teachers and the two other students who testified.

The arbitrator was impressed by the support shown for the Respondent but does not give as much weight to this evidence as he does to the negative findings (of the supervisors).

The arbitrator does not find that the student evaluations submitted by the Respondent prove that she was an acceptable teacher. . . . The arbitrator also wonders whether the evaluations may be biased in favor of the Respondent because of the circumstances under which they were given. Some were in small classes where the anonymity of the students is not fully protected. It appears also that the Respondent administered the evaluations herself and saw the results before she issued grades. Since the students knew this would be the case, they may have been less frank than they would have been under other circumstances.

Since the Respondent was dismissed before the middle of the semester, he [the arbitrator] wonders why the evaluations were made. The arbitrator suspects that the evaluations were given just before the dismissal was effective but after the Respondent knew that she was going to be terminated and were given for the purpose of acquiring data that might be supportive of the Respondent's position. As such, these evaluations carry little weight. [pp. 29–30]

The arbitrator in this dismissal case of a tenured faculty member gave little credence to student evaluation. From a legal standpoint, the students were also anonymous and could not be brought in for a hearing such as this arbitration hearing.

Peer Evaluation

In a summary of the research available on peer evaluation — where teachers evaluate each other — Centra (1979) found this type of evaluation to be weaker than student evaluation. His investigation showed that peers are even more generous than students. Faculty often evaluate their peers without entering the classroom to see how they present their lectures or how effective their teaching techniques are.

Peer evaluation also played a role in the *Sever* case just mentioned. The arbitrator called its reliability into question:

> The arbitrator took note of the positive evaluations of two teachers who visited her classes and the favorable testimony of those teachers who testified.
>
> The arbitrator was impressed by the support shown for the Respondent [from both students and faculty] but does not give as much weight to this evidence as he does to the negative findings of Uebel, Andrews, and Allen. It seems normal for teachers to support another teacher with whom they have been associated for some time even though the teacher may be guilty of the charges made against her by the employer. [p. 29]

The arbitrator responded more favorably to the supervisor's evaluations that followed board of trustee policies and procedures. The policies did not include either student or peer evaluation as elements of the process and, therefore, set the stage for much stronger legal support for the administrative role in the process leading to the dismissal.

Administrative Evaluation

Two-year colleges and technical institutes are teaching institutions. Classroom instruction is therefore what needs to be assessed. Good faculty are not intimidated by such evaluation and expect it if they are to improve. But faculty have a right to expect quality evaluation carried out by administrators who have been good instructors and understand the teaching/learning process. Andrews (1986, p. 2) presented a Bill of Rights for teachers as it relates to evaluation:

1.   Competent evaluators should be expected and used.

2. The evaluators and faculty members should have a clear understanding of the evaluation system and the instruments to be used.
3. Consistency should be expected.
4. Fairness is a "must" element of the system.
5. Both verbal and written evaluations should be part of the feedback to teachers.
6. A chance to disagree needs to be present, both verbally and in writing.
7. Feedback from the evaluator should be expected to occur in a reasonably short time.
8. Positive types of recognition for excellence in one's work should be given.
9. A reasonable amount of time should be given for those areas of teaching that may need some form of remediation due to a weakness.
10. Dignity between faculty and administrative professionals should permeate the process.
11. Privacy of results should be expected — except when an open meetings act may call for board action on a notice to remedy, or on a dismissal of personnel action being recommended.

This guide provides a legally defensible evaluation system with due process procedures. It evolved from much board, faculty, and administrative input over a number of years.

Developing an Evaluation Model

In determining what goes into "model" two-year college evaluation systems, Andrews (1985) presented a range of approaches two-year colleges use to define "effective characteristics of teaching." The City Colleges of Chicago had surveyed thirty of its exemplary faculty members; Guskey and Easton (1982) reported the results. The following picture of ideal teachers emerged:

1. All of them were highly organized, planned carefully, had unambiguous objectives and high expectations for their students. Each class had a clear design:

    a.   an introduction at the beginning;
    b.   a summary at the end; and
    c.   a clear sequence of development in between.

2. All of them emphasized the importance of expressing positive regard for their students:
   a. Most used some time during their first class session to become familiar with their students and continued to exchange personal information throughout the semester.
   b. They generally learned their students' names very early in the semester and addressed them by name.

3. They had an emphasis on encouraging student participation:
   a. They consistently asked questions during class to stimulate involvement.
   b. They also monitored student participation at frequent intervals to gain information as to whether the class was going well or if a change was needed.

4. In addition, they strongly emphasized the importance of providing students with regular feedback on their learning and rewarding learning successes.
   a. Feedback was generally provided through written comments on tests or papers.
   b. They frequently asked their students to see them after class to discuss learning problems.
   c. Written comments were also used to praise students' efforts and to make special note of improvements. [pp. 3–4]

Poole and Dellow (1983, pp. 20–21) added the following items in describing the North County Community College system of evaluation of full-time faculty:

1. Generating an enthusiasm in and establishing rapport with students

2. Making maximum use of library resources, audio-
    visual aids, laboratory equipment, and so on
3. Using a variety of teaching techniques to achieve
    the desired objectives
4. Keeping course materials, including textbook se-
    lection and reference reading lists, up to date
5. Providing instruction in such a way that it is effec-
    tive to the greatest possible number of people.

Stodolsky (1990, p. 181) concluded that instead of placing excessive emphasis on reliability and objectivity, a teacher
observation system would better be determined "by the match
between the school district's view of teaching and the adequacy
with which the instrument reflects that view." In agreeing with
Stodolsky, I have found that faculty and administrators working together can usually come up with a system that brings
ownership to both groups and support for the system as it becomes part of the evaluation system.

Community College District 513 in Illinois utilized faculty
members selected by the American Federation of Teachers union
to help the instructional administration define quality teaching
in that district. It turned those quality teaching traits into a
questionnaire that administrative evaluators could use in their
in-class evaluation process. The questions in Exhibit 21.2 were
included as open-ended questions that evaluators had to answer
as specifically as possible.

The type of inquiry outlined in the exhibit continues
through a dozen questions and also provides for questions relating to "other professional responsibilities." Three of these are
outlined in Exhibit 21.3.

The college faculty leaders applauded the use of open-
ended questions that must first be responded to with specific
written observations, both positive and negative. The faculty
leaders also felt strongly that the follow-up sessions with the
faculty allowed for face-to-face discussion that would ultimately
lead to the improvement of teaching.

Andrews and Wisgoski (1987) reported that this system
of evaluation at Community College District 513 has resulted

Exhibit 21.2. Sample Questions on Teaching Effectiveness.

1. What evidence is there that the person *is* or *is not* prepared for this class, lab, or counseling activity?

   COMMENTS: _____

2. Is there evidence that there is appropriate homework, class participation, and other expectations of the students?

   COMMENTS: _____

3. Does the person use good teaching techniques and provide a good learning environment?

   COMMENTS: _____

4. Does the person demonstrate an *adequate knowledge* of the subject, activity, or skill?

   COMMENTS: _____

5. Is the discussion or activity germane to the *course syllabus*?

   COMMENTS: _____

6. How has the person encouraged student participation?

   COMMENTS: _____

Source: Andrews, 1985, pp. 163–165.

in thirteen probationary faculty not making it to tenure and twelve tenured faculty being "evaluated out" or "fired" for just cause after due process proceedings. But over thirty-five faculty have been recognized for outstanding contributions to teaching and other job responsibilities and given board-sponsored "merit recognition" awards as a result of their supervisors' evaluations.

In summary, developing this model evaluation system first requires a college to define what it feels constitutes "outstanding teaching" and other job responsibilities. The next step is to create an evaluation instrument around those outstanding teaching traits. Faculty involvement is key, since this means that faculty and administrators have jointly defined quality teaching and bought into the evaluation system as it is developed.

Impact of Negotiations on Evaluation

An area of erosion of board management rights and responsibilities is in contract negotiations related to evaluation processes.

Exhibit 21.3. Sample Questions on Other Professional Responsibilities.

---

1. Does the person attend and participate in faculty meetings, division meetings, and college committees?

   COMMENTS: _____

2. Does the person keep current on the latest developments in his or her field of study?

   COMMENTS: _____

3. Does the person exhibit a positive working relationship with colleagues and the administration?

   COMMENTS: _____

Source: Andrews, 1985, p. 166.

Strike and Bull (1981) urged boards of education not to negotiate away legislated board prerogatives and to be careful that the resulting agreement does not violate a statute or a strong public policy. They further stated that "the substantive criteria of evaluation are usually not negotiable" (p. 328). A competent union can circumvent these conditions during negotiations if board representatives are not vigilant.

Cohen and Brawer (1982) expressed their concerns about how complex faculty had made evaluation procedures as they gained more power. They saw faculty as primarily responsible for introducing the peer and student evaluation models. Protecting their members, rather than enhancing professional development, appeared to be the main goal. This was seen as a strain on higher education's ability to police itself and to eliminate weak or incompetent faculty (p. 75).

In his sampling of community college evaluation plans, Andrews (1985) found that a number of colleges had indeed started allowing evaluation to be included in negotiations with faculty. In a follow-up study in 1991, he found that a total of 87 out of the 132 colleges in eight states reported negotiated evaluation processes. Thirty-seven of the 87 administrative leaders (42.5 percent) said no, that they were not satisfied with the negotiated language. Over half of these colleges' administrators reported that they had been "hindered" in their evaluation efforts (Andrews, 1991, p. 10).

Faculty Responses to Evaluation

In a study of 158 faculty leaders, Licata and Andrews (1990) found overwhelming support for the idea of posttenure evaluation. Some 96 percent agreed that "there should be periodic post-tenure evaluation of competence and faculty developmental needs" (p. 51). But a total of 77 percent disagreed with the statement that "post-tenure evaluation leads to the weeding out of incompetent faculty." The same faculty leaders felt strongly about the need to tie evaluation to a faculty development program. Such comments as "give consequences to the results, both pro and con" and "the present plan only pays lip service" clearly indicate weaknesses faculty saw in their evaluation systems. A total of 19 percent of these leaders also argued that evaluation should be used for making merit compensation or merit recognition decisions for faculty (pp. 49–54).

Summary

The governing board of a community or junior college can guarantee quality improvements by means of clearly defined policies in all phases of the college operations. There is no area where these policies will make a greater difference than in the area of personnel. Clearly defined policies that allow for open searches for new personnel and provide for effective evaluation practices for all personnel will help ensure a quality institution.

Boards will improve their colleges by establishing faculty evaluation systems, knowing that research shows faculty leaders to be highly supportive of posttenure evaluation if it is fair, if it addresses faculty development needs, and if it provides recognition for outstanding faculty and allows for remediation or termination for those who do not perform competently. While student evaluation and peer evaluation are prevalent in many colleges today, administrative (supervisory) evaluation should be considered the cornerstone of a system if it is to be effective and legally defensible. Colleges wishing to combine administrative, student, and/or peer evaluation elements should give the greatest weight to administrative evaluation. Faculty development, remediation, and dismissal efforts do not receive adequate attention with student and peer evaluation.

Although colleges are starting to allow faculty evaluation procedures to be negotiated into faculty contracts, boards must be careful not to negotiate away their legal rights and responsibilities in guaranteeing a public policy of quality classroom instruction.

References

Andrews, H. A. *Evaluating for Excellence.* Stillwater, Okla.: New Forums Press, 1985.

Andrews, H. A. "A Proposal: Faculty Evaluation Bill of Rights." *Administrative Action,* 1986, *1*(2), 2.

Andrews, H. A. *Negative Impact of Faculty Contract Negotiations on Community College Faculty Evaluation Systems.* Los Angeles: ERIC Clearinghouse for Community Colleges, 1991. (ED 343 628)

Andrews, H. A., and Wisgoski, A. "Assuring Future Quality: Systematic Evaluation and Reward of Faculty." *Journal of Staff, Program, and Organization Development,* 1987, *5*(4), 163–168.

Bates v. *Sponberg,* 547 F.2d 325 (6th Cir. 1976).

Board of Regents v. *Roth,* 408 U.S. 564 (1972).

Centra, J. A. *Determining Faculty Effectiveness: Assessing Teaching, Research, and Service for Personnel Decisions and Improvement.* San Francisco: Jossey-Bass, 1979.

Chung v. *Park,* 377F. Skupp. 218 (M.D. Pa. 1974).

Cohen, A. M., and Brawer, F. B. *The American Community College.* San Francisco: Jossey-Bass, 1982.

Guskey, T. R., and Easton, J. Q. "The Characteristics of Very Effective Community College Teachers." *Center for the Improvement of Teaching and Learning: City Colleges of Chicago Center Notebook,* 1982, *1*(3), 36.

Hocutt, M. O. "De-Grading Student Evaluations: What's Wrong with Student Polls of Teaching." *Academic Questions,* 1987–88, *1*(1), 55–64.

Jasiek, C. R., Wisgoski, A., and Andrews, H. A. "The Trustee Role in College Personnel Management." In G. F. Petty (ed.), *Active Trusteeship for a Changing Era.* New Directions for Community Colleges, no. 51. San Francisco: Jossey-Bass, 1985.

Jawa v. *Fayetteville University,* 426F.Supp. 218 (E.D.N.C. 1976).

Jenkins, N., and others. *Formal Dismissal Procedures Under Illinois Teacher Tenure Laws.* Springfield: Illinois Association of School Boards, 1977.

Katz v. *Board of Trustees of Gloucester County College,* 118 N.J. Super. 398, 288 A.2d 43 (1972).

Kauffman, J. F. "Strengthening Chair, CEO Relationships." *AGB Reports,* 1983, *25*(2), 17–21.

Knowles, L. W., and Wedlock, E. D., Jr. *The Yearbook of School Law.* Topeka, Kans.: National Organization of Legal Problems in Education, 1973.

Krizek v. *Board of Trustees of Community College District No. 513,* 445–447 N.E. 2d 770 (Ill. 1983).

Lehman v. *Board of Trustees of Whitman College,* 89 Wash. 2d 874, 576 P. 2d at 397 (1978).

Licata, C. M., and Andrews, H. A. "Faculty Leaders' and Administrators' Perceptions on Post-Tenure Faculty Evaluation." *Journal of Staff, Program, and Organization Development,* 1990, *8*(1), 17–22.

Lipka v. *Brown City Community Schools,* 271 N.W. 2d 771 (Mich. 1978).

McGrath, C. P. "How to Talk to Faculty and Students." *AGB Reports,* 1977, *19*(2), 25–28.

Murrell, P. H., and Crawford, R. L. "Ten Tenure Myths." *AGB Reports,* 1987, *29*(3), 34–36.

North Orange County Community College District. *Academic Hiring Policy.* Board policy memo. Fullerton, Calif.: North Orange County Community College District, 1992.

Olswang, S. G., and Lee, B. A. *Faculty Freedoms and Institutional Accountability: Interactions and Conflict.* ASHE-ERIC Higher Education Research Report No. 5. Washington, D.C.: Association for the Study of Higher Education, 1984.

Perry v. *Sindermann,* 408 U.S. 593 (1972).

Piele, P. K. *The Yearbook of School Law.* Topeka, Kans.: National Organization on Legal Problems of Education, 1979.

Piele, P. K. *The Yearbook of School Law.* Topeka, Kans.: National Organization on Legal Problems of Education, 1980.

Poole, L. H., and Dellow, D. A. "Evaluation of Full-Time

Faculty." In A. B. Smith (ed.), *Evaluating Faculty and Staff.* New Directions for Community Colleges, no. 41. San Francisco: Jossey-Bass, 1983.

Rebell, M. "Legal Issues Concerning Teacher Evaluation." In J. Millman and L. Darling-Hammond (ed.), *The New Handbook of Teacher Evaluation: Assessing Elementary and Secondary School Teachers.* Newbury Park, Calif.: Sage, 1990.

Saunders v. Reorganized School District No. 2 of Osage County, 420 S.W. 2d 29 (Mo. 1975).

Sever v. Board of Trustees, Illinois Valley Community College District No. 513, Statute No. 103B, AAA Case #51-39-0179-83B, (Ill. 1984).

Shaw v. Board of Trustees of Frederick Community College, 549 F.2d 929 (4th Cir. 1976).

Stasny v. Board of Trustees of Central Washington University, 32 Wash. App. 239, 647 P.2d 496 (1982).

Stodolsky, S. "Classroom Observation." In J. Millman and L. Darling-Hammond (ed.), *The New Handbook of Teacher Evaluation: Assessing Elementary and Secondary School Teachers.* Newbury Park, Calif.: Sage, 1990.

Strike, K., and Bull, B. "Fairness and the Legal Context of Teacher Evaluation." In J. Millman (ed.), *Handbook of Teacher Evaluation.* Newbury Park, Calif.: Sage, 1981.

Wagner v. Department of Educ. State Personnel Bd., 549 S.W. 2d 300 (Ky. 1977).

Chapter 22

Managing
Educational Operations

Alfredo G. de los Santos, Jr., Scott Finger

Because the primary function of a college is education, the thoughtful and efficient management of educational operations is vital to the success of the whole college. This chapter on educational operations includes sections on strategic goals, yearly objectives, regular assessment, multiunit operations, and single-unit operations.

Strategic Goals

Based on a clear vision—and legislative mandates—each community college needs to develop strategic goals. These are statements of general directions that the institution needs to pursue in order to achieve its mission and to respond well to both its internal and external environments.

The mission statement of a community college gives a brief outline of its reason for existence. It should be in harmony with the mission of the state board of education. A good example is the mission statement for Maui Community College. The college's goal is "to provide for its community the best possible post-secondary education in order to promote and preserve

422

democratic ideas and the growth of individuals as citizens and as participants in their civilization and culture. It is a basic assumption that all citizens should have vocational and general education available to them at whatever level they desire and are able to attain" (Pezzoli, 1990).

Strategic goals turn the mission statement into a framework and provide the direction for institutional operations. Strategic goals need to be developed to cover three areas: the students, the community, and the policies of the institution. All types of students need to be considered in goal setting: those who are planning to transfer, those who want occupational training, and those who take classes for personal enrichment. Goals relating to the community need to address the ways the college can serve the community, by training people to fill employment and social service needs, and by being a resource for information and recreation for members of the community. There must also be goals for the system of the institution to make sure that future policies will be developed and reviewed in accordance with the mission and main objectives of the school. For example, Los Angeles Mission College aims to "provide meaningful participation for faculty, staff, students, community in the decisions affecting the development of the college" (Los Angeles Community College District, 1988, p. 6).

The Los Angeles City College mission statement presented for 1986–87 is "to offer a comprehensive program of occupational and transfer curricula, developmental and continuing education, and community service programs which serve the educational needs of its 'community'" (Los Angeles Community College District, 1988, p. 6). The goals developed to fulfill this mission are broken into two categories: student performance goals and institutional process goals, with goals relating to the larger community classified under the latter.

The student performance goals stress personal growth in problem-solving skills, values, communication, and use of leisure time. The goals for academic performance are quantifiable: instead of a vague "the student should do well in school," the goal is to "have the knowledge and skills necessary to be successfully employed or succeed in upper division study." Institutional process goals include offering career programs based on projected employment needs, developing alternative learning styles to meet the individual needs of students, making the college facilities and resources available to the community for their educational and recreational use, and providing opportunities for all members of the community to participate in campus governance.

Other examples of strategic goals include the following, developed by the Pennsylvania College of Technology (1992, pp. 39, 49, 78).

- STUDENT SUPPORT: To develop an atmosphere in which all students are encouraged to identify personal goals and define a plan for achieving them through an active commitment to learning. . . . To provide a program of student support to accomplish a smooth progression through the recruitment, admission, career definition, financial planning, social and cultural development, and job entry processes for each student.
- PUBLIC SERVICES: To serve as a catalyst for community economic, social, and cultural development through meetings, seminars, cultural events, technical consulting services, applied projects in the community, and other activities as appropriate.
- ACADEMIC SUPPORT: To maintain a system of academic support services of sufficient depth, breadth, and caliber to help achieve fully effective instructional services; within this support system, to include course and curriculum development and evaluation, academic personnel development (including faculty development), library services, academic computing, media services, academic administration, experiential learning, and other activities as appropriate.

Yearly Objectives

Based on the strategic goals, more specific objectives are developed and implemented every year. These objectives are the pragmatic expression of an institution's strategic goals; therefore, they are the foundation of the institutional planning and achievement.

If one of the strategic goals at a community college is to "provide improved access for a diverse community," the objectives might include the following:

1. The Admissions/Recruitment area will work with students and staff to create easy and efficient access to admissions. Outreach efforts to high schools and community-based organizations that work with diverse students will be increased.
2. The Counseling Office will offer special seminars for minority students on study strategies, job interviews, and career planning.

Maricopa Community Colleges set forth a goal to "establish formal processes for working with external agencies affecting occupational education" (Maricopa County Community College District, 1981, p. 14). Some of the yearly objectives created to reach this goal were as follows:

1. Establish liaisons to interact with high schools and universities to improve student entry into and transfer from programs, to market programs, and to maintain working relationships among faculty and others at all levels.
2. Establish and formalize a district process to interact with all levels of government bodies which have a controlling impact upon the operation of the District.
3. Establish and maintain a framework for formal and extensive contacts with local business/industry, trade associations, and professional groups. [p. 14]

An action plan is the part of the yearly objective by which a community college carries out the objective and thus its strategic goals. Action plans are detailed, specific statements of steps that need to be taken in order to achieve each objective. Such plans outline each step, the individual responsible for coordi-

Exhibit 22.1. Steps Leading to an
Action Plan for a Community College Goal.

MISSION STATEMENT	To provide the surrounding community with educational and personal enrichment opportunities.
STRATEGIC GOAL	To provide opportunities to analyze the educational experience in terms of the students' own goals.
YEARLY OBJECTIVE	To develop an evaluation form that students can fill out at the end of each course, indicating in which ways the instructional methods used were effective and to what degree the materials taught helped them to reach their personal goals. Responsible Agent: Dean of Instruction. Work Group: five or six individuals chosen by the dean, perhaps including faculty, administrators, and students. Timeline: May-June 1994.

---

nating the effort, the person or group who will do the work, the fiscal resources required, and the completion date.

Thus, all the steps leading to a plan of action for a community college goal might include those listed in Exhibit 22.1. Another sample plan is illustrated in Exhibit 22.2.

At many institutions where the same work has been done over and over again, detailed action plans are not necessarily developed, principally because the work has become routine. For example, developing a schedule for each semester might not require a written action plan. But from time to time, it is fruitful for such plans to be developed, even for routine matters, in order to assess the procedures used, with the goal of finding better, more efficient or effective ways of carrying out the work.

Regular Assessment

Periodic evaluation of the whole educational master plan ensures that the issues that the strategic goals aim to address are still issues and that the continually changing needs of the community are being met. When the trustees of the San Diego Com-

Exhibit 22.2. Alternative Sample Plan for a Community College Goal.

MISSION STATEMENT	To provide the surrounding community with educational and personal enrichment opportunities.
STRATEGIC GOAL	To improve services to students who wish to transfer to four-year colleges and universities.
YEARLY OBJECTIVE	To arrange several field trips for potential transfer students to visit nearby university campuses and talk with admissions counselors from those schools. Responsible Agent: Dean of Student Services. Work Group: staff at the Transfer Center. Budget: $500. Timeline: Trips scheduled by September 30, 1993. Trips completed by April 1, 1994.
MISSION STATEMENT	To provide the surrounding community with educational and personal enrichment opportunities.
STRATEGIC GOAL	To provide modern equipment and facilities for the students to use as an aid to learning.
YEARLY OBJECTIVE	To purchase three new computers for the computer science laboratory. Responsible Agent: Purchasing Director. Budget: $5,000. Timeline: Price comparisons completed by June 1994. Computers purchased by September 1994.

munity College District reviewed their educational master plan through a joint committee in 1988, they found that some issues that were concerns in 1976 (when the plan was formulated) were now viewed as naive or superficial. They also determined that some objectives were incompatible with the stated goal and that the objectives were not given in measurable terms. This led to a reevaluation and revision of the master plan (San Diego Community College District, 1988).

Regular assessment of attainment of yearly objectives is also important. Institutions must verify completion of the targeted goals and objectives, substantiating fiscal appropriations and ensuring a cohesive district direction. Generally, administrators and faculty work together in committees to review the yearly objectives for the institution. Depending on the department that developed the goal, the chairperson or administrative analyst might be the best person to do the reviewing of specific goals. Evaluation should be an ongoing process. Every year, as last year's plans are being implemented and plans for next year are taking shape, a review of the success of the goals and actions of the year before would be helpful.

Even before the end of the year, some evaluations can be made. For example, immediately after the beginning of the semester, the deans could meet with the department/division chairs to review the schedule of classes for the semester. Which classes had to be canceled because of low enrollment? Was it necessary to add sections for some course offerings? At what time of day? Why? Is it possible to identify trends in student interest? Are some types of courses not as popular now as they were a few years ago? Why? Analyzing the answers to these questions might provide valuable information that could require changes in the action plan.

The responsibility for developing goals and plans and for conducting the evaluations of them can fall to many different offices, depending on the institution. At many schools, the trustees are given the task of determining strategic goals, leaving it to individual departments to make specific action plans and review their own procedures.

Multiunit Operations

Multiunit community colleges usually support geographically and academically separate units that operate under a common framework of governance (see Figures 22.1 and 22.2). The units are like permanent, campus-type facilities, placed strategically throughout a geographic area. The dispersion of units throughout a rural or metropolitan area is in lieu of dividing the area into several tax bases, each supporting a separate community college. Though each unit is smaller than a single-unit college would be, it has available to it all the resources of the whole rural or metropolitan area. This reduces the duplication of human resources, programs, and facility equipment, because all the colleges can coordinate and plan their efforts.

Some of the dangers of multiunit campuses are more bureaucracy, less local autonomy, and less flexibility. As Kerr

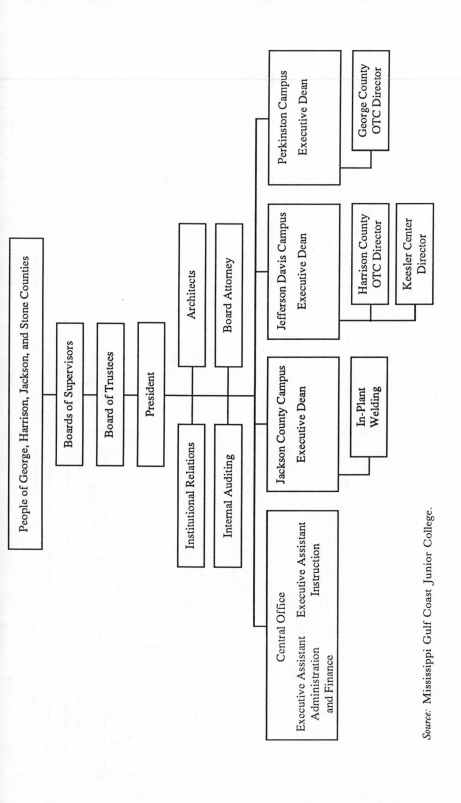

Source: Mississippi Gulf Coast Junior College.

Figure 22.2. Sample Organizational Chart for a Multicollege District.

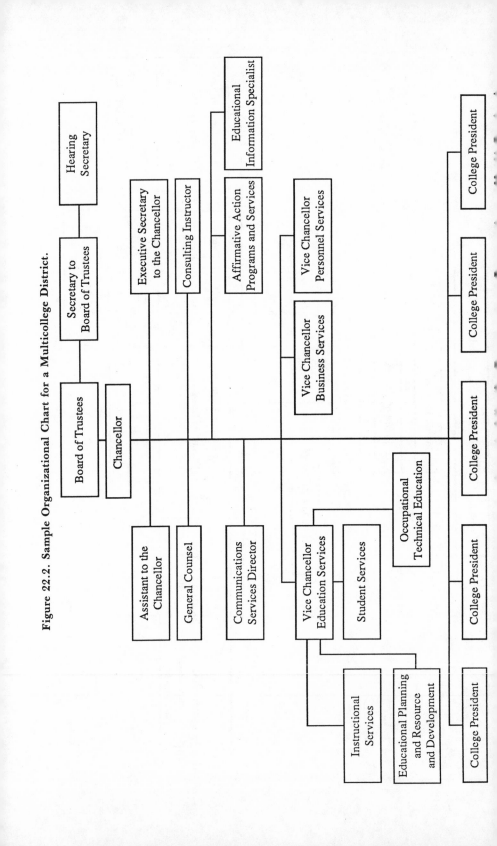

reports, a multiunit system "is strong on the possible positive results — diversity, specialization, cooperation, effective use of resources, advance planning . . . and weak on the negative aspects of the process — bureaucratization, disenfranchisement of faculty and student information influence, complexities in administrative relationships, political interference" (in Lee and Bowen, 1971, p. xiii). Also a concern is the problem of programs at different campuses overlapping to the extent of wasting resources (Rossmeier, 1976).

Because of the extra level of administration, questions arise about the extent to which decision making should be centralized or decentralized to make the individual units and the whole college most effective. Who has the power, the central staff or the units? In their classic study, Kintzer, Jensen, and Hansen (1969) found that a highly centralized college is characterized by efficiency, uniformity, economy, and impartial treatment of units but also tends to create low morale and depersonalization of members. Conversely, high decentralization encourages creativity and the relevance of programs but can also cause duplication, communication gaps, and excessive competition.

A carefully planned balance between centralization and decentralization is the most effective way to reach the goals and objectives of the school. Who makes the final decision is not as important as how involved all staff members feel in the decision-making process. The more influence and input people feel they have, the more likely they will be to work hard to solve problems creatively and to work together toward a common goal.

In a multiunit system, the strategic plans and goals of each individual unit can emphasize the areas of weakness and strength unique to that particular environment. In addition, the planning process guarantees that the colleges are adequately serving the needs of the communities that the whole district was created to serve, as the goals of each unit support the district mission and districtwide strategic goals.

One way of dealing with the problem of program overlap among units is to provide in each unit a basic core of the most important occupational programs along with a full range of college transfer, general education, and community service programs. Each unit could also have a specialized occupational-technical emphasis. Thus, one unit could specialize in health and human services studies, another in law enforcement courses, and another in communications and design (Rossmeier, 1976). Miami-Dade's Medical Center and New World School of the Arts are examples of specialized campuses functioning as magnet schools for students interested in careers in the areas they emphasize (Mese and Spano, 1989).

Single-Unit Operations

Single-unit campuses have fewer administrative levels than multiunit institutions, so all strategic issues filter from faculty through the middle managerial ranks (chairpersons) to the president and the governing board (see Figure 22.3). The middle management position between the top administrator and the faculty has always been a difficult spot to occupy because the department or division chair has to please both groups. The plethora of types of duties, from faculty evaluation to student-flow data management, and the typical practices of being named to the job without having been trained for it, add to the difficulty. Portolan (1992) confirmed that the instructional administrators she studied seemed to be experiencing a middle manager syndrome of feeling ineffective and powerless. Faced with changing student populations, limited resources, and a range of faculty issues they had not been prepared to handle, they were developing feelings of alienation toward their work.

From the administrator's point of view, the chairperson is immediately responsible for the health of the department, the welfare of the instructors and supporting personnel, and the progress of the students — all of which ultimately mean responsibility for the instructional program. The chairperson is part faculty, part administrator, and must ensure the faculty's loyalty to the department above anything else and maintain good relations with the administration. If this balance can be reached, it will be much easier for the chair to effectively improve the instruction in the department (Cohen, 1992).

Recognition and encouragement of faculty members influence the attitude of instructors toward their work, the department, and the institution. Not only do personal congratulations, sympathy, and advice create healthy morale, but so do replacing worn-out equipment and refurbishing labs and offices (Lombardi, 1992).

Evaluating instruction can be done by as many objective instruments or methods of data as are available. If the college has a research director, that person may have information on the inputs and outputs of the educational process. An examination of data on students' aptitudes and learning progress and observations of the physical surroundings will reveal areas of both strength and weakness.

If the college requires formal evaluation, the chairpersons can use this in a strategy for improving instruction. This requires more than the check marks or single sentences that usually characterize evaluations. The report must commend the strengths of the instructor and suggest ways to overcome weaknesses. It might also be helpful if faculty evaluation were not only associated with retention or separation of instructors, but primarily with instructional improvement.

Merit pay, advancement to tenure status, promotion in academic rank, distinguished teacher awards, and grants and sabbaticals for experimentation, research, and study are all important incentives and rewards for the improvement of instruction. Many of these originate outside the department, but the chairperson also plays a key role in the selection or recommendation of instructors for these rewards, which usually have monetary value (Lombardi, 1992).

Though no one method of good teaching exists, the chair of a department can work to see that the students do learn, through a variety of teaching and learning methods. Through evaluation, instructor incentives, and a commitment to the mission and goals of the college, middle-level management can have a direct impact on educational operations through instructional improvement.

Figure 22.3. Sample Organizational Chart
for a Large Community College.

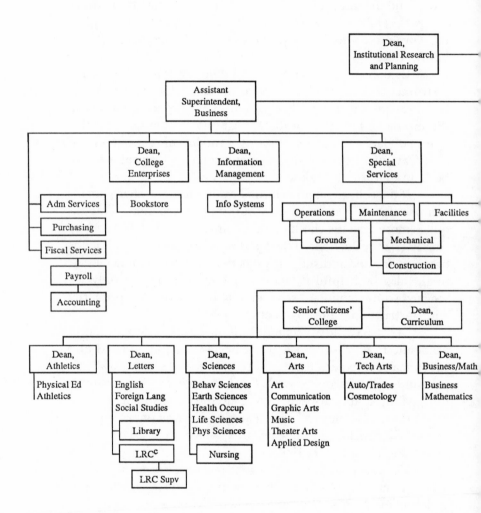

**Figure 22.3. Sample Organizational Chart
for a Large Community College, Cont'd.**

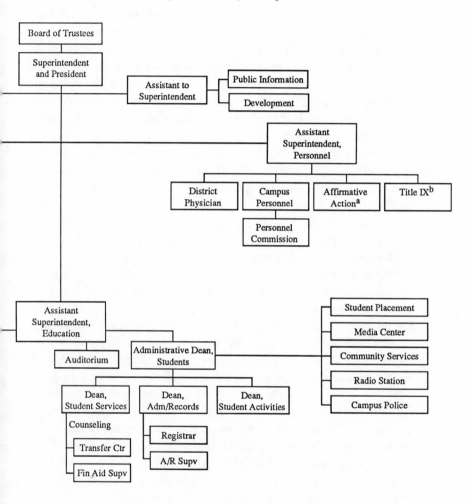

Source: From A. M. Cohen and F. B. Brawer, *The American Community College* (San
Francisco: Jossey-Bass, 1989), pp. 98–99. Reprinted with permission.

[a]Affirmative Action/Dean, Student Services.
[b]Title IX/Dean, Arts.
[c]Learning Resource Center.

Summary

Educational operations, like any other operations, should follow a procedure in order to be effective. The mission statement of a community college gives a brief outline of its reason for existence. It shows the main aims of the school and sets the direction for the rest of the planning process. Based on the mission statement, strategic goals are developed, usually covering three areas of concern: the students, the community, and the policies of the institution.

From the framework of the strategic goals, specific, yearly objectives can be formulated. These are the pragmatic expression of an institution's strategic goals; therefore, they are the foundation of the institutional planning and achievement. Yearly objectives contain action plans, which are detailed statements of steps that need to be taken in order to achieve each objective. Such plans outline each step, the individual responsible for coordinating the effort, the person or group that will do the work, the fiscal resources required, and the completion date. Once put into operation, a goal must be assessed to see if the need it was intended to fill is being met in the most efficient manner possible.

Goals must take into account whether the institution is a multiunit district or a single-unit campus. The many levels of administration at a multiunit school make it extremely important that everyone feels part of the decision-making process. Leaders there must work hard to minimize feelings of depersonalization and alienation that often accompany large organizations. In the single-unit campus, much of the responsibility for educational operations falls to the department chairperson. This can be a frustrating position, since the chair is part faculty, part administrator, and must balance loyalty to the department and good relations with the administration. The encouragement of faculty, incentive and rewards, and instructional evaluation are all tools that can be used to improve the educational process at the college.

Wisdom and insight are needed to determine an area of weakness, plan a course of action to overcome it, and assess the outcome perceptively, but solid planning pays dividends in the quality of education delivered.

References

Cohen, A. M. "A Contemporary View of the Issues." In A. M. Cohen (ed.), *Perspectives on the Community College: Essays by John Lombardi.* Los Angeles: ERIC Clearinghouse for Junior Colleges/Washington, D.C.: American Association for Community and Junior Colleges and American Council on Education, 1992.

Kintzer, F. C., Jensen, A. M., and Hansen, J. S. *The Multi-Institution Junior College District.* Washington, D.C.: American Association of Junior Colleges, 1969.

Lee, E. C., and Bowen, F. M. *The Multicampus University.* New York: McGraw-Hill, 1971.

Lombardi, J. "The Role of the Department Chair in Improving Instruction." In A. M. Cohen (ed.), *Perspectives on the Community College: Essays by John Lombardi.* Los Angeles: ERIC Clearinghouse for Junior Colleges; Washington, D.C.: American Association for Community and Junior Colleges and American Council on Education, 1992.

Los Angeles Community College District. *College Annual Reports, 1986–1987.* Vol. 1: *Narrative Descriptions.* Los Angeles: Office of Research, Planning, and Analysis, Los Angeles Community College District, 1988. (ED 302 276)

Maricopa County Community College District. *Occupational Education Master Plan, 1981–1986.* Phoenix, Ariz.: Office of Occupational Education, Maricopa County Community College District, 1981. (ED 210 074)

Mese, J. H., and Spano, C. M. "Retention Through Intervention: A Strategic Plan for Retention of High-Risk Students." Paper presented at the National Institute for Staff and Organizational Development Conference on Teaching Excellence, Austin, Tex., May 1989. (ED 305 978)

Mississippi Gulf Coast Junior College. *1982–83 Annual Report.* Perkinston: Office of Institutional Research/Resource Development, Mississippi Gulf Coast Junior College, 1983. (ED 245 754)

Pennsylvania College of Technology, Williamsport. *Long Range Plan: 1992–1995.* Williamsport: Office of Planning and Research, Pennsylvania College of Technology, 1992. (ED 346 897)

Pezzoli, J. A. *An Academic Development Plan for the Island of Molokai in Hawaii.* Kahului, Hawaii: Maui Community College–University of Hawaii, 1990. (ED 319 429)

Portolan, J. S. "Developing a Statewide Organization for Instructional Administrators in California Community Colleges." Unpublished doctoral dissertation, Graduate School of Education, University of California, Los Angeles, 1992.

Rossmeier, J. G. "Perspectives on Multiunit Colleges." In B. Heermann (ed.), *Changing Managerial Perspectives.* New Directions for Community Colleges, no. 13. San Francisco: Jossey-Bass, 1976.

San Diego Community College District. *Review of the San Diego Community College District Educational Master Plan.* San Diego, Calif.: Office of Research and Planning, San Diego Community College District, 1988. (ED 300 094)

Chapter 23

Building Relationships with the Community

Billie Wright Dziech

Whatever their sizes, wherever their locations, the greatest achievements and most devastating failures of community colleges have always emanated from relentless exploration, from the pursuit of ideals that have sometimes proved too high for reality and human nature to accommodate, from experimentation and trial unprecedented in American education. Precisely because the exploration has been so vast and their achievements and failures so distinct, community colleges, poised on the brink of a new millennium, must again pose questions about their identities, their priorities, and their positions in unpredictable external environments. If they are to survive the enormous challenges posed by limited resources, unprecedented change, and ever-accelerating technology, they cannot avoid this process of soul searching.

This is especially true of that area of the community college mission that involves responding to the needs and demands of the community. Such a vast array of activities is included in this category that "knowing" and assessing the quality of each is difficult and time consuming. In some respects, it is a "phantom" function, occupying a "now-you-see-it/now-you-don't" position in the community college experience. Lauded by some as one of the unique characteristics of community colleges, community response functions are seldom as well conceived, organized, integrated, or successful as their proponents claim.

Definitions and Missions

This chapter reviews some of the ways that community colleges have responded to their localities. The term *community services* may encompass all areas of response to community needs, or it may be used in a more limited sense to refer to "educational, cultural, and recreational services which an educational institution may provide for its community in addition to its regularly scheduled day and evening classes" (Harlacher, 1969, p. 12). This latter definition excludes adult or continuing education and builds on Basler's (1955, p. 428) concept of community services as "the provision of a variety of services to the community through media other than courses and regular classes." *Community services* and *community education* are sometimes differentiated and sometimes used synonymously. To complicate matters, *adult education, lifelong learning,* and *continuing education* are often used interchangeably, while some prefer one descriptor over the other. The more recent terms *community development* and *community renewal* only increase the confusion.

   One way of bringing a semblance of coherence to the rhetorical chaos is to consider Brawer's (1980) system of classifying community response components according to the intentions of participants. She proposes that such functions be labeled in three ways:

1.   Credit programs for those pursuing degrees, certificates, college or university transfer, general education, and career upgrading
2.   Credit-free programs designed for those seeking adult basic or high school diploma education, recreational/avocational instruction, cultural enrichment, personal development, social interaction opportunities, and skills enhancement

3. Community-based programs to accommodate those desiring access to institutional expertise, facilities, and equipment; specialized training; problem-solving techniques; and coordination with other community organizations

A survey by the Center for the Study of Community Colleges uses ninety-five randomly selected public, two-year institutions to provide a "cautious estimate" (Cohen, 1987, p. 43) of adult enrollments in the nation's public community colleges and discusses the ways in which various programs are funded and initiated. It also provides specific examples of various types of credit and credit-free instruction community colleges offer.

1. Adult Basic Education (including adult literacy classes and high school equivalency programs);
2. Short-Term Vocational Classes (including non-credit occupational courses—such as tax seminars for small business operators or short-term training for the unemployed—that are designed to teach specific job skills and are not part of certificate or degree programs);
3. Continuing Education for Professionals (including recertification or relicensure classes for real estate agents, nurses, and other members of regulated professions);
4. Recreational and Avocational Courses (including noncredit classes in such areas as aerobics, dancing, knitting, and other hobbies);
5. Customized Job Training (including classes offered on a contractual basis for employers at local industries);
6. Distance Learning (including courses by television, newspaper, and radio); and
7. Programs for special populations (including senior citizens, prisoners, displaced homemakers, and other targeted groups). [p. 2]

The scope and variety of these services are great enough to perturb anyone hoping to implement a sound community response program. Nevertheless, far greater challenges are currently being proposed to community colleges by those who demand that they move beyond attempts to fulfill community educational needs and embrace roles of leadership in "community development" or "community renewal." Extensions of Brawer's (1980) community-based program concept, these terms suggest that college leaders should serve as catalysts or, at the very least, partners in discovering solutions to communities' social, political, and economic problems.

Given the scope and variety of activities included in the community response function, the administrators' initial priority must be to determine the tasks their institutions can and should accomplish. They must engage their institutions in strategic decision making that reconciles collegiate ideals and interests with practical needs and constraints. Keller (1983, p. 153) offers sound advice in this respect: "You need to know what your college . . . can or cannot do and what it wants to do. Last, you need to decide what it will do."

Keller's message is especially crucial to colleges attempting to define their responsibilities to their communities. He points out that there is great danger in an institution's allowing its internal aspirations alone to determine academic strategy:

Strategic planning looks outward and is focused on keeping the institution in step with the changing environment. This is strategic planning's single most important contribution to organizational decision making. For decades most colleges and universities have been inner-directed, formulating their aims on the bedrock of their own religious commitments, traditions, faculty desires, and ambitions for growth, largely ignoring the world outside. . . . While an institution's own hopes and the outside forces of history are not exactly "opposed," anyone planning strategically for a college . . . needs to keep two incongruous bodies of facts and ideas — internal aspirations and external conditions — in mind at the same time and act to move the institution ahead nonetheless. [p. 145]

At this juncture in history, the "external conditions" affecting community services programs are, of course, myriad and complex. Business and industry are making extraordinary demands on higher education as they brace for a shortage of adequately trained workers. Constantly expanding and accelerating technologies render even the educated obsolescent before the ink on their diplomas dries. Women, senior citizens, the handicapped, immigrants, the culturally and economically disadvantaged, and even the incarcerated are making separate but equally great demands on colleges' resources and attention. One of the greatest errors an institution can make—and community colleges are among the most guilty—is attempting to be all things to all people, to regard the issue of "What should or would we like to do?" as taking precedence over the more pragmatic, "What can we do, given our limited resources?"

Community colleges are no strangers to messianic aspirations and hyperbolic rhetoric. In *The Community Dimension of the Community College* (1969, p. 4), Harlacher traces the community services function to Socrates who took "his wisdom into the streets and the marketplace, where he created a student community representative of the people and actively concerned with the social and moral issues of the time." Gollattscheck and his colleagues (1976, p. 4) criticize colleges for being "*in* but not *of* communities." They propose "a college for community renewal [that] must be linked to the community in such a manner that it determines its direction and develops its goals through college-community interaction, uses the total community as a learning laboratory and resource, serves as the catalyst to create in the community a desire for renewal, provides a vehicle through which the community educates itself, and evaluates its successes by citizen successes that are recognized as significant by the community itself" (pp. 6–7). Gottschalk castigates colleges for "democratic rhetoric" (p. 11) that disguises a refusal to deal with high-risk problems at the expense of "the poor, the undereducated, the unemployed, and those who seek societal reforms on their behalf" (p. 11).

Where does such discussion leave college leaders who wish to respond to community needs but are beset with fiscal, personnel, and human constraints? Perplexed and intimidated! Yet if they analyze individual areas of the community mission, they can more readily prioritize and plan. Instituting or improving credit programs is considerably different from working with credit-free offerings, and both are vastly dissimilar to initiating or participating in community-based programs that emphasize development and/or renewal activities. Rather than restate the already established in each of these areas, it might be more beneficial to consider their relative stability and stature and to examine the special problems intrinsic to each.

Credit Programs

Credit programs for nontraditional students are the oldest, best supported, most successful and thus the least problematic of institutions' community response functions. Many contend that the adult-education movement originated as far back as the early nineteenth century or, at the very latest, in 1926, when the American Association for Adult Education was established (Monroe, 1972, p. 130). Over the years, institutions of all sorts, especially community colleges, have committed themselves to providing lifelong learning for constituents in their service areas. They do so out of long-established American faith in the value of education as the most effective means of achieving an enlightened, law-abiding, personally fulfilled citizenry dedicated to democratic principles.

Participants in these programs tend to be older individuals with varied educational backgrounds. They may have completed or interrupted their formal educations and regard the return to school as a means of developing personal or professional potential. They are distinguished from traditional learners in that while many concentrate on certificates, degrees, or licenses, some do not focus on credits or credentials and are inclined to use education intermittently to serve a variety of goals. They may be content to work within the traditional curricular framework or may seek more innovative curricula and pedagogical approaches. Because most operate under more personal constraints than nontraditional students, they may prefer courses that are offered at unconventional times, in unique sequences, or at off-campus locations.

What might be described as the who? what? how? when? where? process of providing credit programs is not all that difficult, since so many models and precedents are already in place. Nevertheless, many institutions fail to give adequate attention to the "who" of credit programming. This means that courses are provided sporadically and conducted traditionally as faculty interest and experience dictate. The effective administrator must always ensure that the institution places the student at the center of the learning experience. An extraordinarily heterogeneous group, nontraditional students bring to higher education diverse backgrounds and experiences that must be respected and valued. Individuals who set aside crucial family, career, and social obligations to pursue education are entitled to the best community colleges have to offer. They deserve energetic, committed instructors who understand their needs and priorities and can make coursework stimulating and relevant. Since their students are more likely than ever before to come from heterogeneous backgrounds, contemporary community colleges also face the urgent responsibility of accommodating learners from a multicultural perspective.

Selection of faculty is thus crucial to establishing effective credit programs. Too often, courses are staffed by inexperienced instructors or adjuncts whose pedagogy is poorly suited to learners. Lacking supervision and evaluation, they muddle through without mastering the techniques necessary to reach their students. Ironically, many administrators and professors discover that they themselves must become learners if they are to cope with unconventional students. Selection and training of faculty are not the only personnel issues, however. Administrators must also concede the importance of incentives. If financial or professional remuneration is inadequate, faculty cannot be expected to make significant contributions to this area of the institutional mission.

In addition, it is important to note that the most successful large-scale programs are administered by experienced, qualified personnel who are free of other responsibilities. In the best of all possible worlds, a director or dean would have support staff to aid in conceptualizing offerings, marketing programs, servicing students, recruiting faculty, overseeing and evaluating activities, and carrying out the innumerable daily operations required of an administrative unit. At the very least, one individual must be employed part time or given released time to oversee the program, for the final product will be contingent not only on faculty's skills and commitment, but also on the administrative support services available.

Curriculum (or the "what") is, as Monroe (1972, p. 133) and innumerable others have pointed out, "unlimited." The Cohen survey and all other recent data indicate that the greatest current demand is for occupational course offerings. In some cases, institutions can meet these needs by adapting existing curricula; in others, they are required to design new courses. Community colleges have an enormous advantage over baccalaureate institutions in this respect because they have always been freer to improvise and innovate. More consumer oriented than their four-year counterparts, they are more likely to view the student as customer and to acknowledge the primacy of consumer demand. The administrator's task then is to inspire, encourage, and reward faculty innovation and awareness of community needs.

The unlimited scope of potential course offerings does create drawbacks. In other words, the "how" can be more complex than simply deciding what courses should be taught, assigning instructors, and scheduling times and locations. As Keller (1983, p. 145) has observed, "Strategic planning looks outward." Thus, college leaders must provide the resources to conduct and then continually update community needs surveys and must encourage interaction with external groups that can provide insight into community demands. At the same time, they must ensure that academic standards are maintained so that taxpayers can never accuse them of frivolously awarding credit to noncollegiate instruction.

Experience has demonstrated that the "when" and "where" of providing services are theoretically easy to cope with. Nontraditional students require flexible schedules to accommodate conflicting demands on their time and energy and convenient locations to minimize transportation time and costs. Nevertheless, such demands are easier to recognize than to satisfy, since availability of faculty and space may be limited. As collegiate budgets continue to shrink, the prospects for providing class space and remunerating faculty to teach at nontraditional hours may also decrease.

Credit-Free Programs

This will not be an unusual occurrence, for community response programs have always been subordinate to transfer, technical, and — especially now — remedial offerings. A quarter century ago, Clark (1968, pp. 56–57) used the term *marginality* to depict the "insecurity" of adult programs in most institutions. Today, as much as ever, the terms are appropriate descriptors for all components of the community response function, but "insecurity" is even more characteristic of credit-free programs than it is of those offered for credit. The one exception is adult basic education, which lacks traditional academic stature but is accorded acceptance and resources because contemporary needs are so great. Legislators and the public are far less inclined to support recreational or personal development activities. Unlike credit programs, which generally support themselves through a combination of tuition and revenues from state and local governments (and sometimes external agencies), credit-free programs occupy a far more precarious position. Some receive no direct aid and depend entirely on participant or agency contracting with the institution, and those that do enjoy tax support do so through enrollment formulas that are much lower than those for credit programs.

Directors of credit-free programming seldom lack vision and creativity; what they do need are the resources, especially monetary, to realize their aspirations. Vaughan (1983, pp. 14–15) makes this point when he observes that "perhaps more than any other factor, funding influences the shape of the mission. 'Form follows function,' a once-popular tenet of architecture, might be rephrased for the community college, 'mission follows funding. . . . ' Probably the best example of how funding influences mission is in the area of community services. If the state or locality funds community services or if the college is able to earn additional revenue through community services, the college emphasizes this aspect of the mission; if no funding is forthcoming, little emphasis is given to community services." Vaughan concludes, "If the campus leadership is to play a major role in charting the direction of the community college of the future, leaders must be sensitive to the role funding plays in shaping the mission and must seek funds for that part of the mission which they feel is worth fighting for" (p. 16).

Herein lies the difficulty. While community college leaders are sophisticated at articulating missions and dreaming impossible dreams, they have been less adept at strategic decision making, organizational planning, and evaluation. Without such knowledge, they have only a limited perception of what is "worth fighting for," and they are hard pressed to make their case to those who fund educational endeavors.

Most, if not all, of the directives applicable to credit programs also fit credit-free endeavors. Some need to be stated even more emphatically. Instructors may or may not come from faculty ranks but must possess expertise in dealing with nontraditional students. Curricula must meet diverse needs and yet measure up to collegiate standards. Most important is recognizing that if experienced, enthusiastic directors are necessary to successful credit programs, they are even more crucial to the success and survival of credit-free programming. Because the public and many academicians themselves do not understand the principles governing or the components comprising credit-free programming, directors are responsible for fostering such understanding, as well as for carrying out other daily operational tasks.

In one of the most perceptive articles written to date on the topic of community services, Cohen (1972, p. 10) points out,

Community services in the community college is a puzzlement to many people. What does the term mean? What is the community to be served? And by whom and in what ways? Community services directors may have ready answers to these questions, but it should come as no surprise that their perception of the community and the types of

service to be provided are not widely shared within or outside the college. Community services . . . enjoys the du-
bious distinction of being the community college function
least coherently defined, least likely to have finite goals,
least amenable to assessment of effect.

These observations are obviously true of the credit-free
component of the community response mission. Conference
presentations and journal articles herald the occasional successes
of glamorous credit-free offerings that have attracted public attention. What they frequently neglect to mention is how these
isolated programs fit within the larger mission of the institution and what their staying power will be when they come into
conflict with transfer, technical, and remedial programs that
dominate faculty and legislative agendas. Cohen comments that
while advocates of community service (credit-free) programs
"lack a philosophy, [they] do have a modus operandi — they accept all comers. Anything that the college offers other than its
traditional courses and programs is considered a community
service — hardly a solid foundation on which to build a co-equal
function" (p. 12).

There is a Land of Oz flavor to much credit-free programming. Anyone can travel the yellow brick road so long as he
or she is willing to endure the tribulations along the way, but
at the end of the journey, some, like Dorothy, discover that they
have no need of the Wizard after all, that they could have taught
themselves to knit or could have joined the local senior citizens
group if they wanted social interaction. The Wizard may be
just another ineffectual bungler making claims to power he does
not possess. If the intention is truly to serve, community colleges and their leaders must be certain that they know their communities and their needs thoroughly, that they have assessed
their own abilities and inabilities to meet those needs, and that
they can articulate and prioritize the programs they intend to
provide.

Because community environments differ so radically,
effective credit-free programming must emanate from knowledge of the community. There is a wealth of literature explaining

how to assess community needs and interests and how to deliver services. Article after article stresses the importance of maintaining communication with constituents through surveys, advisory councils, and steering committees. Yet much of the discussion is pure rhetoric. Cohen and his associates (1975, pp. 48–49) found that while "continuing education directors repeatedly stress the importance of what they call 'entrepreneurial' or 'proactive' efforts to maintain contacts with the community, and promote college services that meet those needs, in most cases those efforts seemed to be informal. . . . More formal mechanisms, such as community surveys, are used only rarely."

Sound credit-free programming begins with the college's leaders insisting that accurate, authentic data drive planning. Warm, fuzzy images of audiences entranced by productions of *Rumplestiltskin* or *Snow White* will not fill auditoriums if parents are disinclined to support children's theater. An institution may design the most sophisticated television instruction or senior citizens program in the country, but neither will flourish or survive without constituent interest and response. An aerobics class at the local community college may prove enormously popular in an isolated Arkansas community, while in Los Angeles, it will be about as unique as traffic.

A college may survey its constituents and evolve a series of moderately to highly successful credit-free endeavors and still fail to achieve any end other than attracting warm bodies to promote its image in the popular or professional media. Elitist though it may sound, educational institutions exist to accomplish more than satisfying the transitory whims of their faculties and communities. Even the most trivial activities must somehow fit within a well-articulated, shared conception of community mission. Otherwise the community college becomes simply a participatory version of cable television.

Twenty years ago, Cohen (1972, p. 14) saw this as the fate of most community service programs.

Faced . . . with an institution that frequently is little more than a conglomeration of self-interested administrators defending their own programs, faculty members whose perceived mission is to offer courses and advice only, and students whose primary concern is to accept what is offered, the community services director is not in a position to influence policy through power or persuasion. His administrative colleagues typically fail to comprehend his broader aims; the instructors and counselors may ignore him totally; and the students are most likely unaware of his existence. His college's fiscal and personnel resources will not stretch to accommodate another co-equal function. The community he would serve is fractionated with most of its elements anticipating at best traditional educative services for their tax dollars. And, unkindest cut of all, his national spokesmen advocate little more than uncoordinated program aggrandizement, tending in the main to ignore critical analysis, definitive objectives, and philosophical appraisal of that which they are promoting.

The more scarce resources become, the less possible it will be for credit-free programs to achieve parity with credit programming or for that matter to survive unless concerned administrators ensure that they are clearly integrated with the mission, possess definitive objectives, and are periodically evaluated. These goals must be accomplished not simply for cosmetic reasons, not just so that programs will look meaningful, organized, and well coordinated on paper, but so that when hard decisions must be made, programs can be honestly assessed and prioritized. One general rule that the administrator can employ is to be wary of what Gleazer (1980, pp. 103–104) called "soft" areas:

Two questions are much debated . . . as the mission of community colleges is given new and searching attention. What are the truly legitimate services which institutions should provide? And who should pay for the services? Legislators tend to refer to some services as "soft," or "leisure," or "luxury." An analysis of responses yields a number of clues to what are considered to be soft areas. Among them are education for human fulfillment, social services, expansion of self, personal fulfillment, keeping people busy in old folks' homes, self-actualization, adult hobby-type courses, leisure time programs, and nondegree-oriented activities.

To retain support, administrators are increasingly forced to consider that the public is most likely to favor programs that are "socially useful, as opposed to individually beneficial . . . [that are] verifiably educative programs, as opposed to . . . predominately recreational [or providing] credentials offering the illusion of learning . . . [and] which are not readily available elsewhere for members of the population served by them" (Cohen and Brawer, 1989, pp. 280–281). Given the vast scope of community needs and the limited resources available to meet those needs, the future of credit-free programs thus cannot lie in devising high-visibility, glamorous offerings and outreach experiences. Rather it rests with careful data collection, thoughtful analysis, reasoned decision making, and administrators' willingness to lead community colleges in knowing when to invest in a vision and when "to just say no" (Ernst, 1991, p. 41).

Community-Based Programs

Knowing when to say no is even more crucial in the case of programs that Brawer termed *community based,* a phrase that is expanded here to include community renewal and community development. Brawer (1980) used the original term in a somewhat narrower sense than those who contend that the community college must assume responsibility for solving community problems. As the dilemmas confronting Americans have grown increasingly weighty, they have cast about among a variety of institutions to discover resolutions. It is predictable that, under duress, they would turn for answers to educational establishments because from the nation's birth, its people have had enormous faith in education's power to alter individual and collective destinies.

Committed to the belief that community colleges must move beyond the confines of classrooms into the larger arena of social action, many have challenged them to become agents of community renewal and development, to fulfill their egalitarian missions by immersing themselves in the potentially vola-tile economic, social, environmental, political, and cultural con-cerns of their communities. The Land of Oz quality in much of the rhetoric about credit-free programming is heightened in discussions of community renewal and becomes almost reminis-cent of a screening of *Star Trek*. There is an exhortative tone to much of the literature written about this function, and while development and renewal are clearly consistent with the com-munity college vision, they must, in practice, be defined and approached with caution.

One reason for such prudence is that public institutions cannot survive if they become aligned with competing community interests. Years ago, Harlacher (1969, p. 9) argued eloquently that the community college is the logical home for community initiatives because it is "disinterested in . . . the community power structure, [with] no profit motive . . . no axe to grind. . . . It is the unified force that casts aside red tape, apathy, jealousies, and asks what the community problems are and how 'all of us together [can] solve them.'" While his assessment might have seemed appropriate in 1969, it appears somewhat naive at the turn of the century. Contemporary community colleges are, of necessity, beset with red tape, interest in various community power structures, and constant financial and political pressures. To immerse themselves in too partisan a manner in what Gotts-chalk (1978, p. 6) calls "high-risk problems" may be to court disaster.

Nor do most possess the resources to affect rapid solu-tions to the dilemmas facing their communities. Talbott (1976, p. 89) is correct: "To take on the role of an omniscient social welfare agency strains the credibility as well as the resources of the college. It is not set up to revamp the courts, to change the traffic pattern, to purify the water, to clean the air of smog." At a time when the public is questioning educators' aptitudes in performing the most basic teaching functions, they are ill-advised to set themselves up as gurus capable of resolving the world's dilemmas.

None of this implies, however, that college leaders should abandon their communities and deny society's afflictions. Brawer points out that community-based programs are designed to accommodate those desiring access to institutional expertise, facilities, and equipment. This means that the institution provides the educational components to analyze alternatives and aid in problem resolution. It does not, as Gottschalk (1978, p. 9) observes, suggest that education itself propose solutions:

> The educational component is . . . a knowledge function. It helps individuals and groups to educate themselves to vital social and environmental relationships within their community. This is the college's major contribution to community development. It is based on the assumption that positive change or progress is the product of rational men and that only by understanding their present condition can men hope to improve their futures. Once this educative function is complete, the college as an institution disengages itself from the problem. . . . As opposed to prescribing what ought to be, the task of the community college is to help define present situations within an atmosphere of objective inquiry.

Summary

Ideally then, the most crucial developmental role an institution can play is simply to do what it does best — to educate, to bring together heterogeneous groups and encourage them to explore and reason together until mutually acceptable solutions to problems evolve. This is not as exalted a calling as some would prefer, but its pragmatism and self-imposed limits may protect the college from inevitable, unnecessary failure.

In the final analysis, the community response function remains largely enigmatic. Intrinsic to the community college's self-image, it occupies a precarious position at a time when, as Keller (1983, p. 145) notes, "Three quarters of all change at most institutions of higher learning is now triggered by outside forces such as directives from the state board of higher education, an economic recession, migration patterns, a change in the supply of gasoline, the wider use of records and cassettes, a governor's change of politics, a new law from Washington, a sweeping court decision about a major affirmative action case, and the shifts in jobs markets." Any of these factors alone may exert a tremendous effect on community programs, thus illustrating why institutions are increasingly forced to switch "from a self-assertion model of their existence to a biological model of continuous adaptation to their powerful, changing social environment" (Keller, 1983, p. 145). If they are to be more than mere shadows of a function, community response programs must commit themselves to external and internal exploration, planning, and evaluation. Only then will they truly "know themselves" and be genuinely able to serve their communities.

References

Basler, R. "Consistent and Increasing Adaptability of the Junior College." *Junior College Journal,* 1955, *25,* 427–429.

Brawer, F. B. *Familiar Functions in New Containers: Classifying Community Education.* Topical paper no. 71. Los Angeles: ERIC Clearinghouse for Junior Colleges, 1980. (ED 187 412)

Clark, B. R. *Adult Education in Transition.* Berkeley: University of California Press, 1968.

Cohen, A. M. "The Twilight Future of a Function." *Community Services Catalyst,* 1972, *3*(2), 7–16.

Cohen, A. M. *Community College Involvement in the Education of Adults: A Progress Report Submitted to the Carnegie Foundation for the Advancement of Teaching.* Los Angeles: Center for the Study of Community Colleges, 1987. (ED 277 428)

Cohen, A. M., and Brawer, F. B. *The American Community College.* (2nd ed.) San Francisco: Jossey-Bass, 1989.

Cohen, A. M., and Associates. *College Responses to Community Demands.* San Francisco: Jossey-Bass, 1975.

Ernst, R. J. "Know When to Just Say No." *AACJC Journal,* 1991, *61*(5), 40–44.

Gleazer, E. J., Jr. *The Community College: Values, Vision, and Vitality.* Washington, D.C.: American Association of Community and Junior Colleges, 1980.

Gollattscheck, J. F., Harlacher, E. L., Roberts, E., and Wygal,

B. R. *College Leadership for Community Renewal: Beyond Community-Based Education.* San Francisco: Jossey-Bass, 1976.

Gottschalk, K. "Can Colleges Deal with High-Risk Community Problems?" *Community College Frontiers,* 1978, *6*(4), 4–11.

Harlacher, E. L. *The Community Dimension of the Community College.* Englewood Cliffs, N.J.: Prentice-Hall, 1969.

Keller, G. *Academic Strategy: The Management Revolution in American Higher Education.* Baltimore: Johns Hopkins University Press, 1983.

Monroe, C. R. *Profile of the Community College.* San Francisco: Jossey-Bass, 1972.

Talbott, L. H. "Community Problem Solving." In H. M. Holcomb (ed.), *Reaching Out Through Community Service.* New Directions for Community Colleges, no. 14. San Francisco: Jossey-Bass, 1976.

Vaughan, G. B., and Associates. *Issues for Community College Leaders in a New Era.* San Francisco: Jossey-Bass, 1983.

Chapter 24

Educational Planning and Assessment

James C. Palmer

Contemporary college management places considerable emphasis on the systematic organization and interpretation of information. Indeed, the history of higher education administration
after World War II can be traced in its successive adoption of
information gathering techniques such as program planning
budgeting systems, zero-based budgeting, strategic planning,
environmental scanning, and (most recently) Total Quality
Management. All connect decision making to data collection,
stressing the analytical observation of the college as a system
with identifiable inputs, processes, and outcomes.

The analytical tradition of the manager, however, has done
little to prepare community colleges for the current "outcomes
assessment movement," spurred on in the 1980s by growing demands for information on student learning and development.
Data analysis and evaluation, long viewed as an administrative
and budgetary imperative, have rarely guided educational thinking at any level of the organization. In the classroom, few faculty
members employ behavioral objectives to guide instruction and
document student learning (Cohen and Brawer, 1989). At the
institutional level, presidents seldom articulate a concise educa-

tional mission for the college, explaining the purpose of the curriculum and its intended effects on students (Vaughan, 1989). Without a history of planning and evaluating instruction on the basis of goals specifying what students will learn and how that learning will be documented, community colleges are hard pressed to augment data on enrollments, funding, and other indicators of the magnitude of the educational enterprise with data on student mastery of the curriculum, student advancement to higher levels of education, or other indicators of student achievement.

This heritage is reflected in the goals community college leaders set for their institutions and in the indicators that have been proposed as measures of institutional effectiveness. Many institutional goals offer little more than reaffirmations of commitment to curricular comprehensiveness, open access, responsiveness to community needs, and other tenets of the community college canon. And while many indicators of educational outcomes have been proposed, most are not yet formulated according to consistent definitions that would allow colleges to gauge trends in these outcomes over time. The application of information management to educational planning and assessment is still at an incipient stage, lagging far behind the expectations of accrediting agencies, state policy makers, and others who demand that colleges demonstrate institutional value in terms of student success.

Functional Versus Educational Goals

This chapter describes the uses of functional goals and offers examples of institutions where such goals have been implemented. Used in their traditional sense, goals help tie staff or faculty work to institutional purpose. They occupy a middle position in a planning hierarchy bounded by broad mission statements on one end and by measurable objectives on the other end (Fenske, 1980). In setting goals, college leaders communicate and explain the institutional mission so that actions appropriate to that mission can be planned and carried out. Distributed to external constituencies, goals can also "help explain and relate the organization to its publics" (Fenske, 1980, p. 178).

Community colleges often structure goals within this hierarchical framework. The ERIC collection includes master plans, accreditation self-study reports, and other documents that relate goals to the institutional mission; many take the further step of organizing objectives under specific goal statements. For example, Honolulu Community College's Academic Development Plan for 1987–1995 (Kessinger, 1988) begins with a discussion of the history and mission of the campus, followed by a delineation of twelve goals, each with its own listing of associated objectives. As another example, Blong and Friedel (1991) detail the results and procedures of a project involving faculty, staff, and community representatives in the formulation of a "collective image" of what the Eastern Iowa Community College District (EICCD) should focus on in the future. Starting with the district's mission statement, the participants first developed ten broad goals that were in turn used to establish goals in the narrower areas of instruction, student services, administration, research and planning, and community services. Blong and Friedel (1991, p. 24) stress the linking function of the original ten goals, noting that they "are extensions of the EICCD Mission, and [that] all current and future activities will be encompassed by these goals."

But a review of the goals established at these and other community colleges suggests that despite this hierarchical organization, goals often say more about institutional functions (What shall staff do?) than they say about institutional purpose (To what ends are these functions aimed?). These functional goals fall into five categories, each reflecting a distinct facet of institutional life. Some goals relate to the *college as bureaucracy,* a view implicit in goals that are managerial in nature and call for the "effective and efficient utilization of resources" (Blong and Friedel, 1991, p. 25) or for the development of "effective marketing strategies . . . that serve as a communications link to prospective students" (Liston, 1989, p. 59).

A second category of goals posits the *college as community resource* for economic development, cultural enrichment, or occasional educational needs. Such goals stress action in "continuing an active partnership in the economic development of the local and statewide community" (Grunder, 1991, p. 4), encouraging "student and community participation in the visual and performing arts while serving as a focal point for community cultural activities" (Grunder, 1991, p. 4), or "meeting other (nonacademic) community needs" by opening college recreational and library facilities to the public, encouraging faculty to serve as consultants for local enterprises, and offering clinical services to the public (Blasi and Davis, 1986).

Other goals reflect the *college as point of access to higher education,* highlighting institutional responsibility to provide "adult residents of [the state] with open access to postsecondary education (Liston, 1989, p. 17), increase "the participation of minority students" (Indiana State Commission for Higher Education, 1988, n.p.), or ensure "that the college maintains an open-door policy for all who can benefit from our programs and courses while at the same time providing organized developmental work which will improve skills and attitudes so that success in a course or program may become possible" (Colorado Northwestern Community College, 1989, p. 40).

The role of the *college as provider of educational services* is communicated in goals stressing student services, curricular offerings, instructional improvement, and the maintenance of a campus climate conducive to student learning. Typical are goals that stress provision of "student development services necessary to encourage and enhance the success and well-being of a diverse and ever-changing student population" (Grunder, 1991, p. 4); expansion "of retention practices that enhance opportunities for student success" and expansion of "intake services to ensure that students matriculate in an expeditious fashion and are prepared to successfully undertake their choice of college studies" (Pennsylvania College of Technology, 1990, pp. 27, 30); provision of "quality instruction for students through systematic instructional planning, effective instructional delivery, and responsible instructional management which maximizes students' attainment of their educational goals" (Williamsport Area Community College, 1988, p. 9); creation of an "atmosphere that encourages personal well-being and active participation in extracurricular, social, cultural, recreational, and learning activities" (Colorado Northwestern Community College, 1989, p. 41); or provision of "the highest quality of technical and applied science education, leading to the Associate of Science degree and/or Certificates of Training" (Grunder, 1991, p. 4).

A fifth goals category posits the *college as interpreter of individual needs* and stresses institutional responsiveness to students' objectives. Here colleges assert that "students will achieve their stated learning objectives" or stress institutional responsibility to "consistently identify the objectives of students and clients who come to the college for educational services and focus instruction on those objectives" (Pennsylvania College of Technology, 1990, p. 16).

All of these goals imply important staff actions — managing resources, providing access, providing courses, responding to community and individual needs — but few relate those actions to intended institutional impact. Hence they foster a college culture that sanctions institutional evaluations on the basis of the actions themselves rather than on their results. In contrast, goals focusing on student learning, personal development, advancement through the educational pipeline, or job seeking and career development complete the connection between mission and objectives, giving direction and purpose to staff actions and providing a basis for assessing them. For example, goals established for New York's Schenectady County Community College (1986, p. 8) zero in on student outcomes, albeit broadly, asserting that the college is committed to providing the quality instruction, resources, and encouragement necessary for students:

1. To develop communication skills that enhance one's ability to read with comprehension, write concisely, think logically, and speak clearly and forcefully.
2. To achieve an understanding of the liberal arts and sciences and the technologies.
3. To identify realistic educational and career objectives.
4. To cultivate attitudes, habits, and interests that encourage lifelong learning.
5. To develop awareness of the individual's role in, and responsibility to, the community and the society in which he/she lives. [Schenectady County Community College, 1986, p. 8]

Similarly, West Los Angeles College (California) builds its objectives around the purposes of the curriculum:

> As a comprehensive institution of higher education, the College has established the following goals (not in priority order) which describe the purposes of the institutional functions:
>
> 1. General education shall emphasize learning experiences which help students attain knowledge, achieve skills and develop appreciation, attitudes, and values needed for an effective and well-balanced life in a democratic society. All programs and services for students have been formulated with the realization of this goal in mind.
> 2. Career education shall provide intensive and thorough training leading to employment, the upgrading of skills for persons already employed, or ret[r]aining for employment in skilled, technical, business and service occupations.
> 3. Transfer education shall offer courses that enable students to satisfy the lower-division requirements for upper-division work in accredited baccalaureate institutions. [Los Angeles Community College District, 1988, p. 204]

Like most goals, which take a more general form than objectives, those listed above do not specify operational measures of the outcomes they describe, nor do they indicate which students are expected to achieve those outcomes — all students? students who have earned a minimum number of credits? students who have received the associate's degree? But they do imply measures of goal achievement: student involvement in civic affairs, student knowledge of the liberal arts and sciences, transfer to and success at four-year colleges, and employment and skills upgrading. Course and curriculum objectives can be developed with these ends in mind, and research programs can be designed to assess the extent to which they are met. Whereas functional goals describe the "college as . . . " and call for indicators of courses offered, students enrolled, and other indicators of college activities and processes, educational goals describe the "college for . . . " and call for measures of student learning, personal development, advancement to further education, and other indicators of institutional impact.

Gauging College Progress Toward Educational Goals

Calculating and reporting these indicators represent a key step in tying data collection and institutional research to assessments of educational outcomes. Reported on a regular basis according to consistent definitions, such indicators allow colleges to track trends over time, thus providing baseline data useful in evaluating efforts undertaken to help students achieve desired educational ends. For example, the college that regularly and consistently calculates transfer rates for entering student cohorts has at least some basis for estimating the effects of articulation agreements, student counseling programs, curriculum improvement projects, or other interventions designed to further the college's goal of leading students to the baccalaureate. College progress toward other goals can be monitored through indicators of student experience in the labor market, student knowledge of the arts and sciences, student mastery of basic literacy skills, and other outcomes implied in educational goals.

Several indicators of student outcomes have been proposed, though most are offered as generic indices of community college effectiveness that are not operationally defined or tied to specific educational goals. Doucette and Hughes (1990) suggest a framework for assessing outcomes under each of five community college missions: transfer education, career preparation, continuing education, basic skills education, and the "access mission" (that is, keeping the door of higher education open). For each mission, the authors pose questions and note data sources that can guide colleges in the calculation of outcomes indicators. In the area of career preparation, for example, the authors ask, among sixteen questions, "Are students achieving a broad general education?" They suggest that indicators tied to this question can be drawn from "standardized assessment instruments; [student achievement in] capstone courses; communication and computational skills in course assignments; observation of ability to work cooperatively; [and] follow-up surveys of employers" (p. 17).

In another attempt to provide a framework for outcomes analysis, the National Alliance of Community and Technical Colleges (Grossman and Duncan, 1989) points to potential sources for indicators of institutional effectiveness in six areas: access and equity, employment preparation and placement, college/university transfer, economic development, college/community partnerships, and cultural and cross-cultural development. Suggested indices for the "college/university transfer" function, for example, include the transfer rate of those students who enroll with the intention of transferring, the extent to which students' community college credits are accepted for transfer by baccalaureate-granting institutions, the academic success (in terms of grade-point average and general education competencies) of transfer students in comparison to native university students, and the baccalaureate attainment rates of transfer students.

In addition to these general frameworks, some specific indicators have been calculated and reported. The Ford-sponsored Transfer Assembly project, for example, has involved more than a third of the community colleges nationwide that have utilized a standard definition to calculate transfer rates for entering student cohorts. As Cohen (1991, p. 3) explains, the transfer rate was defined as "all students entering the two-year college in a given year who have no prior college experience and who complete at least 12 college credit units, divided into the number of that group who take one or more classes at a university within four years." The process of calculating the transfer rate according to this definition is straightforward. During 1990–91, each participating college:

1. identified those students who entered the community college with no previous college experience in the fall of 1985;
2. determined which of those students had earned at least

12 credits by the spring of 1989 (these students served
as the denominator of the transfer rate equation); and
3. provided neighboring four-year colleges (either directly
or through a state agency) with a list of these students
(or with a data tape with student identification numbers) and asked if they had been admitted at any time
through the fall of 1989. (Those that had been admitted served as the numerator of the equation.)

Adherence to a specific definition promises to bring consistency
to a heretofore confused picture of student transfer behavior.

Other examples stem from the infrequent institutional
documents detailing indicators of college effectiveness. Recent
examples include reports issued by South Carolina's Midlands
Technical College (Hudgins, 1990), the Florida Community
College at Jacksonville (1989), and Howard Community College (1991) in Maryland. The latter report from Howard Community College (HCC) is by far the most detailed, outlining
indicators for each of thirteen goals. For instance, five indicators are reported for the goal that "evidence of student learning
will be demonstrated, including measures of value-added education" (Howard Community College, 1991, p. 7). These indicators include scores of freshman and sophomore students in
nationally normed tests of student ability in mathematics, reading, writing, and critical thinking; graduate self-ratings of development, "including enhanced self-confidence, clarified goals,
increased learning enjoyment, increased mathematics ability,
improved writing and reading, etc." (p. 22); performance of
graduates on licensing examinations; the proportion of transfers from HCC who remain in good standing at the university;
and employer ratings of graduates' job training. Each indicator is reported on a single page, noting trends in the indicator
over time, the rationale for the indicator, the precise definition
of the indicator, the data source from which the indicator will
be calculated, a three-year performance target, and possible
problem areas. (Figure 24.1 provides an example.) One may
argue with the wording of the goals and the appropriateness of
the indicators, but all is spelled out unambiguously.

Figure 24.1. Example of How Indicators Are Reported at Howard Community College: Academic Standing of Former HCC Students at Maryland Universities.

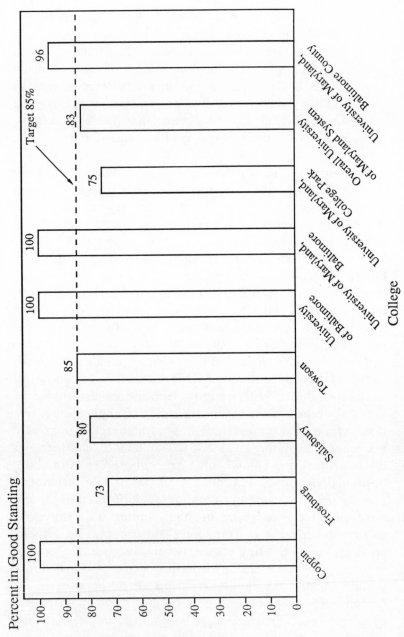

Source: Howard Community College, 1991, p. 24. Reprinted with permission.

Rationale for indicator: The performance of students after transfer to a four-year institution is an indication of how well prepared they were to meet the requirements of senior institutions.

Definition of indicator: Percentage of students who transferred to four-year institutions who are in good standing. Good standing is defined as a grade-point average higher than 2.0. This includes all students who attended HCC prior to transfer regardless of whether they graduated before transferring.

Source: Maryland four-year colleges reporting to the community colleges.

Three-year performance target: 85 percent of transfer students will be in good academic standing.

Performance outcome and analysis: 98 percent of all HCC students at University of Maryland, Baltimore County (UMBC), were in good standing in the spring of 1990. Student performance at UMBC is reported separately from other University of Maryland schools; 83 percent of all Fall 1989 entrants were in good standing at other University of Maryland schools in Spring 1990. Overall results indicate that the college is meeting its goal. Since all HCC students, regardless of credits earned, are included in the transfer numbers, the success rate is lower than it would be for just graduates or for those who had taken a large number of credits at the college. Although the overall success level is good, two problem schools exist, Frostburg and the University of Maryland, College Park. Although few students transfer to Frostburg, the reasons for this lower success rate at College Park should be examined.

These examples, though rare in the literature, point to several imperatives in the development and use of indicators. One is clarity of definition, specifying which students the indicator encompasses and how. For example, colleges participating in the Transfer Assembly Project examined the transfer rates of first-time college students who earn at least twelve units at the community college and who transfer within four years of entering the community college. At Howard Community College, researchers calculate an indicator of transfer success based on the academic standing of all former HCC students enrolled at a public university regardless of their status at HCC prior to transferring (see Figure 24.1). In both cases, attention to definition ensures the consistent calculation of the respective indicators over time.

A second imperative is simplicity. Definitions that are easy to understand and that base the calculation of indicators on readily available data minimize the time that must be devoted to their calculation and lend credibility to the end result. This is a key tenet of the Transfer Assembly Project, which rejects the temptation to figure student educational objectives into the calculation of transfer rates. Though many argue that transfer rate data are meaningful only when calculated for those community college students who enroll with the intention of transferring (Walleri, Seybert, and Cosgrove, 1992), student intent adds a measure of instability because it varies greatly depending on how intentions are assessed and when during the student's college career that assessment takes place. Hence the focus on an indicator whose calculation requires data only on (1) the previous educational experience of students enrolling at a specific point in time, (2) the number of credits those students earn at the community college within four years of entrance, and (3) their enrollment at a four-year college within the same four-year period. All are easily understood and obtainable.

A final imperative is the reporting of indicators in clear and neutral formats that specify exactly how the indicators are defined and recognize their value-free nature. Howard Community College's accountability report is a good example (Figure 24.1). Readers are told what the data mean and, by implication, what their limitations are. No attempt is made to use the data to make facile judgments about HCC's effectiveness in leading students to transfer. Rather, *potential* problems are noted for further investigation. Unless indicators are treated in this manner, too much may be expected of them, and many will fear their misuse. As Ewell (1983, p. 62) points out, "The indicative quality of most student outcomes research is probably the aspect least well understood by its critics. . . . Most procedures for gathering data on student outcomes are indirect and will provide only partial information on a given outcome. Information gathered in this manner is ordinarily much more useful for the questions it raises than for the answers it provides."

Defining Institutional Purpose

Setting educational goals and tying data collection to those goals are logical responses to the outcomes assessment movement. Defining institutional purpose in terms of desirable student outcomes related to learning, personal development, career achievement, or transfer and subsequent baccalaureate attainment focuses college means on college ends, partially satisfying accreditation requirements calling for self-assessments of institutional impacts on students. In addition, college goals focusing on student outcomes and developed with faculty input may encourage similar thinking at the classroom level, leading to a reconsideration of the use of objectives in documenting classroom learning. For example, Banta (1991, p. 219) observes that the process of setting college-level goals for general education outcomes has had its greatest impact on faculty, "who have learned that they must be more systematic in stating their goals for general education, in auditing the means of implementing the goals, and then in assessing outcomes in ways that provide evidence that can be used to confirm or to modify original goals."

But the replacement of functional goals with educational goals and the addition of data indicative of student outcomes to the store of data available on institutional size and growth may require fundamental changes in the institutional culture of the community college. Of primary concern is the tendency to confuse mission (institutional ends) with responsiveness (institutional means), thus positing a college at which there are as many outcomes as there are students. This is evident in goals that stress student achievement of their own objectives and (by implication) abrogate any institutional responsibility to prescribe curricular paths leading to college-defined ends. At best, this leads to an emphasis on "value-added" indicators, which, though well intentioned, imply no standards against which to assess college work with students. At worst, it sanctions the tendency to beg the question of college responsibilities to students entirely. As Aquino (1991, p. 2) notes, by insisting on "the relativity of student success, they [community colleges] have tended to avoid confronting the issue of exactly what is meant by the term 'student success' in the community college context."

A second problem lies in the political nature of college administration, leading many to view information on student outcomes as a potential public relations threat rather than as a requisite for professional self-evaluation and improvement. The need for baseline data required for meaningful assessments of college efforts to lead students to desired ends may be overshadowed by fear of untoward comparisons between colleges, particularly in the area of transfer rates, or of media misuse of outcomes indicators as absolute measures of institutional effectiveness. Oddly, the proactive view of setting goals and collecting data accordingly as a way of controlling and strengthening public relations is often forgotten. In response to critics who fear media misuse of transfer rates, Cohen (1991, p. 11) argues that colleges must take matters into their own hands: "When an institution has its own database and does its own calculations, its spokespersons can say, 'This is what we contribute to student progress.' They do not have to depend on outsiders to define their mission or the success of their mission. . . . There is a great difference in public image when the external reporters are forced to confront sound institutional data instead of generating figures first and forcing the college spokespersons to react."

Finally, there is the tendency to view data collection and institutional research as externally driven processes designed to meet state and federal reporting requirements rather than as internally driven processes designed to assess the link between educational goals and student outcomes. State-mandated indicators of institutional effectiveness, reviewed by Friedlander and MacDougall (1990), as well as federal "right-to-know" legislation requiring colleges to report graduation and transfer rates according to a prescribed methodology reinforce this reporting mentality. Though desirable as a means of documenting college adherence to minimum standards, which is a government's obligation to the public, single-minded attention to these growing and changing requirements can have untoward consequences. Of particular note is the tendency of colleges to create open-ended data collection programs that organize all available student data so that the college will be prepared to respond to newly emerging government mandates for information. This is evident in the establishment of unwieldy student tracking systems designed not for the purpose of reporting predetermined indicators of student achievement but for the purpose of creating unit record systems that can be manipulated to produce cross-tabulations on any number of student variables that might be of future interest (Palmer, 1990). Without educational goals as an organizing principle, outcomes data cannot be meaningfully interpreted and used to inform assessments of the extent to which colleges are fulfilling their educational missions.

Summary

This chapter has reviewed the need for and the process of setting measurable goals for the community colleges' educational programs. The key challenge posed by those demanding information on student outcomes does not lie in the question "What data will meet these demands?" Rather, it lies in the question "What are the educational purposes of the college and how can those purposes be tied to data collection and institutional research?" The college that has no articulated educational mission beyond the mere provision of courses and that offers no indicators of student achievement beyond those that are occasionally required by funding agencies may ultimately be held responsible — rightly or wrongly — for any number of outcomes deemed appropriate by legislators, media representatives, or others scrutinizing the higher education establishment. The institution that views itself as a passive agency shaped by the way students happen to use it is similarly vulnerable to outside interpretation. While it is admittedly difficult to prescribe educational ends for an institution that is often used by students who meet occasional educational needs without following curricular paths (Adelman, 1992), the alternative is to ask the public to accept the "college as . . . " on faith and to leave the enterprise vulnerable to the criticisms of those who, in the absence of guidance of college leaders themselves, see their expectations unfulfilled.

References

Adelman, C. *The Way We Are: The Community College as American Thermometer*. Washington, D.C.: Office of Educational Research and Improvement, U.S. Department of Education, 1992.

Aquino, F. J. "Operationalizing a Student Topology: Steps Toward Building a Community College Success Model." Paper presented at the thirty-first annual forum of the Association for Institutional Research, San Francisco, May 1991. (ED 336 023)

Banta, T. W. "Contemporary Approaches to Assessing Student Achievement of General Education Outcomes." *JGE: The Journal of General Education*, 1991, *40*, 205–223.

Blasi, J. F., and Davis, B. "Outcomes Evaluation: A Model for the Future." *Community College Review*, 1986, *14*(2), 53–57.

Blong, J. T., and Friedel, J. N. *2020 Vision: The EICCD Moves into the 21st Century*. Davenport: Eastern Iowa Community College District, 1991. (ED 327 249)

Cohen, A. M. "Deriving a Valid Transfer Rate." In E. Jones (ed.), *A Model for Deriving the Transfer Rate: Report of the Transfer Assembly Project*. Washington, D.C.: American Association of Community and Junior Colleges, 1991.

Cohen, A. M., and Brawer, F. B. *The American Community College*. (2nd ed.) San Francisco: Jossey-Bass, 1989.

Colorado Northwestern Community College. *The CNCC Plan of Action. 1989–90 to 1993–94.* Rangely: Colorado Northwestern Community College, 1989. (ED 321 819)

Doucette, D., and Hughes, B. (eds.). *Assessing Institutional Effectiveness in Community Colleges.* Laguna Hills, Calif.: League for Innovation in the Community College, 1990.

Ewell, P. T. *Information on Student Outcomes: How to Get It and How to Use It.* Boulder, Colo.: National Center for Higher Education Management Systems, 1983. (ED 246 827)

Fenske, R. H. "Setting Institutional Goals and Objectives." In P. Jedamus, M. W. Peterson, and Associates, *Improving Academic Management: A Handbook of Planning and Institutional Research.* San Francisco: Jossey-Bass, 1980.

Florida Community College at Jacksonville. *Strategic Performance Indicators.* Jacksonville: Florida Community College at Jacksonville, 1989.

Friedlander, J., and MacDougall, P. R. "Responding to Mandates for Institutional Effectiveness." In P. R. MacDougall and J. Friedlander (eds.), *Models for Conducting Institutional Research.* New Directions for Community Colleges, no. 72. San Francisco: Jossey-Bass, 1990.

Grossman, G. M., and Duncan, M. E. *Indicators of Institutional Effectiveness: A Guide for Assessing Two-Year Colleges.* Columbus: Center on Education and Training for Employment, Ohio State University, 1989. (ED 325 193)

Grunder, P. *Measuring Institutional Effectiveness Through the Strategic Planning Process.* Gainesville, Fla.: Santa Fe Community College, 1991. (ED 336 134)

Howard Community College. *Assessing Student Learning Outcomes: Performance Accountability Report.* Columbia, Md.: Howard Community College, 1991. (ED 337 227)

Hudgins, J. L. *Institutional Effectiveness: Mastering the Process Before It Masters You.* Columbia, S.C.: Midlands Technical College, 1990. (ED 322 981)

Indiana State Commission for Higher Education. *Proposed Institutional Performance Objectives for 1989–91.* Indianapolis: Indiana State Commission for Higher Education, 1988. (ED 322 814)

Kessinger, P. R. *Academic Development Plan, Honolulu Community College, 1987–1995.* Honolulu: Honolulu Community College, 1988. (ED 302 271)

Liston, E. J. *Community College of Rhode Island Management Letter.* Warwick: Community College of Rhode Island, 1989. (ED 308 891)

Los Angeles Community College District. *College Annual Reports. 1986–1987.* Vol. 1: *Narrative Descriptions.* Los Angeles: Office of Research, Planning, and Analysis, 1988. (ED 302 276)

Palmer, J. *The President's Role in Student Tracking.* Leadership Abstracts, vol. 3, n. 12. Laguna Hills, Calif.: League for Innovation in the Community College, 1990.

Pennsylvania College of Technology, Williamsport. *Long Range Plan: 1990–1993.* Williamsport: Office of Planning and Research, Pennsylvania College of Technology, 1990. (ED 319 470)

Schenectady County Community College. *Schenectady County Community College Overview, 1985–1986.* Schenectady, N.Y.: Schenectady County Community College, 1986. (ED 217 174)

Vaughan, G. B. *Leadership in Transition: The Community College Presidency.* New York: American Council on Education/Macmillan, 1989.

Walleri, D., Seybert, J., and Cosgrove, J. "What Do Students Want? How Student Intentions Affect Institutional Assessment." *Community, Technical, and Junior College Journal,* 1992, *62*(4), 29–31.

Williamsport Area Community College. *Long Range Plan, 1988–1991.* Williamsport, Pa.: Williamsport Area Community College, 1988. (ED 303 217)

Chapter 25

Conclusion:
The Future Context
for Administration

Arthur M. Cohen, Florence B. Brawer

Cries for change in education are becoming more and more strident. Many are coming from outside the formal education establishment — for example, from well-funded groups fostering plans to divert public funds to the support of private academies. Voucher plans, enabling parents to choose whatever school they deem best for their children, are being forwarded for legislative action. Curriculum revision is underway in several states. Education reform is being pursued at the national level through the U.S. Department of Education's efforts in setting standards and developing broadscale testing programs. On the local scene, charter schools are growing, with parents becoming active participants in their children's education.

　　Some of these efforts will undoubtedly affect the ways education is practiced in the elementary and secondary schools. And their influence will certainly reverberate in higher education, since students' earlier preparation determines what they bring to postsecondary education. Thus, any major changes in lower-school curriculum, standards, and access will extend to community colleges and to other institutions of higher education.

475

How does the future look for American community colleges? What new developments will affect their operating styles and the varied functions they perform? While the answers can only be verified over time, the overriding demand appears to be the need for flexibility in administrative style and approach. All college leaders must have a vision for the institutions they manage. This vision must include a total understanding of the ways their institutions presently function and the ways they could function better. Administrators—in whatever office they hold—who fail to acknowledge current or impending changes in education will not be able to adequately and creatively manage their institutions. The ability to see alternative views, to accept new challenges, to vary old ways of management, to introduce new concepts and new ways of putting these concepts into operation will be crucial for administrators in the twenty-first century.

Planning involves not only setting goals, but also finding practical means to accomplish them. Planning includes developing a system arranged so that all involved feel part of the process. The shared ownership of goals and policies is a motivating force for everyone from faculty to board members. The system must safeguard against any party feeling slighted or overlooked. The days of the hierarchical power struggle are gone. This is the age of cooperation, of seeing power as the ability to empower others. Policies must allow for the equal hearing of ideas. The community college is an institution of service, and leaders need to have the mindset of a servant—self-sacrificing yet not compromising on the principles and policies they feel are vital to an outstanding college.

Changes in institutional size are particularly disruptive because everyone is affected. Managing growth in enrollment, staffing, and budgets is always easier than managing decline. Growth means that decisions about which programs are more important than others can be ignored merely by adding additional programs and maintaining extant ones. Decline, on the other hand, forces choices, which are often impossible to make on a scale of values. Which programs and courses should be cut in the face of a reduced budget? Student counseling or financial aid management? Courses in fine arts or in psychology?

All are worthy. Fortunately for the administrators' well-being, external events often dictate these decisions. The state legislature or board of governors decides to stop funding a certain program. Or the student attendance pattern shifts so that enrollment in an area of study dries up, making that program or those courses impossible to defend. Still, they cause disruptions for which the administrators must be prepared.

Sometimes, long-term trends affect colleges in predictable ways, creating an opportunity for the administrator to exert leadership even while the events are forcing decisions. State-mandated enrollment caps or changes in tuition, for example, can shape college programs and operations drastically regardless of any administrator's style or preference. The effective leader anticipates these events and encourages programmatic and organizational changes before the events reach crisis proportions.

Several chapters in this handbook have alluded to affirmative action and to the concept of multiculturalism. These references are certainly in tune with the times, reflections of the past few decades when public figures, corporate managers, and educators became aware of the need for equity along gender, racial, and other lines. The quest for such equality will undoubtedly continue until measures of parity are established in all public enterprises and major businesses in the country.

These efforts are both laudable and necessary. At the same time, it is important that we recognize the varying characteristics of people as individuals. Alfred Adler (1924) proposed a notion of individual differences decades ago, when he urged that teachers, in particular, look at all people in terms of their own idiosyncracies. This approach is perhaps even more necessary today. Despite the fact that student personnel services have been reduced in many colleges because of financial constraints, those in charge of these services must make it clear to all their staff members that their students should be seen as individuals functioning in the educational world. Whether the students are African-American, Asian-American, European-American, or any other hyphenated American, they are still individuals. The needs, frustrations, and successes of a particular student are not mirrored in all other members of the group. All bring unique requirements and aspirations to the college, and they must be dealt with directly in terms of who they are, as individuals living in a world where both multiculturalism and individuality must be acknowledged.

The colleges' democratizing efforts should reach beyond their developing programs and procedures to assist members of various ethnic groups. Although their data on access and outcomes are usually assembled and the arguments marshaled along lines of ethnicity, the issue of equity is more accurately described in terms of social class. There is an underclass in America, doing the work that people in the other classes do not want to do. Individuals may escape it, but it is continually being replenished with immigrants and young people and through discriminatory actions. To the extent that individuals perceive that they can move into another class by virtue of their own educational or entrepreneurial efforts, the ideal of mobility is being served.

The community college's position as the point of first entry to higher education for most of its students makes it a battleground for ideas surrounding equity in education. Who participates? Who benefits? How can the educational system assist in the unending struggle to reduce differences between classes or at least make it easier for individuals to move out of the stratum into which they were born and reared? The way these questions are answered shapes American society. More than in any other sector, they are being answered in the community colleges.

The national trend toward outcomes assessment will affect colleges. For example, plans for a national collegiate assessment system are well underway. This system will demand data not only on degree completion rates, but also on students' ability to think critically, communicate well, solve problems, and perform specific job skills.

The implications for indicators of college outcomes are direct. Without waiting for demands from external agencies, every college should be able to answer a few basic questions. How many students from various social groups in our district used our college to: Obtain a new job? Upgrade themselves in a field in which they were already employed? Gain credit toward a baccalaureate? Enhance their literacy? Generally accepted definitions of measurements in each of these areas are readily available. The data can be used to support powerful arguments on behalf of the colleges' contributions.

Trends and Directions

The forward-looking administrator will cast a careful eye on trends that may demand major changes in colleges. A shift in the funding base is the most obvious and far-reaching. Other public agencies have become more competitive. Prisons, health care, welfare, and special aid programs all have a growing claim on state monies. The public community colleges, already shaken by the proprietary schools' access to student aid monies, face further competition. The private academies that have grown rapidly at the K-12 level may reach into the community college domain. If the idea of publicly funded private academies spreads, the college administrators will face direct competition for state funds more formidable than the indirect competition from other public agencies. The administrators should now build coalitions to support the idea of public funding for public education and at the same time continually try to demonstrate that the publicly funded, open-access community college can operate efficiently and with a view toward responsible administration of a public trust. Providing data on institutional outcomes is only one of the essentials that must be pursued.

The question of paying for education looms in another way. For many years, community college supporters were able to hold the line on tuition increases that lagged behind those of the university sector. More recently, the concept of low tuition in community colleges has been severely challenged by legislators trying to resolve state budget problems by forcing the students to pay an increasing proportion of the cost of their own education. But the states' budget problems are only part of the reason for the tuition increases. The notion of low tuition as evidence of a concern for the social good is rapidly being converted to one holding that the individual who benefits should assume more of the costs. This major shift in public policy seems likely to continue regardless of the state of the nation's economy.

Tuition, which accounted for 9 percent of the colleges' total income in 1950, had reached 19 percent by 1989 (Alsalam, Ogle, Rogers, and Smith, 1992, p. 134). The idea that all people should be educated at the public's expense to the limit of their desire or ability—basic to the community colleges over the years of their development—can no longer be viewed as a bedrock principle.

Competition from the private sector, increasing tuition, and state agencies whose functions are considered more essential all come together as the greatest challenges facing college managers. The issues go beyond their short-term seeking of budgets that will tide them over the next fiscal year. These problems underscore the urgency of developing alternative sources of funding. The community colleges have never received much money from grants, contracts, rentals, sales, or services provided to other public agencies or to business corporations. College leaders may point with pride to the great numbers of adults returning to take advantage of college programs, but heavily subsidized education for everyone on a recurrent basis is not a feature of community colleges anywhere else in the world. The most farsighted leaders will work to develop alternative sources of funding much greater than the minuscule proportion their institutions now enjoy. The public trough will not support them in the style to which they have been accustomed.

The colleges may change notably, but not because of innovations in management. Institutional restructuring demands changes far beyond rearranging the format of the committees, lines of authority, or decision-making routes within the institutions. A major upheaval, such as the quadrupling of tuition or the reduction of public support by one-half or more, may be forthcoming. The college leaders will then be forced to make some crucial decisions regarding college structure.

Perspicacious leaders should position their colleges to take advantage of school-workplace combinations, an educational demand that is certain to grow. The northern European model of intermittent schooling and apprenticeships is being put forth as a desirable direction for American schools to take. But total wage and nonwage costs in the manufacturing sector in those countries are higher than in the United States, and, in the 1990s, unemployment was higher as well.

The model must be adapted to accommodate contemporary realities. The freedom to choose the type of job and the amount of time one wishes to devote to it is the answer to mankind's prayers to be released from lifelong toil. Few would return to the industrial era when every able-bodied person worked continually for subsistence or to the earlier period when women and ethnic minorities were barred from all but menial jobs. The educational problem now is not as simple as training people to fill industrial jobs. Instead, it is to show young people that employment is as attractive as unemployment, that entrepreneurship can be vital to one's social well-being, that self-esteem is intertwined with work-related activities. Workforce development goes far beyond contract or apprenticeship training or measures in productivity. It is an essential element in social cohesion and human dignity.

New Structures

The mystique and the history of the community colleges have held that the institutions can have fixed curricula directed toward baccalaureate studies or job entry and, at the same time, be open-access, community-responsive institutions. But a full-time faculty and a fixed curriculum, coupled with continued attempts to respond to changed environmental conditions, may be more than most single institutions can sustain. Economic and political forces are mandating smaller institutions as well as restrictions on program entry. At the same time, opportunities keep opening up for rapid response to community, governmental, and commercial agencies and organizations that can provide funds for specialized activities: contract training, basic literacy development, immigrant education, and facilities rental, to name only a few.

The future may not allow for these disparate forms within the same institution. A splitting of the colleges might see new institutional types growing out of the ashes of the comprehensive college. One type would be a smaller institution with selective entry into prebaccalaureate programs centering on the liberal arts, occupational programs around the middle-level positions dominant in the health and business fields, and remedial studies that would include life management skills. A full-time faculty would be central to college operations. Such colleges could obtain support through traditional channels and could establish firm links with the secondary schools and with the universities.

Another institutional type would be one that has separated completely from its roots in the public schools. This institution would have program coordinators supervising part-time instructors with no employment security. Their funds would be derived from a number of sources, including tax revenues, donations, tuition, rents, and sales, with none dominant. Their management structure would be an amalgam of the patterns now seen in university extension programs, ad hoc spectator events, and museums. Low-cost employees and volunteers would be essential to the enterprise. The curriculum would be anything for which anyone was willing to pay.

One way for the comprehensive college to thrive might be as a collectivity of specialized schools. The concept of the magnet school, the most successful innovation in public education in recent memory, has not been tried sufficiently in community colleges. A few outstanding examples are available: Miami-Dade's Medical Campus (Florida) and Coastline College (California) are focused forms within comprehensive districts. Gaining support for boutique colleges with distinctive purposes and results is quite feasible. If such far-reaching reorganization cannot be achieved, college planners can at least differentiate programs more blatantly, providing each with its own staff, facilities, budget, and mandate for outcomes assessment. The times call for distinctiveness.

Overall, the comprehensive community college, common in larger states such as Florida, California, and Illinois, may give way to the more specialized institutions now seen in Wisconsin, Kentucky, and Indiana. Two-year colleges organized as branches of the state university, technical institutes, and adult basic education centers can function apart from each other. Nowhere outside the United States and Canada is the comprehensive community college the dominant form. In most nations, separate institutions accommodate prebaccalaureate studies, technical education, trade and industry training, and community social education. These functional differences far override the differences between colleges that derive more or less support from the public sector. Yet it is just that support, or lack of it, that will determine the future of institutions.

References

Adler, A. *The Practice and Theory of Individual Psychology.* Orlando, Fla.: Harcourt Brace Jovanovich, 1924.

Alsalam, N., Ogle, L. T., Rogers, G. T., and Smith, T. M. *The Condition of Education 1992.* Washington, D.C.: U.S. Department of Education, 1992.

Index

485